W9-AFY-526

INSIGHT GUIDE

SOUTHAFRICA

APA PUBLICATIONS

Part of the Langenscheidt Publishing Group

L

ABOUT THIS BOOK

Editorial
Project Editor
Melissa de Villiers
Editorial Director
Brian Bell

Distribution
UK & Ireland
GeoCenter International Ltd
The Viables Centre
Harrow Way
Basingstoke
Hants RG22 4BJ
Fax: (44) 1256-817988

United States
Langenscheidt Publishers, Inc.
46–35 54th Road
Maspeth, NY 11378
Fax: (718) 784-0640

Worldwide
APA Publications GmbH & Co.
Verlag KG Singapore Branch, Singapore
38 Joo Koon Road
Singapore 628990
Tel: (65) 865-1600
Fax: (65) 861-6438

Printing
Insight Print Services (Pte) Ltd
38 Joo Koon Road
Singapore 628990
Tel: (65) 865-1600
Fax: (65) 861-6438

© 1998 APA Publications GmbH & Co.
Verlag KG Singapore Branch, Singapore
All Rights Reserved
First Edition 1992
Third Edition 1998

CONTACTING THE EDITORS
Although every effort is made to
provide accurate information in
this publication, we live in a
fast-changing world and would
appreciate it if readers would
call our attention to any errors or
outdated information that may
occur by writing to us at:
Insight Guides, P.O. Box 7910,
London SE1 8ZB, England.
Fax: (44 171) 620-1074.
e-mail:
insight@apaguide.demon.co.uk

In April 1994, South
Africa – previously
regarded as something of
an international pariah –
was reborn. Full elections
marked the death of a
political system which
had stained the continent
for more than half a
century. The end of
apartheid has fuelled a massive
influx of visitors, eager to see this
beautiful country for themselves;
consequently, the team behind this
Insight Guide set out to pick their
way through the rubble of the past
and provide a fair, entertaining and
accurate portrait of the present.

How to use this book
New guidebooks to South Africa
are now appearing
virtually every
week, so we were
determined to
produce one that
distinguished
itself from the
crowd.
Fortunately, we
had one great
advantage:

Insight Guides' proven format of
highly informative, entertaining and
well-written text combined with an
exciting photojournalistic
approach.

The book is carefully structured
both to convey an understanding of
the country and its culture and to
guide readers through its sights
and activities:

◆ To understand South Africa
today, you need to know about its
past. The first section covers its
History and **People**, with **Features**
on South African culture and

Nature. These lively,
authoritative essays are
written by specialists.

◆ The main **Places**
section provides a full
run-down of all the
attractions worth
seeing. The principal
places of interest are
coordinated by number
with full-colour maps.

◆ The **Travel Tips** listings section
provides a convenient point of
reference for information on travel,
hotels, restaurants, sports and
festivals. Information may be
located quickly by using the index
printed on the back cover flap – and
the flaps are designed to serve as
bookmarks.

◆ **Photographs** are chosen not only
to illustrate geography and
attractions but also to convey the
many moods of South Africa and
the activities of the people who
live there.

The contributors
The task of
assembling the
team who put
together this
edition of *Insight Guide: South
Africa* fell to project editor **Melissa
de Villiers**, a South African travel
writer and editor now living in
London. Thoroughly revised and
updated, this book builds on the
original edition produced by
Johannes Haape, who today runs a
tour company in Germany
specialising in sub-Saharan Africa.
Both bring an insider's knowledge
to bear on this extraordinarily
diverse, fast-changing country.

The editors sought out writers
with the ideal combination of

affection for, and detachment from, their subject that distinguishes the Insight Guides series. Several have forged successful careers in the media:

David Bristow, editor of *Getaway*, Africa's leading travel and leisure magazine, covered Cape Town, Durban, Swaziland and Lesotho. **Wendy Toerien**, staffer on South Africa's acclaimed *Wine* magazine, wrote on the Cape's grape. Writer and television producer/director **Gary Rathbone** described the intricacies of "Living Together", as well as his twin passions: the city of Johannesburg and the national sporting scene. Prolific local travel journalist **Bridget Hilton-Barber** took time off from exploring the sub-continent's wilder reaches to write on a variety of topics including Zulu culture, township life, the black middle class, and *dorps*.

Other writers included **Christopher Till**, former director of the Johannesburg Art Gallery; **Ian** **MacDonald**, chief executive of WWF South Africa; and ecotourism management consultant, **Vincent Carruthers**. Art historian **Sabine Marschall** wrote on architecture; author **Stephen Gray** contributed the chapter on South African literature.

The History section was written by **Jeff Peires**, former ANC MP and the author of two books on the history of the Xhosa people, and **Rodney Davenport**, emeritus professor and editor of the standard work, *A Modern History of South Africa*.

The fact-packed Travel Tips section was compiled by travel journalist **Roderick Mackenzie**, assisted by **Inge Glaue**.

Many of the photographs in this book are the vision of **Gerald Cubitt**, who has published numerous successful books of his work. Other photographs came from **T.J. Lemon**, a national newspaper photographer with a passion for black South African music and dance; **Anthony Bannister**, whose images grace a wide range of South African publications; and **Chris Ledochowski**, who has exhibited his images of township homes and culture. Picture research was by **Hilary Genin**.

Map Legend

── ‑‑	International Boundary
── ‑‑	Province Boundary
⊖	Border Crossing
─•─	National Park/ Nature Reserve
── ──	Ferry Route
✈	Airport
🚌	Bus Station
🅿	Parking
ℹ	Tourist Information
✉	Post Office
♦	Church/Ruins
♀	Mosque
✿	Synagogue
♦	Castle/Ruins
∴	Archaeological Site
⋂	Cave
★	Place of Interest

The main places of interest in the Places section are coordinated by number (e.g. ❶) with a full-colour map and a symbol at the top of every right-hand page tells you where to find the map.

Contributors

De Villiers   Rathbone

Hilton-Barber   Bristow

CONTENTS

Young South Africans in a township near Cape Town

Information panels

Insight on....

Places

Travel Tips

THE SHAPE OF GOOD HOPE

South Africa's natural beauties are legendary. Now it offers visitors the chance to witness a nation being reborn

The news from South Africa, wrote one observer after a visit, "is absorbingly interesting at the moment." The writer was Matthew Arnold, and the year 1879, but the remark is particularly relevant today. Perhaps no other country in the world is undergoing quite such dramatic change as South Africa, where, after 40 years of white minority rule, a clutch of cultures – interlinked, but powerfully divergent – try to heal the wounds of apartheid and find a communal voice.

Today's visitors have the chance to be present as a new nation is created in all its richness and diversity, rooted in the indigenous cultures that suffered such dismal neglect during the apartheid years. Now, instead of relying on the United States and Europe for inspiration, there is much-welcome official support for African art, music, dance, drama, crafts – and political debate.

For many first-time visitors, their imaginations fed by media coverage of the country's political dramas, South Africa's pristine natural beauty will come as a welcome surprise. Starved of tourists over the past few decades – many people were put off visiting, thanks to the apartheid regime – it has largely escaped the sort of environmental degradation common to countries with a highly-developed holiday industry.

South Africans are proud of their conservation record, and a good deal of debate goes on in the national press on how to preserve the national heritage, while ensuring that the economic benefits of tourism can be passed on to underdeveloped communities and conservation agencies. "Ecotourism" is the buzzword visitors will hear most often; it's the strategy promoted by the government on the basis that the gross returns per hectare from wildlife tourism are much higher than from any other form of land use. It also provides all South Africans with a very real incentive to conserve the country's wildlife and wild places.

What of the future? Apartheid's legacy still looms large as Mandela's government struggles to create jobs, improve health and education, and remove the last vestiges of racial discrimination. Not everyone's expectations have been met, but the mood remains optimistic. Certainly, the world will be watching developments closely after Mandela retires at the next election in 1999.

What is clear is that South Africa has much to offer, and that few visitors will leave disappointed. The news is indeed absorbingly interesting.

PRECEDING PAGES: golden arches in the Cederberg; springbok herds in the Kalahari; surfing the KwaZulu-Natal coast; bringing home the harvest.
LEFT: African magic.

Decisive Dates

Circa **8000 BC:** San hunter-gatherers inhabit the south-western regions of southern Africa.

From AD 200: The semi-nomadic Khoikhoi begin farming the land.

From 1100: Other African peoples migrate into the southern African region from the north.

1488: Portuguese navigator, Bartholomew Diaz, circumnavigates the Cape and lands at Mossel Bay.

1497: Another Portuguese explorer, Vasco da Gama, discovers a sea route to India via the Cape.

1652: Jan van Riebeeck sets up a supply station at the Cape for the Dutch East India Company, thus founding Cape Town.

1659: The first wine from Cape grapes is pressed.

1667: The first Malays arrive at the Cape as slaves.

1668–1700: Huguenot refugees settle in the Cape.

1779: First skirmishes between the settlers and the Xhosas, followed by eight further frontier wars.

1795: The British annex the Cape.

1803: The Cape Colony reverts to Dutch rule.

1806: Britain reoccupies the Cape, the start of 155 years of British rule.

1814: The Cape is formally ceded to Britain by the Dutch government.

1815: Shaka becomes king of the Zulus.

1820: British settlers arrive in the Eastern Cape.

1820–30: Shaka extends his territory, vanquishing other tribes and leaving large areas devastated and depopulated in his wake.

1824–25: Port Natal (later renamed Durban) is established in Shaka's kingdom by British traders.

1828: Shaka murdered by his half-brothers, one of whom – Dingaan – becomes king.

1833: Slavery abolished in all British territories.

1836–54: The Great Trek. Over 16,000 Voortrekkers travel northwards in wagons from the Cape in order to escape British domination, settling mainly in the north and what is now KwaZulu-Natal.

1838: On December 16th, a party of Voortrekkers under Andries Pretorius defeat the Zulus under Dingaan at Blood River in Natal.

1843: Natal becomes a British colony.

1848: British sovereignty proclaimed between the Vaal and the Orange rivers.

1852: Several parties of Boers move further east and found the Zuid-Afrikaansche Republiek.

1854: The Boer Independent Republic of the Orange Free State founded.

1860: The first Indian indentured workers arrive in Natal to work in the sugar-cane industry.

1867: Diamonds found near Kimberley.

1877: Britain annexes South African Republic.

1879: Zulu impis wipe out a British force at Isandlwana. The British retaliate by defeating the Zulus at Ulundi, in what is now KwaZulu-Natal.

1880–81: The Transvaal declares itself a republic. First Anglo-Boer War.

1883: Boer leader Paul Kruger becomes the first president of the Transvaal.

1886: Gold in great quantities is discovered on the Witwatersrand. Johannesburg is founded.

PARTIES AND ORGANISATIONS

AWB: Afrikaner Resistance Movement, a neo-Nazi white group.

COSATU: Congress of South African Trade Unions.

IFP: Inkatha Freedom Party, the Zulu political party which clashed violently with the ANC in the 1980s and 1990s.

NP: National Party, the white, mainly Afrikaner political party which ruled South Africa from 1948–94.

NUM: National Union of Mineworkers.

SACP: South African Communist Party, formed 1921, banned 1950–90.

PRECEDING PAGES: San rock art.
ABOVE LEFT: Stone Age tools found at Thulamela.

1899–1902: The second Anglo-Boer War, in which the Boers are beaten and their settlements destroyed.

1910: The Union of South African proclaimed.

1912: The South African National Congress is formed, known after 1923 as the African National Congress (the ANC).

1913: The Native Land Act is passed, limiting land ownership for blacks.

1920: South African Indian Congress founded.

1925: Afrikaans replaces Dutch as the official "second language" after English.

1948: National Party under D.F. Malan wins general election. Acts enforcing apartheid follow.

1950–53: Apartheid is further entrenched via a series of acts such as the Group Areas Act, and the forced removal of numerous communities.

1952: The ANC launches the Defiance Campaign.

1960: On 21 March the police shoot and kill 69 of the participants in a demonstration staged against passport laws in Sharpeville, Transvaal. The government bans the ANC.

1961: South Africa becomes a republic, and leaves the Commonwealth. The ANC launches armed struggle. Albert Luthuli awarded Nobel Peace Prize.

1964: Following the 1962 arrest of lawyer and ANC president Nelson Mandela, his original prison sentence of five years is commuted to life for "high treason and sabotage" in the Rivonia Treason Trial.

1966: Apartheid's arch-proponent, Hendrik Verwoerd, assassinated in Parliament. B.J. Vorster succeeds him as Prime Minister.

1967: Professor Chris Barnard performs the world's first human heart transplant at Cape Town's Groote Schuur Hospital.

1975: Zulu cultural movement *Inkatha* revived by Chief Mangosuthu Buthelezi in Natal.

1976: On 16 July, Soweto schoolchildren protest against Afrikaans as the medium of instruction in black schools. Police violence ignites resistance across the country. At least 600 people lose their lives.

1976–81: The homelands of Transkei, Bophuthatswana, Venda and Ciskei are given nominal independence from South Africa and become "separate countries".

1983: A new Constitution provides for a tricameral Parliament for whites, coloureds and Indians. The United Democratic Front is founded.

1986: Various "petty apartheid" acts abolished, including the ban on mixed marriages.

1984: Anglican Archbishop Desmond Tutu is awarded

ABOVE RIGHT: the unlikely architects of a revolution, F.W. de Klerk and Nelson Mandela.

the Nobel Peace Prize. State repression is stepped up nationwide and a State of Emergency declared.

1989: Resignation of President Botha, who is succeeded by F.W. de Klerk.

1990: De Klerk announces plans to scap apartheid and release Nelson Mandela. The state of emergency is ended, and organisations including the ANC unbanned. The ANC suspends armed struggle. *Inkatha* becomes a political party, the Inkatha Freedom Party.

1991: All apartheid laws still in force (racial separation, separate living areas) are repealed. UDF disbands Declaration of Intent signed at the Convention for a Democratic South Africa (Codesa).

1993: President de Klerk and Nelson Mandela are

jointly awarded the Nobel Peace Prize; international sanctions are lifted.

1994: The first democratic general elections are held. On 10 May, Nelson Mandela is sworn in as the first black President of South Africa. De Klerk and Thabo Mbeki become joint Deputy Presidents, and Buthelezi, Minister of the Interior.

1995: Truth and Reconciliation Commission appointed under Archbishop Desmond Tutu. South Africa hosts – and wins – World Cup Rugby Tournament.

1996: De Klerk pulls the NP out of government and joins the Opposition benches.

1997: South Africa's new Constitution comes into effect on 3 February. De Klerk steps down as NP leader. Nelson Mandela steps down as ANC leader.

1998: Truth and Reconciliation Commission ends.

BEGINNINGS

The first African cultures were established much earlier – and were more sophisticated – than the apartheid theorists cared to admit

Apartheid theorists were fond of describing South Africa as an empty land, peopled by immigrants. Apartheid maps showed fat black arrows depicting waves of Africans migrating into South Africa from the far north, while much thinner white arrows discreetly indicated the European incursions from the sea. The intention, of course, was to give the impression that all South Africans, equally, were intruders of alien origin, and that the white minority had the same moral right to the land as the black majority.

For similar reasons, apartheid theorists were at pains to stress the cultural differences between different kinds of Africans. Black Africans were alleged to belong to "tribes", culturally monolithic and mutually incompatible. These could not be trusted to live in peace, and had to be sharply segregated from each other. One of the ways this was achieved was by dividing South Africa up into ethnically distinct tribal "homelands".

Apartheid theory also sought to disaggregate this African majority into much smaller components so that the white minority no longer seemed like a white minority, but more like one tribe among many other tribes. The fact that the white tribe, a mere 13% of the total population, occupied more than 80% of the total land surface of the country was shrugged off as a mere historical coincidence.

Such crude apartheid theories are rarely met with in South Africa these days, but the underlying stereotypes still persist to a surprising extent. Many of them are the by-products of attempts to romanticise African culture and the African past for the sake of making a fast tourist buck. The stereotype of the "proud Zulu" is a good example.

South Africa's people are naturally conscious of their diverse origins, and consciously seek to preserve all that is positive in their heritage. The importance attached to the country's 11 official languages in the very first chapter of the 1996 constitution is a case in point.

However, the industrial revolution which followed the discovery of gold in 1886 and created Johannesburg, South Africa's first non-racial

city, fused all these diverse pre-existing elements into a single social formation with a common destiny. The white ruling class joined together in the Union of South Africa in 1912. The black majority joined together in the African National Congress of 1912. Ever since then, South Africans have been South Africans first and foremost, although it is true that every now and then, glimpses of more retrograde tribalisms do appear.

Moreover, having suffered for so long at the hands of a government which tried to slot everybody into ethnic boxes, most South Africans today rightly resent the question "Which tribe do you belong to?"

LEFT: a ceramic head, dated to AD 500, found on an Early Iron Age site near Lydenburg, Mpumalanga.
ABOVE RIGHT: San hunters armed for an expedition; from a painting by Samuel Daniell, about 1830.

The Peopling of South Africa

The earliest known varieties of humankind emerged in Africa. Physical anthropologists call them hominids, meaning that they were more than apes but less than humans. More than 300 hominid remains, some dating back about three million years, have been found at the Sterkfontein Caves near Krugersdorp just west of Johannesburg, a site well worth visiting.

But not all hominids were the same. The *Australopithecus* (an "upright-walking small-brained creature") co-existed in South Africa with the more sophisticated *Homo Habilis* for more than a million years before finally biting

in relative isolation in the southwestern corner of the continent for about 40,000 years. These are the so-called Khoisan peoples, who once inhabited substantial parts of what is now South Africa, Namibia and Botswana.

The Khoisan were shorter and lighter-skinned than most other Africans, their languages contained clicks and other unusual consonants, and they knew nothing of agriculture or iron-working. They were mostly hunter-gatherers, and they lived in very small nomadic bands following the migration patterns of wild game.

The Khoisan peoples concentrated mainly in what are today the Western Cape and Northern

the dust – surely a worthy theme for a high-tech, big budget movie!

Remains of our own direct ancestor, *Homo Sapiens Sapiens*, have also been found widely distributed throughout South Africa. African variants of *Homo Sapiens Sapiens* display genetic markers which are called Negroid by comparison with the Mongoloid and Caucasoid variants found elsewhere. Crudely put, this implies that black people have been living in South Africa for about 100,000 years.

Within the Negroid genetic constellation, however, different groups developed in relative isolation from each other. One sub-group which we particularly need to notice must have lived

ENTER MODERN MAN

About three thousand years ago, one group of Khoisan living in northern Botswana were initiated into cattle-keeping by other Africans. Being herders rather than hunters, they multiplied and dispersed very rapidly. They called themselves *Khoikhoi* ("men of men"), and they called the remaining hunter-gatherers *San*. The Dutch called them Hottentots and Bushmen, but these terms are now regarded as insulting and should no longer be used. Similarly, the word *Bantu*, a perfectly respectable term outside South Africa when used to describe the cultures of the sub-continent, is not socially acceptable at home.

Cape provinces. Most of South Africa was occupied by other African peoples who were darker-skinned and more technologically sophisticated. They spoke languages which clearly indicate their cultural links with the rest of Sub-Saharan Africa.

Internationally, these languages are known as Bantu languages, a perfectly respectable term outside South Africa. But in South Africa the word "Bantu" was so abused by the apartheid governments that it is not socially acceptable in any context.

The African emphasis on custom and tradition was a natural recourse of people who

finds Venda, which is a relative of Shona in Zimbabwe, and Tsonga, which is related to the languages of southern Mozambique.

Reputable social scientists attribute many cultural differences between the Sotho-Tswana and the Nguni to the different natural environments in which they lived. Water is relatively scarce in the interior. Hence the Sotho-Tswana tended to live in bigger settlements and to build in stone. The coastal lands, however, are punctuated by many rivers running from the mountains to the sea. This permitted the Nguni to live in more dispersed settlements, and to change their dwellings more frequently.

lacked the means to record their political and legal codes on paper. It did not prevent innovation, but tended to change according to circumstance.

For example, most black South Africans speak either the Sotho-Tswana languages, which are found mainly on the interior plateau, or else they speak the Nguni languages (Zulu, Xhosa, Swazi), which are found mainly along the coast. In the Northern Province one also

Left: Zulu Kraal near Umlazi, Natal, by G.F. Angas.
Above: Ndebele warriors attacking, by C.D. Bell. The Ndebele troops carried large, oval, Nguni-type shields and short stabbing spears.

Another good example of the way in which environment influenced customs is that of marriage practices. Among the Sotho-Tswana, cattle were relatively scarce and society was more hierarchical. It therefore made good sense to marry one's cousins and keep the cattle in the family.

Among the Nguni, however, homesteads were more dispersed, and it made more sense to forge alliances by marrying into other families and exchanging cattle with them. These small examples show that African cultures were well adapted to their local circumstances, and that they were far more flexible than the apartheid theorists cared to admit.

THE COLONISATION OF THE CAPE

Two centuries of European settlement failed to unite South Africa – yet the seeds of apartheid were sown

European colonisation of South Africa began in 1652 when the Dutch East India Company opened a refreshment station at Cape Town. The first Commandant, Jan van Riebeeck, was unable to maintain good relations with the neighbouring Khoikhoi, and he took two decisions of great importance to the future of South Africa: he established a class of permanent white settlers, and he imported slave labour. He also went to war with the Khoikhoi, and he imprisoned their leaders on Robben Island. This was the beginning of South Africa's most notorious penal settlement.

The slaves at the Cape soon came to outnumber the white population. They came mostly from the Dutch East Indies (modern Indonesia), and they intermarried with Khoisan, Africans and renegade whites to form a new community, known today as the Coloured people. There were no slave plantations at the Cape, and very few big farms. Most of the slaves lost their indigenous culture and adopted the language and religion of their masters.

However, a minority of slaves, mostly political exiles and skilled artisans who had bought their freedom, adhered to their Islamic heritage. This "Cape Malay" community still predominates in parts of Cape Town such as the Bo-Kaap, which has a distinctive style of architecture.

The first white settlers farmed wheat and wine on relatively small holdings near Cape Town. But as soon as settlement expanded beyond the mountains into the drier grazing-lands of the interior, it accelerated at a frightening speed. The settlers referred to themselves as "Boers" (farmers) or "Afrikaners" (Africans) to distinguish themselves from the Netherlands officials. They took whatever land they pleased and treated the Khoisan as vermin, killing the adults and raising the children as household servants. There was very little control by the fee-ble Dutch East India Company, and Boer interests were well served by their local *Heemraaden* (magistrates' council).

The Huguenots

Meanwhile, the colony continued to expand. In 1688, the first of 220 French Protestants, known

as Huguenots, arrived at the Cape. They were fleeing religious persecution because Louis XIV of France had revoked the Edict of Nantes, the last guarantee of immunity for Calvinists living in France.

The impact of this small group was more significant than might be imagined: for one thing, it increased the European population by about 15 percent. Yet the Huguenots also brought with them valuable know-how, including the knowledge of how to cultivate wine. The names of wine-farms in the vicinity of Franschhoek ("the French Corner") still recall the places of origin of some of these settlers.

LEFT: The arrival of the Dutch East Indiaman *Noordt Nieuwlandt* in Table Bay on 21 August 1762.
ABOVE RIGHT: A typical Boer frontier family with Khoisan servants in attendance.

Britain takes control of the Cape

The British presence at the Cape was initially strategic. During the War of American Independence, an increasing number of French vessels visited the Cape on their way to India. This development greatly disturbed the British government, then on the brink of hostilities with Napoleon. When the Dutch East India Company was finally liquidated in 1795, British forces took control of the Cape as allies of the Prince of Orange, and, although briefly returning it to the Netherlands in 1803-1806, they eventually decided to keep it.

The British were infinitely more powerful than their feeble predecessors. One of the first loose ends they decided to tie up was the Eastern Frontier. Several Xhosa chieftains, headed by a rebellious ex-Regent named Ndlambe, had penetrated deep into colonial territory, defying all the attempts of the Dutch authorities to dislodge them. Colonel John Graham was instructed to inspire "a proper degree of terror" in "these savages", and to chase them over the colonial boundary. He did just that, also founding, in 1812, the town which still bears his name today.

To accelerate the region's integration into the British colonial system, the government in London decided to sponsor emigration programmes to the Cape. Accordingly, in 1819, some 4,000 people – mostly artisans and ex-soldiers – were granted land in the area known as the Zuurveld, bordering on the Great Fish River. Between 1820 and 1824, the settlers were shipped out from the mother country, issued with basic rations, tents and farming tools and quickly dispatched to their new frontier "farms".

The settlers were, on the whole, a literate and articulate group who were to make a lasting impression on the development of education,

A Tougher Enemy

The Xhosa proved a tougher enemy than the Khoisan, being better led, better armed and more numerous. Nor did they die from European diseases in the same way. In North America and Australia, for example, whites not only defeated the native inhabitants but came to outnumber them because the diseases they imported proved to be deadly. This did not happen to black South Africans, who are still by far the largest racial group in the country.

the press and the legal system in South Africa. However, frontier life was harsh and uncompromising. Few of the settlers were experienced farmers, and many drifted towards towns such as Bathurst and Grahamstown. Those who remained on the land had to contend with a fickle climate, regular crop failures and constant raids on their stock by marauding Xhosas.

Despite petitioning the government in the Cape to provide them with adequate protection, the settlers' pleas were to no avail. Instead, the government decreed they should use their own horses and equipment while engaged in punitive expeditions. What's more, farmers were still expected to pay their normal taxes, which only added to their grievances.

The Boers shared with the new immigrants a common resentment against the administration in Cape Town. Beforehand, as already noted, they had done more or less whatever they wanted and taken more or less whatever they could, particularly land and labour. But from 1822 onwards, a British Commission of Inquiry initiated a series of reforms designed to destroy the Boer's preferred way of life. These included more effective taxation, land allocation and more determined magisterial authority. Ordinance 50 of 1828 abolished forced labour and proclaimed authority before the law regardless of colour, paving the way for the abolition of slavery in 1834.

The Boers could read the writing on the wall, and they turned their eyes to the lands beyond the Orange River which were still outside the British sphere of control. Already, small bands of Coloured people known as Griquas, who had left the Colony to escape racial discrimination, had set up de facto states beyond the Orange. They dominated the surrounding black nations by virtue of their access to horses and guns. From about 1834, Boer leaders such as Piet Uys and Louis Trichardt started to send out exploratory parties to reconnoitre new territories. By 1836 the mass migration of Boers, known to history as the Great Trek, was under way.

A Time of Troubles

Meanwhile, a very different kind of revolution was taking place north of the Thukela River in the present province of KwaZulu-Natal. It culminated in the reign of Shaka Zulu (1818-1828), but it did not begin with him. The critical element in the rise of the Zulu kingdom was the militarisation of youth associations called in Zulu *amabutho*, and usually translated as "regiments". Some recent historians have maintained that this militarisation was due to the presence of Portuguese slave traders at nearby Delagoa Bay (now Maputo). But this argument falls down on chronological grounds, because the slave trade only began in the 1820s, at least 25 years after the events which led up to the formation of the Zulu state.

The decade of the 1790s saw a series of increasingly ferocious wars fought between increasingly ferocious chiefs, concluding with

Male regiments were, in fact, twinned with female regiments and their deprivation was social rather than sexual in nature. Although the Zulu warriors were physically mature men, they were not regarded as independent adults but as the children of the king who had to be available at all times to do his bidding.

Shaka thus obtained a degree of despotic control over his people which was unprecedented in southern African history. Legends of his cruelty abound, and although these must be treated with caution, it does seem that he became increasingly erratic as time went on. It is quite certain that his nearest and dearest conspired

the establishment of the Shakan despotism in 1818. Shaka did not originate the regimental system, but he elaborated it to its highest point of perfection. He erected military headquarters throughout his kingdom, in which the various regiments were housed.

The nature of these establishments has been greatly misunderstood by romantic and reactionary writers alike, more especially the fact that Zulu warriors were not allowed to marry until their regiment was dissolved by the king.

ABOVE: Table Bay in 1683, by Aernaut Smit, with the ship *Africa* in the foreground. The castle is depicted with the original entrance facing the beach.

against him, which tells us something. Shaka was assassinated in 1828 by his brother Dingane, with the active assistance of his other brother, his father's sister and his personal manservant.

By this time, the Shakan method had become well understood, and it was copied by a number of mini-Shakas who carved out their own despotism in diverse parts of southern Africa, including Mozambique, Swaziland, Zimbabwe, Zambia, Malawi and Tanzania. On the other hand, wiser and more tolerant chiefs built up their power by offering succour and defence to homeless refugees. Moshoeshoe, the founder of Lesotho, is the most famous example of this kind of chief. This period of South African history is sometimes called the *Mfecane*, after a word meaning "crushing", but this term has lately fallen out of favour.

Piet Retief, leader of the Boer trekkers, or "Voortrekkers", attempted to negotiate with Dingane to obtain land in Natal south of the Thukela River. But Dingane distrusted the Boers and ordered the murder of Retief and his negotiating party. The Boers rallied their forces under Andries Pretorius, who gave his name to the South African capital. They defeated the Zulus in 1838 at the Battle of Blood River.

Later, in the 1930s, Afrikaner historians and politicians turned the events of 1838 into a nationalist and racist myth. Retief's murder became an act of primitive savagery, and Pretorius' "miraculous" victory over the Zulus a sign that the Voortrekkers and their descendants were God's people who alone had the right to rule South Africa.

The birth of the Boer republics

After their victory, the Boers in Natal set up a new republic which proved short-lived. The British were not yet ready to surrender their imperial hegemony over southern Africa, and so they annexed Natal in 1845. The Boers, how-

ever, refused to accept this. They headed across the Drakensberg into the far interior, where they founded two republics, the Orange Free State and the South African Republic (later known as the Transvaal).

The independence of these republics was soon challenged by the British. Claiming that their jurisdiction extended to the 26th south parallel, in 1848 a British invasion force annexed the entire territory between the Orange and the Vaal rivers. Eventually, however, a change of government in London contributed to the British recognising Boer independence north of the Vaal in 1852, and south of the river in 1854. The move effectively awarded sovereignty to the Boer republics.

The character of these republics may be inferred from Article 9 of the constitution of the South African Republic (1858). This stated unequivocally that "the people are not prepared to allow any equality of the non-white with the white inhabitants, either in Church or State."

Other laws of the South African Republic also show very clearly the goals which the Boers set themselves when they embarked on the Great Trek. Every Boer who had participated in the Trek was entitled by right to two farms, which he demarcated himself. Black chiefdoms defeated by the Boers were obliged to supply them with tribute labour. The old tradition of child labour in the form of indentures (called the *inboekstelsel* because the names of the children were recorded in a book) was continued.

And if that was not enough, in 1870 the SAR legislature passed a law called the *kaffer wet,* whereby each farmer was entitled to labour service from five black families living on his farm. This was the origin of the system of labour tenancy which still faces the post-apartheid government in the present day.

The Frontier Wars

Back in the Cape, Britain was still continuing what is now known as the "Hundred Years War" against the Xhosa people on its Eastern Frontier. Both the Xhosa and the settlers were stock farmers, dependent on sufficient grazing. After a series of devastating droughts, the white farmers started trekking eastward, encroaching on tribal land. Subsequently, they were subjected to stock raids of increasing intensity.

The settlers, blaming the British administration for the lack of adequate protection, took matters into their own hands. Between 1819 and 1853 four frontier wars erupted in the border area, claiming thousands of lives and debilitating traditional Xhosa society for generations to come. Attempts by the British administration to reassert its authority were met by equally strong resistance from the farmers. Their feeling of alienation from the Cape was aggravated by their anger over lack of compensation for their losses.

In 1856–1857, the extraordinary incident known as the Xhosa Cattle-Killing occurred. A young girl, Nongqawuse, prophesied that if the people killed all their cattle and destroyed all

ensure that Xhosa power was finally destroyed.

The manifest failure of Xhosa traditionalism following the cattle-killing set the scene for increased co-operation between settler traders and progressive Xhosa farmers. British missionaries were very active in the Eastern Cape and they encouraged the growth of an African peasant class. Here, British commercial interests led to the liberalisation of the laws of the Cape Colony – there was even a non-racial franchise, although it included only the very well-educated.

In the British colony of Natal, however, the situation was very different, and policy was not

their crops, the dead would rise, new cattle would rise, and nobody would ever again lead a troubled life. Hard-pressed by the rapid disintegration of their traditional culture under severe pressure from the settlers (claimants of ancestral land) and the missionaries (breakers of traditional custom), the Xhosa resorted to these desperate measures. The failure of the prophecies was manipulated by a particularly ruthless governor named Sir George Grey to

LEFT: Boer leader, Andries Pretorius.
ABOVE: C.D. Bell's depiction of a surprise attack by Zulu warriors on a small party of Voortrekkers encamped near the Bloukrans River.

at all liberal. Here, the British established sugar plantations which were voracious of land and labour. Segregation and "native reserves" were consequently established in the colony before they were even thought of in the Boer republics. And because labour was so scarce, the British added another twist to South Africa's social fabric by introducing indentured Indian labour.

As late as 1867, South Africa did not really exist. There were four white-ruled colonies and innumerable black kingdoms and chiefdoms. Britain was the dominant imperial power, but even she had more pressing concerns elsewhere.

Then diamonds were discovered and everything changed. Completely.

WEALTH AND WELFARE

The discovery of diamonds and gold created wealth,
cities and jobs. It also sparked war

South Africa before the mid-19th century was a thinly-populated land with limited economic resources and a small export trade in such items as wool, ivory and hides. Before 1848 there were few roads, before 1860 no substantial banks, and until 1880 almost no railway lines. Such towns as existed, apart

from the ports, were either seats of magistracy like Graaff-Reinet, or meeting places for the quarterly *nachtmaal* of the Dutch Reformed Church.

Diamond rush

All this changed after 1867, when the first diamond was found north of the Orange River. Speculators from the Cape and Natal, a few Afrikaner farmers, and local Griqua and Tlhaping tribesmen sought to benefit from the river diggings on the Vaal and the dry diggings that soon turned into the vast prospectors' camp of Kimberley. The region became a bone of contention among the British, Free State and Trans-

vaal governments because of its strategic position. That problem was resolved, amid much controversy, by an arbitration court which ordered the proclamation of the diamond fields as the crown colony of Griqualand West.

Successful diamond mining depended on the ability of the claim-holders to control marketing, and this necessity led between 1870 and 1888 to a step-by-step amalgamation of individual claims, which was made more urgent as the mines went deeper and the work became more expensive. Cecil John Rhodes' De Beers Company eventually emerged as the pre-eminent mining house, a position it still holds.

The Kimberley mines drew in the skills of well-paid immigrants and the manual labour of low-paid Africans. The latter were recruited on contract by labour touts in collusion with chiefs, who in turn required payment of their subjects in firearms as well as other goods. The black miners were in due course housed in compounds under strict control, and subjected to close body searches to prevent diamond smuggling. The white diggers won exemption from these searches. Thus there developed a pattern of labour differentiation and control which would set a precedent for much of the industrial life of South Africa in later years.

With the birth of Kimberley, industrial South Africa came into being. It provided an urban market for foodstuffs, at first supplied largely by African farmers. Kimberley's needs also set in motion the railway age.

Gold fever

Gold, like diamonds, had been discovered in 1867, at Tati on the Transvaal border of Bechuanaland, and subsequently in various parts of the eastern Transvaal from 1874. But it was only with the location of the main reef on the Witwatersrand in 1886 that South African gold mining began in earnest. Kimberley supplied the entrepreneurs, the initial capital and some of the expertise to set Rand mining going. But the monopoly conditions necessary for diamond mining did not develop on the Rand.

The Chamber of Mines, established in 1887, went some way to regulate the competition, above all by ensuring that labour was made extremely cheap, and housed in compounds as a control device. But by 1890 the Chamber found itself in opposition to Paul Kruger's government for both political and economic reasons.

The republicans resented the intrusion of foreigners (*uitlanders*), especially when they demanded political rights, which it was reluctant to grant. It sought to

A WHITE LAND

By the end of the 19th century nearly all the land in southern Africa was owned by whites, either through surveyed titles, or through government control.

carved out farms and worked the mineral deposits they had acquired through victory in frontier wars. On the other, there was a contest between Great Britain as the paramount power in the region and the Boer republics for the political control of territory.

The first phase of the Anglo-Boer conflict over territory, which developed after the recognition of republican sovereignty by Britain, was a dispute between Britain and the Free State over the control of Basutoland (Lesotho)

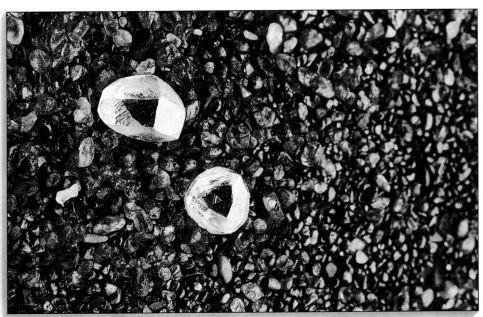

profit from gold mining but drove up production costs by, among other means, the inefficient taxing of explosives. By 1895 it was becoming clear to governments in Europe that the Transvaal had become a focal point of power, just at a moment when the international partition of Africa was gradually moving towards a climax.

The imperial factor

The European occupation of southern Africa was a double process. On the one hand, there was the physical appropriation of the greater part of the land by white colonists as they

---

LEFT: a miner's life. **ABOVE:** diamonds are forever.

and the Diamond Fields. Both territories passed under British control and both were later transferred to the Cape Colony, but Basutoland was made a British protectorate in 1884, as were Bechuanaland (Botswana) in 1885 and Swaziland in 1902.

From 1868 it became a stated objective of British policy to amalgamate the South African territories politically for reasons of defence and economy. In 1875 Disraeli's Colonial Secretary, Lord Carnarvon, sought to do this, but he forced the pace, and failed to win the backing of the Cape government. He had, however, annexed the Transvaal by an adroit move designed to put pressure on the Free State. The annexation proved a fiasco, partly because of poor administration, partly because the Afrikaner leadership under Paul Kruger organised a successful rebellion in 1880–81 and persuaded Gladstone that it would be wise to withdraw. Conventions signed in 1881 and 1884 restored the Transvaal's independence on terms which gave Britain, at best, an ambiguous right to intervene in its affairs.

When gold mining developed on the Witwatersrand, it became apparent that the economic balance had shifted to the north, and that whoever ruled the Transvaal would dominate South Africa. Deep-level mining on the Rand pro-

duced only narrow profit margins, partly due to Kruger's fiscal policy, and this created at least a temptation to overthrow his government.

Cecil Rhodes, prime minister of the Cape from 1890 to 1896, had already unsuccessfully attempted to incorporate the Transvaal in a South African railway and customs union, and then to encircle the republic by purchasing Lourenço Marques (Maputo) from the Portuguese. In 1895 he plotted a rebellion on the Rand to be assisted by an invasion by his British South Africa Company forces from across the border. But the Jameson Raid, planned with the knowledge of the British Government, also failed, and seriously undermined Kruger's will-

ingness to trust the British. Rhodes was discredited and resigned.

The Anglo-Boer War

In a sustained diplomatic face-off in 1899, the British drove Kruger to the brink of war by insisting on the full recognition of *uitlander* rights. Kruger yielded ground to the point at which his pride could yield no more, and anticipated a British ultimatum by invading the coastal colonies in October.

The Anglo-Boer War of 1899–1902 at first went well for the Boers, who scored major victories against a heavily equipped, well-trained enemy. Only when the main British forces arrived were they able to invade the allied republics, occupying Bloemfontein and Pretoria by June 1900. However, the war dragged on for two more years. Boer guerrilla forces raided across the plateau. The British commander, Kitchener, responded by moving Boer women and children into concentration camps. These were a disaster, their poor sanitation causing the deaths from disease of close on 28,000 Boers and many thousands of black refugees. Finally, and bitterly, the Boers surrendered in 1902. Their two republics, and the gold fields, became part of the British Empire.

The conflict had a profound effect on the moulding of South African political attitudes. Most Boers believed that they were the victims of a monstrous British injustice; that the British had set out to destroy them as a people. Latter-day Afrikaner nationalism was born out of a determination to put right these wrongs by making sure that South Africa became an Afrikaner country, not a British one.

However, the myth that it was a "white man's war" which didn't affect blacks has little historical evidence to support it: blacks were recruited as labourers and scouts by both sides in the conflict, though the Boers were more reluctant than the British to issue them with arms. Blacks also suffered directly and in large numbers during the sieges and from the destruction of farms, as well as from the concentration camps, where more than 14,000 died. But their hardships went relatively unnoticed in the published accounts, and, when the war was over and the peace treaty signed, they had little to expect for their sufferings.

LEFT: for three years, the Boers kept the British at bay.

Kruger and Rhodes

With his baggy black suit, straggly beard and enormous pipe, Paul Kruger was caricatured by the world press as a typical "backveld" Boer, but critics who underrated his undoubted political skills did so at their peril.

Born in 1825 in the Cape Colony to a Boer family of German origin, Kruger was a veteran of the Great Trek. As he liked to remind his audiences, he had seen the circle of wagons, the children melting lead to make bullets, and the women hacking off the arms of those Zulus who tried to break through the thornbushes between the wagons at the Battle of Blood River.

With no formal education, his first "profession" was that of lion-hunter, but he quickly rose within Voortrekker ranks by showing his mettle on commando, in battles to subdue various African chiefs. At 26 he was elected as a delegate to the Sand River Convention, and withing 10 years was appointed Commandant-General. In 1877, when Britain annexed the Transvaal, Kruger emerged as the Boer's national champion, and was twice sent to London to try to persuade the British to abandon their policy. In 1883 he was elected President of the South African Republic – an office he was to hold for four terms.

A Calvinist to the core, with an unshakeable belief that his "volk" were God's chosen people who alone had the right to rule South Africa, Kruger was a forceful personality, but Afrikaner as well as British opponents found him headstrong and autocratic.

Provoked into declaring war on Britain in 1899, it was Kruger's misfortune to lead his beloved Republic to defeat. When the war started to go badly he went into voluntary exile, following events closely to the final defeat of the Boer forces in 1902. Refusing to submit to British rule, he remained in exile, dying in Clarens, Switzerland in 1904. His remains were brought home for burial at Heroes Acre in Pretoria.

If ever there was a *bête noire* almost custom-made for Kruger, it was Cecil John Rhodes. Born in Hertfordshire, England in 1853, the son of a vicar, Rhodes was first sent out to Natal to recuperate from tuberculosis. The sickly youngster soon found his way to the new diamond fields at Kimberley, where he conceived an ambitious plan to gain total control of the entire diamond industry. By 1889, Rhodes and his mining company, De Beers Consolidated, had achieved his goal.

Obsessed with furthering the cause of British imperial expansion, Rhodes combined his commercial genius with an equally ruthless career in politics. Made prime minister of the British Cape Colony in 1890, he used intrigue and war to grab the lands of the Matabele and Shona north of the Limpopo, and establish under Royal Charter his personal states of Northern and Southern Rhodesia (now Zambia and Zimbabwe). This effectively blocked Kruger's South African Republic from expanding north of the Limpopo.

But a scheme to topple Kruger and seize the Republic's goldfields for the British led to Rhodes' downfall. The Jameson Raid of 1895, in which Rhodes tried to organise a committee of leading *uitlanders* (dissatisfied immigrants) to overthrow Transvaal government with the help of a column of British police, failed dismally – Kruger's government got wind of the plot before it even took place. This fiasco not only marked the end of Rhodes' political career, it also helped to alienate British and Afrikaners across the whole of South Africa.

Rhodes died in his Muizenberg cottage in 1902, his dreams of a British "Road to the North" unrealised. Paradoxically, the financial empire he built continues to be a mainstay of South Africa's economy.

RIGHT: Paul Kruger, the "Wounded Lion".

UNION AND RESISTANCE

By the turn of the century, white domination had finally been achieved – despite the fact that blacks far outnumbered whites

The Peace of Vereeniging registered the victory of the Empire over the Boers shortly after white domination of South Africa was finally achieved. The 20th century would witness a speedy Afrikaner return to power, and then – after 90 years of assertive white dominance – the start of an impressive black resurgence.

Britain annexed the former Boer republics in 1902, but made it possible for them to regain autonomy. This was largely the achievement of Generals Louis Botha and Jan Smuts, who saw the need for conciliation among whites – between Empire and Boer, Boer and English speaker, and rival groups within Afrikanerdom – but left the problem of dealing with blacks to the "stronger shoulders" of the future. The British government thought that extending the vote to blacks would jeopardise their aim of conciliating the whites.

Meanwhile, black political organisations watched resentfully as Britain first allowed the Transvaal and Orange River Colony to acquire white-controlled constitutions in 1907–08, and then agreed after the National Convention of 1908–09 to a constitution for a united South Africa, which did substantially the same thing.

Britain aimed to restore the South African economy by bringing the mines back into production and resettling the uprooted on the land, thereby coaxing the Afrikaner back into the imperial fold. Black labour might be essential for this task, but not black voters. Reconstruction therefore took place, conciliation among whites began to work, and the Union of South Africa took its seat with the other white dominions in the British Commonwealth of Nations.

As a member of that imperial system, South Africa took part in two world wars and played a leading role in the evolution of dominion autonomy between 1917 and 1934. The involvement of prime ministers Louis Botha, Jan Smuts and Barry Hertzog in the consultations of the Empire were themselves a clear indication of how well conciliation had worked. But it operated only on the surface, and could not contain the groundswell of opposition underneath.

The Union of South Africa in 1910 was an embryonic industrial state, with mineral exports (especially gold) far exceeding agricultural, and with a developing manufacturing industry producing mainly for the local market. These years also witnessed a parallel townward movement by both Afrikaners and black South Africans.

Resurgence of Afrikaner power

Afrikaner republicanism was reborn soon after union, on a platform of opposition to the imperial connection and a demand for the effective recognition of Afrikaans language rights. The former found expression in the rebellion of 1914, triggered by the government's decision to invade German South West Africa, while the founding of the secretive Broederbond in 1918 led to a spread of Afrikaner cultural and economic organisations, the latter with a focus on the rescue of poor whites.

Both found a political mouthpiece in the National Party governments of General Barry Hertzog between 1924 and 1939: first in alliance with the white Labour Party and after 1932 in alliance with General Smuts (until their fused United Party was split asunder when Hertzog tried to keep South Africa neutral in World War II).

Hertzog's strident nationalism was toned down once he had seen that South Africa could remain within the British Commonwealth without the rights of the Afrikaner necessarily being threatened. But this wasn't the view of a new "purified" National Party, which grew after 1934 under the leadership of Dr D.F. Malan.

Malan's party, the voice no longer just of the poor whites but also of a new brand of Afrikaner entrepreneur seeking economic power, won the

LEFT: the proudly-named "Union Express", symbol of a newly-united country, carried passengers from Cape Town to Johannesburg.

1948 election and remained in power without a break until the first democratic elections for all South Africans in April 1994. Afrikaner voters, some of whom had been attracted to Leninism in their poverty of the 1920s, had entrenched themselves not only on the land but also in the civil service and the professions, and more recently in business too. English speakers, by contrast, remained politically marginal, though their business dominance remained strong.

Roots of black opposition

But the main catalyst for change, which gradually came to monopolise the attention of the

by the Land Acts of 1913 and 1936. Thus tied down, blacks found it hard to organise themselves effectively to promote political or economic change.

During World War II, it seemed that segregationist policies might be reduced under pressures generated by the Atlantic Charter. The wartime government of General Smuts tried to ameliorate the conditions of urban blacks, ceased briefly to enforce the pass laws, began to build black secondary schools, made a start with black pensions and disability benefits, and professed its rejection of the principle of segregation.

white political establishment, was the numerical growth and townward movement of black South Africans. A small minority in all urban areas at the time of union, blacks were in the majority in nearly all of them by mid-century, though they were required nearly everywhere to reside in "locations" away from the towns proper.

Blacks were also effectively debarred by law from political and trade union activities, and controlled in their movements by pass laws. This ensured that many could not move from white-owned farms to towns. The majority, who remained in the tribal reserves, were also prohibited from acquiring land outside the reserves

But in the run-up to the general elections of 1943 and 1948, the Smuts government could not contain the rising propaganda of the National Party. Smuts's failure to initiate a change of direction led to a major confrontation with the African Mineworkers' Union in 1946, in which lives were lost. This broke black trust in Smuts. His government's attempts at policy changes, on the eve of the 1948 election, were neither sweeping enough to attract black backing nor cautious enough to prevent the white electorate from casting their votes decisively for Malan.

ABOVE: Two Afrikaner generals: Smuts (left) and Herzog.

Gandhi

The development of the sugar-cane industry in the 1860s in what is now KwaZulu-Natal meant that large numbers of indentured Indian labourers were imported by the British colonial authorities to work in the plantations. As they finished their contracts and settled in South Africa, establishing small businesses, trade connections with India grew. Durban, in turn, developed into South Africa's most distinctively multi-cultural city.

In 1893 a 24-year-old advocate named Mohandas Karamchand Gandhi came to South Africa to act in a lawsuit between two Indian trading firms. Having landed at Durban, he caught a train to Pretoria in connection with the suit. He had a first-class ticket, but during the journey a white passenger objected to his presence in the compartment, and he was ordered to move to a third-class coach.

Ignorant of South African racial prejudice, he refused – and was promptly ejected from the train for his pains. He spent the night at Pietermaritzburg station. The incident made such an impression on Gandhi that in later life, he declared it had been the single most important factor in rousing his spirit of protest and determining his political career.

Gandhi's subsequent involvement in the Indian community's struggle for civil rights kept him in South Africa for 21 years. It was here that he first developed the philosophy of *satyagraha* which made him world-famous, and which later played such a key role in India's struggle against British colonial rule.

Satyagraha means "keep to the truth". Gandhi considered truth a central life-principle – one which meant, in practice, resisting injustice not with force, but with the superior powers of love and spiritual conviction. Hence his conception of passive resistance as a form of political protest.

The community of Indian entrepreneurs in Natal was a flourishing one, but deeply resented by white traders who disliked undercutting. Attempts to establish Indian businesses in the Transvaal were met with restrictions on residential and trading rights; Natal also imposed a hugely unpopular £3 tax on Indians who wished to stay in the colony after the expiry of their indentures.

The young Gandhi quickly became one of the Indian community's most articulate and influential leaders, founding the Natal Indian Congress in 1894. He also pursued his professional career with great success, first in Durban, then in Johannesburg.

But it was in protesting against the Immigration Act of 1913, restricting Indian settlement in the Transvaal, that his passive resistance campaign reached its climax. Strikes were organised in the coal mines of Northern Natal, which soon spread to sugar and other plantations. Finally, on 1 November, more than 2,000 *satyagrahis* started a march to the Transvaal with the intention of breaking the law and being arrested and imprisoned. The authorities could do little beyond make mass arrests,

thereby seriously threatening work on the sugar estates. Gandhi himself was sentenced to nine months' imprisonment.

The net result of all the upheaval, the Indians' Relief Act of 1914, addressed some of the community's chief grievances, such as the hated £3 tax and the fact that Indian marriages were not recognised. However, Indians were still denied any sort of official political representation.

Nonetheless, Gandhi considered his work in South Africa completed and returned to India, where he immediately threw himself into the struggle against British rule. His ideal was finally realized in August 1947, when India became independent. Tragically, only a few months later in January 1948, he was assassinated by a Hindu fanatic.

RIGHT: the philosopher-politician Mahatma Gandhi.

THE RISE AND FALL OF APARTHEID

More than three centuries of white domination finally ground to a halt
in 1994 – without the predicted bloodbath

The National Party headed by Dr Daniel François Malan, a preacher and journalist before becoming a politician, won the 1948 general election by a narrow margin, against expectations. The bulk of support came from recently urbanised whites who feared the challenge of blacks in the market-place, espe-

cially as the African National Congress (ANC), in association with the African Mineworkers' Union, showed signs of growth during the 1940s.

The new government's response was to bring out a legislative programme designed to entrench white (and by implication Afrikaner) dominance. The principles of apartheid (separateness) dominated the government's legislative programme from the start. It enacted a Population Registration Act to slot everybody into an appropriate race group, as well as to outlaw interracial matrimony or sexual relations, and a Group Areas Act to divide every town in South Africa into defined sectors where only members of particular groups could own or

occupy property. This required the physical removal of many Coloured and Asian households, but few whites. Most resented of all were the "pass laws" which restricted the movements of blacks. The legislation was buttressed by laws designed to undercut political resistance, beginning with the Suppression of Communism Act. It was followed by measures which would restrict individuals and organisations, while denying them right of appeal to the courts.

After Dr Hendrik Frensch Verwoerd, a chief promoter of apartheid legislation, became prime minister in 1958, the policy was developed to promote territorial partition so that the African reserves could be turned into "independent homelands" whose citizens could on that pretext be deprived of access to political rights in the South African heartland. Verwoerd tried to establish border industries to enable blacks living in the homelands to find employment in "white" South Africa with minimal daily travel; but he would not allow white capital to finance such development. His successor, Balthazar Johannes Vorster, a lawyer and staunch supporter of traditional Boer principles, removed this restriction; but by 1970 it was clear that job creation in the homelands fell far short of providing a living for the number of Africans required by government policy to live there.

Growing black resistance

Such policies strengthened support for the ANC. The oldest existing political party in the coun-

PASSIVE RESISTANCE

A campaign against the pass laws during the war eventually led to the launching of a Defiance Campaign in 1952, a well-orchestrated passive resistance tactic by African, Asian and Coloured movements to offset the white tercentenary celebrations. Its forceful suppression led to the public adoption of a Freedom Charter at Klipfontein, near Johannesburg, in 1955 – a broad social democratic affirmation designed to achieve wide public support.

try, it had formed for six decades the vanguard of black political aspirations. It was in January 1912 that representatives of the country's major African organisations met in Bloemfontein to form the Native National Congress. The movement, soon renamed African National Congress, had its agenda cut out. Two years earlier the Union of South Africa had been forged out of the ashes of the Boer-British struggle, but had ignored the position of the vast majority of the country's citizens.

The ANC spent its first years protesting the historical errors committed at Union. But its critics accused it of being an organisation of

marked the beginning of a new strategy of direct, non-violent confrontation.

Documents confiscated by the police when they broke up the Klipfontein gathering (*see box, page 38*) formed the basis for the first of a number of "treason trials" which marked the next 35 years. The defendants were all found innocent in 1961, but in the meantime divisions opened up within the ANC. A group of "Africanists" led by Robert Sobukwe were disturbed by communist influences on ANC policy, arguing that if a racist government was in power the assertion of African nationalism was the real note to strike. Driven out of the ANC in 1958,

elderly men fighting to preserve their hard-won, middle-class privileges. Impatient activists joined the fledgling labour movements that advocated more radical action. In 1943 the ANC Youth League was formed by a group of young men whose political legacy is still felt: the brilliant Anton Lembede, Oliver Tambo, Walter Sisulu and an enigmatic young lawyer, Nelson Mandela. They were soon strong enough to stage an internal coup and to get their candidate, Dr James Moroka, elected president. This

LEFT: Grand Vizier of apartheid, Dr Hendrik Verwoerd.
ABOVE: Sharpeville, 1961. Police bullets killed 67 protestors, hitting many in the back.

they broke away to form the Pan-Africanist Congress (PAC).

When the government launched its campaign for a republic in 1960, the ANC and PAC were at daggers drawn, yet both were angling for mass support by promoting anti-pass demonstrations linked to wage demands. Some 30,000 Africans marched on the Houses of Parliament in Cape Town. Police bullets killed 67 protesters at Sharpeville, near Vereeniging on the south Rand, on 21 March, and the government, clearly frightened, banned both the PAC and the ANC, driving them underground. The world condemned the Sharpeville shootings, and South Africa's ostracisation in world affairs began.

White responses

In a whites-only referendum, Dr Verwoerd obtained a narrow victory to proclaim a republic and his government subsequently decided to leave the British Commonwealth. Sharpeville had shown the inadequacy of passive resistance and drove the African resistance movements into violent opposition. In 1963, however, the police captured the underground leaders of the ANC, headed by Nelson Mandela, in Rivonia, outside Johannesburg, as they were planning to disrupt public life. After an eight-month trial, they received life sentences in the notorious Robben Island prison.

The ANC and the PAC set up bases in exile in Lusaka, Dar-es-Salaam and London, but they found it difficult to make much impact locally or internationally. For almost 10 years the South African government managed to keep a lid on black political activity. Activists were rounded up and held under "90 Days" detention without trial.

In September 1966, Hendrik Verwoerd was stabbed to death in the House of Assembly by a parliamentary messenger. His successor, B.J. Vorster, was better at silencing opposition than developing strategies for change. But, when capital started to flow back into South Africa, he tried to revive the socio-economic aspects of apartheid. Investment corporations were set up to develop the homelands. The expansion of black businesses, black housing, black schools and black immigration into the white area was made harder.

By 1970 the number of jobs created in the homelands was seen to be nowhere near that required if Africans were to be able to "flow back" from the white areas. The government decided to press ahead with homeland "independence", starting with the Transkei in 1976. The aim was to create alternative allegiances, thus depriving all citizens of "independent" homelands of their South African citizenship even if they still lived in the Republic.

The tide turns

On a cold winter's day, 16 June 1976, Soweto, the large African residential location outside Johannesburg, erupted after a government decision to enforce the use of Afrikaans as a language medium in schools, though the grievances were far wider and included objections to homeland independence. Much of the drive came from a new Black Consciousness Movement led by Steve Biko, an activist from the Eastern Cape.

Over a period of 18 months the burning of public buildings, schools, liquor outlets and cars had most of the African townships in flames and the conflagration soon also spread into Coloured and Indian residential areas. The government again clamped down heavily. On 18 August 1977, Biko was arrested by the security police. Twenty-six days later he died from head injuries sustained during interrogation.

Black consciousness was too well-rooted to be effectively extinguished; it re-emerged in other forms, linking Africanist aspirations to a socialist ideal. Many young activists fled the country, joining the waiting structures of the ANC in exile. This influx of new blood rejuvenated and strengthened the movement considerably. Led by Oliver Tambo, the ANC redoubled its onslaught against the government on two fronts: the military, where they achieved moderate successes with sabotage attacks on strategic installations; and international isolation, where they continuously pushed for strong punitive measures – economic sanctions, arms embargoes and cultural and sporting boycotts.

Internally, black opposition re-emerged in 1985 with the formation of the United Democratic Front (UDF), a loose federation of anti-apartheid movements, linked ideologically to the ANC. A new generation of black leadership – "the '76 generation" – came to the fore. When they were restricted, trade unions became a focal point of political activity, leading to the creation of the giant Congress of South African Trade Unions (COSATU). Church leaders emerged as vocal spokesmen for black aspirations, with men like Archbishop Desmond Tutu and Dr Allan Boesak becoming household names across the world. Tutu became the second South African to win the Nobel prize for peace (the first, in 1960, was Albert Luthuli, a

Nations which had started soon after World War II. Talk of international sanctions, beginning with an arms embargo in 1963, was spreading to include economic and cultural boycotts. Almost the whole world condemned the Republic's policies.

Vorster's government fell after disclosures of serious financial mismanagement in the running of its propaganda activities. The scandal divided the ruling National Party and propelled the Defence Minister, Pieter Willem Botha, to the premiership. Botha restored effective control over government. He also tried to rebuild the economy, which went into deep recession from

Natal teacher who had become leader of the ANC in the 1950s).

World opinion

In the 1960s and 1970s, Vorster's government had offended world opinion by refusing to support sanctions against the white rulers of Rhodesia, and by holding out against the transfer of power in South West Africa (present-day Namibia), in a dispute with the United

LEFT: Hector Pietersen, the first victim of the riot police at Soweto, 16 June 1976.
ABOVE: a groundswell of public violence was a hallmark of the apartheid years.

1982 as a result of a sustained drought and a dramatic fall in the gold price, aggravated by a move among the world's banks to impose a stranglehold on South Africa's borrowing.

Far from trying to abolish apartheid, Botha attempted in 1983 to make it irremovable. He secured white electoral support for a new constitution which not only made him an executive president (as distinct from the largely formal office created in 1961) but also created ethnically distinct houses of parliament for whites, Coloured people and Indians, with no representation for Africans.

This led to renewed violence in the new Coloured and Indian constituencies when a general election was held in 1983. By then, the ability of black organisations to conduct effective resistance had markedly increased as industrial workers and resistance leaders in the townships began to act together.

The ANC, for its part, was now concentrating on building up its links with the international community, setting up missions in many parts of the world where the South African government was not represented, even acquiring diplomatic recognition in some.

Furthermore, the homeland structures, Verwoerd's brainchild, were beginning to collapse as "independent" states – in some instances

confusion on the eve of a general election which had been forced upon it by a deadlock with the Coloured House of Representatives arising out of the terms of the 1983 constitution.

Apartheid in reverse

Botha's mantle fell on the shoulders of the Transvaal leader of the National Party, Frederik Willem de Klerk, who won the 1989 white general election by an outright majority over opponents of both left and right after seeking a mandate for unspecified reform. Educated and confident, de Klerk was an example of a new generation of Afrikaners who came of age after

through the exposure of corruption, in others through the overthrow of ruling dynasties – ground to a standstill. In Natal, even though KwaZulu's Inkatha movement had opposed independence, something like open warfare developed between Inkatha and ANC supporters as each side attempted to build up its constituency in anticipation of an eventual redistribution of political power.

Paralysed by a manifest inability to keep his policies on course and in the face of a growing threat from a new Afrikaner right wing, P.W. Botha was forced out of office by a ministerial rebellion in September 1989. The future direction of the National Party was thus thrown into

"BLACK-ON-BLACK" VIOLENCE

During the 1980s and early 1990s, parts of KwaZulu-Natal and the Witwatersrand were turned into battlegrounds as something like open warfare raged between members of the Zulu Inkatha movement (later, the Inkatha Freedom Party) and the Xhosa-dominated ANC. Most of the disputes were concerned with local government, as the ANC-supported "civic" movements fought to discredit councillors (Inkatha members) elected under the unpopular local government legislation of 1983. Although the level of violence has now declined, sporadic outbursts still occur.

the introduction of apartheid and began to question the very basis of the system they inherited.

Because he was known to be a supporter of narrow, white "group interests", many doubted his will to go for real change. But South Africa could no longer afford to maintain apartheid in an increasingly hostile world, with a weakened economy, and with a ruinously expensive war which had broken out on the South West African border against members of the South West African People's Organisation (SWAPO).

Opening the parliamentary session of 1990, de Klerk undertook to remove apartheid, promising sweeping reforms. He planned to

attended the independence celebrations as South West Africa became Namibia, ending a deadlock that had lasted more than 40 years.

De Klerk found a willing negotiating partner in the pragmatic Mandela. Opening the South African Parliament in February 1990, he declared the government's willingness to negotiate a new constitution with equal political rights for all. The ban on political opponents was lifted and the leaders of the liberation movements released from jail or allowed to return from exile. Despite these moves, a groundswell of public violence was a constant reminder that the transition would not be easy.

move cautiously, consulting the ANC leadership step by step. On 11 February he unconditionally released Nelson Mandela, the last of the imprisoned ANC leaders, after he had served 27 years in jail. It was a momentous decision because it signalled to a world which had long regarded Mandela's imprisonment as a symbol of apartheid's evil that a milestone had been passed. Six weeks later de Klerk removed another source of international protest: he

LEFT: ANC supporters campaign for non-racial, democratic elections.

ABOVE: a first-time voter proudly displays proof of her newly-won democratic rights.

The odd couple

Hopes for the country's future centred to a remarkable degree around de Klerk and Mandela – a fact the outside world recognised by awarding them jointly the 1993 Nobel Peace Prize. But could de Klerk neutralise groups such as the Afrikaner Resistance Movement, who still referred to the ANC as "the AntiChrist"? And could Mandela reconcile the ethnic rivalries cemented by centuries of violence?

Mandela called his election manifesto "A Better Life for All". It promised 10 years of free education for all children, a million new homes, and a public works programme to provide jobs for 2½ million people. These were unrealistic promises, according to de Klerk, who realised better than most that there had been little significant investment in infrastructure for years, and that the annual 6 percent growth of the 1960s had turned into negative growth by the 1990s.

After extensive and prolonged multi-party negotiations – including threats from Inkatha's Mangosuthu Buthelezi that his party would not participate – South Africa's first democratic elections were held between 26–29 April 1994. Described by one official as "unmitigated chaos", many ballot papers went missing, while fraud and malpractice were prevalent.

allowed them unilaterally to rewrite the constitution, but it was still a respectable result. On 9 May 1994, Nelson Mandela, former prisoner 466/64, was elected president. F.W. de Klerk became one of two vice-presidents.

The "marriage" between Mandela and de Klerk lasted until 1996, when de Klerk took the National Party out of government and into opposition. Mandela remained an international hero, being accorded a state visit to Britain in 1996. At home, though, there were accusations of authoritarianism. The big question was how long the black majority would wait for the president to make good his promises to

People who had never seen a ballot paper before queued for hours under a hot sun to cast their vote. Old women, some aged more than 100, were pushed in their wheelchairs to the booths. White women lined up alongside their maids. Archbishop Desmond Tutu danced a jig for the cameras after voting in Cape Town. A Johannesburg radio station played Louis Armstrong's *What a Wonderful World*. After 342 years and 23 days, white rule had come to an end.

Despite the allegations of chicanery, the election had to be declared free and fair. The ANC emerged with 62 percent of the vote. This fell short of the 66 percent which would have

improve their economic well-being. "The wheels of government grind slowly," Mandela said.

But at least they *were* grinding, and the transition to black majority rule, an event which only a few years before had seemed utterly improbable, had been achieved without the predicted bloodbath. What's more, South Africans, white and black, had accomplished the miracle themselves, without the intervention of international tribunals or peace-keeping forces. Hope, although still fragile, had begun to bloom again.

ABOVE: people queue to reach the voting-booths, 1994.

Mandela

Born the son of a chief in 1918 in Qunu, Transkei (now the Eastern Cape), a member of the Thembu royal household, Nelson Rolihlahla Mandela first became involved in politics as a student at the University of Fort Hare. It was here that he met Oliver Tambo, later to become the African National Congress' president-in-exile.

After being expelled from Fort Hare for their role in student strikes, both young men moved to Johannesburg. Here, Mandela met Walter Sisulu, and the three – Tambo, Sisulu and Mandela – became heavily involved in ANC politics, helping to found the ANC Youth League in 1944. The Youth League was extremely influential in pushing the ANC towards adopting a more radical stance on protest action, and, in particular, founding the Defiance Campaign in 1952. Based largely on Ghandian principles of non-violence, the Defiance Campaign involved the deliberate breaking of apartheid legislation, such as the hated "pass laws".

Mandela also completed a BA degree by correspondence and then studied for an LLB at the University of the Witwatersrand, before establishing (with Tambo) Johannesburg's first black law firm in 1952. He married Winnie Madikizela, a social worker, in 1958, and the couple had two daughters.

When the ANC was banned in 1960, the organisation decided that the time for peaceful protest was over. Mandela went underground to form *Umkhonto we Sizwe* (the Spear of the People, commonly known as MK), and to organise a campaign of sabotage. Tambo left the country to re-establish the ANC in exile.

Mandela survived "underground" for 17 months, training as a guerrilla fighter in Algeria and visiting Britain and many African states in search of support for MK. He became famous for staying a step ahead of the police, earning himself the nickname "the Black Pimpernel". But his luck ran out in 1962 when he was caught in a police trap. His links with MK as yet unknown, he was charged with "leaving the country without permission" and given a five-year jail sentence. Then, in 1963, the police raided MK's Rivonia headquarters and discovered evidence of Mandela's role in the organisation. On 12 June 1964 he and eight others, including his old friend Sisulu, were found guilty of plotting to overthrow the state and sentenced to life imprisonment. Mandela was sent to Robben Island prison.

For the next 26 years, the ANC's leaders in exile struggled to keep the organisation active and united. They were helped in no small measure by Mandela's fame as an internationally respected leader and symbol for human rights, which grew the longer he remained in prison.

After his release in 1990, Mandela went on to play a central role during the four long, troubled years of multi-party negotiations, which finally culminated in South Africa's first democratic elections in April 1994. On 10 May 1994 he was inaugurated as South Africa's first black president.

Despite the problems his government has had trying to implement an ambitious programme of reform, Mandela has remained enormously popular, not least with many white South Africans who once regarded him as a terrorist. He has come to be seen as the living embodiment of new, longed-for standards and values in post-apartheid South Africa, and the world will be watching developments in the country closely after he retires at the next election in 1999.

In 1996, Mandela divorced his wife, Winnie, a loyal ANC member whose reputation since the late 1980s has, unfortunately, become increasingly tarnished by scandal, including accusations of torture and murder and even a conviction for kidnapping.

RIGHT: South Africa's first black president.

LIVING TOGETHER

The transition to majority rule hasn't been easy. But the new

Rainbow Nation is as complex as it is fascinating

It's become one of the most difficult questions to answer. That's why most people here have stopped asking it: who or what is the typical South African? Most countries have a stock of comfortable national stereotypes to fall back on when faced with this question. In South Africa the cultural clichés change from suburb to suburb, never mind city to city. Cultural life here is that diverse.

For many, the stock image of Africa starts with the colonial stereotype of the "noble savage": people and cultures both primitive and vibrant, still magically in touch with the ways of the natural world. And let's not forget that crucial sense of rhythm, honed after generations of dancing around ceremonial fires.

As everyone knows, South Africa has an extra element – the whites. White settlers, the people responsible for inventing apartheid, live here too; burly, bearded folk in khaki bush suits, wearing veldt hats and clutching rifles to keep marauding lions, rhinos and the occasional restless native at bay. It's the image most people have of the Afrikaner, and it's the way many people imagine all white South Africans to be.

But these stereotypes have little basis in reality. South Africa is an extraordinary tapestry of race and culture like no other place anywhere in the world. And despite the problems of the past, it's a society that's beginning to find great strength in its diversity.

A complex culture

Diversity was definitely what the country's first democratic election was all about. No less than 19 different parties, representing practically every aspect of the political, religious and social spectrum, presented themselves to the voting public. And seven of them found enough support among this public to gain representation in parliament.

Diversity of language and culture was further recognised by the newly elected government in giving equal official status to 11 of the languages spoken throughout the country: English, Afrikaans, Zulu, Xhosa, Sotho, Venda, Tswana, Tsonga, Pedi, Shangaan and Ndebele.

Switch on the television in South Africa today and you'll find news broadcasts coming at you in each of the four main language groups – English, Nguni (Zulu and Xhosa), Afrikaans and Sotho – while radio tells it like it is in all 11 languages. Switch over to a local soccer match and you'll get your commentary broken up into 15-minute slots, alternating between Zulu and Xhosa, English and Sotho. Diversity? I think South Africa invented the term.

So the one thing first-time visitors shouldn't pack is the preconception of a nation divided into two basic groups of blacks and whites. Nothing is simple in South Africa. It's a far more fascinating place than that.

PRECEDING PAGES: Durban's beachfront; Cape Town's Minstrel's Carnival.
LEFT: Northern Cape farmer.
ABOVE: Hindu traditions, proudly preserved.

Melting-pot – or divided society?

Broadly speaking, the racial and cultural enigma that is South African society consists of people of African origin, those of European descent and a third stream of mixed origin, known as "Coloureds". Of a total population of some 38 million, around 76 percent are black. Whites represent about 12.8 percent, Asians 2.6 percent and those of mixed origin 8.5 percent.

The key division in black South African society is between *Sotho* people (South Sotho, Bapedi, Tswana), and the *Nguni* (Zulu, Xhosa and Swazi). Originally, academics split nations between these two groups on the basis of

language, location and settlement patterns – the early Nguni settlements tended to be widely dispersed in scattered homesteads and villages, while the Sotho lived in more concentrated settlements and towns.

Although the terms "Nguni" and "Sotho" cover most of the black passengers riding the South African cultural bus, there are also societies such as the Shangaan-Tsonga, who belong to neither major group. Nor do the enigmatic people of Venda, made up of about 30 independent chiefdoms including the Lemba, who claim to be one of the lost tribes of Israel.

White South African society is no simple homogeneous grouping, either. As in black society, there is a key cultural divide – between English-speaking South Africans, and the small, stubborn tribe known as the Afrikaners.

It was inevitable that the Dutch colony established at the Cape in 1652 should soon spill over the Hottentots-Holland Mountains, its natural border. Those settlers who left the Cape became nomadic cattle-farmers and hunters. Under these extreme circumstances, a new language was born, based on the Dutch of medieval Flanders with European, African and Oriental additions. The settlers called it "Afrikaans" and themselves "Afrikaners", or "Africans". A surprisingly streamlined Germanic tongue which, like English, has rid itself of most of its declensions, Afrikaans is the world's most modern language.

The Napoleonic wars in Europe altered the course of South Africa's history and brought new people and a new language to the country. In order to safeguard its interests, Britain took possession of the Cape towards the end of the 18th century. This prompted a large-scale migration movement; the new arrivals were mostly settled in the Eastern Cape. Whereas the Afrikaners were mostly stock farmers and hunters, the new immigrants included merchants and artisans. With the discovery of diamonds and gold, the English-speakers were well-equipped to develop the fledgling mining industry. Right up until 1994 – the end of the apartheid era – the language of the business community remained predominantly English while the language of politics and administration was to a large extent Afrikaans.

Other, smaller groups abound. South Africa's Jewish community (about 130,000 strong) has made an indelible impression on cultural and economic life, with men like Barney Barnato and Alfred Beit playing an important role in the establishment of the diamond and gold mining industries. A sizeable group of Jewish refugees from the Baltic settled in the country after World War I and became involved in trading and manufacturing, laying the foundations for one of the most prosperous sectors of the local economy.

The years immediately following World War II brought a number of new settlers from Europe. These included Dutch immigrants of a strict Reformed persuasion, searching for a new country where they could practise their beliefs; and a significant number of Germans – most of them highly skilled in engineering and the sciences – looking for a place to start afresh, away from their war-ravaged fatherland.

Without these skilled European minorities, South Africa would probably not have succeeded in establishing a highly industrialised society with such technical achievements as its petro-chemical industry.

The 1960s saw an influx of Lebanese, Italian and Greek settlers (mainly from Cyprus), as well as Portuguese from the island of Madeira and the former Portuguese colonies in Africa. The Soviet invasions of Hungary (1956) and Czechoslovakia (1968) also brought a number of new immigrants from central Europe to

indentured labourers – the Indians to work on the sugar farms of KwaZulu-Natal in the 1860s, and the Chinese as mineworkers on the Witwatersrand in 1904.

Shaped by conflict

A series of wars – including the Frontier Wars of the Eastern Cape, the Zulu Wars and the Boer Wars – originally established the basis of the relationship between South Africa's different communities, both black and white. This bleak history, along with the 1913 Land Act and the brutal legacy of apartheid, pretty much defined South African society as it is today.

South Africa. All these people played an important role in the economy by supplying new skills and helping to create job opportunities.

The term "Coloureds" is used to refer to South Africans of mixed descent, but it also includes a number of people from other subgroups, such as the Cape Malays. Most of this 200,000 strong community live in Cape Town's Bo-Kaap district.

Our profile also includes people of Asian descent, mainly from India but also a small number from China. Both groups arrived as

LEFT: Zulu dancer in imaginative headgear.
ABOVE: Griqua woman, carrying home the firewood.

SURVIVING AGAINST THE ODDS

The last surviving San and Khoikhoi communities fall into the "Coloured" category, although their numbers are now so small that they can no longer be said to represent distinct social groupings. A few small bands of San still roam the arid Kalahari desert, pursuing their traditional nomadic hunter-gatherer lifestyle. Of the Khoikhoi, several communities of Griqua (one of the main clans) have settled around Kimberley in the Northern Cape province; while the last surviving Nama, another key group in this category, live in an area situated near Steinkopf on the northwest coast.

However, what the Afrikaner Nationalists who devised apartheid completely failed to grasp was that this diverse and somewhat motley conglomeration of people who settled at the southern end of the continent actually belonged together. Paradoxically, years of conflict has only served to create a stronger sense of history shared.

Due in no small part to the apartheid system, which tried to confine 42 percent of South Africans on 13 percent of the land in the so-called tribal homelands, the country's various social groupings are found in highly specific geographic locations. Fairly obviously, you'll

Province, Free State, Northern Province and parts of Mpumalanga have the largest white Afrikaans communities (Afrikaans is also the language spoken by the Coloured community).

KwaZulu-Natal, often referred to (proudly or disparagingly, depending on how you like to take your tea) as the Last Outpost of Empire, has a solidly British flavour. In addition, this is where you'll find the great majority of South Africa's Indian population.

The Eastern Cape, home to most of the original British settlers who came here in the early 1800s, is pretty much evenly split between English- and Afrikaans-speaking whites.

find the Zulus in the southeastern coastal province of KwaZulu-Natal. The Eastern Cape and parts of the Western Cape is traditional Xhosa territory. Sotho and Tswana people inhabit the area that covers the Northern Cape, North Western Province and most of the Free State between the countries of Botswana and Lesotho. In the north, in Mpumalanga and the Northern Province, you will find the Venda, Lemba, Pedi, Shangaan and Ndebele peoples.

The Coloured people live mainly in the Western Cape, but there are also large Coloured communities in the Northwestern and Eastern Cape. The Western Cape, Northern Cape, North West

Finally, there's Gauteng. As the centre of the South African universe, it's home to everyone and anyone. It represents multicultural South Africa at its most vibrant and diverse.

But remember: these are just broad, simplistic outlines in a country where nothing is that simple. For example, that last bastion of English colonialism and the home of Shaka's Zulu ancestors, KwaZulu-Natal, also has a conservative Afrikaans element in the farming communities of the northern parts of the province. Similarly, while the Western Cape is the domain of Afrikaans speakers, both Coloured and white, it has a significant English-speaking population, particularly in and around Cape Town.

A new way of life

So how does this fantastic jigsaw that is South African society fit together? How does all this diversity get along on a daily basis? Well, it's a relatively new experience for most. Apartheid tried to confine everyone to discrete ethnic boxes, which meant that despite the fascinating cultural variety, people kept themselves to themselves. Back then, a trip to a middle-class white suburb in any city would leave you thinking you'd arrived in an Australian, European or American Midwest suburb. The only black faces belonged to the people who did the laundry, washed the dishes and mowed the lawn.

Since democracy and a new, open-plan approach to government and culture has come into being, the barriers have come down. That's not to say that everyone has been flooding across them, but the overwhelming impression is of a nation coming to terms with its multicultural identity and – well, liking it.

Land of many tongues

When it comes to understanding each other, South Africans are faced with a situation that makes the lot of those ancient Babylonian tower builders seem simple by comparison. After all, this is a country with 11 official languages. It

Similarly, for most whites, a trip to a black township – in their imaginations, at any rate, since very few whites ever visited one– would have been the equivalent of visiting hell; a place filled with angry people ready to rob and mug you, if roast you over their coal fires. In the apartheid realm, people weren't supposed to know how the other half lived, unless the information came through an official media mouthpiece.

LEFT: Ndebele women tend the fire. The traditional cast-iron *potjie* cooking pots are a feature of many a modern *braaivleis*, too.
ABOVE: *Kappies* like these are worn for church.

might sound bizarre, but fortunately, no-one is really expected to communicate in all 11 of them. It's just part of the democratic dispensation that strives to recognise all the various pieces of the population equally.

Language is the first clue you get that the differences between people here are not simply a matter of black and white. Not all black South Africans can understand each other in their own languages. Xhosa is as separate from Venda as German is from Spanish. And the same goes for whites. If it wasn't for the English language's propensity to gobble up bits and pieces from other languages and culture around it, it would have as much in common with Afrikaans as Italian would with Chinese.

The reality is that English is by far the main language used by everyone – officially and unofficially. Afrikaans, Sotho and the Nguni languages, Zulu and Xhosa, are the other tongues in common use on a wider scale. The rest are generally confined to their regional bases.

Of the black languages, Zulu is probably the most widespread. KwaZulu-Natal is the most populous province and the Zulu influence on culture is everywhere, thanks mainly to Shaka's "how to win friends and influence enemies"

Today it's a pervasive part of everyday township lingo, full of coded names and expressions: the ever-present minibus taxis are called "Zola Budds" (because they're always crashing into each other, as athlete Zola Budd did, colliding with Mary Decker at the Los Angeles Olympics). The small 200-ml bottles of spirits commonly sold at shows and sporting events and in shebeens are called "cellulars", because they fit into your pocket like a cellphone.

When things are renamed like this, it signifies a lasting acceptance into local culture. The same principle applies to people, particularly soccer stars. A player without a nickname has

campaign of conquests during the previous century. It's also very similar to Xhosa, with which it shares its Nguni roots, as well as sharing common traits with Ndebele and Shangaan.

The cities, especially in the Gauteng area that has attracted people from all over the country thanks to mines and industries since the turn of the century, have their own distinctive styles of communication. The townships of the Witwatersrand gave rise to the colourful street-slang known as Tsotsi-taal (Gangster, or Bad-Boy language). Combining elements of Afrikaans with African languages and the more expressive bits picked up from American gangster movies, it typifies the style of the ultra-cool modern youth.

obviously not touched the hearts of the fans. Popular nicknames include "Chippa", which implies the skill to chip or bend a shot beyond an opponent's defence. "Dancing Shoes", or "Shoes", is another, given to players whose skill with the ball allows them to "dance" past opponents with it. A unique nickname was "Codesa 2", given to Kaiser Chiefs' and one-time national team captain Neil Tovey (a white South African in a predominantly black team) after the 1991 negotiations in which the principles of a new, non-racial South Africa were hammered out.

Another fascinating form of street lingo is the expressive language of the Cape Coloureds.

Combining their mother tongue of Afrikaans with English and African phrases, it is both powerful and humourous, You haven't really been sworn at until you've been sworn at by a "Capey".

Culture clashes

All this "living together" business has presented more than a few problems and misunderstandings between people. While the growing black middle class has meant that these days the Jones's have to keep up with the Khumalo's, the Jones's

the khaki that Jones is wearing is his scouting uniform and the rifle is part of his father's collection of antique guns. The meat the Khumalo's are barbecuing *(braaing)* for the relatives who've come to celebrate was bought, pre-packaged with a spicy marinade sauce, from the local butcher. But still, caution prevails, and it will be a few generations yet before people feel completely at ease across the cultural divide.

One popular generalisation that often comes up is the idea of "African time", which observes

aren't too sure how much of their traditional ways the Khumalo's have brought into the suburbs with them. So they peer cautiously over the fence to make sure the Khumalo's aren't about to slaughter a goat in the back garden in honour of the birth of a new child.

Similarly, the Khumalo's remain suspicious about young master Jones's propensity to dress up in khaki and clean his rifle on the front porch. Of course, in most cases the reality of it is that

LEFT: jubilant voters queue at a Gauteng polling station during the first democratic elections, 1994.
ABOVE: rugby fans, their faces patriotically painted in the colours of the new South African flag.

that it's no use making appointments with black South Africans for a specific hour, as they will invariably be late and arrive, unapologetically, whenever it suits them. When this happens, you're supposed to shrug your shoulders and roll your eyes heavenwards and say, "Well, that's African time". It's a generalisation based on two myths. The first is the old racist stereotype of blacks as lazy and uncooperative. The other, often propagated by black South Africans themselves, is that "This is Africa, man. Relax... don't be white and uptight. Everything will get done in good time".

These different understandings of the nature of "African time" are at the heart of a bigger, two-sided, cultural debate concerning how South African society should be getting things done. On the one hand there are those arguing that a more Afrocentric approach is called for. On the other hand is everyone else who believes that Africa, and South Africa in particular, is part of a much larger modern world which requires people to shift away from a more traditional mindset and get into step with the rest of the planet. The Afrocentric corner calls this lot Eurocentric.

While they debate themselves into a self-important and meaningless lather, the reality on the ground is that South African society already

is a fascinating blend of African tradition and modern principles. In the suburbs, a white householder calls in a traditional healer, or *sangoma*, to prepare charms to protect his home from being robbed after the sophisticated alarm system has failed to do the job. Across town, a black mother-to-be is putting her faith in her Jewish, London-trained, gynaecologist rather than the rural midwife her mother went to.

And at the local stadium, black and white fans are urging on a player, kitted out by Adidas and anointed with a secret *muti* (traditional medicine) by the team's *sangoma*. In another world, the soccer boots and secret *muti* are as far removed from each other as the opposing

viewpoints in the Afro/Eurocentric debate. On the field they become partners in the same cause – victory in the football match.

African traditional medicine still plays a big part in society and if the Afrocentrics have achieved anything it has been to get white South Africans to look at the traditions of Africa not as quaint, curious and outdated but as real and powerful.

But not all traditional beliefs make the modern South Africa feel comfortable. Attitudes to homosexuality, for example, are still almost medieval in rural black communities, where some conservative elements simply refuse to acknowledge that such a thing exists. Still, at least things have come a long way since the days when homosexuals were thrown into the communal cattle-kraal to be trampled to death. In the major urban centres, most black communities now accept the gay culture as a part of life.

Coming together

For all the in-fighting that goes on down here, there can be no doubt that South Africans of all races and cultures have a grudging, but mutual, respect for each other. It's certainly evident in the sporting arena, where sports like soccer, cricket and boxing bring South Africans of all colours, political shapes and ideological sizes together in a frenzy of adulation for the sporting heroes of their new, united South Africa.

Supporting your country in sport is something most people would take for granted. Yet it's important to remember that until the end of apartheid, it was common for South Africans to support foreign teams instead of the local sportsmen and women, who, it was perceived, represented only white South Africa.

Despite the differences in traditions and languages, South Africans of all races and cultures remain very much the same kind of people at heart. On most Saturdays and Sundays you'll find the average male, black or white, standing around the braai drinking beer and talking sport. The brand of beer might be different; the white man may be talking about rugby, the black about soccer, the Indian about cricket and the gay man about the latest Milanese fashions, but in the end they're all living the South African way of life.

LEFT: *Sangoma* grinding herbs, Mai Mai market.

The Zulus

According to South African journalist Khaba Mkhize, "there are two types of Zulus – postcard Zulus, and the type of Zulu who is running away from the postcard". South Africa's largest black nation has been subjected to some particularly crude stereotyping in the past, from the caricature of the rustic, cattle-herding peasant to that of bloodthirsty tribalist, sporting leopardskin and waving a spear.

Based on fragments of apartheid propaganda, bolstered by the "tribal" souvenirs mass-produced for the tourist market, such images have little bearing on reality. Most Zulus today view themselves as citizens of South Africa, rather than identifying themselves first and foremost as members of a particular tribe. For one thing, many aspects of the traditional way of life were so abused by the apartheid government, whose policy it was to force every black person to adopt a tribal identity and a "homeland" address, that they have become permanently tainted. And in any case, as more and more people opt for an urban lifestyle, the old customs and traditions are fast being displaced by "Western" ways.

What is certainly true is that the Zulus were once a mighty military power. The late 18th and early 19th centuries were characterised by almost constant Zulu warfare – against neighbouring clans, against the Afrikaner Voortrekkers, and against various British regiments (KwaZulu-Natal's historic "Battlefields Route" bears fascinating and sometimes chilling testament to these torrid times). Legendary leaders such as Shaka are still a source of fireside tales and a symbol of both resistance and national pride.

This legacy has been rather clumsily linked by some social analysts to the "black-on-black" violence so prevalent in KwaZulu-Natal and on the Witwatersrand during the 1980s and early 1990s. Some onlookers saw this as the latest stage of an ancient feud between the Zulus (who dominate the Inkatha Freedom Party) and the Xhosas of the ANC. Yet insiders will tell you that the violence first arose out of disputes relating to issues of local government. In reality, it involved two political movements struggling for control of the townships, each attempting to build up its constituency in anticipation of an eventual redistribution of political power.

RIGHT: Zulu leader Chief Mangosothu Buthelezi.

The fact that some IFP Zulus were being paid and trained in secret by members of the apartheid security forces did little to clarify these muddy waters.

Yet not all Zulus have traded in their cultural roots for a briefcase or a factory job. Millions remain faithful to at least some semblance of custom and culture, consulting *nyangas* (traditional healers) and paying *lobola* (the traditional "bride-price" paid by a bridegroom to his father-in-law). Notwithstanding urbanisation and Christianity, a belief in ancestral spirits is still strong.

Today, as the whole issue of ethnicity becomes less of a hot potato in post-apartheid South Africa,

something of a indigenous cultural renaissance is getting underway. Post-apartheid, there is official support for all aspects of traditional black culture, from music and theatre to traditional healing. "Cultural villages" have been set up to promote indigenous crafts and customs – at Simunye Pioneer Settlement in KwaZulu-Natal, for example, visitors can spend time listening to tales of battles with the British from a Zulu perspective, filled with "unofficial" oral history. Most importantly, thanks to a post-apartheid update of the history books, black schoolchildren are now able to take pride in their tribal heritage without being patronised or politically branded for it.

At long last, it seems South African Zulus can turn their backs on those postcards.

THE SPIRIT OF RELIGION

The scope of belief is as wide as South Africa's communities are diverse,
with traditional beliefs still holding a surprising amount of sway

Countless religions have taken root in South Africa in the course of the country's history. Even in the smallest villages, steeples or minarets reach like fingers toward the sky; and in the shadow of the skyscrapers which shape the skylines of major cities, houses of worship stand ready for believers to congregate for devotions and prayers.

Today, the constitution guarantees complete freedom of worship to all, and reflects the diversity of South Africa's communities. As in most other parts of Africa south of the Sahara, Christian denominations form the largest group: four out of five South Africans belong to a Christian church or organisation, although a sizeable minority has no religious affiliation.

Despite a softening of approach in recent years, Sunday observance laws are still in effect in the country, and they govern both trading hours and entertainment.

Traditional beliefs

Traditional African religion is based on an holistic conception of the universe. Religious practices are supposed to preserve and reinforce harmony within the web of an individual's relationship to himself and his family, to his society and environment, to the realm of spirits, good and evil – and ultimately to God. Keeping damaging influences at bay and healing damaged relationships is therefore extremely important.

The animistic conviction that natural elements and objects such as water, trees and wind possess souls also plays a large part in traditional beliefs and ceremonies. But the central tenet is a belief in a Supreme Being, who can only be reached by people on earth through the agency of their ancestors.

Because the ancestors are already with the Godhead, they are venerated as the "living

dead" who may pass along the requests of their earth-dwelling descendants on important matters like rain, health and fertility.

But first the ancestors have to receive a sign. Traditionally, this was given by slaughtering an animal, which was then divided communally and consumed – with the dead ancestors duly

receiving their portion. The head of each household functioned as family priest; in matters concerning the whole community, the chief took the role. He killed the cow or goat with a spear reserved for the purpose, and conveyed the requests of the living to the ancestors.

Traditional beliefs still hold a good deal of sway in South Africa, particularly in the rural areas, but among many people who are urbanised and "Westernised" as well.

Traditional healers

Diviners and mediums have always played – and still play – an important role in traditional religion. According to popular belief, people

LEFT: Stellenbosch's *Moederkerk*, the town's first Dutch Reformed church.
RIGHT: the largest Indian community outside Asia – both Hindu and Muslim – lives in KwaZulu-Natal.

are most vulnerable to illness, often caused by sorcery, when their ancestors are "facing away". Traditional healers – *inyangas* or *sangomas* – give instruction in the rituals which will placate the ancestors and ensure good health, as well as prescribing *muti* (medicine).

There are an estimated 300,000 traditional healers ministering to the physical and spiritual needs of South Africa's black community. These include herbalists or *inyangas* (usually male), and diviners or *san-*

HEALTHY OPTIONS

Since 1994, growing numbers of medical aid schemes have allowed their members to claim for treatment by traditional healers.

traditional remedies, animal and bird parts are used in them as well.

Today, traditional healing is enjoying a growing respectability in health care circles. Many conventional medical practitioners recognise the wisdom of the traditional healer's holistic approach, which incorporates psychological, social, cultural and spiritual facets in the healing process. It's also recognised that, thanks to a critical shortage of qualified doctors, a very large proportion of the rural population

gomas (usually female), who specialise in divining the illness and its causes by spiritual communication with the patient's ancestors. Both kinds of healer will have a comprehensive knowledge of herbal remedies and of the plant species used to make up so much of pharmaceutical medicine today.

The most common treatments administered by traditional healers are infusions, hot and cold; powders which are rubbed into parts of the body where incisions have been made; and poultices, lotions and ointments. Healers also prescribe blood-letting, enemas and emetics to flush impurities out of the system. Although plants are the basis of most of the

currently depends on herbal remedies. Some South African universities have therefore introduced traditional healing as a medical school subject, to train students in the importance of using natural resources in primary health care.

Christian churches

South Africa's first encounter with Christianity occurred when Dutch settlers colonised the Cape of Good Hope, bringing with them strong Calvinist beliefs. At first, they observed these so strictly that they tolerated only the Reformed Church within their sphere of influence. But as time progressed, countless mission societies came along,which competed with each other for converts.

Today, South Africa is home to followers of nearly every kind of Christian belief. Most denominations have established their own churches in the country; yet, while safeguarding their own religious identity, they keep up strong ties with churches abroad.

The Reformed churches

The family of Dutch Reformed Churches (DRC) is the oldest Christian establishment in the country, the first church being founded just three years after the arrival of Jan van Riebeeck

The DRC's habit of citing biblical writ in justification of apartheid meant that for decades it was ostracised by most of the world's Protestant communities. It also produced some powerful critics from within its own ranks – men such as Beyers Naude, a former DRC minister who broke away to found the Christian Institute. However, in 1986 the DRC publicly rescinded its apartheid views, and apologised to black South Africans for its past stand. Today, its 3½ million members and followers make it one of the country's largest denominations. The DRC still preaches a Calvinism based on strict Old Testament teachings.

on 6 April 1652. Its congregation was mainly Dutch, who remained true to their language in their religious life; their Dutch evolved into Afrikaans, still spoken at home and in church.

In 1826 the first official mission was established in South Africa; two smaller churches branched out of the Dutch Reformed Church in the middle of the 19th century. As apartheid became more established, "daughter churches" were set up for different – or "non-white" racial groupings.

LEFT: Sundays are sacred.
ABOVE: tools of the trade: a traditional healer's medicine kit.

The Lutheran churches

The first missionary of the Lutheran family, Georg Schmidt, travelled from the Brotherhood of Count Zinzendorf to South Africa in 1737 and founded the Genadendaal Mission, near Cape Town. Today, congregations of the brotherhood are still found predominantly in the Cape Province. Although its followers are not numerous – around 100,000 – this movement exercises some influence on South African Christian life as a result of its book of proverbs, which many families use as a devotional text.

The first Lutheran congregation was established in Cape Town in 1779. In the early 19th century, the work of missionaries, most of whom came from Germany (Berlin and Hermannsburg) and Scandinavia, helped spread the religion rapidly; over the years, this led to the development of independent churches. The Lutherans set great store by their native tongue. Even today, in some of the communities originally settled by Germans, one can still attend services in German.

British churches
Thanks to South Africa's sizable population of British immigrants, as well as British and Amer-

Many Anglican churchmen played a leading role in the anti-apartheid movement, the best-known being Nobel Peace Prize-winner Desmond Tutu, who was the first black Archbishop of Cape Town and head of the Anglican Church in southern Africa.

On his retirement in 1996, Tutu was succeeded by Archbishop Winston Ndungane, Bishop of Kimberley and Kuruman. Prior to training for the ministry, he had served a three-year prison term on Robben Island for furthering the aims

ican missionary work, the full spectrum of British churches is represented.

The Scottish Presbyterians first arrived in 1806 during the second wave of English colonists. They were particularly concerned with academic and technical education for the young; while disputes about segregated education in South Africa were taking place, they developed their own school system. Today the Methodist Church has about 2.3 million members, including the largest number of black followers of all the Christian denominations.

The Anglican Church was established in South Africa in 1749, while the local diocese has been independent since 1876.

of the banned PAC. Today, the Church of the Province of South Africa has about 1.3 million members.

The Roman Catholic Church
Another denomination to come out strongly against apartheid was the Catholic Church. This church's cross was first raised in South Africa a very long time ago: Bartolomeu Diaz did so on the island of Santa Cruz (Holy Cross) in Algoa Bay in 1486, as did Vasco da Gama in Mossel Bay in 1498.

Today, this denomination has 2.5 million members and is governed by a council of bishops under the jurisdiction of the Vatican.

The council also administers other countries in southern Africa.

Also well established are the Baptists, the Salvation Army and the Greek Orthodox Church. With over 2 million adherents, the charismatic and Pentecostal movements are the fastest-growing denominations.

The African Indigenous Churches

The African Indigenous Churches (AIC) are run by and for black South Africans, independent of the mainstream churches. Key features include a belief in prayer healing and baptism by total immersion, along with a general prohibition on

that there were only 900 branches country-wide 40 years ago gives some idea of the AIC's rapid growth. The movement has no all-encompassing parent organisation.

It began in 1883 when one Nehemiah Tile broke off from the Methodist Church and founded, with the support of his chief, the National Thembu Church. In 1885, the Native Independent Congregationalist Church separated from the London Missionary Society; in 1889, the Lutheran Bapedi Church declared its independence from the Berlin Mission, taking their missionary Johannes Winter with them.

tobacco, alcohol, medication and pork. Hundreds of small congregations, each with a different name and colourful uniform, gather for weekend services throughout South Africa.

The AIC have had a presence throughout sub-Saharan Africa for over a hundred years. Their strongest followings are in Nigeria and in South Africa, where there are about 2,000-plus congregations, mostly in Gauteng. Soweto alone has 500 such church groupings. The fact

LEFT: the initiation ritual of a *sangoma*, a female traditional healer.
ABOVE: in an ancient ceremony, the *sangoma's* lips are smeared with a chicken's gall bladder.

Mangena Maake Mokone, who "emancipated" his followers from the Methodist Church in Pretoria in 1892, called his denomination the Ethiopian Church. Ethiopia, the symbol of African independence, became a catchword – and this first great flowering of the AIC became renowned as the "Ethiopian" movement. Its followers established ties with the Afro-American churches which had been founded in America by descendants of the slaves. White South Africans perceived all this as "the black danger", but the movement flourished in spite of their opposition.

In 1910, the second great wave of AIC activity spread throughout the country in the form of the Zionist movement. This is not related to the Israeli brand of Zionism; the name stems from an American Pentecostal church, the Christian Catholic Apostolic Church of Zion, whose missions were active in South Africa around the turn of the century.

Various groups were founded by charismatic leaders, who gathered a steady stream of converts in the course of their intensive missionary work. The Zion Christian Church, established in 1914, is the largest AIC grouping in the country today, with its own settlement established at Zion City Moria, near Pietersburg in Northern Province.

round hut accommodates the proceedings, its central pole replacing the tree. These "temples" are found in both rural areas and big cities.

Healing and religion are closely interrelated. As Christians, however, AIC members make it clear that they do not pray to ancestors for intervention; on the other hand, like followers of traditional religion, nor do they put much store in conventional medicine.

Rather, they believe in the power of faith-healers (*umthandazi*) and prayers for the sick. Prayer meetings are usually held after every service, while some people also undertake long journeys to their central church, to sacred

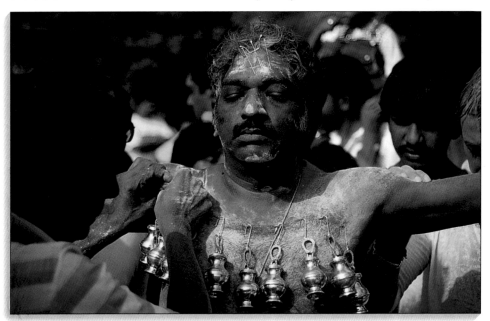

Fusion of traditional elements

The incorporation of elements of traditional African religion is an essential part of the AIC belief system. For instance, the circle is a powerful symbol both in traditional beliefs and here.

As the AIC does not have recourse to large amounts of foreign aid, its financial means are generally adequate only for the bare essentials – which precludes the erection of elaborate churches. AIC "temples" usually consist of a simple circle of whitewashed stones set around a high tree, which stands in for the church steeple.AIC members congregate for worship within this circle, sitting and kneeling on simple grass mats. If the weather's bad, a

springs, or to the coast, where the sea is said to have particularly curative powers. Healing rituals of this nature are often seen on Sundays at sunrise on the beach at Durban.

The biggest churches not only have a number of faith-healers with immense reputations and constantly overcrowded consulting rooms, but also have their own range of herbal treatments, coffee, tea and strict rules for healthy living. Although professed Christians, faith-healers do not always undergo training.

Another very significant element taken over from tribal religion is the AIC's emphasis on harmony with God and peace with one's fellow man.

Judaism

Until the middle of the 19th century, South African Jews were denied the right to practise their religion; they did not build their first synagogue until 1863. Gold and diamond mining and the growth of the cities brought increasing numbers of Jewish immigrants, especially from Eastern Europe, Britain and Germany. Apart from a small group of reformed Jews, today's Jewish population of more than 120,000 is predominantly Orthodox.

A LONG WAIT

Islam arrived in South Africa as early as 1658, but repressive conditions meant the first mosque was only erected in 1804.

quently, many others from India and other parts of Africa also came to South Africa to find work. Today, there are approximately 400,000 practising Muslims in the country – they form about 20 percent of the Asian population.

Asian religions

Many of the great religions of the East have taken root in South Africa. Three-quarters of the contracted Indian labourers brought into the country in 1860 were Hindu; today, they

Islam

Islam was the second of the "world religions" to have settled in South Africa. It arrived as early as the 17th century, when Dutch settlers brought slaves, soldiers and convicts (many of them from Indonesia) to the Cape. The descendants of these involuntary settlers are known today as Cape Malays.

Among the Indian labourers imported to work in the sugar fields of KwaZulu-Natal in the 1860s were hundreds of Muslims. Subse-

LEFT: a Hindu fire-walker gets ready to perform.
ABOVE: twenty percent of Indians and Cape Malays follow the Islamic faith.

form 68 percent of South Africa's Asian population. They have kept their original languages – Tamil, Hindi, Telegu and Gujarati – alive for use at worship and at home.

While Hinduism is the religion of some 650,000 people in South Africa today, Buddhism and Jainism are adhered to only by tiny minorities. There is a Buddhist ashram in Ixopo, KwaZulu-Natal, which is mostly attended by whites. The Jains are followers of Mahatma Gandhi, who spent over 20 years in South Africa at the turn of the century, fighting for the rights of Indian contracted labourers using his famous *satyagraha* policy of non-aggression. *(See page 37.)*

RICH MAN, POOR MAN

There's not enough wealth to go round, but the goals of the new economic policy are emphatically redistributive

South Africa is passing through a curious economic transition. After more than four decades of apartheid and 15 years of economic decline, re-entry into the global economy and the end of white rule bring a somewhat uncomfortable mix of pressures for policy change and new market opportunities.

South African Trade Unions, the ANC in government has relied strongly on private investment and market-based reforms as foundations for its economic policy. The goals are undoubtedly redistributive: the flagship Reconstruction and Development Programme (RDP) sets out ambitious targets for creating jobs, building

Apartheid attempted to separate communities, social services, business activity and political life along ethnic lines. Bringing these fragmented threads together is a major social and economic project, not unlike the transformation challenge facing eastern European countries in transition. But South Africa does have the advantage of comparatively well-established market networks and economic infrastructure. It has the disadvantage of an extreme inequality of incomes and wealth, and considerable backlogs in education, health, housing and job opportunities.

Despite a continuing alliance with the South African Communist Party and the Congress of

houses, extending electricity and telecommunications lines, redistributing land and improving basic education, health and welfare services. But the policy framework depends on opening up income-generating opportunities and reducing state subsidisation of privilege, rather than re-engineering a failed interventionist blueprint.

Where National Party rule was built on hegemonic principles, ultimately centred on a State Security Council, South Africa under the ANC is characterised by surprising new partnerships. The prominence of former unionists in powerful business alliances, the emergence of Malaysian and other non-traditional investors backing industrial and infrastructural initiatives, the privatisation of state enterprises and concessioning of new projects, reliance on non-governmental organisations to spearhead social and developmental campaigns, a commitment to opening trade and investment flows within Southern Africa, and innovative relationships with foreign donors are all features of the new environment.

Diverse Strategies

South Africa's fortunes through most of the past century rose and fell with gold and diamonds.

DIVIDED SOCIETY

Busy metropolitan city centres and plush, tree-lined suburbs coexist alongside vast slums and sprawling shanty towns.

Early signs are that the economy has undergone a decisive turnaround. After falling by 20 percent since 1980, income per capita has increased steadily, reaching around US$ 3,000 by the late 1990s – somewhere between Turkey and the Czech Republic in the international league tables.

After a decade in which gross domestic fixed investment fell from 27 percent to just over 15 percent of GDP, private capital formation has recovered strongly. Non-gold merchandise

As recently as 1990, as much as 70 percent of export earnings derived from mining, of which more than half came from gold mines. Achieving greater competitiveness in manufacturing and services sectors is central to the new government's economic strategy. Protective tariffs have come down, industrial subsidies and support measures are more carefully targeted and a new skills development strategy is under way.

LEFT: the good life: Johannesburg suburb, dotted with swimming pools.
ABOVE: there's no indoor plumbing – yet – for this Cape Coloured family in the village of Arniston.

exports have been growing not more than 10 percent a year. Inflation came down to just over 7 percent in 1996, its lowest level in more than two decades.

Yet while rich commercial farmlands expand production to be air-freighted to European markets, smallholders in former homelands lack access to water, technical support or markets. Commercial and financial services are well-integrated into global markets, but credit extension to small businesses and the lower end of the housing market remains patchy. Health care and education providers have been amongst the strongest performers on the Johannesburg Stock Exchange, but services in many communities are appallingly badly managed. The resolution of a protracted political liberation struggle has coincided with the escalation of violent crime in South Africa.

Social progress: the building-blocks

The first census to be conducted subsequent to dismantling the apartheid "constellation" of homeland states resulted in a count of 38 million, well under most analysts' expectations. Fertility has fallen sharply over the past decade, bringing population growth below 2 percent annually.

The 1996 census also showed that urbanisation is proceeding rapidly, reversing the effects of "influx control" and other barriers to the mobility of black people. But the shadows of South Africa's migrant labour system – broken families and dysfunctional townships – continue to threaten local economic developments. Crime and social conflict all too often undermine the evolution of more integrated towns and cities.

Expansion of educational opportunities over several decades also tells a mixed story. South Africa has near-universal enrolment for 10 years or more of schooling, and participation in higher education now exceeds 850,000. But rapid growth of the system has increased education spending by government to nearly 7 percent of GDP – high by any international comparison – and has contributed to strains in management capacity and some glaring qualitative deficiencies. Science and mathematics teaching is woefully inadequate; resource constraints threaten the government's ambitious "Curriculum 2005" reform programme.

Electrification, improved water supplies to low-income communities and extensions to the network of primary health clinics are the most striking successes of the ANC government. Over 300,000 additional households per year can switch on lights and run electrical appliances. By the end of 1996, 700 water projects were in the pipeline, bringing safe water to over 6 million people. Charges have been eliminated in the primary health system and 270 new clinics have been built or are under construction.

Less impressive has been the pace of delivery of housing projects. A strategy aimed at bringing private sector capacity and finance to the programme, underpinned by a limited state subsidy scheme, has proved both difficult to implement and open to abuse. There has been some acceleration in new housing starts in 1997, however, together with the first steps towards a coordinated municipal infrastructural investment programme.

Jobless growth?

Despite an improved growth performance, job losses continue to dominate the headlines. The most widely reported measure of employment shows a persistent downward trend in private sector jobs, partially offset by government employment. The public sector accounts for 1.8 million of the 5.3 million jobs in the formal non-agricultural employment series. Mining employment is now 560,000 – 30 percent below its level in the late 1980s. Manufacturing and construction have also shed labour since 1990, while jobs in trade and services have grown by about 2½ percent per year.

Spearheaded by the "strategic" investments of the apartheid siege economy – a major arms industry, oil-from-coal technology, iron and steel plants, off-shore gas and oil exploration – South Africa has followed a capital-intensive growth path over the past three decades. The off-shore schemes have, in the main, been expensive blunders, but most projects supported by the state's Industrial Development Corporation – Sasol and Gencor, for example – are now important sources of foreign exchange earnings.

South African manufacturing includes a well-established food-processing sector, chemicals, motor vehicle assembly, clothing and textiles, pulp and paper and diverse minerals-based industries. Strong export growth in recent years has been spread across a wide range of products, taking advantage of a more competitive exchange rate, favourable regional and global

HIGH UNEMPLOYMENT

The unemployment rate is 29 percent, making this by far South Africa's most important source of poverty and inequality.

accelerating economic growth, promoting greater labour market flexibility and investing in labour-intensive development projects.

There is a tension, however, between dismantling labour market rigidities and securing protection for black workers whose rights and remuneration were undoubtedly repressed under minority rule. Labour market reforms since 1994 have been focused on strengthening the industrial bargaining system and outlawing exploitative working conditions. For the work-

market trends and a range of export incentives. Manufacturing output growth has been steady, and annual investment in manufacturing plants has grown by 30 percent since 1994.

South Africa has acknowledged expertise in managing large-scale industrial projects. But the spin-offs for job creation are just not adequate to meet South Africa's labour market challenge.

The government's macroeconomic strategy aims to turn the employment trend around by

LEFT: hawker outside the tall glass needle of the Johannesburg Stock Exchange.
ABOVE: small businesses like this township barber's are one of the economy's fastest-growing areas.

ing poor, government is investing in housing and social infrastructure, protecting minimum wages, shortening working hours, increasing overtime rates and mandatory leave benefits. But for the jobless, there is the threat that improved labour standards will further weaken the prospects of finding work at all.

As in many developing countries, the official statistics have gaping holes. Household survey data show that total employment is about 10 million – nearly double the total measured by the regular data series. Agriculture, household employment, informal activities and large parts of the private services sector are not tracked in the employment numbers. The regulatory environment has had the unintended effect of encouraging labour-only contracting and some casualisation of employment – trends the statistics do not capture.

Trade – heavily repressed a decade ago – now flourishes on the streets of South African towns. Formal industry may not be creating employment, but there is a complex balance to be struck between promoting technological progress and global industrial penetration, and ensuring that income-earning opportunities extend into townships and rural areas. But economic progress must also be built on established strengths and industrial development capacity.

Future prospects

Finance Minister Trevor Manuel's "Growth, Employment and Redistribution Strategy" has come under fire from the left for its stringent deficit reduction targets, privatisation and implied labour market reforms. The South African Reserve Bank has also come in for criticism for keeping interest rates high in the face of slower economic growth and falling inflation. But the strategy has been welcomed by business and international commentators, although questions about its effective implementation remain to be answered.

The main elements of the strategy are an opening of the economy to international trade and investment, a disciplined monetary and fiscal policy framework, continuing labour market reforms and investment in vocational education and training, privatisation of enterprises that do not belong in the public sector and an overhaul of government aimed at more efficient service delivery, accelerated infrastructural investment and sustainable employment creation. Although presented in the context of economic projections to the year 2000, this is really a framework for a transition to a stronger economy in the next millenium.

Can South Africa succeed in creating a dynamic economy, faced with popular spending pressures and the uncertain financial environment of today? One answer lies precisely in the tension between meeting development challenges and addressing the concerns of foreign investors. South Africa has well-developed financial markets that attracted some US$ 4 billion in portfolio investment in the first half of 1997. Economic expansion depends on capital inflows, as the current account of the balance of payments runs a deficit when firms are investing and importing capital and intermediate goods. But investment flows are sensitive to perceptions regarding policy trends and progress towards implementing policy commitments. Over-ambitious spending plans or incompetent management of economic reforms are punished swiftly in modern financial markets. Of course, there is no particular justice or supreme rationality in capital market movements; it is rather that the new global environment encourages prudence and facilitates the kinds of partnerships and pragmatic reforms that are needed if this economy is to make the transition from its fragmented past to a more prosperous integrated future.

South Africa has come a long way since 1994. Transformation ideals have given way to the more tedious projects of building institutions and reconciling public spending goals to the available means. Black business interests are rapidly making more money than their unreconstructed competitors. Career prospects are now more prominent than political struggles in the minds of ambitious students. South Africa's past still casts shadows over the country's prospects, but its policy debates are firmly focused on the challenges of the future.

LEFT: black gold: the Sasol oil refinery.

The rise of the Black middle class

The tall glass building of the Johannesburg Stock Exchange soars up from a bustling western corner of the city. Outside, a designer-suited black man buys a bag of fruit from the sidewalk stall of a black woman hawker. It's more than a simple transaction – it's a metaphor of the changing face of South African business.

In just a few years, the economy has undergone a dramatic metamorphosis. From the formation of black-owned investment consortiums to the key role now assigned to the informal sector, the buzzword of the day is black economic empowerment.

A new government, South Africa's reconnection with global markets and new national economic development strategies (the ANC is committed to a moderate economic programme providing for the privatisation of many state assets – reflecting a desire to play down its fighting and rather socialist past and play up its readiness to work with big business) have created a rising black middle class, along with powerful aspirations of economic self-reliance across the board.

At grassroots level, the "new deal" means the right to hawk goods as simple as a household broom without coming up against the impediments previously imposed on black entrepreneurship by apartheid laws. For others, it's the chance to spot a gap in the market and act on it – opening up a hair salon, for example, or a mobile hotdog stand, or a street-stall offering telephone services in competiton with the official callboxes, which are all too often vandalized or out of order. Small businesses such as these have been a key area of black economic growth; the little *spaza* shops (small general dealers) that pepper the townships a colourful symbol of entrepreneurial spirit unleashed.

In mining, publishing and electronic media, black South Africans are increasingly prominent. A small but growing number of companies listed on the Johannesburg Stock Exchange are now controlled by black investors. Increased black ownership of private businesses, joint ownership ventures between farm workers and farmers, and trade union shareholder schemes also exemplify the new trend.

RIGHT: a home in Diepkloof Extension, Soweto's very own "Beverly Hills".

The government's controversial "affirmative action" policy, which aims to ensure that black South Africans are employed in all sectors of the economy in a ratio more consistent with the country's demographics, has been an important factor here, despite all the debate it has generated and its unpopularity with many whites. It has also gone some way to achieving its aim of breaking down racial barriers in the workplace.

In Sandton City, Gauteng's most up-market shopping mall, the elegantly-tiled floors resound to the clip-clip of well-heeled black South African professionals. They earn handsome salaries, drive smart cars, sport cellphones (nicknamed "Gauteng

earrings", so ubiquitous are they) and designer clothes. Some cashed in political exile and jobs abroad for a stake in the new South Africa; others have made their way into posts previously held by whites. Many have moved into the smart northern suburbs and joined the corporate cocktail circuit.

It is a far cry from 1953, when the Grand Vizier of apartheid, Hendrik Verwoerd, declared in a speech to the South African Senate that "the Natives will be taught from childhood to realise that equality with Europeans is not for them ... What is the use of teaching the Bantu mathematics when he cannot use it in practice ... There is no place for the Bantu child above the level of certain forms of labour." From the boardrooms to the backstreets, black South Africans are finally taking control.

FACING THE FUTURE

The pitfalls are many, yet with shrewd leadership, South Africa
could yet become the continent's true powerhouse

For a long time South Africa was, at core, a very simple place to understand. A minority of the people ran the show. The majority stood outside the gates of citizenship. Not surprisingly, perhaps, most South Africans grew up in the expectation that apocalypse loomed – first, there would be a revolution; and second, everything would become different.

It was widely taken as inevitable that the state would clamp down on resistance ever tighter, become ever more besieged, until finally something would snap. Then a new world would follow. Some white people took it for granted that the new world would mean their destruction; the end of survival. Some black people took it for granted that the new world would mean nirvana. In the middle, the majority of the population waited with caution, believing that apartheid was the source of ill, hoping that after apartheid things would be better, although always less than wholly confident.

But the revolution evaporated, as quietly as a puddle drying up. History will pinpoint a moment – 2 February 1990, when President F.W. de Klerk said in effect: "Oops, reverse gear." But history is written in short sentences; the puddle had in fact been drying up for years.

A new challenge

Now we have a new environment, a new mode of thought, and a new task. It's an environment where, for instance, the children often live in a world as wide as their parents' was narrow. And the task is truly daunting: no longer a matter of fighting for or against the status quo, for or against the revolution, but of making a shared country a success against odds any bookmaker would laugh at. The national mood skids from high to low and back again. Much depends on the daily news. But not all is a hostage to the headlines, and that is the saving grace.

Take South Africa's new Constitution, which came into effect almost exactly 7 years after De

LEFT AND ABOVE: the future belongs to all South Africans, both black and white.

Klerk announced his plan to scrap apartheid, on 3 February 1997. It is a major democratic milestone, recognising that all South Africans are entitled to a common citizenship in a sovereign and democratic constitutional state in which there is equality between men and women of all races, where all can exercise their fundamental rights and freedoms. Its provisions can only be changed by 75 percent of the members of the National Parliament.

The Constitution also contains a Bill of Rights guaranteeing freedom of movement; freedom of opinion, religion and belief; equality and equal protection before the law. It aims for a balance of power between the arms of government (Parliament, the Executive and the Judiciary) by a clear separation of their powers.

In terms of policy, it is the government's stated objective to create jobs, improve health and education, end racial discrimination and achieve national reconciliation between the races. Accordingly, a Reconstruction and

Development Programme (RDP) has been put in place – a hugely ambitious 25-year plan designed to normalise South African society and the economy. By the year 2000, it hopes to have built at least a million low-cost houses, redistributed 30 percent of agricultural land amongst blacks, established more health facilities and a better education system, and supplied electricity, water and sanitation to 2.5 million more households.

What of the ordinary lives lived amidst these grand designs? Ben, the gateman at the parking lot, has a new house with electricity and water and can't help breaking out into a grin as he

But the wheels of government grind slowly. The sheer enormity of the task of unravelling the disastrous social engineering of the past 50 years means many black households – especially those in the rural areas – are unlikely to see electricity and piped water for years to come. The RDP, critics say, has a delivery crisis on its hands; yet it is on that ability to deliver that the government will be judged by the masses at the 1999 general election.

The ANC: a new mode

The threats are gigantic, and it all boils down to the political basics: the lack of jobs, the fact that

explains the transformation it has wreaked. Jonas the milkman always answers the routine "How are you?" with a vigorous "Hundred percent!" Frank, the barman at the tennis club, is frantic about whether he's done everything right for his daughter's wedding next week.

These people – black city-dwellers – are, by and large, optimistic about the future. They see the white man more as a provider of jobs than as brutal oppressor. They pay practically zero attention to the great political issues of our times except when these things burst through their living-room doors, which has been happening recently more often than they might like.

more than 45 percent of South Africans live below the poverty line, the near-collapse of the forces of law and order in the face of exponential increases in crime, the gap between the government's theories of social justice on the one hand, and the dismal reality of corruption on the part of those who make the laws and those who administer them.

At the same time, there has also been a substantial upsurge of "conservative" and/or "cautious" black political expression, which had remained invisible during the era of the fight for black liberation.

Needless to say, there are those who think this shift represents a betrayal of the ANC's socialist principles, and there are those who think it has not gone far enough. It is the latter group who, for example, point to the fact that foreign investment has been slow to materialise, claiming this is largely due to the government's unwillingness to take any action which might jeopardise its alliance with the South African Communist Party and the powerful trade union federation, COSATU.

Yet given the ANC government's shift away from its state interventionist policies of the 1980s, it seems clear that its relationship with its left-wing allies will not be plain sailing. It is expected that deputy President

the official policy of "affirmative action", designed to "redress past imbalances and to ameliorate the conditions of individuals or groups who have been disadvantaged on the grounds of race, colour, gender or disability". Whites have complained that in the civil service and universities, particularly, black people are being catapulted into jobs for which they are unqualified. As a consequence, many professionals are emigrating.

Then there's "cross-subsidisation", the policy whereby ratepayers in traditionally "white" areas have seen their service charges rocket, while municipalities supply the same services

Thabo Mbeki – tipped to succeed Nelson Mandela after his self-imposed one-term presidency comes to an end in 1999 – will have his work cut out to keep this much-vaunted alliance from tottering.

White fears
Nor has majority rule eliminated the anxieties which always have and always will be felt by some whites living in Africa. Top of the list is

LEFT: working together.
ABOVE: unravelling the disastrous social engineering of the past 50 years is a slow process; many poor black households won't see much benefit for years to come.

SHIFTS IN POLICY

ANC policy since 1996 has moved away from its former commitment to nationalisation. The government now tends to play down its socialist past and play up the fact that it is committed to a moderate, growth-driven economic programme which will provide for the privatisation of many state assets, as well as a reduction in the size of the civil service. The so-called "route of Africa" – the typical snap replacement of a right-wing settler regime by a left-wing liberation movement which soon displays feet of clay – seems to have been short-circuited in the case of South Africa.

free to black communities – who simply refuse to pay for them.

Facing the future

It is easy to dismiss grumbles about this sort of thing as the predictable response of an embittered minority who have seen their privileged lifestyle slip away.

Yet, slowly but surely, the diminishing importance of what was once considered the holy grail of colour-blindness is working to South Africa's benefit. Traditionally "non-racialism" was taken to mean a wholesale scrapping of community existence. This idea spread terror

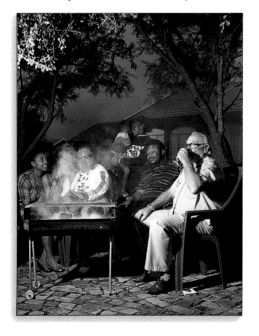

among minorities who perceived their way of life being simply wiped out, but nowadays this notion is being replaced by maturer recognition of the need to seek justice and interracial respect rather than enforced denial of ethnic bonds.

Other hugely heartening changes include the slow emergence of a new tradition of artistic and cultural exchange between Africans of all colours, and between Africa and international artists.

The end of the apartheid era has fuelled a large influx of tourists to South Africa, with the British leading the trend: in 1995, a quarter of a million Britons visited the country. Tourism is the world's fastest-growing industry and

largest employer, and this new development offers South Africa a glimpse of a potential economic goldmine.

On the whole, though, it is accepted that the country's largely "Third World" nature spells hard times in the competitive world economy of today and tomorrow; that the South African situation is unique and wherever it's going is necessarily unprecedented.

A few other scenarios are widely debated, such as the possibility of a descent into outright wheelspin. South Africa's frighteningly high levels of violent crime – explained by some analysts as a sort of backlash against the "peaceful" ending of apartheid; as an expression of collective rage at the long years of vicious and organised racism – is certainly a factor here. But, for the most part, predicting South Africa's future is an individual concern. No-one knows better than anyone else.

The most salient fact of all, however, is that the country has acquired a democratic political foundation – very probably a foundation more democratic than is conventional in the established, less pressured, democracies, in the sense that it looks for such things as a fuller and freer accountability to ordinary people, with a higher level of balancing of local, regional, and national interests and powers.

For the first time, decision-making now involves not a white state imposing its will on a black minority, but a primarily black democracy in which the aggrieved will be contesting the decisions ratified by their own relatives and communities. But corruption, whether perpetrated by criminals or simply by various indigenous groups trying to do the best for their own people, will prove difficult to root out.

A fully-fledged democratic electorate could, given strong and united leadership, remove much of the continuing violence. And if stability could only be reasonably assured, the economic decline of the past two decades could be checked. Investor confidence would return.

Yet South Africa has the potential to become the true powerhouse of Africa, and possibly the world's most dramatic case of a Third World country catapulting to a secure First World status. The pitfalls are many; but, if shrewdly reconnoitred, the outcome could be a resounding success.

ABOVE LEFT: facing the future together.

Truth and Reconciliation

Yasir Henry is a traitor. He betrayed the whereabouts of his friend, Anton France, to the authorities, and on 4 September 1984, his friend died in a hail of police bullets. Now Henry is seated before a microphone in a gloomy public building somewhere in Gauteng. Tears trickle down his face; the members of the public listening to his testimony are hushed. Yasir Henry betrayed his friend after being tortured by the police. Ever since, he's been tortured by the image of Anton dying with a single unanswered question on his lips: "Who betrayed me? Who gave me away?"

The line between victims and criminals is a thin one in South Africa. It seems scarcely possible that the scars left by 40 violent years of apartheid could ever be healed, yet the South African government is attempting to do just that. The Truth and Reconciliation Commission, established in 1995 under the chairmanship of Nobel Peace prizewinner Desmond Tutu, aims to investigate gross human rights violations committed by all parties between 1 March 1960 and 10 May 1994. It also aims to recommend reparation for victims.

The regular televised regional sittings of the Commission have included shocking disclosures of atrocities committed by senior officials in the National Party, the police and the Defence Force, as well as members of the Inkatha Freedom Party, the ANC and PAC and other organisations involved in the anti-apartheid struggle.

Yet, extraordinarily, the Truth Commission is not geared towards punishing offenders. Instead, they are granted amnesty and indemnity if their crimes can be proved to have been "politically motivated" – while victims are given the chance to speak out about the injustices done to them and so liberate themselves from the burden of their memories.

Tutu's insistence that the Truth Commission's emphasis is less on "settling things legally" and more on allowing all South Africans to come to terms with the past in a cathartic spirit of reconciliation has angered some of the families of apartheid victims, who have indicated that they would instead prefer to see justice done. Yet he has been adamant in his espousal of a Christian philosophy of forgiveness. And while critics say

RIGHT: Nobel Peace prizewinner Desmond Tutu.

hearings have also been disappointing in terms of extracting candid confessions from apartheid's worst sinners, most would nonetheless agree the Commission has been a vital first step in the process of creating a new national morality. "South Africa cannot step confidently into the future unless and until it has made an honest effort to come to terms with its past. And the TRC is that effort," noted the *Star* newspaper in an editorial in 1997.

Human rights activist Alex Boraine, who designed the structure of the Truth Commission, spent several years researching the task. He studied 15 similar bodies worldwide, in countries such as

Guatemala, El Salvador, Chile and Argentina, and reached a somewhat depressing conclusion. In most cases, the key perpetrators of human rights abuses – high-ranking military officials – had simply ignored the whole process. "Each commission was supposed to help the victims of an unjust regime start a healing process, but in the end, they all gave up trying. Each has left behind an underclass of victims who have never had any reparation for what they went through," he has noted.

So far, South Africa's Truth Commission may be unique in having found a solution. To date, more than 8,000 people have voluntarily given testimony; people like Yasir Henry – forgiven, at last, by his friend's family, after confessing to his crime.

THE PERFORMING ARTS

Despite swingeing cuts in subsidies to performing arts bodies,
a cultural renaissance is currently underway

For the San, South Africa's earliest inhabitants, drama had a strong religious connection. This took the form of ceremonies to mark important occasions (an impending hunt, for example) where the gods would be asked to ensure success. Led by a "shaman", who was believed to be in direct contact with the spirit world, ceremonies always took place within a circle.

Down the centuries, these sacred acts became more abstract, evolving into rites-of-passage rituals to mark important steps in life. Fertility myths were acted out for the tribe to remind themselves of their origins, and of the purpose of their relationship with the spirit world.

Now into the centre of the circle stepped the first kind of actors – one man representing "good", and another "evil". These "actors" wore masks or face-paint to indicate their "character", and performed dances to show that life always triumphed over death. It was believed that the enactment of these "plays" brought the spring; that things would grow, and that there would be food. In other words, people made a direct connection between the enactment of these dramas and the continuation of life itself.

Indigenous theatre today

In modern times, the growth of indigenous theatre in South Africa has been inextricably linked to the country's political realities. The 1980s, in particular, produced a wealth of "protest plays" focusing on the damaging social and psychological effects of apartheid.

Theatre complexes such as the Market Theatre in Johannesburg became known as avant-garde centres staging original works which reflected the lives and aspirations of all South Africans. It was a laborious process, often hampered by state censorship and not always artistically successful. But it produced some

PRECEDING PAGES: performance of Swazi dancers.
LEFT: government subsidies for the classical performing arts – including ballet – have all been slashed.
ABOVE: modern drama.

memorable theatre that was exported to international stages.

Actors and playwrights to succeed abroad include Athol Fugard (*A Lesson from Aloes*) and the very successful partnership of John Kani and Winston Ntshona (*Sizwe Banzi Is Dead* and *The Island*) who were both honoured with the

American theatre's highest accolade, the Tony Award. An expatriate actor, Zakes Mokae, later won the award for his performance in Fugard's *Master Harold and the Boys*.

Often dubbed "the father of black theatre", Gibson Kente provided through his "theatre of the townships" numerous opportunities for aspiring writers and actors to become major stars. This provided the impetus for talented writers such as Mbongeni Ngema, Barney Simon and Percy Mtwa to take their trailblazing production, *Woza Albert*, onto the international stage.

Works of the playwright Mbongeni Ngema have also been performed across the world.

Ngema's *Asinamali* wound up on Broadway in 1987 and won a Tony nomination for best director. In 1988, he took his hit musical *Sarafina* to New York's Lincoln Theatre and then to Broadway, where it played to capacity audiences for 11 months. *Sarafina* has also been made into a film starring Whoopie Goldberg.

The arts and official policy

Since the advent of democratic government in South Africa in 1994, it has become official policy to support indigenous African art in every sphere, while maintaining the vitality of the Western tradition. It is hoped that by nour-

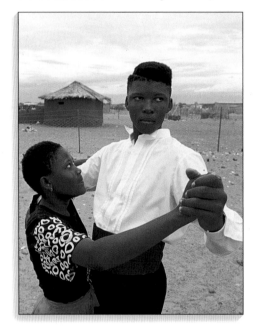

ishing a diversity of traditions, one rich, multi-faceted South African culture will ultimately arise.

However, the government's developmental programme has as its main focus housing, education, land redistribution, health and the general upliftment of the formerly disadvantaged; subsidising the arts is not a priority.

As far as the classical performing arts are concerned, opera, theatre and ballet are officially supported in the sense that a number of important venues, such as Cape Town's Nico Malan Theatre Centre and Pretoria's State Theatre, receive state subsidies. But it is quite possible that in the future these theatres will have

to look to private enterprise for funding. In the long term, though, it is the government's aim to form a national ballet and opera company.

These developments have left South Africa's four apartheid-era, government-subsidised performing arts councils in a state of flux. Official policy now makes new provision for culture, both at the state and provincial level. A national department of Arts, Culture, Science and Technology has been formed, while South Africa's four old provinces have been split into nine, each with its own arts council.

Cultural officers have been appointed in all the main centres to promote the arts – and particularly the Africanisation of the arts (chief of the criticisms levelled at the old arts councils was that they bolstered Western values to the detriment of indigenous culture, mounting only classical performances or well-tested modern theatre). It is expected that the old councils' government subsidisation will shortly come to an end.

New themes for a new era?

The disappearance of apartheid and the lifting of the cultural boycott has proved something of a mixed blessing for the performing arts in South Africa. On the one hand, there has been a resurgence of interest from the world outside, with foreign theatre and dance companies eager to visit, observe and entertain. A new tradition of artistic and cultural exchange is slowly getting underway.

On the other hand, home-grown theatre – so long reliant on the protest genre – seems hard-pressed to find fresh themes. There have been a few interesting departures, among them Athol Fugard's *Valley Song*, which explores issues of individual, rather than simply political, discontent. Paul Slabolepszy's inspired discourse on rugby fever, *Heel Against the Head*, is another noteworthy exception. Yet debacles such as the *Sarafina II* scandal – the Ministry of Health's Aids education play, commissioned from celebrated playwright Mbongeni Ngema, which eventually cost some R14 million to stage – have done little to provide the local theatre scene with that much-needed spur. Nonetheless, the overall standard of production of works by both local and foreign playwrights remains encouragingly high.

Ballet, too, is adapting to the challenges of the post-apartheid era. The school of ballet, which was established at the University of Cape Town in 1934, has now been privatised, and – along with the provincial arts council formerly known as PACT – mounts impressive repertoires of classical works and indigenous ballets. Both companies are committed to maintaining standards of excellence.

Music: a new crossover

Although orchestras have faced particular difficulties as a result of subsidy cuts, they have, in the main, managed to survive. The independently-run Cape Town Philharmonic Orchestra (formed after a merge between the

at this point that their financial futures are secure.

Choral music has found a ready "crossover" market, but perhaps it is the success of the Soweto String Quartet which best typifies the exciting new trend towards the merging of Western and African musical forms. Under the leadership of Sandile Khemese, the quartet gained international recognition with their 1996 hit, *Zebra Crossing*.

Also notable has been the revival of traditional Afrikaans music. Legendary musicians such as Nico Carstens are creating a new fusion between black and traditional *boereorkes* forms.

former Cape Town Symphony Orchestra and the CAPAB orchestra) performs regularly and also serves as a pit orchestra for opera, ballet and musicals.

The Natal Philharmonic Orchestra in Durban and the National Symphony Orchestra in Johannesburg (the latter formerly sponsored by the South African Broadcasting Corporation) are now both privately funded and performing at every opportunity, although there is no certainty

LEFT: ballroom dancers, Kleinsee, the Kalahari.
ABOVE: if both Western and African cultural traditions are nourished, so the thinking goes, one rich, multi-faceted culture may one day emerge.

FRESH HARMONIES

Despite the subsidy cuts suffered by provincial arts bodies since the ANC came to power, a new tradition of artistic and cultural exchange between Africans of all colours, and between Africa and international artists, is starting to emerge. A particularly exciting development has been the interest shown in opera and ballet by black South Africans. New opera productions are being staged, such as those created by Cape Town's Michael Williams, based on Xhosa, Kenyan and American Indian folklore. Many fine black opera singers are also starting to come to the fore.

THE MUSICAL TRADITION

With the richest musical history on the continent, South Africa

offers a potent mix of indigenous and world musical trends

South Africa is distinguished by the richest musical history, the most complex profusion of styles and the best-developed recording industry on the continent. Its music – although deeply influenced by Europe and America – is unique.

Traditional music

Southern Africa's earliest known musicians were the hunter-gatherers known as the San, who sang in a language filled with unusual click sounds, produced a variety of instruments – rattles, drums and flutes – and adapted forms of their hunting-bow for making music.

The Khoikhoi ("men of men"), who arrived in southern Africa some three thousand years ago, seem to have been more sophisticated in their musical tradition than the San. When, on 25 November 1497, the Portuguese explorer Vasco da Gama landed at Mossel Bay on the southwest coast, he was met on the beach by a band of Khoikhoi who treated the expedition to a performance on reed flutes. These were rather like a set of dismantled pan pipes, with each player blowing on one reed to produce a single tone at a set point of time. Probably da Gama heard a set of four different reeds playing a four-note melody.

Five centuries later, the same principle is still used by the Venda in Northern Province. The only difference is that the Venda use a large number of players to each pitch and, since the reeds can not all have the exact bore commensurate with the pitch, the resulting impression is one of a conglomerate of microtonal pitches grouped around four notes.

By the beginning of the 17th century, most of what is now South Africa had been occupied by other African peoples who were darker-skinned and more technologically sophisticated than the San and Khoikhoi. Musically, these people had

a strongly-developed vocal tradition with songs to accompany every occasion, from the initiation of adolescent youths to the exorcism of spirits, from festival days to education through songs. Yet whatever the song, the underlying musical structure was always the same – two or more linked melodic phrases not only repeated ad infinitum, but staggered in relation to each other, producing a simultaneous polyphony. This is the basis of the "call and response" arrangement of many later African-American styles, including gospel, doo-wop and soul.

The arrival of Christian missionaries in the early 19th century provided the first contact with Western music, and – through the mission schools – a Western musical training. Enoch Mankayi Sontonga, who composed *Nkosi Sikelel' i Africa* – one of South Africa's two national anthems – in 1897, was both a pupil and later a teacher at a Methodist mission school.

LEFT: performance by members of the Umzanzi Zulu Dance troupe.

RIGHT: the San adapted the traditional bow and arrow for making music.

The Cape Malay Tradition

The early Dutch settlers at the Cape relied on slave labour; indeed, slaves soon came to outnumber the white population.

They came mostly from the Dutch East Indies (modern Indonesia), and intermarried with Khoisan, Africans and renegade whites to form a new community, known today as the Coloured people.

A minority of the slaves, mostly political exiles and skilled artisans who had bought their freedom, adhered to their

congregation), while others are connected with wedding ceremonies (for instance, the antiphonal *minnat* songs which are sung at an extremely slow pace by a leader and a group of male guests.) But they also preserved songs reflecting their two centuries of serfdom, which have, ironically, been absorbed into the old Dutch repertoire of folk songs.

Township jazz

By the 1930s, a black urban culture was firmly established in South Africa's larger towns,

Islamic heritage. This "Cape Malay" community still predominates in parts of Cape Town such as the Bo-Kaap, and their traditional music still has several marked Eastern characteristics: for example, a couple of rhythmic instruments (the portable drum, or *gomma*, and the large tambourine, *rebana*), an Eastern singing style marked by *karienkels* ("sound wrinkles" of microtonal decorations surrounding certain melody tones), and also by traditional vocal styles which have survived 300 years of estrangement from the original country.

Some of these are of a religious nature (for example, the *pudjies*, antiphonal singing divided between an imam and members of the

despite increasingly strict segregationist laws which controlled the movement of black people and subjected them to a nightly curfew. One of the most important musical expressions of this culture came out of the ghettoes of Johannesburg. Dubbed *marabi*, it consisted of a single phrase built around a three-chord progression, repeated endlessly in traditional style.

Despite its apparent limitations, skilled musicians gave the style depth by varying the theme and by improvisation. *Marabi* was flexible enough melodically to absorb almost anything, from hymns to hits from Tin Pan Alley.

The new music was thrillingly raw and potent, and was performed in unregulated drinking haunts (as opposed to the government-licensed and rigidly-controlled beer halls), and sung by a solo voiceto over an organ or guitar. Drums were improvised and pebble-filled condensed-milk tins provided percussive accompaniment.

Yet the style quickly evolved. Legendary band leader Willard "Zuluboy" Cele introduced modern instrumentation. Later, idioms from American swing were blended in by popular bandleaders such as Zakes Nkosi. Later still, bebop was to prove a big influence, notably in the performances of reed virtuoso Kippie Moeketsi. Dorkay House became downtown

soon developed to become a new musical genre all of its own.

Also in the 1960s, many of the country's most brilliant musicians – Hugh Masekela, Abdullah Ibrahim, Miriam Makeba and Jonas Gwanga among them – left to escape the political pressures of apartheid. Many of these exiles went on to win an enthusiastic following for South African jazz abroad.

At home, the jazz scene mellowed, absorbing the influences of jazz-rock fusion in the style of such bands as Weather Report. In Cape Town, musicians drew on an exotic range of influences from Latin sounds to the music of the

Johannesburg's jazz haven, providing a platform for established players and a training-ground for new ones.

In the 1960s and 1970s, a white audience developed a taste for township *kwela* music – simple saxophone-based jive tunes – and record companies accordingly started to put pressure on artists to record tracks in this style, along with lyrics. Purist jazz saxophonists disdainfully referred to this music as *mbaqanga* – meaning something like "just-add-water-and-stir" – yet the vocal component of *mbaqanga*

local Cape Malay community to create a style which is now instantly recognisable as "Cape jazz".

Today, not only are the returning exiles achieving recognition at home as well as abroad, but a whole new generation is creating a rich mix of South African heritage and world jazz trends. Reedman Zim Ngqawana draws on folk roots; Cape Town-based guitarist Jimmy Dludlu is blending Shangaan guitar and *marrabenta* rhythms with a big-band format. The band Bayete is fast gaining status abroad. New young jazz vocalists such as Gloria Bosman and Busi Mhlongo have come to the fore. In short, the beat goes on.

LEFT: a home band in Cape Town's Malay community.
ABOVE: traditional *isicathamiya* choir, Johannesburg.

BLACK MUSIC

With its rich profusion of styles backed up by a highly developed recording industry, music is one of South Africa's most impressive endowments

In 1959, black South African township music first exploded onto the international stage with the hit musical *King Kong*. With a score by Sowetan pianist-composer Todd Matshikiza, it told the story of South African heavyweight boxing champion, Ezekiel Dhlamini – "King Kong" – who murders his girlfriend and dies in prison. This slice of township life played to enthusiastic audiences not only in South Africa but in London and New York as well.

EXILED BY APARTHEID

The show's remarkable line-up included Jonas Gwangwa, trumpeter Hugh Masekela, saxophonist Kippie Moeketsi and songstress Miriam Makeba, a one-time domestic servant who had paid her dues on the township scene in the 1950s with bands like The Cubans, The Manhattan Brothers and The Skylarks. At the very height of *King Kong*'s success, however, Makeba left South Africa for the United States, where she quickly re-established her career. Large numbers of the cast – including Hugh Masekela – also used the show's London run as an opportunity to flee apartheid and go into exile. The drain of artistic talent had begun.

△ **KING OF REGGAE**
Hugely popular at home, where he has been dubbed "the natural successor to Bob Marley", Lucky Dube's status as an international star was cemented in 1996, when he received the World Music Award for Best Selling African Recording Artist.

◁ **AFRICAN SONGBIRD**
Turning her back on a successful career in America, Miriam Makeba made an emotional return in 1991 with a series of sell-out concerts.

◁ CROSSING THE BARRIERS
The Soweto String Quartet use the format of the classical string quartet to perform songs drawn from both traditional African music and contemporary pop. The result is an extraordinary hybrid of sounds that crosses every musical barrier imaginable. *Zebra Crossing*, their first album, went platinum in 1996.

▽ THE PRINCESS OF AFRICA
With a huge following across the African continent, Yvonne Chaka Chaka's sound epitomises the township pop known as "bubblegum" – a synthesised shebeen jive marrying modern technology and African rhythms. Her star has been somewhat eclipsed in the 1990s by newer forms, such as *kwaito* and hip-hop.

CLASSIC ALBUMS FOR COLLECTORS

• *King Kwela* by Spokes Mashiyane (Celluloid, France). A reissue of Mashiyane's classic 1958 album, featuring uptempo rhythmic jives played on the pennywhistle.
• *The Lion Roars* by Mahlathini and the Mahotella Queens (Shanachie, USA). Culled from the glory days of the 1960s and 1970s, featuring *mbaqanga* king Simon Nkabinde (pictured above).
• *The Best of Sipho Mabuse* by Sipho "Hotstix" Mabuse (Gallo, South Africa). Includes the soul luminary's greatest hits: "Jive Soweto" and "Burn Out".
• *Verse One* by the Jazz Epistles (Celluloid, France), featuring Dollar Brand, Hugh Masekela, Kippie Moeketsi and Jonas Gwangwa.
• *Blues for a Hip King* by Dollar Brand (Kaz, UK). Dedicated to the groovy king of Swaziland.

◁ THE MUSICAL TRADITION
While most South African styles evolved against a backdrop of urban migration, rural music is an important part of the musical range as well. Best known for their "neo-traditional" styles of playing are the Pedi, Sotho, Zulu, Ndebele and the Shangaan. Here, a brightly costumed Ndebele woman sounds a traditional horn.

▽ THE BEAT GOES ON
It is now official policy in South Africa to support indigenous music, rather than look to the USA or Europe for inspiration. Not only are returning exiles achieving musical recognition at home, but a whole new generation is creating a rich mix of heritage and world musical trends.

▽ GODFATHER OF JAZZ
Forced into exile in the 1960s by the policies of apartheid, legendary trumpeter Hugh Masekela returned in 1990 and remains an active promoter of local jazz acts.

◁ ZULU HARMONIES
The brand of a cappella folk harmonies perfected by Ladysmith Black Mambazo – which means "the Black Axe of Ladysmith" – are instantly recognisable. Formed in 1970, their contribution to American musician Paul Simon's 1987 *Graceland* album first made them world-famous.

THE CHANGING FACE OF ART

The ending of the cultural boycott has finally exposed local
talent to the rest of Africa – and the world

The art of southern Africa dates back to pre-history and, it has been argued, represents the human race's longest artistic tradition. This claim is based on San rock art, which developed from this time right up to the second half of the 19th century.

The paintings and engravings of the San people are found mainly in the Drakensberg and its extension from the Eastern Cape to Lesotho and Swaziland, as well as in the mountains of Northern Province and sites on the inland plateau along the Vaal and Orange rivers. The sensitive depictions of animals and human figures painted and engraved in rock shelters are thought to be shamanistic and a link between the real world and the spirit world. There are over 15,000 documented sites in South Africa.

Wood carving, beadwork, basket-making and pottery have for centuries been found here, serving both utilitarian and decorative purposes. You can still find carved sticks and head rests, initiation figures and decorative doors, stools and utensils.

Beadwork is produced by most African people in South Africa but most strikingly by Zulu speakers. This art, originally used as a symbol of status, is increasingly aimed at the tourist market. Highly original patterns, using traditional beads alone, have given way to the use of plastic, safety-pins and other more modern materials, stitched on to decorative blankets.

Western influences

The influence of Western painters and art was first felt when early explorers recorded their adventures. The names of 19th-century chroniclers such as Thomas Baines (1820–1875), Fredrick I'Ons (1802–1887) and Thomas Bowler (1812–1869) are synonymous with early South African painting; their works can be seen in a number of museums and art galleries.

LEFT: interior design, Ndebele-style.

The influence of Europe remained strong, with the Dutch tradition of landscape painting predominating, thanks to Dutch settlers such as Frans Oerder (1867–1944) and Pieter Wenning (1873–1921). They helped establish the South African-born painters J.E.A. Volschenk (1853–1936) and Hugo Naude (1869–1941), as well as artists who reflected the British and French Impressionist landscape tradition, such as Robert Gwelo Goodman (1871–1938).

Anton van Wouw (1892–1945) is commonly regarded as the father of modern Western sculpture in South Africa. A Dutchman who arrived in 1890, his work followed a descriptive realist tradition. Moses Kottler (1896–1977) and Lippy Lipshitz (1903–1980) followed a carving tradition, as did later artists such as Elsa Dziomba (1902–1970) and Lucas Sithole (born 1931).

The influence of Expressionism reached the country in the early 1920s when Irma Stern (1904–1966) and Maggie Laubscher (1886–1973) returned from studies in Weimar and Berlin. The 1930s saw the New Group set out to explore Post-Impressionist influences, following what they believed to be progressive ideals. Gregoire Boonzaier (b. 1909), Terence MacCaw (1913–1976) and Walter Battiss (1906–1982) led the break away from what they perceived to be amateurism in South African art displayed by the naturalistic depiction of landscape.

Among the most prominent black artists of the early 1940s were Gerard Sekoto (b. 1913), who left to live in Paris in 1947, Ernest Mancoba (b. 1910), and George Pemba (b. 1920). All three painted scenes of people and places in a realistic manner.

Township art

Post-war developments saw a move towards abstract art theories current in Europe and the United States in the 1950s. But also present was a figurative expressive style, emanating from a growing body of black urban artists. Their subject matter of crowded black townships and distorted expressive human figures became known as "township art".

Mslaba Dumile (b. 1939) is the best-known exponent. Black sculptors such as Sydney Kumalo (1935–1990) and Michael Zondi (b. 1926) became, together with Dumile, the first black artists to represent South Africa internationally.

A further attempt to combine a European approach and African symbolism took place during the 1960s with artists such as Edoardo Villa (b. 1920), Giuseppe Cattaneo (b. 1929) and Cecil Skotnes (b. 1952) featuring prominently. Villa settled in South Africa from

Italy after World War II and introduced welded metal sculpture.

The 1970s saw the rise of an art which began to protest against apartheid. Despite the country's enforced cultural isolation, black artists such as Leonard Matsoso (b. 1949) and Ezrom Legae (b. 1938) still achieved international recognition. Avant-garde artists tried to reflect the socio-political realities and challenge the social conscience.

A new generation of artists – such as William Kentridge (b. 1955), Penny Siopis (b. 1953) and Keith Dietrich (b. 1950) – came to prominence in the mid-1980s and have used a figurative style in their interpretation of contemporary socio-political events. Personal iconography has been undertaken by artists like Karel Nel (b. 1955) and Paul Shelly (b. 1963).

The phenomenon of formally-untrained rural artists finding their way into the mainstream of South African art can be traced to the 1985 BMW exhibition, *Tributaries*. Black sculptors fron the Venda area in the northern Transvaal were introduced to the urban art world. Among the most original is Jackson Hlungwani (b. 1923), whose religious cosmology and world view are translated through extraordinarily powerful and innovative sculptures.

People's art

The 1980s saw the establishment of a number of non-formal collective projects which tried to adapt teaching to conditions in the townships, providing skills, training and access to resources. The best-known of these were the Thupelo Arts Project in Johannesburg and the Community Arts Project in Cape Town. The Thupelo Art Project, which owed its origins to the Triangle Artists' Workshop in New York, saw the development of an abstract expression-ist, non-figurative style. This caused contro-versy among those who felt a figurative socio-political style was more appropriate to the South African situation.

This tendency found expression with the 1985 unrest in the townships, which saw the emergence of a spontaneous public art known as "people's parks" – places where people could gather for cultural and political activities. Sym-bols of work such as tools were juxtaposed in sculptures with common junk, maps of Africa and home-made wooden weapons. None of these "parks" remain today.

The 1990s have seen the introduction – for the first time in South Africa's history – of a ministry with an arts and culture portfolio. Two of the most important visual arts projects recently supported by the Department of Arts, Culture, Science and Technology were the 1995 and 1997 Africus Johannesburg Biennales, South Africa's first biennales and the largest contemporary art events in Africa.

With the formation of national arts councils in 1997, and with more local artists being rep-resented internationally in exhibitions focusing specifically on South African art, the place of the country's artists on the international art scene finally seems assured.

The first artists

South Africa is home to the largest collection of Stone Age art in the world. Scattered throughout the interior of the country are more than 15,000 rock paintings and engravings created by the San hunter-gatherers, who first made their mark in southern Africa about 40,000 years ago.

It is generally thought that this art has an occult significance, representing the San's strong identification with the animals they hunted and the rituals they used to obtain power over them. Some of the finest paintings depict eland hunts. The eland, largest of the African antelopes, was regarded as having supernatural powers and was the San's special link with the Godhead.

Another common theme is trance-dancing, performed by the clan's shaman in order to activate a supernatural potency which would transform him and allow him to enter the spirit world. Paintings show women clapping and men dancing before an extraordinary half-animal, half-human figure – the shaman, merging with his animal power.

Shamans entering the spirit world experienced a variety of physical and visual hallucinations, a state depicted in their art by such metaphors as "being underwater". "Death" is another, because there were certain similarities between a shaman entering a trance and, for example, a dying eland – both bled at the nose, frothed at the mouth, stumbled about and eventually collapsed unconscious.

Once in the spirit world, it was the shaman's task to cure the sick, resolve social conflict and control the movement of herds of game, including the mysterious rain-animal that brought rain. Such "work" guaranteed the continued existence of San society.

The paintings and engravings depicting trance dances and the symbols of supernatural power were a means by which the shamans tried to communicate what they had undergone to their peers. But they were also regarded as powerful things in themselves, storehouses of the very potency that made contact with the spirit world possible.

Historical events and observations of the newcomers who encroached on the San's living space were also recorded. Nguni warriors and cattle, Khoekhoen fat-tailed sheep, European settlers on horseback with rifles, ships and uniformed soldiers were all captured in surprising detail.

Sadly, the San did not survive the arrival of the white man. When the diminutive hunter-gatherers who had lived in perfect ecological harmony with their environment for so many thousands of years saw the vast herds of game cut down by the settlers' guns, they launched fierce retaliatory raids. But their bows and arrows were no match for guns. The San were hunted from their lands like vermin; and today a few scattered artefacts and the rock-art sites are all that remains of their culture.

Carbon-dating has shown the rock art sites range in age from about 20,000 years to about 100 years old. However, many prime works are at remote sites which are difficult to get to.

Some of the most vivid and detailed paintings are in the Drakensberg mountain range. The Giant's Castle Game Reserve has a good site near the guest chalets, and another at the Sunday's Falls Christmas Cave in the Game Pass Valley, near the south end of the reserve. The Cavern and The Stream shelter in the Cathedral Peak area are also well-known and accessible.

In the Cape, the area around Queenstown has some excellent sites, as does Barkly East. There is a 32-metre-long (105 ft) gallery of paintings on the farm Denorbin, between Elliot and Barkly East, which may be viewed. One of the largest and best-known engraved sites, Driekopseiland, lies on the banks of the Riet River near Kimberley.

LEFT: street art, Soweto.
ABOVE: a Stone Age depiction of an eland hunt.

BLACK ART

From contemporary Western to distinctly African trends, from watercolours to wooden masks, artists draw on an eclectic range of styles and forms

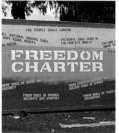

During the 1980s, the fight against apartheid reached its peak. For many artists, playwrights, writers and musicians the act of creation became a political one. This "cultural struggle" was symbolised by images of defiance, painted on walls, recited from stages and printed on t-shirts and badges. Art became a weapon of the struggle to make people aware of the realities of South African society under apartheid.

A NEW MEDIUM

What made this aspect of the cultural struggle so successful was its accessibility to a broader public, a public not used to seeing "art" unless it was hung upon gallery walls or displayed in highbrow journals. Now, coffee mugs, table placemats, badges and walls – even freight containers like the one pictured above – became the new medium for the anti-apartheid message. A host of collectives (of which the best-known were Cape Town's Community Arts Project and Johannesburg's Thupelo Arts Project) were set up to provide the necessary skills. Today, with apartheid a thing of the past, these have become the cornerstone of a thriving independent crafts industry.

◁ZULU CRAFTS
At Dumazulu Cultural Village at Hluhluwe, in the heart of KwaZulu-Natal, you can spend the night in a traditional kraal and watch demonstrations of basket-weaving, beadwork, and clay-pot making.

◁SYMBOLS OF AFRICA
Wooden ceremonial masks like these can be found at street markets in most big cities. Styles vary according to the tribal ritual for which the mask was devised.

▽ "MADE IN SOUTH AFRICA"
Oil by Gauteng artist David Koloane, who has exhibited worldwide with much success. In 1994 he was the winner of the prestigious 2nd Quarter FNB Vita Now award.

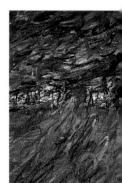

◁ FINE LINES

The cornerstone of both tribal dress and the curio market, you'll find beautiful beadwork like this wherever you go in South Africa. Traditionally, beads are used to denote the status of the wearer and to send messages – the Zulus wear blue for faithfulness and white for love, for example. These bracelets are made by the Ndebele people.

△ TOY ART

A good example of the cultural elevation of craft or folk art in South Africa, these Ndebele dolls can be found in museums and galleries as well as private collections.

△ A WAY OF LIFE

The Ndebele people fill their lives with symbols of traditional culture, using dazzling colours to decorate their clothes, their homes and their household goods.

▷ "THE SHEPHERD"

Bronze by Ezrom Legae, 1995. One of a new generation of black artists whose works embody the synthesis of both Western and African traditions.

ART COLLECTIONS AND GALLERIES

"Innocence", by George Velaphi Mzimba. This Soweto-born artist made his mark in the 1980s with exhibitions in South Africa, northern Ireland, Canada and the USA. His work is currently available through the Everard Read Gallery in Rosebank, Johannesburg (tel: 011 788 4805), one of the best commercial galleries in the country.

Other places to seek out the best in black art are:

• The Gertrude Posel Gallery in Senate House, University of the Witwatersrand (tel: 011 716 3632), which houses collections of both black contemporary art and a superb collection of tribal art, including Xhosa and Zulu beadwork.

• The De Beers Centenary Art Gallery, in the Centre for Cultural Studies at Fort Hare University (tel: 0404 22269), spans works by pioneer painters such as George Pemba to more modern artists such as Sydney Khumalo. A collection with a strong emphasis on social realism.

• The Centre for African Studies Collection, University of Cape Town (tel: 021 650 2310). A wide range of contemporary South African art, from Jackson Hlungwane sculptures to paintings by Helen Sebidi and Tommy Motswai.

LITERATURE

Freed from the constraints of the apartheid years, fiction writers
are engaged in a search for compelling new themes

The first European literature to deal with South African experience is the Portuguese. A significant part of Portugal's national epic, Luís de Camões' *The Lusiads* of 1572, deals with the early navigators' records of rounding the formidable Cape of Storms. Here the African land mass is portrayed as a

hostile and dark giant, threatening to all but the most heroic Christian adventurers. He is given a mythological name, Adamastor, and a part of his body is Table Mountain that guards the entry to the land.

After the settlement of the Dutch there in 1652, the written records of the Cape are mostly in diary form. In the 18th century, this small enclave had a considerable reputation in Europe as a botanical paradise, and several travellers' records portray its slave-holding milieu. Inland over the frontier was an explorer's playground, of which a boastful adventurer like François le Vaillant in 1795 could publish his highly-exaggerated accounts. Nevertheless, the travel-ogue of the Enlightenment included detailed records of the life and customs of indigenous peoples, together with accounts of hunting big game.

British tradition

From the 1820s, with the British colonisation of Southern Africa, a systematic literature began with the introduction of the press. On the Eastern frontier, the first Xhosa-language newspaper began in the 1840s, more or less at the time the emancipation of slaves became general. Missionary endeavour on many fronts, while translating the Bible, preserved the first accounts we have of the earliest oral literature in Xhosa, Zulu, Tswana and Sotho.

The even older poetry and folklore of the Khoisan peoples was first taken down and translated by the German philologist Wilhelm Bleek, whose collection for the South African Library in Cape Town has not yet been exhausted by scholars. The San and Khoikhoi – now practically extinct – provide us in their mythology and history with an absorbing account of the European conqueror from the other side.

The British frontier produced two types of writing which persist even today. Thomas Pringle (1789–1834) introduced a high-flown, romantic style of poetry, starting a tradition which stays in touch with European models, while Andrew Geddes Bain (1797–1864) began a stream of popular songs and satires which used the far more earthy language of the market-place. In Bain's polyglot work we find early forms of Afrikaans, the African language that was to develop from Dutch, as well as English, French and German (the languages of the early settlers), Malay and various spoken black languages.

Continuing the Pringle line of high culture, we have by 1883 the publication of the novel *The Story of an African Farm*, which was really the first great work to be written in the far-flung colonies. It was greeted in the motherland with amazement and controversy, for it was the first work which gave a realistic and credible portrait of the conditions of daily life on an establishment in the Karoo and of the cruel and difficult society, with its educational, commercial and religious institutions, on which it depended. The author, Olive Schreiner (1855–1920), was the daughter of a German missionary and his English wife but considered herself one of the first "South Africans", owing her inspiration to the modern nation she was so influential in building.

Adventure novels

The other popular stream of writing in the late 19th century was particularly productive and successful. With the appeal of British imperialism at its height, many earlier forms became concentrated in the adventure romance. In the hands of an exponent like H. Rider Haggard (1856–1925), this new genre created one of the first modern bestsellers. *King Solomon's Mines* (1885) has been filmed at least five times.

What is so memorable about his original adventures is the skilful way Haggard wrote them. He used an endearing, self-effacing narrator, Allan Quatermain, who was a professional hunter, settled in Durban, always willing to guide newcomers into the interior of Africa. One must remember that it had not been so long since David Livingstone had set off from the Northern Cape to find the inland Okavango Swamps of Botswana and then the great Central Lakes of Africa, nor since Burton and Speke had located the source of the Nile. The imperial adventure romance has everything to do with glamorising these exploits for readers back home.

Directly in the Haggard line is Wilbur Smith, whose adventures (such as *Where the Lion Feeds*) are very widely translated.

The oeuvre of many South African writers has tended to dwell on the burning racial and political issues that have confronted the country. But in the works of Sir Laurens van der Post (born 1906), such debates, if they have arisen at all, have played only a subordinate role. The essence of *The Lost World of the Kalahari* (1958), his famous book and documentary film

on the San, or his gripping adventure tales, such as *Flamingo Feather, A Story like the Wind* (1972) and its sequel *A Far-Off Place* (1974), is far more the enduring culture of southern Africa's indigenous peoples (particularly the San) and the mysteries of the vast landscape in which they live.

The black experience

Parts of this fiction-writing tradition are uniquely African. A black writer, Sol T. Plaatjie (1876–1932), in *Mhudi* (1916), started to reformulate the Haggard-Schreiner heritage, making it sympathetic to a portrayal of black history that

THE WORLD OF CAN THEMBA
edited by Essop Patel

THE MODERN TRADITION

Industrial South Africa, with its sizable cities such as Cape Town, Durban and Johannesburg, has maintained a literature like any modern country's since the declaration of Union in 1910. After Schreiner, a distinctive tradition emerges in fiction, which includes internationally-acclaimed writers like Nadine Gordimer, Breyten Breytenbach, J.M. Coetzee (*The Life and Times of Michael K*) and André P. Brink (*A Dry White Season*). Such writers played a vital role in the apartheid years, giving a picture of South Africa to the outside world – and sometimes even awakening consciences at home.

LEFT: spreading the word.
RIGHT: taking cover: the work of Can Themba, legendary chronicler of life in 1950s Soweto, is still very much worth a read.

white writers had tended to ignore or even destroy. In the same line, magical Bessie Head (1937–1986), who lived the second half of her life in Botswana, was able to recover whole areas of the black experience from oral sources. These she converted into short stories that, while remaining African in spirit, are very acceptable to white readers – *The Collector of Treasures* (1977) is a good example.

Those unfamiliar with South African writing should, however, beware of making simplistic distinctions between "white" and "black" writing, as if these two categories existed far apart from one another. Throughout the 20th century,

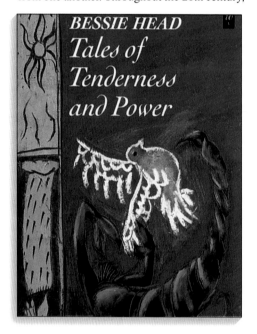

the great theme of South African fiction writers has been precisely that relationship between blacks and whites, so that every writer has, to some extent, been studying and presenting the country as one in which interrelationships are vitally important. The best example is Alan Paton's *Cry, the Beloved Country* (1948), which is still the widest-read South African work of all time.

Afrikaans writing

Poetry in modern South Africa has also proved a distinguished area of its literature, particularly in Afrikaans. Indeed, it is through their poetry that many Afrikaans-language artists have shaped their tongue as a written language. Eugene N. Marais (1871–1936), a founder of lyric verse in Afrikaans, was also a widely respected naturalist whose classic works such as *The Soul of the Ape* (1969) helped to raised the science of zoological observation into an art form.

Another Afrikaans-language poet is C. Louis Leipoldt (1880–1947). Like Schreiner, he was born of German missionary stock. He wrote voluminously in several languages, particularly about Rhenish mission settlements which were such a feature of the Western Cape.

An overt form of political expression later matured in the work of poets such as N.P. van Wyk Louw and Dirk Opperman. In the 1960s a younger generation of writers – led by Breytenbach, Brink and Etienne Leroux – emerged, and their work represented a drastic departure from the conventional Afrikaans tradition.

Modern trends

During the apartheid era, when many artists were driven into exile in Europe and America, the form of autobiography became particularly rewarding among black writers. Peter Abrahams in 1954 published *Tell Freedom* the first of many such works to recount the life histories of black people. *Down Second Avenue* (1959) by Es'kia Mphahlele is another important example of a black man's story of climbing out of a disadvantaged world of poverty and illiteracy to be educated, and ultimately achieve the status of self-made writer.

The enormous political changes that have swept South Africa in the 1990s have not yet made much of an impact on contemporary literature – although the biggest non-fiction best-seller of the decade has been Nelson Mandela's autobiography, *Long Walk to Freedom* (1994). Many novelists still tend to concentrate on themes which explore the painful apartheid past – for example, the best-selling *A Smell of Apples* (1993) by Mark Behr, the story of a white boy growing up in the militaristic 1960s and 1970s.

A new generation of black writers has yet to appear, although significant work is being done by organisations such as the Congress of South African Writers to undo the damage caused by the ravages of "Bantu Education" and the struggle against it, which pitched many youngsters out of school and into street battles.

Nadine Gordimer

When Nadine Gordimer was awarded the Nobel Prize for Literature in 1991, there was worldwide approval of the choice. The warmth of that reaction reflected acclaim for her two lifelong preoccupations: the craft of writing, and a commitment to opposing – both in her writing and on countless platforms at home and around the world – the evils of apartheid.

Born in 1923 in the small mining town of Springs, on the gold-laden reef that runs through Johannesburg, Gordimer had an atypical childhood. Her parents were immigrants: her father a Jewish watchmaker from Lithuania; her mother English. More significantly for her development as a writer, her mother took her out of school at the age of 11 on the pretext of a heart ailment, keeping her at home until she was 16.

The young Gordimer had private lessons at home, and developed a passion for reading and writing. She published her first short story at the age of 13, and her first novel, the autobiographical *The Lying Days*, in 1953.

Subsequently, as well as building up a considerable reputation as a writer of fiction, Gordimer has become known as a tireless worker for, and advocate of, free expression in South Africa.

The Nobel Prize is the most illustrious of a series of awards dating back to 1961, when Gordimer won the W.H. Smith Literary Award for her short story collection, *Friday's Footprint* (1960). Others include the Benson Medal from the Royal Society of Literature and the French international award, the Grand Aigle d'Or. Her 1974 novel, *The Conservationist*, was joint winner of the Booker Prize in the UK.

Yet despite her formidable international reputation, Gordimer is somewhat underrated in her own country. Her refusal to submit her fiction to the duties and slogans of revolutionary action alienated her from many black commentators totally committed to a political agenda. In the 1960s and 1970s, she was also criticised for choosing not to follow other intellectuals of her generation into exile.

Although Gordimer has often explored the theme of absolute commitment to political action in her work, her own position is that she is first and foremost a novelist, not an activist or historian. As she has written, it is through her art that she aims to evoke broader truths about human behaviour. Her works are merely interpretations of real-life culture and historical event; they must be completed by the reader's imagination.

Post-apartheid, Gordimer continues to record and comment on the turbulent present with a resolve that can only be regarded as steely. While much of her early fiction dealt with the impasse (political, cultural, moral) created by white supremacy, her more recent works deal with the complex demands made on a society in transition. Her 1994 novel, *None to Accompany Me*, explores with a ruthlessly honest eye the changes which occur within the individual – nothing less than an abandonment of the

old self – along with the subtle hazards that characterise a transition to a new order.

What surprises many overseas visitors is Gordimer's relative lack of popularity among white South Africans, who until now have constituted the majority of the country's small novel-reading public (small because the literacy level is low, and more whites can afford to buy books – a heavily taxed commodity). There are two chief reasons for this: for readers satisfied with Wilbur Smith's best-selling blend of salacity, racial mastery and romance, her work is heavy going.

More trenchantly, though, it is uncomfortable reading; it "holds the mirror up to nature". If you want to understand white South Africa, read Nadine Gordimer.

LEFT: Bessie Head: a powerful and original voice.
RIGHT: Nobel literature prizewinner, Nadine Gordimer.

ARCHITECTURE

The built environment reflects a rich cultural diversity –
as well as exposing the country's stark economic contrasts

South Africa's architecture clearly reflects the country's distinctly different climatic zones, the cultural diversity of its people and, not least, the stark economic contrasts pervading every aspect of life.

Archaeological research in Northern Province and Mpumalanga has uncovered some remarkable remains of settlements dating back long before the first white settlers arrived at the Cape. However, the oldest surviving building in South Africa today is the Castle of Good Hope in Cape Town, built in 1666.

In response to local conditions of climate and availability of materials the 17th-century settlers of the Cape developed the Cape Dutch style, a truly vernacular architecture. Characterised by a pitched thatched roof, a decorative gable, whitewashed walls and a symmetrical façade with shuttered rectangular windows, the early Cape Dutch houses were often built in the shape of a T; later, the larger H-plan design became more popular.

A fine example is Groot Constantia near Cape Town, the famous homestead and wine farm built for the Dutch governor, Simon van der Stel. First built in 1685, the homestead's decorative pediment was added in 1778 by the German sculptor, Anton Anreith.

Other important historic buildings in Cape Town are the Tuynhuys, today used as the State President's office and residence, the Old Slave Lodge (now the South African Cultural History Museum), the Old Town House on Greenmarket Square, and the South African Library.

After a hugely destructive fire in 1736, thatching was strongly discouraged in Cape Town. As a result, a new house type featuring a flat roof and – sometimes – a decorative wavy parapet became common. The oldest surviving examples are now found in the city's Malay Quarter, the Bo-Kaap. These simple one-storey

---

LEFT: hot property: this futuristic glass tower houses the Johannesburg Stock Exchange.
RIGHT: brilliant colour subverts a soulless street in Khayelitsha township.

buildings originally housed the fishermen, labourers and tradesmen who had come to the Cape as slaves. This district also houses the country's first mosque, the Auwal Mosque, built in 1798. Only a few original walls still survive.

As the frontiers of European settlement pressed northward, a derivative of the Cape

Dutch vernacular developed in the harsh, arid interior. The Karoo house is a flat-roofed yet pedimented building with a *stoep* (porch) and later a verandah. In the Northern Cape, early 18th-century Boer settlers responded to the scarcity of wood by building hut-like structures of corbelled stone, some of which survive in the towns of Williston and Carnarvon.

The British influence

In the 1820s, British settlers arrived in the Eastern Cape, an area previously occupied by Boer farmers. A vernacular architecture soon developed around Grahamstown, fusing the building traditions of the Cape with those of the settlers.

Stone was more readily available here than in Cape Town, which led to Grahamstown's characteristic unplastered stone buildings with slate or shale roofs, some of which also have decorative open trellis-work. In Port Elizabeth, the British influence manifests itself architecturally in terraced houses with elegant Georgian and Regency verandahs.

KwaZulu-Natal: exotic blend

The cities of Durban and Pietermaritzburg also have a pronounced British architectural character, even though the province was settled before 1839 by Voortrekkers. Trees for firing kilns

Asian districts, while the city centre boasts the gigantic Grey Street Mosque.

African vernacular

In the rural areas of KwaZulu-Natal, the original Zulu beehive hut of intricately woven grass has now disappeared. In remote parts, a closely related type can still occasionally be found, consisting of a very low wattle-and-daub cylinder with a dome-like beehive roof. Most common today, however, is the "cone-on-cylinder" type, often built with modern materials, or Western-influenced rectangular houses.

In rural Free State, examples of beautifully

were plentiful in this subtropical region, facilitating the making of bricks and consequently construction with face-brick. Pietermaritzburg, in particular, is famous for its Victorian salmon-coloured brick buildings with corrugated-iron roofs and pretty filigreed verandahs.

In the late 19th century, the economic impact of the growing mining industry resulted in a remarkable building boom, epitomised by the monumental structure of Durban's City Hall (now the Post Office), built in 1884 by Philip Dudgeon in a Classical style.

Yet the city's architectural uniqueness stems from the local Asian population. Well-preserved Hindu temples are scattered throughout the

decorated South Sotho homes are still frequent. Their rectangular shape with low mono-pitch roofs reveal the influence of Western architecture, but construction methods and decoration are still traditionally African.

The most splendid examples of African vernacular architecture are produced by the Ndebele people. These buildings have a complex system of courts and forecourts, reflecting the social hierarchy that structures both family and community.

However, the Ndebele are most famous for their ingenious way of assimilating influences from other cultures, creating a strong identity of their own in the process. This is particularly evident in the colourful decoration of their houses.

Modernism, Gauteng-style

Just as the cities of Cape Town and Durban each have their own unique architectural character, the same is true for South Africa's third major urban centre: Gauteng. At its heart lies Johannesburg, a cosmopolitan industrial centre whose growth and wealth were originally closely connected to the mining industry. Nearby is the smaller, much more provincial city of Pretoria, crowned by Herbert Baker's majestic Union Buildings (1912).

The legacy of apartheid

The 1960s and 1970s was when the bulk of municipal schemes to erect black townships around the cities were carried out. Endless rows of monotonous box-like structures with corrugated iron roofs are a sombre contrast to the much more elaborate homes in white areas.

Providing affordable homes for South Africa's lowest-income population is the single greatest challenge facing local authorities, town planners, developers and architects today. Given the magnitude of the project, this issue will have a considerable effect on shaping the future of South Africa's cities.

Both cities have some fine examples of the architecture of the modern movement. A new period in South African architectural history began when the International Style first took hold at the University of the Witwatersrand in Johannesburg, under the guidance of Rex Martienssen. In Pretoria, architects like Norman Eaton made significant contributions towards the development of a regional style, adapting modernism to local conditions.

LEFT: Boschendal, near Stellenbosch, is one of the finest examples of the Cape Dutch style.
ABOVE: a covering of intricately woven thatch ensures these Zulu homes stay cool during the summer.

A GLARINGLY OBVIOUS STYLE

The period of the 1960s to the 1980s (apartheid's heyday) saw an architectural attitude of defiance in the context of South Africa's international isolation. Every major city centre proudly boasts a number of stark office tower blocks, epitomised by prestigious architect Helmut Jahn's tower in Johannesburg's Diagonal Street (1982), assertively standing up to be measured against the architectural achievements of the rest of the world. And every town, whatever its size, has at least one Dutch Reformed church in a brutal brick and steel design, rearing a relentlessly "modern" spire against the bright blue sky.

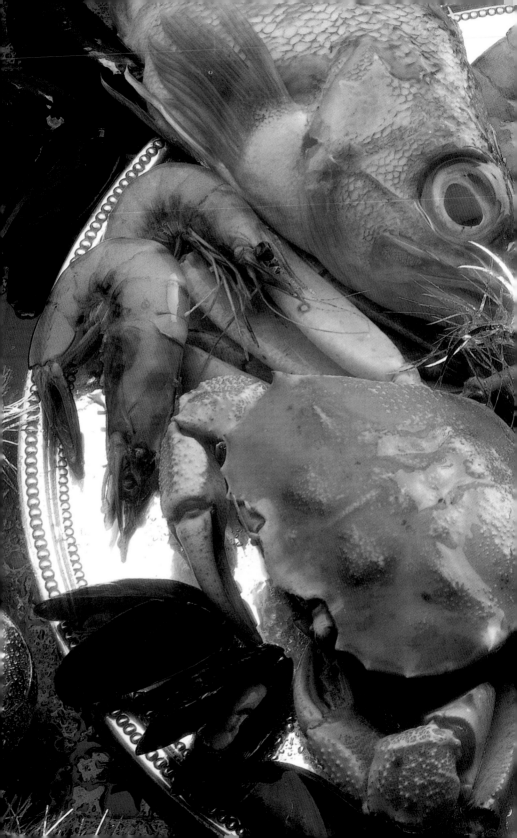

FOOD

From hearty Dutch cooking to Indian curries and black "soul food",

the national cuisine is a delicious mix

Remarkable yet true: the chief reason for South Africa's European colonisation was food and wine. Holland's domination of the East Indies' spice islands created heavy sea traffic past the Cape in the mid-1600s; after three months at sea, crews would stop in Table Bay to take on fresh water from Table Mountain. The vegetable garden started by Jan van Riebeeck, first commander of the Cape, still exists at the top of Adderley Street, although it is now a botanical park.

As the primitive settlement grew first into a seaside village, then into a town, hearty and wholesome Dutch cooking held sway. Gradually culinary ideas from the East Indies were introduced. Stews were enhanced by cloves, cinnamon, pimiento, turmeric, anise and tamarind, as were cakes and homemade sweets, confectionery and preserves.

It was not long before rice was a standard accompaniment to many dishes – a direct legacy of the Dutch/Indonesian *rijstafel* – as well as oriental pickles and condiments. All still play a big role in the preparation of *boerekos* – Afrikaner traditional cuisine.

As well as being moulded by the passing spice trade, Cape food was influenced by East Indian slaves, political hostages and exiles, whose families transformed old Dutch recipes with the flavours of Bengal, Java, Malabar, Ceylon and Malaya. To this day the Malay word *piesang* is Afrikaans for "banana"; small cubes of meat grilled on a short skewer are called *sosatie* (a corruption of Indonesia's *sate*).

A mouthwatering baked meat-loaf, aromatic with mild curry and with a sweet/tart piquancy, is called *bobotie* after its Javanese original and enjoyed with a savoury fruit chutney (*blatjang*).

A French influence arrived in 1688 with the Huguenots, who were fleeing the revocation of the Edict of Nantes. They settled in the beautiful

Franschhoek valley, where they harvested fruit and made wine. Their technique of preserving food by long slow simmering, *confit*, means that all fruits preserved in sugar syrup, including jam, are called *konfyt* in Afrikaans.

To them, South Africa also owes a rich, succulent heritage of biscuits, tarts, cookery with

wine, pastries and a bread roll called *mosbolletjies,* using fermenting wine as a raising agent instead of yeast. Broken into pieces and dried in the oven, this fine-textured speciality is turned into rusks – the standard accompaniment to early-morning coffee all across the country.

Curry is another of South Africa's culinary signature dishes – a speciality of KwaZulu-Natal, where it was first popularised by the Asian community. Unlike the Cape's mild Malay curries, which work well with seafood, the curries of KwaZulu-Natal are hotter, and usually reserved for beef, lamb, chicken or vegetarian dishes. Rice, sambals, masala, crackly *poppadoms, roti* bread, fried *puri* dough,

PRECEDING PAGES: one of the dishes the South Africans do best – succulent seafood platter.

LEFT: mopani worms: crunchy, peppery, rich in protein.

RIGHT: adding *zest* to the national repertoire.

coconut and sliced banana are the signatures of curry restaurants throughout the province.

Indigenous cuisine

In traditional African society, food production and preparation were the responsibility of the women of the house. Women were the agriculturists and took care of the fields. Young girls would accompany their mothers and aunts to collect *veld* foods, and were taught which plants were edible. The best-known plant dish was a stew of wild leaves called *morogo*, or *imifino*.

The most basic African foodstuff was, and still is, maize. A variety of dishes are made with milk), was and still is a favourite dish on its own or with *phutu pap* (crumbly porridge).

Chicken, pork and mutton did not form part of the traditional diet, and fish is another recent addition – except among a few tribes such as the Shangaan, fishing was not generally practised. Another popular source of protein was insects such as locusts, flying ants and mopani worms. These were roasted and eaten on their own or as a snack with porridge.

Gifts of the southern oceans

Fine-textured fish, mussels, oysters, crabs, baby squid and pilchards are all caught along the

it, the most popular being ground-maize porridge (*pap*) and hominy grits (*samp*). Sorghum is another staple, used in dishes such as *ting* (sour porridge) and for making beer.

Beans are another key ingredient in the traditional diet, along with pumpkin, served stewed along its fried flowers and seeds, or mixed with cereal as a porridge. Groundnuts, or peanuts, are also commonly used to enhance dishes such as *morogo*.

In traditional communities, meat and milk were the responsibility of the menfolk. Stock was usually slaughtered on a special occasion only; game and birds were more commonly hunted and eaten instead. Curd, or *maas* (sour

TOP OF THE POTS

Umngqusho is said to be President Mandela's favourite dish. It's made with dried maize kernels, sugar-beans, butter, onions, potatoes, chillies and lemons – all simmered until the ingredients are tender. And on Western Cape menus, the dish to look out for is *waterblommetjie bredie*. The *waterblommetjie*, a kind of pond-weed, is indigenous to dams and marshes here. Best months to enjoy it are July and August, when the buds are at their plumpest. But don't make the mistake of ordering it in its English translation ("waterlily stew") unless you wish to incur serious loss of face.

southern and eastern coastlines, but the finest seafood is to be had between November and April: this is high season for the Cape's world-famous rock lobster (known locally as crayfish), a prized delicacy so sweet and tender that vast quantities are exported to top restaurants worldwide. Similar to North Sea lobster except that it has no claws, it is served in all the traditional ways, such as thermidor, grilled or cold with mayonnaise.

Other summer delicacies are the pelagic fish, found in shoals along the east coast of the warm Indian Ocean. Barracuda, yellowtail, katonkel and shad are all fighting fish and there-

browned snoek chunks, sometimes with a little stewed tomato, always served with rice and tart chutney.

Satisfactions of the hunt

Since the first Dutch farmers cleared the Cape of lion, elephant, buffalo and buck, South Africans have relished the pleasures of meats and sausages grilled over wood coals, of sustaining air-dried venison called *biltong*, of fresh-brewed coffee around a camp fire under the Southern Cross. To this day, in countless gardens, weekend wood fires are lit for the family *braaivleis* (*braai* means to grill or roast, *vleis*

fore popular amongst anglers, but they are overshadowed by the Cape's pungently flavoured *snoek*. Named by the early Dutch settlers after the European freshwater pike, this is a long (1 metre, or 3 ft), silvery fighter which is firm-fleshed and delicious.

Served fried, it is traditionally accompanied by sweet *korrelkonfyt*, a luscious jam made of honey-flavoured muscat grapes, which complements the bracing saltiness of the snoek. Visitors should also look out for *snoeksmoor*, a hot, savoury mix of fried onions and potatoes with

Left: exotic roadside stall, KwaZulu-Natal.
Above: the *braaivleis* is part of the South African way of life.

means meat), while there is hardly a picnic spot, campsite or bungalow in the national parks that doesn't have a barbecue.

Lamb chops, curried *sosaties* and freshly-picked corn on the cob are the foundations of this outdoor meal, but it can also include beef fillet, or cuts of springbok, kudu, bush-pig, eland or impala.

Then there's the coarse-minced sausage of spicy beef and pork fat called *boerewors* (*boer* means farmer, *wors* means sausage. The best specimens are usually purchased from rural butchers in the Free State and Northern Province, who make them with the same recipes used by their grandmothers.

WINE

With the advent of a post-apartheid democracy, the world has rediscovered South Africa – and especially its wine

Cape wine has undergone a revolution in the 1990s. It's been borne of another revolution – the political kind. With the ascendency of a man named Nelson Mandela and the advent of a true democracy, the world has rediscovered South Africa, and with it, its wine.

A NEW WORLD WINNER

Until the 1970s, South Africa's wine-making tradition was strongly influenced by Germanic styles, despite a latent French connection (way back in the late 17th century, French Huguenot immigrants brought their skills and expertise to bear in nourishing the local viticulture – first established by Dutchman Jan van Riebeeck in the 1650s). Since the end of the apartheid era, however, wine-makers have been at pains to learn new skills; certainly, the country has all the ingredients to produce the ripe, fruity and accessible "New World" wines modern consumers are thirsting for.

While South Africa is still largely a white wine-producing country in quantity, it's the classical red varieties that produce the finest quality. And the French influence remains strong, with well-travelled young local winemakers constantly arguing the merits of "Old World" structure, elegance and longevity versus "New World" softness, fruitiness and immediate drinkability.

Although the Cape wine producers of the 1940s pioneered cellar techniques such as the cold fermentation of white wine, they subsequently fell behind in the vineyard, with old clones, poor material and bad management causing a dip in wine quality. They were severely shown up upon re-entry into world markets in the early 1990s, although inexpensive wines and the novelty factor wooed the world's pockets and palates. Booming exports have led to local wine shortages: from a target of just one million cases in the early 1990s, Cape wine exports reached 11 million after the last recorded increase of 35 percent. While such success cannot hope to be maintained in an increasingly competitive wine market, this exposure has served to educate, temper and refine Cape wines and wine-makers alike.

The wine revival of the 1990s has drawn ambitious young wine-makers, monied businessmen and major corporations alike to seek out prime vineyard sites, build compact, hi-tech cellars and produce finely crafted wines. Boutique wineries are popping up all over.

There has also been a spate of international vineyard ventures. Burgundian Paul Bouchard has linked up with Pinot Noir and Chardonnay specialist Bouchard Finlayson, in Walker Bay. The Moeiux family of Château Pétrus fame is developing a vineyard with Savanha Vineyards in Paarl. The French Cognac family of Cointreau has rejuvenated the historic Stellenbosch property of Morgenhof. Bordeaux's De Rothschilds and the Ruperts of Stellenbosch, billionaires both, have plans for a Paarl farm called Fredericksburg. Zelma Long of Napa's Simi Winery and Michael Back of Backsberg are involved in a joint Cape venture. Needless to say, competition, export demand and the climb in quality has resulted in a steady rise in price. Good reds hover around R50 a bottle; whites are about R30.

While control over what's in the bottle remains strict, Cape wine producers are now at liberty to plant whatever they wish, wherever they choose. The "Wine of Origin" designation on Cape wine labels indicates the source of the grapes, the most standard being the traditional Cape wine regions of Stellenbosch, Paarl, Franschhoek, Constantia, Walker Bay, Wellington, Robertson and Worcester.

Serious wine-makers are bottling wines from selected vineyard sites, and specific areas within a designated region are being proclaimed, such as Helderberg and Devon Valley – both in Stellenbosch – and Elgin. And virgin territory is being identified as prime land for top-quality wines, including Noordhoek and Stanford along the southern coast of the Peninsula.

Pick of the best? Cabernet Sauvignon is king, with Merlot on the upswing as both a blending partner and a strong, structured wine in its own right. Shiraz is probably the most underrated red, producing wines of consistency and charm, capable of both Rhône-like elegance and that Aussie fruit effrontery. But it's the Cape's home-grown variety, Pinotage, that has made a name for itself with international palates. Bred from Pinot Noir and Cinsaut – mistakenly called Hermitage – it can be sweet and simple, or robust and regal, depending on its treatment. And wine-makers are finally paying it the attention it deserves.

Chenin Blanc, a stalwart in the local brandy industry, still dominates in the vineyards. But the classics are making inroads. Chardonnay is well-established, with styles that have evolved from the heavily wooded wines of the early 1990s to a more Burgundian elegance and complexity. And cool-climate sites are being sought out, producing Sauvignon Blancs combining Kiwi varietal character and Loire delicacy.

Pinot Noir continues to struggle as a red wine, although Walker Bay and Franschhoek cellars make some fine Burgundian examples. But its use as an integral component of fine *méthode champenoise* sparkling wine is putting the Cape's Cap Classiques on the map.

Stellenbosch and Paarl are the main, probably the most versatile wine regions of the Cape, offering the best of everything: rich reds, crisp whites, ports in true Portugese style, Sauterne-like sweet Noble Late Harvest wines and excellent value-for-money Cap Classiques.

Franschhoek, a valley of boutique wineries, offers mostly white wines, with a handful of red gems. Then there's Constantia, conveniently placed in the heart of Cape Town, with a select range of classical whites and reds nurtured in

historic Cape Dutch cellars, in surroundings equalled only by Stellenbosch for natural beauty. Walker Bay is the place for some of the Cape's benchmark Pinot Noirs and Chardonnays, and a taste of pioneering Pinotages.

Calitzdorp in the arid Klein Karoo, about 370 kilometres (230 miles) from Cape Town, is the port capital of South Africa. The Douro-like environment here has encouraged several cellars to plant port varieties and adopt traditional Portugese methods and styles. Robertson and Worcester are the regions to visit for the sweet, fortified dessert wines so common to the Cape's drinking culture. Jerepigo, Muscadel and Sweet Hanepoot are the labels to look for.

LEFT: a sensual delight in a beautiful setting.
RIGHT: the Hex River Valley, classic Cape wine country.

SPORT

Since the end of apartheid, sportsmen and women have made
great strides in the international arena

With its rich sporting traditions and excellent facilities, South Africa is a sports fan's dream.

The friendly climate offers superb opportunities for golf, watersports, hiking and climbing – to name but a few options – while avid spectators can look forward to catching the latest world-class sporting action at famous stadiums like Johannesburg's Ellis Park, or Newlands in Cape Town.

Since the end of apartheid and South Africa's readmittance to the international arena, local sportsmen and women have made great strides. After initial humiliations against foreign teams in soccer and rugby, the South Africans finally came good. In 1995, the national rugby team, known as the Springboks, were crowned world champions at Ellis Park after defeating the favourites New Zealand in the World Cup final. 1996 saw the national soccer side defy the odds to lift the African Nations Cup trophy. Nicknamed Bafana Bafana (a Zulu phrase meaning "the boys, the boys"), the South Africans also reached the finals of the 1998 World Cup.

1996 was also the year of the Atlanta Olympics. Here, swimmer Penny Heyns struck gold twice (in the 100 metres and 200 metres breaststroke), while marathon runner Josiah Thugwane stunned everyone by taking the gold medal in that most Olympian of events, the marathon. In the 800 metres, track star Hezekiel Sepeng came from behind to snatch silver in breathtaking style.

Then there is golfer Ernie Els, who followed in the footsteps of legendary South African golfer Gary Player by winning the US Open in 1994 – a feat he repeated in 1997. Els, winner of the World Matchplay tournament three years in succession, is consistently ranked among the top three golfers in the world.

LEFT: sailing off the coast of Durban.
RIGHT: football has always commanded the fanatical support of South Africa's black community – this Kaizer Chiefs fan is an elegant example.

Other sports stars to achieve success since the moratorium on international contact came to an end are IBF World Junior Featherweight champion Vuyani Bungu; Junior Flyweight boxer Baby Jake Matlala, who has won both the WBO and IBF world titles in his division; hurdler Llewellyn Herbert and javelin thrower

Marius Corbett – silver and gold medallists respectively at the 1997 World Athletics Championships in Athens.

The challenge at home

Yet while much has been made of South African sporting success since the end of the era of isolation, the biggest challenge facing sport in the country has not been abroad, but at home. For years, only white players and the sports in which they predominated (such as rugby and cricket) received the necessary money and facilities for development. The vast majority of South Africans were given little opportunity to make an impact on the sporting scene.

Although South Africa's sporting bodies have now made an effort to unify their racially-divided administrations and create a more equal sporting society, none has been as diligent, committed and successful as cricket. The United Cricket Board of South Africa has launched an impressive development programme in the townships and rural areas, resulting in the game expanding both its player and fan base dramatically. A rising generation of black cricketers will now add a new and powerful dimension to the sport in years to come.

Considering that South African cricket has already made a huge impact internationally

since readmission, and is regarded as one of the top sides in both Test Cricket and One Day Internationals with such stars as Alan Donald, Sean Pollock, Brian Macmillan and Hansie Cronje, the future looks bright.

Football: the people's game

Soccer has always commanded the fanatical support of South Africa's black community, who are loyal to teams with such exotic names as Kaizer Chiefs, Moroko Swallows and Orlando Pirates. As the largest participatory sport in the country, football has a showpiece stadium – Soccer City – halfway between Johannesburg and Soweto near the Expo Cen-

tre show grounds. It is an eye-opener for any visitor with a passion for the most popular game on the planet.

While soccer has always attracted white fans too, they've tended to avoid local league action, deeming it inferior to the European game available on TV. But that perception began to change when Bafana Bafana won the African Nations Cup, storming into the top 20 of the FIFA world rankings in the process. The introduction of the fully professional Premier Soccer League has also led to better organisation and huge sponsorships in the sport. All this has helped cement the game as the number one sport amongst all South Africans.

Key events and venues

Apart from regular internationals in soccer, cricket, rugby and athletics, South Africa hosts two major annual world sporting events. The Comrades Marathon, held on 16 June every year, is rated by some as one of the greatest ultra-marathons in the world – a 90-km (55-mile) pilgrimage made by more than 14,000 runners every year between the coastal city of Durban and Pietermaritzburg, provincial capital of KwaZulu-Natal. It's run "up" one year from Durban and "down" the next, in reverse.

On that day in June, the country comes to a standstill as millions of TV viewers watch the road-race drama unfold. The Comrades Marathon has made a hero of Bruce Fordyce, the world's most accomplished ultra-distance runner, who has won it a record nine times. Russian Dmitri Grishine, who won the race in 1996, is the only runner apart from Fordyce to have completed the race in under 5 hours, 30 minutes.

Then there is the Sun City Million Dollar Golf Challenge. Held in December each year on the Gary Player-designed course at the famous Sun City resort northwest of Johannesburg, it offers 12 of the world's top golfers a chance to compete for the richest prize in international golf. Past winners include Seve Ballesteros, Bernhard Langer, Nicky Price and Nick Faldo.

Years of international isolation resulted in a powerful provincial sporting system. The "big six" are Northern Transvaal, based in the capital, Pretoria; Transvaal (Johannesburg), Western Province (Cape Town), Eastern Province (Port Elizabeth), KwaZulu-Natal (Durban) and Free State (Bloemfontein).

If you're a cricket fan, the venues to head for are The Wanderers in Johannesburg (just off the M1 motorway at the Corlett Drive turn-off; graceful Newlands in Cape Town; historic St George's Park in Port Elizabeth, overlooking the city centre; and Kingsmead in Durban, on the Old Fort Road heading for North Beach.

In Cape Town, Newlands Rugby Ground is just a block away from the cricket stadium, while Durban's King's Park Stadium (which also hosts local soccer team, Amazulu) is a 3-km (1.5-mile) drive up NMR Avenue from Kingsmead. In Johannesburg, rugby action happens at Ellis Park, the venue that staged the

A long coastline and plentiful inland dams and rivers mean that South Africa is the venue for some exciting and testing canoe races, the most challenging of which is the four-day, 228-km (142-mile) Berg River Marathon from Paarl to Veldrif, which includes stretches of "white water". This is usually held in July.

The course hacked out of the bush at Sun City is a challenge no golfing enthusiast can pass up; another equally demanding layout – designed by Gary Player – has now been built nearby for the Lost City leisure complex. Durban's plush Country Club also has a fine course, rated among the top 100 courses in the world.

1995 Rugby World Cup Finals. Take the Harrow Road turn-off from the M1 South, and follows the signs – and the fans.

The Ellis Park precinct is also home to the major tennis venue, the Standard Bank Arena, as well as the country's premier athletics venue, Johannesburg Stadium (which, coincidentally, hosts the popular soccer team, Kaizer Chiefs). All this makes for a lot of sporting action in just a few square kilometres of Johannesburg.

LEFT: survivors of the tough Comrades Marathon.
ABOVE: rugby – traditionally seen in the townships as a "whiteman's game" – has many dedicated followers amongst the Coloured community in the Cape.

KEEPING UP WITH THE GAME

If you prefer the sedentary approach to your favourite sport – taking in the action in front of the television – South African broadcast networks between them offer one of the widest ranges of televised local and international sporting action you are likely to find anywhere in the world. Live soccer, tennis, golf, cricket and rugby are beamed in from local venues and across the globe, so you're not likely to miss any action from back home while you're out here on holiday. In the big cities, you could also head for one of the numerous "sports bars", often crowded with very vocal supporters.

THE CALL OF THE WILD

From the tiny shrew to the mighty African elephant, wildlife on

the tip of the continent is simply spectacular

South Africa is endowed with an extremely rich mammal fauna, comprising some 230 land and 43 marine species. Put another way, 7 percent of the world's known mammals can be encountered on just 1 percent of the earth's land mass.

This variety stems from the country's great ecological diversity, which includes two major oceanic currents and no less than six major land biotic zones. These range from desert in the northwest to the Cape *fynbos* region with its winter rainfall in the south; from the central semi-desert of the Great Karoo to the grassland of the Free State; from the eastern montane and coastal forests to the ecologically complex and diverse woodland savannah of KwaZulu-Natal, Mpumalanga and Northern Province.

Nearly all of Africa's classic big-game species can be found in South Africa's parks and reserves. The Kruger National Park boasts the widest selection, but many of the country's smaller parks contain almost as many species, often with peculiar regional specialities.

Unusual species

About 60 percent of species are small, and each has adapted to suit a particular environmental niche. The 20-plus species of mole found in the country are endemic to Africa and all have short, cigar-shaped bodies, underdeveloped eyes and no external ears. Their presence in an area is conspicuously confirmed by mounds of excavated earth pushed to the surface from newly constructed tunnels.

Bats are the only mammals to have achieved the ability of true flight; they are the masters of the night skies. They cannot fly as fast as birds but are more agile and acrobatic, thanks to their wings – elongated forelimbs, with a double layer of tough skin between the fingers and between the forearm and torso.

PROCEDING PAGES: a trunk-to-toe mud coating keeps things cool in the hot summer sun.
LEFT: neck and neck.
RIGHT: these birds warn buffalo of impending danger.

All bats become active at night and the insectivorous species manage navigation by means of echo location – emitting ultrasonic pulses through the mouth. In South Africa there are at least 75 species. Eight are fruit-eating; the others feed on insects. Insectivorous bats remove thousands of tonnes of harmful insects from the

environment, while fruit bats are important pollinators and seed-dispersers of endemic trees.

Elephant shrews are so-named because of their movable, elongated snouts. They have large eyes and soft pelts, and satisfy their voracious appetite on insects. These timid creatures are active during the cooler parts of the day, and their slender and elongated limbs facilitate lightning movement. In spite of a superficial resemblance to mice, they are not rodents.

Rodents are distinguished by their protruding curved upper incisors; South Africa's wide array of species have had to adapt to their diverse environments. At 25 kg (55 lbs), the porcupine is by far the largest African rodent, while cane rats can grow to a mass of 3–5 kg (6–11 lbs), making them a delicacy among some local peoples. Other species are small – less than 100 gm (4 oz) – and unobtrusive, but they form an important link in the ecosystem, both as consumers of large quantities of vegetable material and as prey for medium-sized carnivores.

Rock-dwelling hyraxes (or "dassies") are found where there are suitable rock crevices for safe retreats, and boulders to provide basking-places in the sun. Hares are also quite common, the plains species distinguishable by long, well-developed hindlegs. The riverine rabbit is very rare and only occurs in the Karoo.

control the sophisticated structure of the troop and protect it against predators such as leopards.

The smaller, pale-coloured vervet monkey prefers open woodland, whereas the medium-sized, darker samango monkey is a forest dweller. The lesser bush-baby and the thick-tailed bush-baby are both nocturnal and entirely tree-living. Both of these bush-babies are exceptionally agile and capable of enormous jumps when moving from one tree to the next foraging for various types of insects, small reptiles, fruit and gum. Bush-babies get their name from their loud wailing contact call.

Popular primates

Many an enjoyable hour can be spent in a South African game reserve, watching the antics of a baboon troop. Primates are often favourites with tourists, probably because they display so many human-like qualities.

Only five primates occur in South Africa. The chacma baboon, the samango monkey and the vervet monkey are diurnal and live in well-organised groups. Mutual grooming is an integral part of their social behaviour and helps maintain communal order.

The predominantly terrestrial chacma baboon is the largest of the three species and is found throughout the country. Dominant adults

Meat-eaters

Modern man has always been fascinated by carnivores, perhaps because his ancestors had to struggle to protect human lives and livestock from predatory raids. Human behavioural traits are often likened to those of carnivores – for example, through the use of phrases like "as cunning as a jackal", or "brave as a lion". Certainly, few sights on earth can match the majesty and confidence of a lion strolling to water at dusk after a long day at rest, or the steady stealth of a pride of lions on the hunt. And needless to say, tall tales about confrontations with lions abound throughout southern Africa.

In earlier times, lions were widely distributed throughout the region, but because of poaching they are now on the whole confined to the large game reserves. A large male may weigh up to 180 kg (400 lbs), while the lioness, who does most of the killing, is somewhat smaller and without the distinguishing mane.

Only the secretive leopard can match the lion in stealth. Its fluidity of movement, its agility and its strength enable it to carry large prey into a tree with no more than a few easy bounds. But the *pièce de résistance* of many wildlife films is the cheetah, which chases its prey at speeds of up to 120 km/h (75 mph) over open

suricate in the arid regions, have been the subject of several rewarding studies.

African plains are dotted with termite mounds, and it stands to reason that some mammals will utilise this abundant and rich source of nourishment. Although the aardwolf, the scaly anteater (pangolin) and the aardvark (ant bear or great anteater) are not related, they are all nocturnal with retiring habits and all rely on termites and formicid ants for nourishment. The pangolin rolls in a tight ball when disturbed, relying on its scales for protection. The ant bear can justifiably be regarded as nature's building contractor, as a large array

plains. To ensure the continued survival of this graceful feline, cheetah-breeding stations have been established at the Hartebeespoort Dam near Pretoria and north of Nelspruit in Mpumalanga.

No less interesting to observe are the many smaller carnivores such as jackal, caracal and the serval cat. The close collaboration and intricate social system of the dwarf and banded mongoose of the woodland savannahs, and the

---

LEFT: few – if any – of the smaller antelope can match the balletic grace of the little steenbok.
ABOVE: don't be fooled by the tubby hippo's benign appearance – when threatened, it can be formidable.

DOGGED SURVIVORS

One of the rarest and most misunderstood creatures found in the South African bush is the wild dog. Far from being man's best friend, it has been regarded with loathing by farmers because of its forays on domestic stock. As a result of widespread extermination it is now an endangered species, its numbers almost entirely confined to the Kruger National Park. Wild dogs live and hunt in nomadic packs, wearing down their quarry in a protracted chase and often ripping the flesh from the exhausted victim while the prey is still fleeing. Small antelope are the most common prey.

of other animals rely on its numerous burrows for refuge.

The African elephant

Local elephants are much larger than the Indian species, with an average bull measuring up to 3.5 metres (11 ft) at the shoulder with tusks weighing between 30 and 45 kg (65 and 100 lb) each – although a mass of 107 kg (236 lb) has been recorded.

Recent research has shown that lone elephant bulls remain in touch with herds led by matriarchs by means of infrasonic sound. Such solitary bulls are not, therefore, outcasts or

rogues, but often the prime breeding bulls and very much part of the social system of an elephant population.

All elephants in South Africa are protected in game reserves. Culling has been practised by conservation authorities for some 30 years to prevent elephant populations exceeding the carrying capacity of their enclosed environment. The proceeds of the cull – especially ivory – was used to fund the conservation effort.

In most other African countries, elephants are threatened by illegal ivory hunting, and in the late 1980s an international ban was placed on the sale of ivory to try to curb poaching. The measure was effective, but in South Africa,

Zimbabwe and Namibia, conservation bodies argued for the right to earn funds from legitimate culling.

The bitter controversy was resolved in 1997 when limited, closely controlled sales were once again permitted. It remains to be seen whether the reopening of the market will cause an upsurge in illegal poaching.

Hippos, pigs and rhinos

Until recently, both species of rhinoceros were on the verge of extinction. At one stage a group of only 60 square-lipped (white) rhinos remained in the Umfolozi Game Reserve. Thanks to an extensive conservation campaign, their numbers have grown steadily and rhinos are now exported to game parks all over the world. The smaller, but more aggressive, hook-lipped (black) rhinoceros is still subject to intensive conservation measures.

Large rhinos can weigh up to 5,000 kg (5 tons) and despite their ferocious appearance are inoffensive and myopic creatures that would rather turn and lumber off than charge. The horn – which can grow to more than 1 metre (3 ft) in length – is composed of tightly-packed fibre growing from the skin and resting on a hollow base in the skull. Coveted by poachers for its so-called aphrodisiac qualities, it may also sometimes be knocked off in fights or accidents.

Two species of wild pig occur in the country. The aptly-named warthog, with its characteristic curved tusks and – when in flight – aerial-like tail, is least likely to win a beauty contest. The russet-coloured bush-pig is a shy forest animal that is seldom seen.

Characterised by an ungainly body and large head, the hippopotamus is capable of large-scale destruction in cultivated fields and is consequently largely confined to conservation areas, although a few wanderers remain close to water sources in remote areas.

Hooved animals

Zebras are best known for their dramatic black-and-white striping, with Burchell's zebra of the woodland plains distinguishable by the shadow stripe in the white. The mountain zebra is an endangered species and is protected in the Mountain Zebra National Park near Cradock.

The giraffe, with its greatly elongated neck and reticulate colour pattern, is unmistakable. The buffalo features prominently in the writings of early explorers and adventurers, who described large herds trekking across the plains of the interior. The arid-adapted oryx (gemsbok) is thought by some to be the origin of the "unicorn" myth, because in profile only one of its curved horns can be seen. Equally stately are the sable and roan antelopes frequenting woodland savannahs.

Herds of blue wildebeest are often observed grazing in close association with Burchell's zebra and waterbuck – easily distinguishable by the white circles around their tails – in open woodlands. The black wildebeest prefers the grassland plains of the central highveld.

occur in healthy numbers throughout the country. However, the plight of the petit grysbok and especially the oribi is less secure. The nyala is a beautiful but very elusive antelope that can be spotted occasionally in the game reserves of KwaZulu-Natal and Kruger National Park.

Marine mammals

Schools of bottle-nosed dolphins are often seen off beaches as they relish playing in the surf. These creatures – one of 43 marine mammals occurring off the South African coastline – are believed to be highly intelligent, a claim

Early explorers wrote vivid accounts of springboks moving across the open central and arid western plains in their millions in search of grazing, often springing into the air in the characteristic "pronk". Indeed, the springbok's grace and spryness has so inspired South Africans that it has been adopted as the national emblem of the country's national rugby team.

Kudu and impala are common game species in the northeast of South Africa. Of the smaller antelope, the grey duiker and steenbok still

easily accepted when their performances in dolphinariums in Port Elizabeth and Durban are observed. In the wild, bottle-nosed dolphins may travel in groups of several hundred.

The number of southern right whales has increased since whaling was stopped around the South African coastline in the early 1970s. These 15-metre (50-ft) long whales have perfected the ability to remain under water for extended periods – often up to 90 minutes. Like dolphins, they communicate with each other by means of a highly sophisticated language of clicks and whistles. They normally give birth to a single, well-developed calf that swims immediately, following the mother.

LEFT: family resemblance.
ABOVE: over short distances, the cheetah is the fastest mammal on land.

AMPHIBIANS AND REPTILES

South Africa has an incredible variety, as well as large numbers of species exclusive to the sub-continent

South Africa's ecological diversity guarantees a large number of amphibian and reptile species – most of them exclusive to the subcontinent.

As most amphibians are nocturnal, it can be hard to spot any of the 100 known species. However, during spring and early summer, visitors are often treated to the extraordinary range

At the other extreme to the aquatic platannaare is the rain frog, which can live quite independently of water, even for reproductive purposes. It makes its nest underground, which is where the entire larval development takes place until a small froglet emerges from the burrow. Eleven species of rain frog can be found in South Africa.

of night sounds made by frogs. Some species occur in huge numbers, creating deafening choruses. Each makes its own unique sound, from the booming call of the African bullfrog to the snoring rasps of certain gutteral toads, from the ringing chorus of reed frogs to a whole cacophony of noises described by experts as "a raucous cackling", "a wooden tapping", "a rapid chattering" and the intriguing-sounding "an explosive tick".

The aquatic platanna is common but not often heard, as it lives, feeds and breeds under water. Tongueless, it uses its agile fingers to cram food such as frogs and fish into its mouth. It also feeds on dead animals.

The potential danger some reptiles pose to humans should not be underestimated – but if they are are treated with respect, confrontation can be avoided. The much-feared Nile crocodile is nowadays largely restricted to game reserves. In recent years, crocodile farming has become a popular and prosperous venture which helps to reduce the pressure on natural populations.

The sub-continent has an exceptional variety of tortoises, including five marine turtles and five freshwater terrapins. The importation of the American red-eared terrapin for sale in pet shops has meant the growth of isolated colonies of discarded purchases.

Twelve species of land tortoise are found in South Africa, the highest number in any one country. The smallest species of all does not quite reach 10 cm (4 inches) in length, even when fully grown.

Amongst the lizards, the geckos predominate. Most are nocturnal. Many have adhesive pads under their toes, enabling them to hang upside-down on a ceiling or walk up a window pane. Geckos are usually welcome house guests because of their voracious appetite for insects. The tropical house gecko,

ON THE LINE

The geometric tortoise, which occurs on the Cape Flats, is currently South Africa's most threatened reptile species.

crag lizards and the brightly-coloured flat rock lizards. If you're lucky, you may see the country's largest lizard species, the Nile monitor, or leguan – a conspicuous creature usually found near water.

Snakes, represented by about 130 species on this sub-continent, hold a morbid fascination for many people. Yet only 14 species possess a potentially fatal bite, which means that the vast majority of snakes are harmless or not seriously dangerous. Many species, such as the dwarf adders, the harmless

a common lizard, is often seen seen on walls near lights after dark in the Kruger National Park.

Chameleons occur only in Africa and Madagascar. Sixteen species are found in South Africa, of which 14 are endemic. One of the oddest-looking creatures is the Namaqua chameleon, which lives in the arid semi-desert region running parallel to the Cape's west coast.

Girdled and plated lizards are also exclusively African. Most common are armadillo lizards,

ABOVE and **LEFT:** the hunter and the hunted. Keep your distance from the cobra (above) – its poisonous venom can prove fatal if treatment is not administered.

egg-eating snakes and also the dangerous varieties of cobras, are in fair demand with snake keepers. Stringent measures have been introduced by conservation authorities to curb the commercial exploitation and illegal exporting of snakes, which threaten to deplete sparse resources.

Cases of snake-bite are rare and mostly result from people trying to handle snakes. The puff-adder is short, fat and lethargic – not aggressive, but it does bite when trampled upon. Adder bites can be lethal, but their venom acts slowly and allows time for treatment. Fortunately, the dangers of snake-bite have been greatly reduced by the excellent quality of modern serum.

BIRDS IN THE BUSH

*As a result of the country's location at the tip of a mighty continent,
some unique forms of birdlife have evolved*

Visitors with an interest in bird-watching can look forward to spending hours in South Africa enjoying a rich variety of species – from the northeastern savannah where birds of prey soar effortlessly above herds of big game, through the arid interior where species have adapted to cope with semi-desert condi-

tions, to the Western Cape, which sustains so many beautiful birds with its floral wealth.

Thanks to South Africa's position at the southern end of one of the world's largest land masses, its birdlife has evolved plenty of unique forms – some of which can now be found on other continents too. Families endemic to South Africa include the hamerkop, the secretary bird, louries, wood hoopoes, sugarbirds and whydahs.

The northeastern lowveld

About 60 percent of the African continent is savannah – or "bushveld" – so it's not surprising that most indigenous species (including the birds of prey, the bustards and korhaans, kingfishers, bee-eaters, rollers, hornbills and bush shrikes) are found in this type of environment. Much of the Kruger National Park's vegetation is classic bushveld; almost half of the 718 bird species found in South Africa can be seen here, making it one of the most productive birding spots in the world.

As far as birds of prey are concerned, it is possible to see a good range of species in the course of a normal day's drive through the lowveld. One of the most striking is the bateleur, a snake eagle with a black body, white underwings and bright red face and legs. The best-known scavengers are, of course, the vultures, which can be seen wheeling high in the sky all day long, on the lookout for dying or dead game However, contrary to what most pople believe, lion kills make up only a fraction of vultures' food.

Other large birds of prey include the tawny eagle, generally found on the plains, and the smaller African hawk eagle, which lives in denser woodland along the rivers.

Riverine trees often include the giant fig, which attracts fruit-eating birds like the green pigeon, louries, hornbills, barbets and bulbuls. Also keep a lookout here for the vivid, graceful bee-eaters, which usually perch conspicuously on top of leafless twigs of bushes or trees (or on telephone wires), and so are easy to photograph from a vehicle.

Surprisingly, most of Africa's kingfishers are woodland birds. Along the major rivers both giant and pied kingfishers are common, but in woodland areas you can see at least five species, including the grey-headed and the rare pygmy kingfisher.

Another essentially African group includes the rollers and hornbills. All five southern African roller species – easily recognised by their brilliant blue wings – occur in the Kruger Park. Like the bee-eaters, they perch conspicuously in the open. The exceptionally beautiful lilac-breasted roller is the most characteristic bird of the Kruger Park.

Hornbills are common over most of the park, especially the yellow-billed and red-billed varieties. One to watch out for is the extraordinary ground hornbill, a very large, black bird with white wings and a rather grotesque red-wattled face. These tend to stick together in solemn groups of around five to 10 birds, feeding on insects, reptiles and other small animals.

Another common sight at camp-sites are the metallic-blue starlings with their glossy plumage and yellow button eyes, scavenging for hand-outs from visitors. The

LONG-HAUL TRAVEL

Every year, the ringed plover flies more than 10,000 km (6,000 miles) from Siberia to the western Cape.

along with the bigger Kori bustard – is still sometimes hunted for its meat.

The magnificent, if somewhat ponderous, long-tailed widow, or sakabula, can often be seen sweeping across the grasslands, while the snow-white egret can be seen among grazing herds, picking at grasshoppers that the cattle disturb.

The secretary bird, which has long plumes resembling quill pens at the back of its head, is a splendid sight to behold. You may be lucky enough to witness the dramatic

distinctive sound of the red-chested cuckoo, or *Piet-my-vrou*, can also be heard throughout the spring and summer.

The highveld

The beautiful blue korhaan is one of the most distinctives bird of the open grassland, which covers much of Mpumalanga and the Free State. One of the rarer members of the bustard family in Africa, it's quite common here, and indeed –

LEFT: you'll find the yellow-billed hornbill in northern KwaZulu-Natal and Northern Province.
ABOVE: the flamboyantly crested African hoopoe is one of South Africa's best-loved birds.

spectacle of a battle between a secretary bird and a snake, the bird using its long legs to try and stamp the reptile to death.

Quite a few highveld birds can also be found in the mountains to the east and in the Karoo to the west. Several of the chats fall into this distributional pattern and so does the endemic ground woodpecker, a curious bird that never perches in trees, feeding off ants on the ground. It nests in an earth burrow in a vertical bank or a steep hillside.

From mountains to sea

The eastern slopes of the Drakensberg mountain range, and the dense evergreen forests and deep valleys at its foothills, provide a dramatic backdrop for some rich birdlife. The forests harbour sunbirds, flycatchers and the shy bush blackcap, a species that may be found only in wooded valleys bordering clear mountain streams.

Orange-breasted rock-jumpers and Drakensberg siskins are endemic to the mountains of the eastern escarpment. On the grassy slopes here, you'll see grey-wing francolins, orange-breasted long-claws and cisticolas.

If there are protea bushes around, it is likely that you'll catch a glimpse of Gurney's sugarbird, whose squeaky song breaks the mountain silence. The brightly coloured forest weaver, emerald cuckoo and Knysna lourie are also found here, and in the Tsitsikamma Forest National Park.

South Africa's national bird, the blue crane, nests on the flatter tops of grassy spurs, laying two mottled eggs on the bare ground or rock. Overhead, the bearded vulture, black eagle and Cape vulture wheel about in search of food.

The crowned eagle in action is another extraordinary sight. After waiting in a tree to ambush an unsuspecting victim, it swoops down on its prey, carrying it off in its strong claws with the aid of its enormous wings.

FEEDING FRENZY

At Giant's Castle Game Reserve high in the Drakensberg Mountains, a unique "vulture restaurant" provides carrion for the endangered bearded vulture (*lammergeyer*) in winter. Bones are scattered on a high cliff-top by the Parks Board, to protect the birds against accidental death from poisoned carcasses left out to kill jackals. It's an excellent opportunity for birdwatchers to photograph them from a comfortable hide fitted with one-way glass and specially-cut ports for telephoto lenses – and as there are only about 200 pairs of *lammergeyers* left, this is not a sight to be missed.

The KwaZulu-Natal midlands are largely given over to farming but provide some excellent birding spots. Close to Pietermaritzburg lies Game Valley, which has over 300 bird species, including waterbirds (kingfishers, wagtails and the hamerkop), grassland birds (long-claws, cisticolas and guineafowl) and forest birds (trogons, robins, bush shrikes and many more). It is one of the best birding places in KwaZulu-Natal. Tracts of bushveld in the northern parts of the region are much like the Kruger Park in vegetation and avifauna. The reserves on the north coast are rich havens for waterfowl, pelicans, flamingos and the majestic fish-eagle.

In Ndumu Game Reserve, on the border of Mozambique, you can find such subtropical specialities as the purple-banded sunbird, yellow-spotted nicator and Pel's fishing owl. Here, too, are tropical waterbirds, including the African finfoot and all kinds of storks, herons and bitterns. Reserves such as Umfolozi, Hluhluwe, Mkuzi and Lake St Lucia also boast prolific birdlife.

The arid lands

Bird-watching is relatively easy in the dry, open Karoo and the arid western parts of the country. Perhaps the most eye-catching birds here are Ludwig's bustard and the Karoo korhaan. A roadside stop will almost certainly produce some arid-zone specialities like the rufous-eared warbler, Layard's titbabbler and chat flycatcher. Travelling westward, chances improve of seeing some of the endemic larks, such as Sclater's lark (around Vanwyksvlei and Brand-vlei) and the red lark (in the red sand dunes near Kenhardt and Aggenys).

At the Karoo National Park near Beaufort West, you can step out of the front door of your chalet and be greeted by white-backed mouse-birds, Karoo robins and the ubiquitous *bok-makierie*, a member of the endemic African family of bush shrikes.

The region's best-known inhabitant is the ostrich, the world's biggest bird. Males reach a height of about 2.5 metres (8 ft) and weigh up to 135 kg (300 lbs). Although the birds are generally docile, the male – distinguished by its black plumage – can be temperamental during the mating season. Its skin may turn bright pink and it is likely to make a roaring sound – not unlike that of a lion – when approached by intruders. If all else fails, it may deliver a formidable kick with deft accuracy.

Ostriches are known for their speed and can reach up to 50 km/h (30 mph) – which explains why "ostrich derbies" are such popular events at farms in the Oudtshoorn area. A major part of the local economy around here is dependent on the ostrich industry, in which every part of the bird has a use: the skin is used for leatherware such as handbags and shoes, the feathers

for dusters, the meat for dried *biltong* and the massive eggshells sold as curios.

The sandy Kalahari, dotted with low shrubs and some bigger acacia bushes and trees, has an abundant supply of small and large mammals, which make birds of prey a significant feature of the avifauna.

Undoubtedly the most astonishing avian spectacle here are the huge nests of the sociable weaver bird, perched like untidy thatched roofs in the bigger camelthorn trees. These communally built structures can be up to 4 metres (12 ft) in diameter, and house anything up to 200 weavers. They live in these nests all year round,

breeding there after suitably good rains. The dainty pygmy falcon, Africa's smallest raptor, makes its home here too. A pair of falcons may take over one or two chambers in the weaver's nest, the two species living side-by-side.

The nests are dry and well-ventilated, but vulnerable to attacks by predators such as snakes and honey badgers, who frequently raid them in search of eggs and young birds.

If you position yourself near a water-hole shortly after sunrise, you may see huge flocks of sand grouse flying in to drink, sometimes in their hundreds or even thousands. Sand grouse are unique in their habit of carrying water in their belly feathers for their young to drink – the

LEFT: the secretary bird kills snakes – an important part of its diet – by stamping on them.
RIGHT: the white pelican is found all around the coast, and in huge numbers at St Lucia Bay.

feathers are specially designed to take up large amounts of water in the manner of a sponge. The males wade into the water to soak before flying back to their thirsty chicks, which drink water from the feathers.

The *fynbos* region

Large tracts of land in the southern Cape hillsides and mountains are covered by a characteristic growth of low shrubs and bushes, known as *fynbos*. Many are pollinated by birds which come to the flowers to feed on the abundant nectar, especially of the proteas and heaths. Two of the endemic nectar-feeders are the Cape sugar-

bird and the orange-breasted sunbird. Also endemic are the protea canary, a seed-eater, and the insectivorous Victorin's warbler.

Further north, into Namaqualand (famous for its show of spring flowers), the *fynbos* assumes a more arid character. This is where one can find the cinnamon-breasted warbler and the fairy flycatcher, but bird-spotters must take a scramble into the dry, rocky hills for these special birds.

Coastal birds

The Benguela current along the southern and southwestern coastline supports a rich supply of fish, which in turn attracts large numbers of seabirds. Large flocks of cormorants can often

be seen perching on rocks or flying in a characteristic V-formation in search of shoals. When one is spotted, the whole flock descends upon it in a frenzy, diving into the water to gorge on their catch. Some garrulous and noisy gulls inhabit the shores, the most impressive being the kelp. These large birds often drop molluscs from great heights on to the rocks below, exposing the edible animals inside.

Large colonies of Cape gannets are found at Lambert's Bay and on small islets such as Bird Island and Malgas. This beautiful bird, with creamy plumage and distinctive black markings on the face, can often be seen swooping down on fish in the waves below. Arctic terns or sea swallows migrate from the Arctic to the Antarctic every year, using the South African coastline as a stopover. Other, smaller birds include the African black oystercatcher, the sanderling and the white-fronted plover.

Bird migration

Every summer more than 100 species of bird migrate from the northern hemisphere to the South African shores. The most common migrants are waders of the sandpiper family, but they also include other birds ranging in size from herons to shrikes.

The journey from South Africa to Europe may take a small bird five to seven weeks to complete. They travel at ground speeds of 40–75 km/h (25–45 mph) and often fly for up to 100 hours non-stop over inhospitable stretches of ocean and desert. Small birds must use flapping flight, but larger species, such as storks and eagles, can soar and glide. This is much slower, but this way they expend less energy – a useful method of travel for birds whose size does not allow them to store a great deal of fat. Travelling these vast distances, a bird may burn up to 40 percent of its body mass.

Big soaring birds migrate by day when the heat of the sun generates thermals from the ground below, and they can utilise the rising warm air for lift. Small birds usually migrate at night at heights of up to 2,000 metres (6,500 ft) above the ground. For navigation, they use the position of the sun and stars, assisted by other environmental factors such as magnetism, wind direction, smell and landmarks. This process remains one of nature's great mysteries: young birds instinctively know how to find the correct route, even in the absence of experienced adults.

Insects

With an estimated 80,000 species of insect, South Africa is the continent's most exciting country for entomologists, collectors and photographers alike.

The subtropical bushveld savannah in the far north of the country is home to the largest variety of insects, from the giant termite and the huge baboon spider to the cleverly camouflaged stick insects and praying mantises; from the beautiful emperor moths and butterflies to the barely visible lice, ticks, fleas and aphids.

less Colophon beetles inhabit the mountain peaks – some species so rare that they are known only from the fragments of a solitary dead beetle. The protea, South Africa's national flower, plays host to a variety of beautiful chafer beetles. Forests here are home to the velvet worm, the most primitive living arthropod, which has survived almost unchanged for the last 400 million years.

Arid Namaqualand is highly regarded among entomologists for its wealth of insects and arthropods. Best-known is the colourful bottlebrush beetle.

Wherever you are in South Africa, it's wise to give all small shiny, spherical spiders a wide berth

Here you can see an astonishing variety of vividly-coloured dung-beetles push their dung-balls along with their hindlegs, while columns of matabele-ants stage raiding parties on neighbouring termite nests before they themselves are waylaid by robber flies.

The tropical region of KwaZulu-Natal's east coast harbours an endemic fauna which takes some truly exotic forms. From web-throwing spiders and multicoloured fruit chafers to glamorous butterflies, this narrow strip of coast supports an amazing range.

Down south, the Cape's unique floral kingdom supports some equally fascinating insect life. Wing-

in case they should turn out to be members of the genus *Latrodectus* – the button spider. The poisonous black variety is most commonly found in the wheatfields of the western Cape; you'll recognise it by a red stripe or spot on the tip of the abdomen.

Well over 100 species of mosquito are found in South Africa, including the genus *Anopheles* – some species of which are transmitters of malaria. They're confined to the northernmost parts of the Cape and KwaZulu-Natal as well as the lowveld.

Tick-bite fever may be transmitted by the bite of the red-legged tick as well as the common dog-tick. The disease is most widespread during the summer, when humans spend most time outdoors in grassy or wooded areas.

LEFT: the pretty little white-fronted bee-eater is confined to the Lowveld; look out for it near rivers.

ABOVE: a colourful member of the leaf-eating fraternity.

FLOURISHING FLORA

Thanks to its ecological diversity, South Africa is graced

with some of the richest and most varied flora in the world

The flora of southern Africa is one of the richest, most beautiful and vulnerable in the world. Popular species include the red-hot poker, the bird of paradise flower, the arum lily, the gladiolus, agapanthus and sweet-scented freesias. Most of these were first introduced into European botanic gardens and private collections in the 18th century. More recently, plants such as the richly-coloured gazanias and the shy osteospermums, which open their petals only when the sun shines, have found favour abroad.

The Floral Kingdom

Located around Cape Town on the southwestern tip of the continent, the Cape Floral Kingdom or *fynbos* region covers about 70,000 sq. km (27,000 sq. miles) – an area the size of the Republic of Ireland – and is home to 8,600 kinds of flowering plants.

On the Cape Peninsula alone, 2,600 indigenous species have been counted: more than in many considerably larger countries. Renowned for its proteas and heathers, this is also where you'll find South Africa's most famous orchid, the red disa, known as the "Pride of Table Mountain". This area receives most of its rain in the cold seasons of the year, between April and October. Kirstenbosch National Botanical Gardens in Cape Town is an excellent place to see *fynbos* in its natural habitat.

The semi-deserts

North of the winter rainfall zone lies the arid area known as Namaqualand, running parallel to the Cape's west coast as far as the lower Orange River Valley. This is a dry land which receives, on average, about 50–150mm (2–6 inches) of rain a year. The correspondingly sparse vegetation is dominated by succulents, especially shrubs with fleshy leaves.

Mesembryanthemums (*"vygies"* in Afrikaans), grow here in abundance. Other natives include the pebble plant (Lithops), plants of the similar Conophytum families, and many species of daisies, which have adapted to their parched surroundings by germinating and flowering only after good spring rains. All produce splendid blossoms of shimmering, metallic red-violet, yellow, white or copper-coloured petals, which appear in one burst in the spring.

Trees are, in general, rare in this region; but the tree-like *Aloe arborescens* (candelabra plant) can be found in large quantities in certain parts to the north. The Karoo National Botanical Garden, at the foot of the Brandwacht Mountains near Worcester, is an excellent introduction to the local flora.

Ranking a little higher on the vegetation scale is the Great Karoo, the vast semi-desert stretching up from the Northern Cape into the Free State and beyond. The rainfall here averages between 125–375mm (5–15 inches) a year, and plant life is dominated by small shrubs, mainly members of the family Compositae, such as the camellia, the silk-cotton (kapok) bush and the quassia.

Great silvery plumes of feather grass and ostrich grass are a common sight here, while in the deeper valleys you will often encounter the sweet thistle, which produces a beautiful display of yellow blossoms in the summer months.

The savannah

Covering some 959,000 sq. km (374,000 sq. miles) from the Kalahari basin right across to the east coast, with a narrow strip reaching down into the southern Cape, this is the subcontinent's largest floral region. Rainfall, which occurs primarily in summer, averages about 25 cm (10 inches) a year.

FLOWER POWER

24,000 plant species – nearly 10 percent of all the flowering plants on earth – are found here on 1 percent of its land area.

LEFT: the cycad is the dwindling remainder of a group of plants that were the dominant vegetation type 300 million years ago. Individual plants may live for hundreds or even thousands of years.

This is an area of mixed vegetation, consisting mainly of grassland, with scattered trees and drought-resistant undergrowth. Although isolated trees and shrubs are the norm, there are also large patches of savannah forest – the classic "bushveld". The vegetation covering much of the Kruger National Park is a good example.

Thorny acacia trees, often with a distinctive umbrella crown, are characteristic in dry parts of the region. The bizarre baobab, with its mighty trunk which often attains a diameter of several feet, can be found in the extreme north, along with the marula, the fever-tree and the ubiquitous dark-green mopani.

The grassland

Covering an area of some 343,000 sq. km (133,770 sq. miles), the grassland area encompasses Lesotho, western Swaziland, and large parts of the Free State and Northern Province. Rain falls virtually only in summer; frost occurs on most nights in winter. Even so, about one-tenth of the world's 10,000 species of grass are indigenous to the area.

The grasslands can be roughly divided into a western and an eastern region; of these, the western receives less than 660 mm (26 inches) of rainfall annually, while the eastern receives more. The grasses of the west are generally

Eye-catching grass varieties, such as red grass, pepper grass and ostrich grass, are all common. During the dry season – when many trees and bushes lose their leaves – these grasses take on a yellow or reddish colour, which has a corresponding effect on the overall landscape. Each year, large areas are burned off; but at the beginning of the rainy season, these bleak, blackened patches are covered virtually overnight with a colourful carpet of spring flowers and fresh green shoots. The Pretoria National Botanical Garden, located in an area where savannah gives way to grassland, has examples of the plant life of both regions – as well as over half of the country's tree species.

ROOTED IN THE CAPE

Many of Europe and America's favourite garden plants have their origins in the botanical treasure-house which is South Africa. This is thanks to the endeavours of a number of 18th-century plant-collectors and explorers (many of them Dutch) who scoured the Cape for colourful flowers that would be suited to colder climates. One of the best-known plants introduced in this way was the pelargonium (commonly called geranium), first brought to Europe in 1690 and which now brightens gardens and window-boxes all over the world.

designated "sweet" or "white", while the eastern, moister region produces "sour" or "purple" grasses. The descriptions are farming terms and refer to the grasses' value as fodder.

The forests

Forests are in short supply in South Africa; most of the relics (victims of man's depredations) are now protected by law. Only in the southern Cape, in the vicinity of George, will you find extensive woodland.

There are, however, small, generally isolated areas of forest in the belt which extends between the coast and the mountain ranges on the which extend northwards from the eastern Cape up into Northern Province – there are many patches of what was once a larger forest, above all in the deep gorges and on sheltered, humid slopes. Such areas are dominated by coniferous species, such as *Podocarpus*, known locally as yellowwood. These trees can grow into forest giants, reaching heights of up to 40 metres (130 ft) and with massive trunks. Species of the olive family also grow here, as well as the stinkwood (*Ocotea bullata*), so-called because it has an unpleasant odour when it has been freshly cut. Stinkwood furniture is a much sought-after feature of the Knysna area.

periphery of the continent, from the southwest Cape north of Cape Town, east and then on up to the north through Natal and Mozambique.

Along KwaZulu-Natal's east coast, you can still see isolated remnants of mangrove forest, growing in mud and sand. Further inland, you can see the remains of evergreen forests, where milkwood, ebony and wild bananas grow. Among the peripheral ranges – the long chain of the Drakensberg Mountains, for example,

FAR LEFT: the orchid *Disa uniflora*, which flowers just below the cloud-line on the southwestern Cape's highest mountains. **LEFT:** the red-hot poker.
ABOVE: the protea, most famous *fynbos* plant of all.

The desert

The huge and desolate expanses of the Namib, a true desert, lie outside the Republic's borders, stretching parallel to the coast of Namibia. In this region, almost entirely without rainfall, vegetation is scarce or entirely absent. When rain does fall, the soil comes alive with grasses whose seeds have lain dormant for years.

In places, you will see the Namib's most famous plant, the welwitschia, which resembles a giant carrot with two broad flat leathery leaves growing out of the top. It is an extremely long-lived plant, often surviving for centuries, and its appearance is all the more weird because of the way the desert wind erodes its leaves.

THE CONSERVATION RECORD

Nature conservation has always been taken seriously here,

and the time of transition is proving no exception

A recent survey of overseas visitors to South Africa revealed that nine out of 10 came primarily to experience its wildlife and unspoiled natural areas. When one realises what a wide variety of wild plants, animals and ecosystems the country has to offer, this statistic is not at all surprising. However, although wildlife is extremely significant as a cornerstone of the rapidly growing tourist industry, the importance of conserving it does not rest on this consideration alone.

Why conserve?

Nature conservation is essential for the preservation of one of the world's richest centres of genetic diversity, and for the maintenance of natural resources on which many of the country's people depend for their livelihood. Nature conservation is accordingly taken very seriously and South Africans have much to be proud of, at least in recent times.

Not only is the area exceptionally rich in species, but many are found nowhere else (these are called "endemic species"). Thus about 80 percent of the plants are endemic to South Africa, 30 percent of the reptiles, 15 percent of the mammals and 6 percent of the 600 bird species breeding in the country. The plants of the southernmost tip of the continent are so different from those found anywhere else that the area has been defined as one of the six floral kingdoms of the world – the Cape Kingdom. This tiny area, only 46,000 sq. km (18,000 sq. miles) in extent, is thus considered equivalent, for example, to the Boreal Kingdom which includes all of Europe, North America and northern Asia, an area of more than 53 million sq. km (20 million sq. miles).

This high concentration of unique wild species places South Africa on a par with the much-discussed tropical rainforest areas, such as those of the Amazon Basin, as an area of international significance for conservation.

The conservation record

Africa, and thus South Africa, is most famous for its amazing variety of antelopes and other grazing mammals and the large carnivores that prey on them. These herds of antelope used to graze from the Cape Peninsula in the south to the Limpopo Valley on the northern border.

The conservation record is not so good for native plants: at least 60 species or subspecies have become extinct since their discovery.

As the herds of wild ungulates began to be reduced by hunters in the 17th and 18th centuries, they were replaced by flocks of sheep and herds of cattle. The larger carnivores – lions, spotted and brown hyenas, cheetahs and Cape hunting dogs – came increasingly into conflict with livestock farmers. These species were soon restricted to the remaining unoccupied or sparsely occupied portions of the country. Of all the larger carnivores, only the wily leopard has managed to persist in reasonable numbers outside the larger national parks and nature reserves, mainly in mountainous areas.

Today the large carnivores, the elephants, the rhinoceroses and the large herds of wild antelopes are restricted in main to the larger protected areas, particularly those in the country's northern savannahs. The greatest of these is the Kruger National Park. At 19,485 sq. km (7,500 sq. miles), this park is almost as large as the

GONE FOREVER

The huge herds of springbok and quagga (a now-extinct subspecies of the still-widespread plains zebra) that used to roam the Karoo soon disappeared before the guns of the European colonists. Those dark days before the dawning of the conservation ethic also saw the extinction of the endemic bluebuck, a relative of the sable antelope. This is the only endemic vertebrate animal known to have become extinct in South Africa.

PRECEDING PAGES: drives in open-topped Land Rovers are a special feature of the private game reserves.
LEFT: zebra are unique to Africa; South Africa has two species. Here, a Burchell's zebra crosses a river.

state of Israel and larger than Kuwait, or the nearby kingdom of Swaziland. This enormous savannah park constitutes a quarter of the country's total area under formal protection for nature conservation.

In the Kruger National Park, visitors can view – from their own vehicles or from a variety of hides – some of the finest spectacles of African wildlife still available to the average tourist anywhere on the continent.

The park has a range of different savannahs, and the well-prepared visitor can spend many days exploring its vastness, its diversity and its unending series of wildlife interactions, without ever becoming bored. Within this park alone, it is possible to see up to 132 native mammal species, 438 species of birds, 104 reptile species and 1,771 plant species, including 357 species of trees and shrubs.

Kalahari Gemsbok Park

Kalahari Gemsbok National Park is the country's second largest national park (at 9,600 sq. km or 3,700 sq. miles). Situated in the Northern Cape Province, the park is bordered by Namibia on the west and Botswana on the east. The latter border is along the normally dry bed of the Nossob River and is unfenced, the Botswana side of

the border being the western boundary of that country's even larger Gemsbok National Park (24,800 sq. km or 9,500 sq. miles). The stark beauty of this semi-desert area is remarkable, with its red sand dunes dotted with low thorn trees, covered in good rainfall seasons with vast waving strands of sun-bleached grasses.

Here can be seen such dry country specialists as the majestic gemsbok, the red hartebeest and the springbok. Amongst the birds, the sociable weavers are probably the most characteristic. Their enormous communal nests not only provide accommodation for themselves but also harbour a whole community of "hangers-on", including the diminutive pygmy falcon, which

CONSERVATION AND NATIONAL PARKS

If the level of a nation's civilisation is at any moment measured by the care with which it preserves its heritage, then South Africa has a fair record. A total of 72,700 sq. km (28,000 sq. miles) enjoys formal protection for nature conservation, in more than 580 nature and game reserves around the country. This may sound like a very large expanse, yet in reality, it means that only 5.8 percent of the surface area of the land is protected for conservation – far less than the 10 percent set as the minimum national requirement by the International Union for the Conservation of Nature.

appropriates and then nests in one of the many individual chambers built into the weavers' nests.

The tall acacia trees that grow in these riverbeds concentrate the larger birds of prey that abound in the open savannahs. There are few places in Africa where one can meet with such densities of large eagles, vultures, falcons, hawks and owls. Family parties of ostriches are frequently met with as they slowly pick their way across the dune veld or run energetically along a shimmering pan. In the dry heat of mid-day the pace of life slows right down in these silent savannahs. At this time Kori bustards,

Jewels of the east

In the east of the country there are many smaller savannah reserves, including Africa's oldest surviving game reserves, Hluhluwe and Umfolozi. Both were proclaimed in 1895, just 13 years after Yellowstone National Park was established in the United States as the world's first. Proclaimed primarily to protect the last remaining populations of rhinoceros in Natal, these parks have succeeded beyond their originators' wildest expectations.

The square-lipped rhinoceros found its last sanctuary in the Umfolozi Reserve and this population was thought to have been reduced to

Africa's largest flying bird species, fly in from the surrounding dune veld to stand gasping in the shade of a gnarled old *kameeldoring* tree.

Mammalian predators are also easily located along these sparsely-vegetated river-beds, and this is probably one of the best places in South Africa to observe the cheetah hunting. This is also the major sanctuary for the only large carnivore which is endemic to southern Africa: the brown hyena.

LEFT: preparing tranquilliser darts for elephants.
ABOVE: without man's help, the black rhino faces extinction in Africa.

fewer than 20 individuals early in the 20th century. By careful protection and through the development of methods to capture safely and transport these enormous creatures, the Natal Parks Board, which administers these reserves, has built up the world population of this species to its current total of more than 8,000 individuals. There are 1,800 to 2,000 of these rhinos in the Hluhluwe and Umfolozi Reserves.

More than 3,500 have been captured and safely transferred to other conservation areas in Africa and to zoos and parks throughout the world. The population of more than 900 individuals currently in the Kruger National

Park all stem from individuals translocated from these two remarkable little reserves. This is one of the few instances worldwide where conservation measures have been so successful that it has been possible to remove a species from the IUCN Red Data Book of endangered species.

These two KwaZulu-Natal reserves have also played a significant role in the conservation of the South African population of the black or hook-lipped rhinoceros. With the current deterioration of nature conservation programmes elsewhere in Africa, what was once the relatively insignificant population of about

Maputaland

On the northeastern coastal plain of Maputaland there are a variety of different conservation areas to visit. Africa's largest estuary, Lake St Lucia, holds the country's most important hippopotamus and Nile crocodile populations. Waterbirds inhabit this enormous shallow lake, including large breeding colonies of white pelicans and the striking Caspian tern. If the water levels are low, vast flocks of flamingos can be seen. Rest camps are located at several points around the lake.

South of the estuary mouth, Mapelaan Nature Reserve preserves a diverse dune forest on what

600 black rhinos held by South Africa has suddenly become the only relatively secure wild population in existence. A massive conservation effort is continuing.

These reserves are not only famous for their rhinoceros populations. Other mammals abound, including the most attractive of the African antelope, the nyala, found only in the dense thickets of the southeastern lowlands. The variety of birdlife is astounding, and breathtaking hours spent in the hides at waterholes in these reserves during the winter dry season will never be forgotten. The nearby Mkuzi Game Reserve is also renowned for its hides.

are said to be the world's highest forested sand dunes.

North of the estuary mouth stretches a series of coastal reserves, with a proclaimed marine reserve preserving the adjacent offshore wonders. Submerged coral reefs and the associated myriad tropical fish species and other sealife abound in the crystal clear waters of the warm Mozambique Current that washes these golden beaches fringed by lush dune forests. Each summer, hundreds of loggerhead and leatherback turtles haul themselves up these beaches to bury their clutches of eggs in these protected sands. After 25 years of strict protection by the Natal Parks Board, which each year monitors and safeguards their breeding activity, the populations are thriving.

To witness a huge turtle heave herself out of the surf and up the beach, the moonlight glistening off her wet carapace as it must have done each year for countless millennia, and then to silently watch her go about this age-old ritual of reproduction, is to experience something which cannot fail to confirm the importance of maintaining the full diversity of life on earth. There is something in the turtle's heroic exertions which drives home the message that this tenacious life-force must not be summarily terminated through mankind's exploitation or pollution.

yellow-barked fever trees are filled with an amazing variety of waterfowl, and provide sanctuary for many hippopotamuses and crocodiles.

The fig forests that fringe the rivers and pans and the thickets that cover most of this relatively small reserve (110 sq. km or 42 sq. miles) hold a great variety of birdlife. More than 390 species have been recorded from the reserve, and in the summer wet season (November to March) when migrant species are present, one may easily record upwards of 200 species within a few days. Ndumu has the added advantage of allowing access to much of the reserve

The coastal lakes of Sibayi and Kosi Bay lie close behind the forested dunes that back the turtle-nesting beaches of the Tongaland Marine Reserve. Small rest camps are located on the shores of these lakes as well as in Ndumu Game Reserve, located an hour's drive inland on the Usutu River, the country's border with Mozambique. This, the most tropical of the Natal reserves, is probably the premier bird reserve in South Africa. A series of pans lined with

LEFT: celebrated game wardens Dr Ian Player and Magqubu Ntombela.
ABOVE: Laura Stanton in her Lowveld clinic with a rehabilitated black eagle.

on foot under the supervision of a trained game guard; many of these guards are expert fieldsmen and will much improve the visitor's ability to detect the often unobtrusive birds and mammals in the reserve's dense forests.

The high grasslands conservation areas have much else to offer. For instance, those of the Drakensberg mountain range that form KwaZulu-Natal's inland boundary with the mountainous kingdom of Lesotho are virtually all included in various reserves and wilderness areas. Here are found many of the country's most beautiful landscapes – huge, towering amphitheatres set above rolling grassy slopes, with numerous sparkling mountain streams running through tranquil forested gorges to fall tumbling over cascading waterfalls.

These mountains and grasslands are home to a fabulous variety of wild flowers and several of the country's endemic bird species, such as the yellow pipit and the Drakensberg siskin. The majestic lammergeyer is still secure here, too.

The arid interior

Further west one can visit the Mountain Zebra National Park or the Karoo National Park as well as several provincial reserves, such as the Goegap Nature Reserve or Rolfontein Nature Reserve, to obtain a glimpse of the semi-arid

in such an area provide an unforgettable spectacle.

Ironically, whereas in most other countries it is the semi-desert ecosystem which are best conserved in national parks, in South Africa the converse applies. This situation may soon be rectified, and the planned Richtersveld National Park (in the arid mountainous region just south of the Orange River border with Namibia) is one of the few large areas protected in the drier portions of the country.

The Augrabies Falls National Park, higher up the Orange River, is certainly worth a visit but it is not large enough to ensure the long-

Karoo ecosystem, now mainly used for sheep farming. The Karoo is probably the most characteristic of South Africa's ecosystems. For those who enjoy wide-open spaces and stark semi-desert landscapes, a trip through the Karoo, with planned stopovers at several of the relatively small reserves found here, will be well worthwhile.

Most of the Karoo's animal and plant life is unique to this area. Those visiting the region soon after good rains can witness levels of biological activity unsurpassed in any of the other ecosystems of South Africa. The fields of brightly coloured flowers, a host of insects and flocks of nomadic birds breeding

term survival of the rich semi-desert fauna and flora of the country's western arid zone.

Forests, lakes and *fynbos*

Further south still, one has the well-watered coastal strip in the Eastern and Western Cape Provinces. Here are found the country's largest evergreen forests. The Tsitsikamma Forest National Park, as well as the nearby Tsitsikamma Coastal National Park, allow the visitor a chance to see the region's dense temperate forests. The enormous yellowwood trees, their canopies often festooned with "old man's beard" lichens and the forest floor beneath them damp and mossy, are a far cry from the semi-desert Karoo ecosystems which are located only a few hours drive inland. The Coastal Park not only boasts a spectacular five-day hiking trail – called the "Otter Trail" after the Cape clawless otters which can sometimes be seen feeding along this coastline – but also has an underwater trail for skin-divers or scuba-divers. The Knysna Lagoon and the Wilderness Lakes both fall within the major temperate rainforest areas of the southern Cape; these verdant forest landscapes only add to the beauty of the area.

The mountains in these southern Cape areas are almost all located within proclaimed and protected mountain catchment areas or

feeling uneasy about the conservation future in South Africa. Within a single lifetime, the Cape Flats, which lie between the Cape Peninsula and the Hottentots-Holland Mountains to the east, have been engulfed by a spreading wave of humanity. What used to be an area of exceptional wetlands and a veritable garden of wild flowers is now virtually completely covered by factory land, suburbia and small agricultural holdings.

Wattles introduced from Australia choke the native vegetation on the last remaining scraps of uncultivated land. Sadly, many of the plants and animals of this area and the adjacent

state forest areas. Clad in the unique *fynbos* vegetation that holds the proteas, ericas and other renowned plants of the Cape Floral Kingdom, these mountains are traversed by a series of hiking trails. To take a four- or five-day hike along one of these is to get to know one of the most spectacular ecosystems of the world.

The future

Sitting on the top of Table Mountain and looking down on to the seemingly never-ending suburbs of Greater Cape Town, one cannot help

LEFT AND ABOVE: a feature of any stay in the bush is the distinctive character of the safari camps.

A NEW NATIONAL PARK

Part of the Cape Peninsula is currently in the process of being proclaimed a national park, one which will hold a good representative sample of Cape flora. Species will be protected from such typical threats as agriculture, farming and urban sprawl, fire and marauding alien vegetation. World-famous Table Mountain, which forms the backdrop to the country's mother city, Cape Town, will be the park's focal point. Visitors can take relatively easy day walks some way up the mountain (the easiest route starts in Kirstenbosch Botanical Gardens), or use a cable car to reach the summit.

Cape Peninsula are now threatened with extinction. Indeed, 39 plant species have already been lost from the Cape Peninsula; 15 of them Peninsular endemics.

With a human population which is currently growing extremely rapidly (the population increased from about 18.3 million in 1960 to 42.5 million in 1997 and is expected to exceed 45 million in the year 2000), all the pressures on South Africa's natural environment are now intensifying.

PLANTS AT RISK

About 2,000 plant species are thought to be facing extinction unless trends in habitat destruction are halted.

Kruger Park. It now has over 15,000 members, and runs a variety of high-profile conservation education programmes.

The major fund-raising organisation for the environment in South Africa is the local branch of the World Wide Fund for Nature, or the WWF (*see Travel Tips for contact numbers*).

The new South Africa

When the new government came to power following the historic April 1994 democratic elec-

It is essential that conservation agencies continue to receive the necessary funds to carry out their important task of protecting the natural resources of South Africa for the benefit of all its peoples, including the generations still to be born. A visitor who, having enjoyed the wonderful country and its superb national parks, wishes to do something constructive to assure the future of conservation might consider taking out membership in one of the many local conservation societies.

The oldest and largest of these is the Wildlife and Environment Society of South Africa, which first came into existence a century ago during the initial campaign to establish the

tions, the environment was one of the causes that was set to benefit. The new South African Constitution, for example, contains a clause guaranteeing the "environmental rights" of every citizen; their rights to a clean and healthy environment, and the rights of present and future generations to a well-conserved natural environment.

With the country's readmittance to the international community has come the ratification by South Africa of several important international conventions, most important of which (from a nature conservation perspective) is the Convention on Biological Diversity. Not only was this treaty ratified, but an extensive policy development process was carried out to support its local implementation, ending in the production of a Government White Paper on the topic. Another important treaty recently ratified was the World Heritage Convention, preparing the way for South Africa to nominate several of its important areas as World Heritage Sites.

The time of transition has also allowed several initiatives that have long been stalled to proceed: for example, the new government has approved the proclamation of Table Mountain and the rest of the Cape Peninsula's remaining natural areas as a national park

their experienced conservation professionals as a result of an ill-conceived and poorly executed "downsizing" of the civil service.

Probably the single biggest environmental success story of the "new South Africa" has been the "Working for Water" programme of the National Water Conservation Campaign. Under the visionary guidance of the new Minister of Water Affairs and Forestry, Professor Kadar Asmal, this huge project ultimately aims to remove all alien trees from mountain catch-ment areas throughout the land, thus solving South Africa's most serious single nature conservation problem. Involving an

(a move that was first mooted in the 1920s!). Similarly, the long, drawn-out debate on the possibility of mining the dunes on the eastern shores of Lake St Lucia was ended when the new Cabinet ruled that this mining would not be permitted. The long-awaited national park for the Highveld Grassland biome has also finally been created (in an area near Potchefstroom).

Unfortunately, not all the recent changes have been so positive, with many of the provincial conservation agencies losing the majority of

amazing number of different institutions, within six months this campaign had mobilised over 6,000 unemployed people, most of them women.

It has not only benefited our streams and rivers, but also the native plants and animals that would otherwise have been replaced by rapidly spreading stands of invasive alien plants.

In many ways, the "Working for Water" programme epitomises the new government's approach to conservation: doing everything it can to care for the environment, while at the same time taking into account the real needs of South Africa's predominantly poor population.

LEFT: a relaxing end to a good day's walkabout.
ABOVE: a rare shower of rain in the Kalahari.

PLACES

*A detailed guide to the entire country, with principal sites
cross-referenced by number to the maps*

With reliable sunshine, almost 2,000 miles of sandy beaches, a mighty, wooded mountain escarpment criss-crossed with hiking trails and over 500 game farms, parks and reserves, South Africa is an extremely appealing destination for nature-lovers and outdoor enthusiasts alike.

By African standards, it's an easy country to negotiate, with good facilities that are well-organised and efficiently run. The internal infrastructure is excellent, too, all the way from the southern tip to brash Johannesburg, spinning on a hub of gold from the mines that provide so much of the country's wealth. And with a weak rand greatly increasing foreign visitors' spending power, South Africa is very good value for money.

South Africa is an enormous place; roughly five times the size of Britain. Unless you plant to spend a few months in the country, it would be hard to take in the great variety of sights in a single visit. In order to help first-time visitors decide on a basic itinerary, we have therefore organised our descriptions of the country into a series of standard routes – not so much a prescriptive list of stops and sights as a basis for creative improvisation and overlap.

Classic sights? The Kruger National Park and the Kalahari Gemsbok Park are two of Africa's great game reserves. The Cape peninsula, where two oceans meet, must rank as one of the most beautiful and striking sights in the world, let alone the continent.

But make time, too, to head off the beaten track: to explore the far reaches of Northern Province with its sacred lakes, home of the python-god; the Eastern Cape and its long, blond beaches, fringed with indigenous rainforest; the Rip van Winkle stone-built villages of the Free State and the majestic open expanse of the Great Karoo.

It is at last getting easier to cross the racial divide, which in the past meant so much of South Africa's cultural richness and energy was inaccessible to whites. Yet it is also impossible to ignore the statistics which show such worryingly high levels of violent crime. Although most instances occur in townships, visitors should be alert to muggings during the day as well as at night in tourist zones. And while it is not a good idea to visit townships as a lone wanderer, do try and visit with a guide or on an organised tour. Paranoia is not necessary; common sense is.

Lastly, while South Africa's public transport system is improving, it is still pretty limited, and won't take you into the country's most intriguing corners. To get the most out of your trip, it is strongly recommended that you hire a car.

PRECEDING PAGES: Kalahari grasslands; Namaqualand springtime; bushveld sunset.
LEFT: the Outeniqua Choo Tjoe plies a beautiful route between George and Knysna.

158

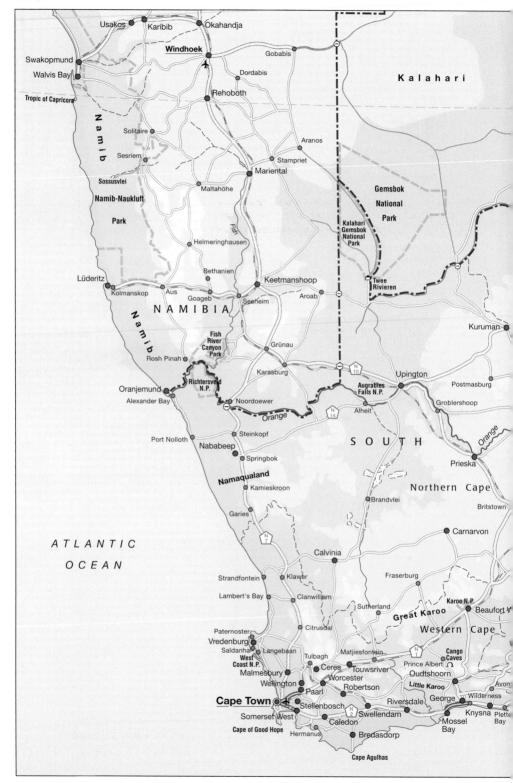

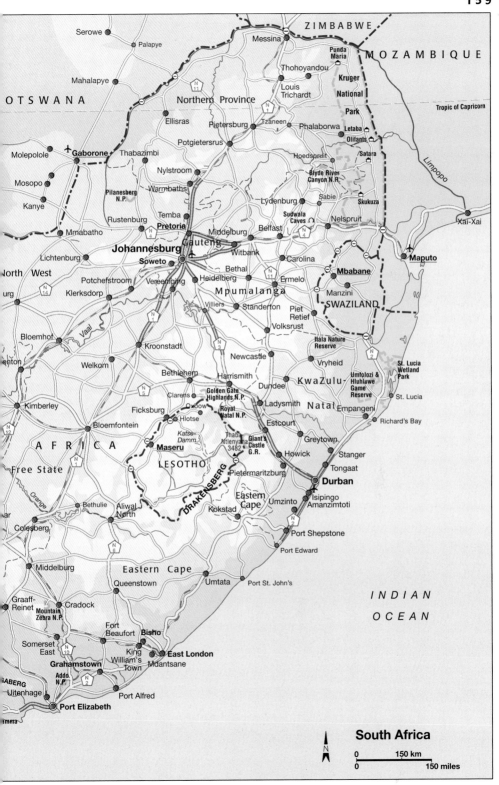

South Africa

0   150 km

0   150 miles

CAPE TOWN AND THE CAPE PENINSULA

Map, page 164

A mountain plateau flanked by two oceans, graced with long, uncrowded beaches and a unique vegetation

When he sailed into Table Bay aboard the *Golden Hind* in 1580, Sir Francis Drake exclaimed, "The fairest Cape we saw in the whole circumference of the earth". To this day, the Cape Peninsula's combination of sea, spreading valleys and purple-headed mountains is still breathtakingly beautiful. All South Africans are proud of it, even Jo'burgers, who nevertheless spend quite a lot of time thinking up rude jokes about Capetonians to wipe the infuriating "we've got it all" smirks off their faces.

Through the centuries it has been called many names: the Cape of Good Hope, by those who survived the journey to enter into the calmer waters of False Bay; the Tavern of the Seas, when fresh produce was shipped in here to enable fleets to continue on their arduous journey to the East; the Cape of Storms, by the Portuguese soldiers who first navigated their way around the treacherous shores at Cape Point.

For most of the year the Cape experiences weather that wafts between pleasant and sublime, but it earned its sobriquet Cape of Storms not without reason. The southwestern Cape is the only section of Africa that falls within a temperate weather zone, and it enjoys a typically Mediterranean climate with long, hot summers and cool, wet winters. The howling southeaster is aptly called the "Cape Doctor": it sweeps away every loose object in its path, cleansing the city of dust and pollution and making its atmosphere one of the healthiest.

The sense that this region is a fresh and fertile world apart is helped by the fact that Cape Town is physically cut off from the rest of the country by a barrier of mountains, in places some 2,000 metres (6,500 ft) high. With their rich clay soils, the valleys they shelter are the nation's storehouse – the centre of its grape, wine, wheat and deciduous fruit industries.

The peninsula is South Africa's oldest European-settled region, and man-made attractions include some of the best shops, hotels and restaurants on the continent. But, like all South African cities, it is a Molotov cocktail of first and third worlds. Cape Town's British-built Georgian buildings, cobbled streets and ancient oaks may look familiar to Europeans, but the vast townships stretching across the plains east of the city could only be in Africa.

The historic city

If ever a land mass was designed to look like the punctuation mark at the end of a continent, it is the Cape Peninsula. That it is not actually certified as the southern tip of Africa doesn't seem to deter the tour guides, who unashamedly point it out to their clients as the

PRECEDING PAGES: Cape Town at night. **LEFT:** the Twelve Apostles at sunset. **BELOW:** the Mother City has more statues than any other in the country.

place where the Indian and Atlantic oceans meet. Technically speaking, however, the dividing line is directly south from Cape Agulhas, some 200 km (120 miles) to the east.

Taking similar literary licence, most accounts of life at the Cape begin with the arrival of the first colonial governor, Jan van Riebeeck, in 1652. Others hoist their sails with stories of Portuguese navigators such as Bartolomeu Diaz and Vasco da Gama, who pioneered a sea route round the Cape to the East in the 15th century. In fact, Khoi herders and San hunter-gatherers had inhabited this corner of Africa from time immemorial. No-one is sure just how long ago, although 40,000 years is a figure often quoted by archaeologists.

The best place to get a handle on this cultural puzzle – indeed, on the entire racial and cultural melting pot that is the "rainbow nation" – is at the **South African Museum Ⓐ** (open daily; entrance fee) in Cape Town's **Company's Gardens Ⓑ** at the top of bustling **Adderley Street Ⓒ**, where evocative dioramas recreate scenes of South African life through the ages. Don't miss the extraordinary Whale Well – a multi-sensual, multi-media display.

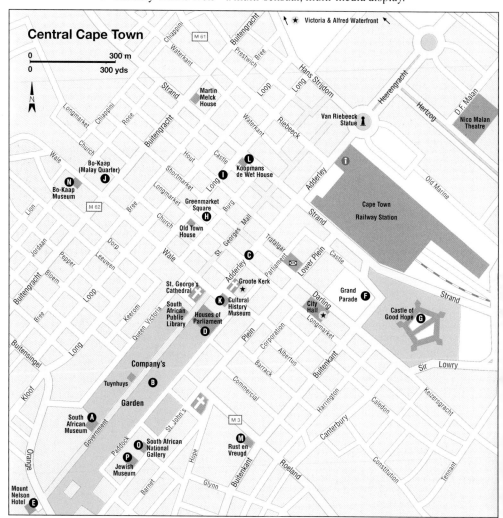

The Gardens were first laid out under the instruction of the Dutch East India Company, who wanted to provide a midway victualling station for its ships on the way to the East. Van Riebeeck duly planted patches of cabbages, potatoes, turnips and grains. As a doctor, he knew how valuable wine and brandy could be in staving off the sailors' curse of scurvy, so he planted grapes as well. The first vintages probably tasted more like tar, but this far from home, a drink was a drink.

Tucked into other secluded, leafy corners are grand buildings housing various museums, as well as the Anglican **St George's Cathedral**, former diocese of Nobel laureate Desmond Tutu. Dominating the area, however, are the **Houses of Parliament** (guided tours Mon-Fri; free), built in High Victorian style and facing on to Government Avenue. Close by is **Tuynhuys**, an official residence of South Africa's State President. And at the southernmost tip of Government Avenue, in the shadow of **Table Mountain**, you'll find the city's best-known hotel, the **Mount Nelson** . After almost a century of service, the pale-pink "Nellie" prides itself on retaining a grand colonial atmosphere, exemplified by the sumptuous afternoon tea.

Walking down Adderley Street towards the harbour, you'll pass the historic **Groote Kerk**, the oldest church in South Africa, containing an elaborately carved pulpit. At the bottom end of the street are statues of **Jan van Riebeeck** and his wife, **Maria**, close by to the **City Hall** with its baroque embellishments and honey-marble façade. It faces **The Grand Parade** ⑤, originally marked out as a place to train military troops but now a thriving open-air market.

On the eastern side of the Parade is the sturdy stone structure of the **Castle of Good Hope** ⑤ (open daily; closed Christmas Day; entrance fee), completed

Map, page 164

TIP

If Cape Town's troops of chacma baboons become dependent on tourist handouts, they can become annoyingly persistent. Please don't feed them.

BELOW: the Houses of Parliament.

You can still take the Penny Ferry (although the fare is no longer a penny) across The Cut, the entrance to the Alfred Basin at the V & A Waterfront.

BELOW: flea market in Greenmarket Square, city centre.

in 1697, making it the oldest surviving intact structure in South Africa. With its 10-metre (30-ft) thick walls and five corner bastions, each named after one of the various titles of the Prince of Orange, the Castle is today a military headquarters; it also houses a military and maritime museum.

Cutting across the courtyard of the castle is the *Kat* balcony, fronting the large reception room which was once a focal point of the colonial governor's official residence and the city aristocracy's social life. For contrast, peek into the dungeons, or "Black Holes", where criminals – and those who had simply fallen out of favour with the colonial authorities – were locked away.

Heart of the old city is **Greenmarket Square** ⑪, abuzz with flea market stalls, buskers, shoppers and cultural voyeurs. Two blocks west lies **Long Street** ❶, slightly down on its luck these days but still lined with lined with fine Georgian and Victorian buildings housing pawnshops and boutiques, knick-knack outlets and secondhand bookshops specialising in Africana and first editions.

West of the city centre, beyond **Buitengracht Street**, is one of Cape Town's most exotic districts – the **Bo-Kaap** ("Upper Cape"), or Malay Quarter ❶. Here, winding, narrow streets are flanked by restored early 19th-century cottages painted in pastels – originally slave quarters, stables and a military barracks. This was where many of the Muslim Batavian slaves imported by the 17th-century Dutch colonists settled, alongside powerful *imams* exiled from Indonesia where they had challenged Dutch colonial rule. Their descendants still live here, and they have, by and large, kept the community's Cape Malay identity intact.

For the best part of 50 years, the **Victoria and Alfred Waterfront** (the oldest part of Cape Town's harbour) lay in a state of disrepair. Then in the 1980s it was given a thorough face-lift, emerging as a multi-faceted playground crammed

with shops, craft markets, up-market hotels, and quay-to-quay pubs and restaurants. It is easily the most successful tourist development in the country. Worth a visit here is the **Two Oceans Aquarium** (open daily; entrance fee), brimming with fish of all dimensions, from the tiny seahorse to the ragged-toothed shark, as well as innovative displays of diverse marine habitats.

On a clear day, **Robben Island** is easily visible from across the bay. Originally a penal colony for errant slaves, it later became one of the most notorious prisons in the world. Many of the present government's top officials were held here – most famously, Nelson Mandela, who spent nearly 20 years in Section B. Now it is a monument to "the struggle" against apartheid, as well as a nature reserve. Boat tours leave the Waterfront daily at 9.30am, 11.45am and 1.15 pm; tickets are sold from the Embarkation Point on Jetty One.

Cutting across the foreshore is **Table Bay Boulevard** – the start of the major N1 Highway that bisects the country 2,000 km (1,200 miles) from the south to the northernmost boundary point at Messina in Northern Province.

Museums and galleries

The **Cultural History Museum** ⓚ (open Mon–Sat; entrance fee) is at the top of Adderley Street, opposite the Gardens. This beautiful 17th-century building (the second-oldest in the city) has had a varied history, being at different times a lodge for slaves as well as the Cape Supreme Court. Today, it houses some fine collections of Cape silverware and furniture amongst its diplays. The tombstones of Van Riebeeck and his wife lie in the cobbled courtyard.

Associated with this museum is a collection of other city houses that have been restored and preserved as outstanding examples of different architectural

Map, page 164

BELOW: Table Mountain, with "cloth".

periods and lifestyles. These include the **Koopmans de Wet House Ⓛ** at 35 Strand Street (open Tues–Sat; entrance fee) and **Rust-en-Vreugd Ⓜ** at 78 Buitenkant Street (open Mon–Sat; free).

The **District Six Museum** (open Mon–Sat; entrance fee), a little further along at 25A Buitenkant Street, presents the other side of the coin: relics of a vibrant inner-city community destroyed during the apartheid era in the name of racial purity. At 71 Wale Street, the **Bo-Kaap Museum Ⓝ** (open Mon–Sat; Sun by appointment; entrance fee) portrays in detail the lifestyle of a wealthy 19th-century Muslim family, complete with prayer room.

The Company's Gardens is the peaceful setting for the **South African National Gallery Ⓞ** (open Tues–Sun; closed Easter and 1 May; free) which during the apartheid era built up an impressive collection of mainly Western art, including works by Gainsborough, Reynolds and Rodin. The current acquisitions policy is now, however, biased against "Eurocentrism" and towards indigenous art. Nearby is the **Jewish Museum** and synagogue Ⓟ, housing a rich collection of items depicting the history of the Cape Town Hebrew Congregation

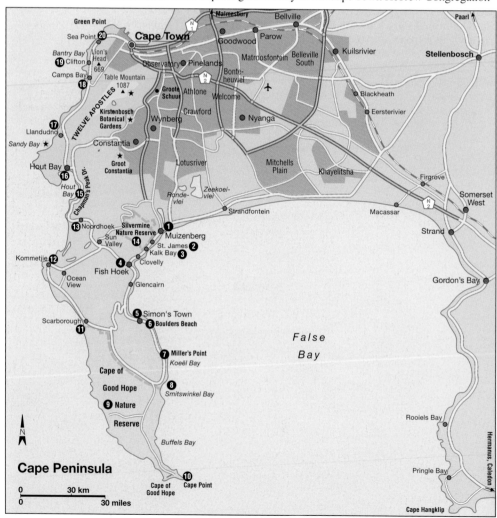

Cape Peninsula

0   30 km
0   30 miles

and other Cape congregations (open Dec–Feb: Tues–Thur, Sun only; Wed and Sun till 12.30pm; March–Nov: Tues, Thur afternoons only; Sun till 12.30pm; closed public holidays; free).

Table Mountain

Locals simply call it "the mountain", for this famous flat-topped block of horizontally bedded sandstone dominating Table Bay is a lodestone to all who live there – a compass, an anchor, a wilderness in the heart of the Mother City. No visit to Cape Town is complete without gaining a view from the top. The journey up takes about six minutes, but expect to queue for up to several hours during the peak summer holiday season, when the cableway ferries, on average, 1,500 people a day up to the 1,000-metre (3,300-ft) summit. To reach **Lower Cableway Station** (open daily, weather permitting; entrance fee; tel: (021) 245148) from Kloof Nek road, turn right along Tafelberg Road and follow the signs.

For those with enough determination there is another way – actually, around 500 ways – of getting to the top on foot. One of the easier hiking routes starts from the botanical gardens at Kirstenbosch, and takes about three hours. Be aware, though, that conditions can change very quickly on the mountain; take suitable protection in case it rains.

The magnificent 560-hectare (1,380-acre) **Kirstenbosch National Botanic Gardens** grace the mountain's eastern slopes. Here, formally laid-out beds display some of South Africa's showiest flora before blending into the natural protea *fynbos* and yellowwood forests on the mountain slopes (open daily; Apr–Aug: 8am–6pm; Sept–Mar: 8am–7pm; entrance fee; tel: (021) 762 1166).

Map, page 168

TIP

Drinking alcohol is forbidden on Llandudno beach. Apply for a special permit from the local police station if you wish to toast the sunset with champagne.

BELOW: beautiful Kirstenbosch National Botanical Gardens.

You're bound to spot dassies on the top of Table Mountain. Also known as the "rock-rabbit", the dassie is, in fact, more closely related to the elephant.

Flanking Table Mountain are the imposing peaks of **Lion's Head** and **Devil's Peak.** It was on the slopes of the latter, according to legend, that a retired soldier named Van Hunk was challenged by the devil to a pipe-smoking contest. The result of their showdown can best be judged in the summertime, when a seemingly motionless sheet of cloud (popularly known as the "tablecloth") often hovers over the mountain-top.

Devil's Peak is also the site of the **Groote Schuur Estate**, once owned by Cecil Rhodes. Bequeathed to the nation on his death in 1902, it now includes a number of ministerial residences as well as the campus of the University of Cape Town. The Groote Schuur hospital and medical school here was the scene for the world's first heart transplant, performed by Professor Chris Barnard in 1967.

Best beaches

Given Cape Town's seductive summer climate, visitors are often surprised by the near-freezing temperatures at the famous bathing beaches of Clifton, Camps Bay and Llandudno, to say nothing of the nudist beach at Sandy Bay.

For those who enjoy swimming in the sea, **Muizenberg** and **Fish Hoek** on the warmer Indian Ocean coastline provides the best spots. The secret is to choose a beach according to the wind direction: if there is a cloud-cloth on Table Mountain it means the southeaster is blowing and one should head straight for **Clifton** or **Llandudno**; but if there is a northwesterly sea fog brewing, go to Muizenberg and environs.

The reason for the Atlantic's chilly waters is more complex than most people realise. It has a lot to do with the whims of the "southeaster" wind. When this

BELOW: surfing on Llandudno beach.

ROBBEN ISLAND

World-famous as the place where Nelson Mandela was condemned to life imprisonment, this little kidney-shaped island 11 km (7 miles) off the shores of Green Point was named by the Dutch for the large numbers of seals ("*rob*") they encountered here. It has a grim history: this was where Jan van Riebeeck kept rebellious Khoikhoi leaders captive; later, the British used it as a general dumping-ground for lepers, paupers and lunatics alike. In the second half of the 19th century, the small village known as Irishtown was built next to the jetty. A military base during World War II, it was finally taken over by the Department of Prisons in 1960, quickly acquiring a reputation as South Africa's most notorious penal colony. Today, South Africa's own Alcatraz has been turned into a national monument and museum, run by the Ministry for Arts and Culture. Ferries and charter boats bound for the island leave Cape Town's V&A Waterfront several times a day, but not all of them are allowed to land. In order to protect the environment (Robben Island is a haven for wildlife, especially seabirds and jackass penguins), visitor numbers are limited to 300 a day. Many boats simply circle the island, providing passengers with a view from about a kilometre (half a mile) out at sea.

wind pushes the warm surface water away from the western shore, the water is replaced from underneath. This phenomenon is called "upwelling", bringing with it the cold Antarctic water of the Benguela Current. Small wonder water temperature can be as low as 12° or even 10°C (54–56°F) after a strong "blow". Ironically, it is in winter – when the southeaster abates – that the Atlantic beaches experience their warmest sea temperatures.

Map, page 168

The Cape's grape

Head out on the Eastern Boulevard or De Waal Drive, both of which become the M3 route. Continue along this road, leaving the city behind you, and climb Wynberg Hill (where Jan van Riebeeck first extended his vineyards), before dropping down into leafy **Constantia Valley**. This is one of Cape Town's most beautiful suburbs, and certainly its most exclusive.

Here, you can visit the site first developed by early Dutch governor Simon van der Stel in 1685 as his private estate. As well as building a modest homestead here which he named **Groot Constantia**, Van der Stel planted vines. A century later, the farm had become world-famous for its wines (a drop of "the finest old Constantia that ever was tasted" soothes Elinor Dashwood's broken heart in *Sense and Sensibility*), and the homestead enlarged and converted into a splendid manor-house. Bought by the Cape government in 1885, Groot Constantia is now run as a model wine farm. The house and old wine cellar are now a museum (open daily; Feb–Nov: 10am–5pm; Dec–Jan: 10am–6pm; entrance fee; extra fee to view the manor-house; tel: (021) 794 5128).

Van der Stel's original farm was later divided into a number of smaller plots. **Klein Constantia**, with its magnificent maturation cellars set inside a

BELOW: Mostert's Mill, Groote Schuur.

TIP

Raise a glass to Table
Mountain to the strains
of live jazz while
cruising the harbour.
Jazz cruises depart
from Quay 6 at V&A
Waterfront. For details,
tel: (021) 419 3122.

mountain, is one of the Cape's most rewarding wineries (open for tastings
and sales Mon–Fri; Sat 9am–1pm; tel: (021) 794 5188), as is nearby
Buitenverwachting. The name means "beyond expectation", and that's a fair
description of this gracious old manor-house in its lovely setting of spreading
vineyards and oak-dotted hillsides. The restaurant it contains is excellent, too
(open for tastings and sales Mon–Fri; Sat 9am–1pm; tel: (021) 794 5190;
restaurant, tel: (021) 794 3522).

Nightlife and entertainment

Cape Town's culinary speciality is Cape-Malay cooking – spicy and fruity, but
seldom hot. Fruit and chutney-enhanced *bobooties* (mince-based casseroles),
skewered-meat *sosaties* (kebabs), *frikkadel* patties and tomato-based *bredie*
with *blatjang* (meat stew with chutney) – you will find all these delicacies at
the Cape Sun Hotel's **Riempies**, in Strand Street; at the **Kaapse Tafel** in Queen
Victoria Street in the Gardens, and at **Biesmiellah** in the Bo-Kaap – the latter
an authentic Islamic institution where no alcohol is allowed.

As far as seafood is concerned, restaurants can offer fresh catches of crayfish
(rock lobster) and *perlemoen* (abalone), black mussels and oysters, prawns and
linefish. **Blues** on The Promenade at Camps Bay is a particularly good bet; the
restaurant also overlooks a pristinely beautiful beach.

Best for authentic African cooking are **The Africa Café** in suburban
Observatory, and the stylishly ethnic **Mamma Africa Restaurant and Bar** in
downtown Long Street.

Cape Town has a vibrant late-night café society, the hub of which is
"restaurant mile" in Kloof Street, in the Gardens area. Also reliably busy and

BELOW: colourful
bathing huts line St
James beach.

bustling is the Victoria and Alfred Waterfront, packed with bars, restaurants and cafés. For some people, the large-format **Imax Theatre** in the BMW Pavilion here may be the epitome of fun; the screen is so large and the digital sound so good, you can experience whale-watching or a volcanic eruption in virtual, virtual reality.

As for the performing arts, the city's chief venue is the enormous **Nico Malan Theatre** complex down on on the Foreshore, housing an opera house and several theatres. **Mannenberg's Jazz Café**, on the corner of downtown Adderley and Church streets, is one of the best places in the city to catch indigenous Cape jazz talent, much of which is exceptional. Night-crawlers looking for late, loud action will find a thriving club scene centred around Loop Street and Long Street in the city centre.

Map,
page 168

The Peninsula

Cape Town's urban areas spread across the extreme northern end of a 100-km (60-mile) sliver of land, whose southern tip is the famous **Cape of Good Hope.** Here, precipitous mountain passes link up innumerable coves and sandy beaches, villages and fishing communities like beads on a necklace.

To make the most of a drive round the Peninsula, set out early – ideally, just as the sun breaches the jagged **Hottentots-Holland Mountains** and dapples the surface of **False Bay**. Staying with the sun, the journey begins at **Muizenberg** ❶ on the east coast, about 20 km (12 miles) from the city centre. This bustling seaside town was a popular resort in Victorian times; it was in a cottage here (now a small museum) that Rhodes spent his last years when his health

BELOW: interior design, Rainbow Nation style.

CAPE TOWN'S KARAMATS

A "magic circle" of *karamats* – the tombs of holy men who once lived and worked within Cape Town's Muslim community – graces the city, forming an important part of local Islamic lore. Muslims believe the circle provides Cape Town with a protective spiritual barrier, helping to prevent natural disasters. Before making a pilgrimage to the Holy City of Mecca (as is required of every Muslim, if he can afford it), local believers will visit each *karamat* in turn. There is a shrine to Sayed Abdurahman Matura, Prince of Ternate, on Robben Island and one to Nureel Mobeen at Oudekraal near Bakoven beach. The tomb of Abdumaah Shah lies by the gate to Klein Constantia farm in the Constantia valley. Of the two shrines on the slopes of Signal Hill, one contains the remains of Tuan Guru, the Cape's first imam and founder of the country's first mosque.

Most revered of all is the tomb of Sheik Yusuf, near Eerste River in the township of Macassar (take the Firgrove turning on the N2 from Cape Town to Stellenbosch). Yusuf was a 17th-century nobleman who, having rebelled against the high-handed authority of the Dutch East India Company in his native Indonesia, was exiled to the Cape for his pains. His tomb was erected as recently as 1925 by Hadji Sullaiman Shah.

prematurely failed him. The beachfront here has become rather tacky, but the surf is still splendid.

Down the False Bay coast, narrow Main Road follows closely alongside the railway line, with **Muizenberg Mountain** crowding in on the left; it passes the pretty villages of **St James ❷**, **Kalk Bay ❸** with its old fishing harbour, and **Clovelly**, until you come to what is arguably the Peninsula's safest swimming beach at **Fish Hoek ❹**. From here, fork left on to the M4, and follow the winding road through **Glencairn** to the historic port settlement of **Simon's Town ❺**. Named after Simon van der Stel, who first recommended it as a safe winter anchorage, it was a Royal Navy base from the time of the second British occupation of the Cape in 1806 until it was handed over to the South African Navy in 1957.

At the southern end of town you'll find **Boulders ❻**, a smaller but more secluded swimming beach than that at Fish Hoek. Here, among the giant granite rocks, jackass penguins have created one of the very few land-breeding colonies of this southern species (open daily; small entrance fee Nov–Feb).

Leaving Simon's Town, the M4 winds up past **Miller's Point ❼** and **Smitswinkel Bay ❽** with wonderful views down to the sea far below. A 12-km (8-mile) turn-off to the left takes you to the **Cape of Good Hope Nature Reserve ❾** (open daily; Nov–Apr: 7am–6pm; May–Oct: 7am–5pm; entrance fee; tel: (021) 780 9100), a modest 7,750-hectare (19,000-acre) park which is, surprisingly, the second-most visited reserve in the country, after the Kruger National Park.

Stand in front of the old lighthouse at **Cape Point ❿** and peer out across the great curve of ocean. You could almost imagine seeing South America to the right, Australia to the left and, yes, far to the south, the thin white sliver of the Antarctic.

The reserve was first proclaimed in 1936 to preserve a chunk of indigenous *fynbos* close to the city and to protect some rare plant species here. It also serves as a breeding ground for rare antelope and the visitor will invariably see some Cape mountain zebra, bontebok and eland on the sandy plateau.

Return to the city along the western seaboard, the "cold side". Turn left as you leave the reserve, then left again where the road forks, 8 km (5 miles) later. This will take you past the hamlets of **Misty Cliffs** and **Scarborough ⓫**, and the fishing village of **Kommetjie ⓬**. Turn left onto the M6 at the next intersection (straight takes you through the Fish Hoek Gap), then left again after 900 metres (half a mile) and you'll reach **Noordhoek ⓭**. This is where Capetonians head if they want to be alone at the beach; it's 7 km (4 miles) long and it's wildly scenic – breathtaking, even.

Worth a detour if you're looking for a picnic spot is the **Silvermine Nature Reserve ⓮** (open daily; Jun–Aug 8am–6pm; Sept–May 8am–7pm; entrance fee), situated on either side of the scenic **Ou Kaapse Weg** ("Old Cape Road"); the turn-off is signposted between Kommetjie and Noordhoek. Somewhat overshadowed by its close proximity to the Cape of Good Hope Nature Reserve, it is nonetheless criss-crossed

It is off Cape Point that the Flying Dutchman, a phantom ship with tattered sails and a broken mast, is doomed to sail until the end of time – a legend which inspired an opera by Wagner.

BELOW: colony of jackass penguins, Boulders Beach.

with good hiking trails through beautiful *fynbos*. The walk to the heights above the reservoir leads to spectacular views across Hout Bay.

Back on the M6, the road snakes steeply upwards on a nerve-racking 7 km (4 mile) journey around **Chapman's Peak ⑮** – arguably one of the world's most spectacular scenic drives. Above the road, vertical sandstone cliffs rise some 700 metres (2,300 ft) to the summit, while below, giant granite boulders seem to hold the road suspended above the glittering sea below.

Down on the other side of the pass you'll see a turn-off to the right for **Hout Bay ⑯**, another fishing village turned satellite suburb. Not only is it the headquarters of the Peninsula's rock lobster fleet, but freshly caught fish of all description are sold daily off the quayside – so it's hardly surprising that the village has some fine seafood restaurants. Heading north from here over **Suikerbossie Hill**, you'll be able to peer down into posh **Llandudno ⑰** with its perfect sickle-shaped beach and rocky points.

This is near the journey's end, but some of the best is still to come. As you pass **Koeëlbaai**, the grand profiles of the **Twelve Apostles** (Table Mountain's western buttresses) come into view, jutting out like the prows of gigantic ships at anchor along the shore. When the southeaster whips its tablecloth over the crags, the clouds look like sea-swells frothing around their tightly berthed hulls.

The M6 now winds through some of the most sought-after and exclusive residential addresses in the country: **Camps Bay ⑱**, **Clifton ⑲** and **Bantry Bay**. The first two also have famous beaches, the sort where high society sun-lovers go more to see and be seen than to frolic in the (very cold) sea. From Camps Bay, the road passes the busy seaside suburbs of **Sea Point ⑳** and Green Point before leading back to City Bowl.

**Map,
page 168**

BELOW: Hout Bay, as seen from the Chapman's Peak Drive.

THE WESTERN CAPE'S COAST OF WHALES

Whale populations are on the increase, and the Cape is one of the best places in the world to see the southern right whale in coastal waters

No fewer than 29 species of toothed whale (*Odontoceti*), including the killer whale, are found off the South African coast, along with eight species of baleen whale (suborder *Mysticeti*). But by far the most commonly spotted are the southern right whales, pods of which seek out sheltered bays along the Cape coastline every year for breeding. Between June and December, there is a good chance of seeing them all the way round the peninsula from Elands Bay on the west coast to Mossel Bay on the Garden Route. On a good day, you might see them "spyhopping" (standing on their tails with their heads out of water), "lobtailing" (slapping their flukes on the water's surface) or "breaching" – leaping out of the sea like a trout.

THE RIGHT WHALES TO CATCH?

The southern right (*Balaena glacialis*) is distinguished by its V-shaped "blow" – the cloud of vapour produced when the whale exhales a large volume of air through its pair of blowholes. They are thought to live for up to 100 years; an adult can reach 16 metres (53 feet) in length. They are called right whales because 18th-century whalers regarded them as the "right" whales to catch: the carcass was oil-rich, and the whalers' task of collecting their booty was made more easy by the fact that the whale floated on the water after slaughter. They were valued for their blubber, which was reduced to oil for use in margarine, soap and linoleum, and for their bones, used to make glue, gelatine and fertiliser. International legislation was introduced to protect the species in 1935, but the southern right has subsequently shown only a slight increase in numbers.

▷ ENDANGERED GIANTS
As many as 80 southern right whales (out of an estimated world population of about 6,000) have been recorded seeking regular refuge in Hermanus' Walker Bay to court, mate and calve. A South African law bans the use of any vessels for whale-watching (anyone caught within 1,000 feet/305 metres of a whale is liable to a hefty fine), and whales now seem unafraid to come close to the shore.

◁ SLAUGHTER AT SEA
South Africa has some of the strictest whale conservation legislation in the world, so sights like this traditional harpooner are thankfully now a thing of the past. As a result, over the past decade the numbers of southern right whales along the Cape coast has increased at a rate of about seven percent per year.

◁ WELCOME BLAST

The Cape village of Hermanus has the world's only official whale-crier, who, during the peak whale season in September and October, parades through the streets announcing new arrivals in Walker Bay with a blast on his kelp-horn. During this period, visitors can also telephone a special "Whale Hotline" (00 27 283 22629) for updates on all the latest sightings. The service covers the coast from Gansbaai to Betty's Bay.

▽ CLOSE ENCOUNTERS

With a unequalled combination of low cliff-tops and clear water at the base of the cliffs, Hermanus offers some of the best land-based whale-watching in the world. Visitors are practically guaranteed a whale sighting – and living here is about as close as you can get to having them in your back garden.

WHERE TO HEAR WHALES SING

Hermanus' Old Harbour – replaced in the 1940s after nearly a century of service – now houses a museum in a row of beautifully restored fishermen's cottages (*above*). As tourism has replaced fishing as the primary industry, so the museum has become a focal point for visitors to the town.

One of the museum's most interesting features is an underwater microphone, attached to a sonar buoy in Walker Bay. The eerie, sing-song sound of whales chatting to one another deep underwater is picked up and transmitted back to a public "audio room" in the museum. There is also a telescope for watching whales far out in the bay.

The new harbour, to the west of the old one, in Westcliff, is a bustling little fishing port, where fresh seafood – including mussels and crayfish – is sold from the docks. Boats can be hired here for deep-sea tunny and marlin expeditions.

Also in Westcliff is the start of Hermanus' famous cliff path, which follows the shore round Walker Bay to the lagoon at Grotto Beach, allowing unrivalled views of whale activity out at sea. The walk takes at least a morning; bench seats are provided along the way and many people take a picnic. There are even grander views along the Rotary Mountain Way, a scenic drive. The tasting rooms of Hamilton Russell vineyards face the Hermanus market-place.

▷ THE WHALING DAYS

A relic of the bad old days. The wholesale slaughter of whales has been so great that by the 1960s, the world's blue whale population had dropped to an estimated six percent of its numbers before whaling began. The last South African whaling station closed in 1975.

THE GARDEN ROUTE

Wild forests and unspoilt beaches lead past hidden valleys and majestic mountains to Port Elizabeth and Grahamstown, the "City of the Saints"

Map, pages 180–1

Johannesburg
SOUTH AFRICA
Cape Town

The "Garden Route" takes a sweeping tour along the Cape's east coast through lush, bountiful scenery. This is very much an African garden – not the manicured lawns of Europe with their neat and formal layouts, but a rich belt of rugged coastline, flanked by indigenous rainforests, blue lagoons, parallel rows of serrated mountain peaks and fields bright with *fynbos*.

The Overberg

This route follows the N2 southeastwards from Cape Town over the Hottentots-Holland Mountains and into the isolated Overberg region. The quickest way to **Hermanus** – which offers the best land-based whale-watching in the world – leads along a well-surfaced road to **Botrivier**, and from there along the R43 down to the coast. The coastal road, however, is much more exciting. After **Somerset West**, follow signs to **Gordon's Bay**, an attractive resort on the shores of False Bay. Whales can often be seen frolicking offshore here during October and November. After Gordon's Bay, the R44 hugs the coastline around Koeël-baai, with some fantastic sea views. Seven kilometres to the east, not far away from the old whaling station of **Betty's Bay** and dramatically situated between the Kogelberg range and the Atlantic coast, are the **Harold Porter National Botanical Gardens** (open daily 8am–6pm; entrance fee; tel: (02823) 29311), which are definitely worth a visit. Waterfalls and small streams splash through a *fynbos*-sprinkled landscape, inhabited by numerous colonies of baboons. Twelve kilometres (7 miles) after the little town of Kleinmond, turn right on to the R43, which leads on to Hermanus.

Hermanus ❷ is the largest coastal town in the Overberg and can get pretty crowded, especially at Christmas time. The best time to visit is spring, when the biggest visitors of all arrive in **Walker Bay**: the whales. The municipality hires a special "whale crier" during September and October who not only keeps tourists up-to-date on whale activity but can even be reached by mobile phone (the "Whale Hotline", tel: (083) 2121074). If you take the 11-km (7-mile) cliff walk at this time of year you're sure to see whales; sometimes far away on the other side of the bay, sometimes only 30 metres (100 ft) away and very clearly visible in the crystal-clear water. An underwater microphone transmits their strange "songs" live back to a room in the **Old Harbour Museum** (open Mon–Sat; entrance fee).

The route back towards the N2 is a particular treat for wine fans, because the R320 goes past the **Hamilton Russell Vineyards** (open Mon–Fri, Sat am; tel: (0283) 23595/23441) in the Hemel-en-Aarde Valley. Here you can sample perhaps the best Pinot Noir in South Africa.

LEFT: a riot of flowers bloom between coast and desert.
BELOW: this graceful antelope has a sanctuary in the Bontebok National Park.

In 1795, Swellendam rejected Dutch authority and formed an independent government. Just 91 days later, the British occupied the Cape and Swellendam's short-lived independence was over.

From **Caledon ❶**, continue along the N2 via **Riviersonderend ❺** to **Swellendam**. If you're keen on seeing South Africa's southernmost tip, however, you should turn off onto the R316. This road leads through the sleepy town of **Bredasdorp**; the **Shipwreck Museum** (open Mon–Fri, Sat & Sun am) here contains a fascinating exhibition of treasures taken from ships wrecked off the stormy coast. The route continues across gently undulating farmland as far as **Cape Agulhas ❸** which officially separates the Indian and Atlantic Oceans. This is where Africa comes to an end – definitively. Portuguese sailors gave it the name Agulhas, meaning "needles", because it is at this point that the needle of a compass points due north, with no deviation. If you're expecting the sort of dramatic landscape you see at Cape Point you'll be somewhat disappointed; apart from a flat, rocky peninsula and a lighthouse (the second-oldest in South Africa, built in 1848) there's very little else to look at. But you can climb the lighthouse (open Mon–Sat, Sun am; tel: (02846) 56078), and the magnificent beach at nearby **Struisbaai** is unforgettable, with its turquoise-blue sea and colourful fishing boats.

Just as rewarding is a detour from Bredasdorp to Waenhuiskrans, also known as **Arniston ❹**. This fishing village with its thatched, whitewashed houses has been declared a national monument. White sand-dunes form a contrast with the bright-blue sea behind, but the southeast wind can blow a little too harshly for comfort.

The route rejoins the N2 roughly 60 km (37 miles) north of Bredasdorp, near **Stormsvlei**. From there it's only another 12 km to **Swellendam ❻**, the third-oldest town in South Africa, and a Cape Dutch architectural jewel. Founded in 1743, the town's Cape Dutch buildings include a particularly fine **Drostdy**

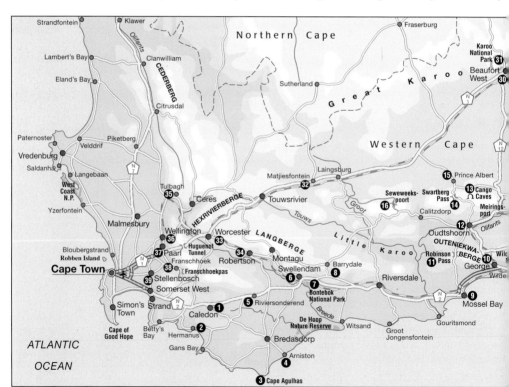

(open daily; entrance fee). Built in 1746, it contains a select assortment of Cape furniture and paintings. An old prison and two Victorian buildings, **Mayville** (1853) and **Auld House**, also form part of the same complex. Even more popular with photographers is the magnificent **Dutch Reformed Church** (Voortrek Street), which dates from 1911; it's a wedding-cake of a building, combining neo-Gothic, neo-Renaissance and neo-Baroque elements with the Cape Dutch style to form an astonishingly harmonious ensemble. The **Town Hall**, also on Voortrek Street, is another imposing Cape-style Victorian building.

Just 6 km (4 miles) south of Swellendam is the entrance to the **Bontebok National Park** ➐ (open daily; tel: (0291) 42735), the smallest national park in South Africa with a surface area of just 28 sq. km (11 sq. miles). You won't see elephant, lion or rhino here – just plenty of graceful little bontebok, a species of antelope hunted almost to extinction during the early part of this century. Springbok and the rare Cape zebra are also found here.

The Little Karoo

If you're in a hurry, take the N2 north from Swellendam and travel via Riversdal to Mossel Bay. It's more rewarding, though, to travel northwest along the R324 over the Tradouw Pass, and then to follow the R62 through the series of fertile valleys known as the Little Karoo. "Karoo" is the Khoi word for "dry", and although it gets blistering hot here in summer, the land has a beauty that comes in many different guises – the serenity of far horizons, a black eagle soaring high above a silent plain, a cool breeze after a stifling day, or just a donkey-cart crunching slowly along an old farm road.

Map, pages 180–1

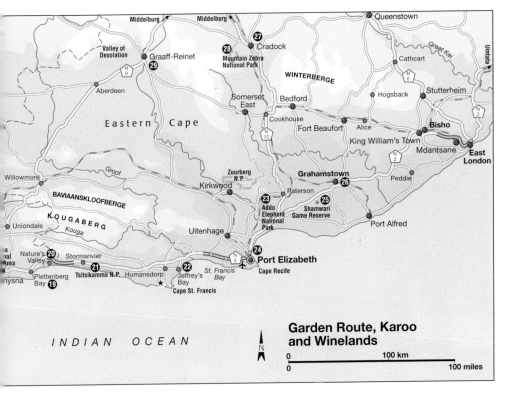

At speeds of up to 78 km/h (48 mph), the ostrich can outrun most of its enemies.

Keep going past pretty orchard villages such as **Barrydale** , Ladysmith and Calitzdorp, until you reach **Oudtshoorn** . This town was once a celebrated ostrich-feather centre: between 1880 and 1910 a number of Eastern European Jewish traders emigrated to South Africa, set up ostrich farms and made a small fortune exporting the feathers to fashion-conscious Europe. The trade generated vast riches – one kilogram (2 lbs) of tail-feathers could fetch up to R200. The **CP Nel Museum** (open Mon–Sat, Sun pm) on Baron van Rheede Street has displays on the history of the ostrich boom.

All this revenue pouring into what had hitherto been nothing more than a remote hamlet helped build a number of "feather palaces", several of which have survived the decline in the market. One such "palace" open to the public is the **Safari Ostrich Farm** (open daily; entrance fee; tel: (0443) 227311), just outside town on the Mossel Bay road. The homestead here boasts teak from Burma, roof tiles from Belgium and marble floors. Lunchtime at an ostrich farm usually means an opportunity to dine on an ostrich steak; you can also try your riding skills on the back of the world's largest bird or watch "jockeys" spur on their mounts in a mock "Ostrich Derby".

Today, the ostrich industry still thrives, but the feathers are used more for dusters than for the hats and boas of high fashion. But while the feather market took a dip the skins of this strange bird have become part and parcel of the world of high fashion. Ostrich skins used in the manufacturing of expensive shoes, handbags and purses now command prices comparable to the highly-prized skins of baby crocodiles.

BELOW: Swellendam is the third oldest city in the country.

The fascinating **Cango Caves** (open daily, hourly guided tours; entrance fee; tel: (0443) 226643), 32 km (20 miles) north of Oudtshoorn, are just one

small part of a massive underground system of limestone caverns that extends under the Swartberg Mountains. An hour-long guided tour introduces you to three of the biggest caves, after which you can either turn back or continue on a more adventurous route, which involves squeezing your way along a series of narrow, hot, damp and stifling shafts. The seat of your trousers gets just as much exercise as your shoes during this operation.

Past the caves, the R328 continues on towards the whitewashed village of **Prince Albert** ⑮ over one of the most beautiful of all South Africa's mountain passes – the **Swartberg Pass** ⑭ (1,436 metres /4,700 ft). Built between 1881 and 1888 and now a national monument, this gravel road climbs 1,000 metres (3,281 ft) in 12 km (7 miles) over the mighty Swartberg range, with very sharp, blind hairpin bends. The views are magnificent, but this is not a drive for vertigo-sufferers. If that's not challenging enough, you could take an alternative route across the mountains via the **Seweweekspoort Pass** ⑯, or by the main road (the R29) through **Meiringspoort**. First opened in 1857, this pass crosses the River Groot some 30 times along its 17-km (11-mile) length, snaking through bare walls of vertical rock which at times stretch hundreds of metres high. Twisted bands of red sandstone and milky quartz loom above the road, their yellow-lichened crags glowing in the sun. Check the status of the road before you set out to drive through the gorge, though; it's often closed after heavy rains.

By comparison, the trip over the **Robinson Pass** ⑪ (859 metres /2,818 ft), down to Mossel Bay is relatively tame. Here, you cross the Outeniqua Mountains, the northern slopes of which are brown and parched and the southern slopes wooded and green, marking the Garden Route which you will be following from now on.

Map, pages 180–1

BELOW: the Cango Caves stretch deep beneath the Cape's Swartberg range.

The N2 arrives at the seaside near **Mossel Bay** . It was here, in 1488, that the Portuguese navigator Bartholomeu Diaz first landed, the first European to touch South African soil. The **Bartholomeu Diaz Museum Complex** (open Mon–Fri, Sat am, Sun pm), housed inside a converted granary, is dedicated to his memory. Displays include exhibitions of shells and shipping; best of all is the full-scale replica of Diaz's caravel (entrance fee).

Mossel Bay is still a popular holiday resort, even though it contains a sprawling industrial centre thanks to the discovery of oil and natural gas reserves off its coast. Write postcards, nevertheless, because the local mail system has a long tradition: in 1500, a Portuguese sailor named Pedro d'Ataide placed a letter inside an old boot and hung it beneath a milkwood tree. A year later, another sailor found the letter and was kind enough to forward it. Today the tree is part of the Diaz museum, and if you post your cards in the boot-shaped letterbox provided, the "oldest post office in South Africa" will process them promptly – naturally, with a suitable stamp.

Posting a letter in Mossel Bay's unique boot-shaped postbox.

As the route continues to **George** ⑩, which author Anthony Trollope once called "the finest village in the world", the scenery grows increasingly wilder. This former lumber village now has a population of over 100,000, and could not by any stretch of the imagination be called a village. Yet there are still several fine historic buildings to visit, such as the Dutch Reformed **Moederkerk** with its magnificent carved stinkwood pulpit, and the elegant **Public Library** (1840) – although the latter's books have, unfortunately, all been moved to Cape Town. Outside the library is the mighty Slave Tree, one of the broadest oak trees in the southern hemisphere, beneath which a slave market was once held. And since we're touching on a dark chapter of South African history, the **George**

BELOW: the Holy Trinity Church at Belvidere, Krysna.

Museum (open Mon–Fri, Sat am) on Courtenay Street has an exhibition devoted to the years of apartheid rule under President P. W. Botha, the last of the hard-liners, who retired here in 1989.

Much nicer times are to be had on the **Outeniqua Choo Tjoe**, a popular nar-row-gauge railway. Here, a steam locomotive dating from 1928 takes passen-gers from George through several attractive, wooded ravines along the coast to Knysna. The trip takes two and a half hours, and it's advisable to book tickets in advance (tel: (0441) 738288).

The railway and the N2 both pass through **Wilderness** ⓱, a bustling little holiday resort which has a magnificent, 8-km (5-mile) long sandy beach, as well as an excellent nature reserve, the **Wilderness National Park** (open daily, 8am–5pm; tel: (0441) 8771197). These wide open waterways, reed beds and marshes, as well as the surrounding bush and forests, provide a rich source of food and varied habitats for a wide array of birdlife. Most attractive of all are the large wading birds that scour the shallows for food; pockets of pink flamin-gos, drifting across the metallic water, straining the surface for tiny algae and crustaceans, and African spoonbills that rake the mud with their peculiar-shaped bills. Of the 95 species of waterfowl recorded in South Africa, 75 can be seen bobbing about on the lakes here.

A little further east lies the busiest resort on the Garden Route: **Knysna** ⓲, founded at the beginning of the 19th century by a certain George Rex, rumoured to be a bastard son of George III. Wooded hills, dotted with holiday homes, surround pretty Knysna Lagoon, connected to the ocean by a single narrow waterway. The mouth of this canal is flanked by two huge sandstone cliffs known as The Heads, and it is thanks to them that Knysna never became an

Map,
pages
180–1

BELOW: angling for dinner near the Tsitsikamma National park.

The strong cheek teeth of the Cape clawless otter make short work of bones and crab shells.

BELOW: ancient yellowwoods dream in the lush Tsitsikamma Forest.

important harbour town: access by sea was simply too dangerous. The eastern cliff is the only one open to cars (along George Rex Drive), and the view from the top is fantastic. The western cliff, in the unspoiled **Featherbed Nature Reserve**, can only be reached by ferry.

A good place for crafts, pottery and woven fabrics round here is Thesen House, a historic townhouse named after one of Knysna's oldest and most influential families. However, the area is chiefly known for its natural wood products, and especially hardwood furniture. The best-quality products are manufactured by hand by master craftsmen, using yellowwood, dark stinkwood and ironwood judiciously culled from the surrounding forests.

Another popular photo opportunity here – although it's rather surreal for Africa – is the Holy Trinity Church in the elegant little suburb of **Belvidere**, which looks very much like an 11th-century Norman implant. And don't leave Knysna without sampling the excellent oysters from the lagoon, either. Thus fortified, you'll be ready to visit **Plettenberg Bay** ⓭, South Africa's most upmarket seaside resort, 32 km (20 miles) east of Knysna. Although the town lacks Knysna's charm, the perfectly rounded "Baia Formosa" (Beautiful Bay) with its golden beaches has been a favourite with holidaymakers ever since the Portuguese arrived here – which is why it's rather depressing to see the hideous multi-storey Beacon Isle Hotel dominating the entire coastline from its rocky promontory. During the Christmas holidays, "Plett" is extremely popular, but out of season the place is often utterly deserted. At any time of year, the rocky Robberg Peninsula (to the west of Plettenberg Bay) is a fine place for hikes.

From Plettenberg Bay you can take either the N2 toll road that cuts a fairly straight path through forests and across the high coastal plain, or the byway (the

R102) winding downwards past the Grootrivier and Bloukrans gorges and through secretive **Nature's Valley** ⑳. The single-span arch concrete bridges over the Storms, Groot and Bloukrans rivers had the distinction – when they were each newly completed – of being the biggest such structures in the world.

Those who take the back road will be rewarded by the experience of sinking deep down into the forest's cool microclimate. Beneath the giant yellowwoods, the shaded floor is thick with proteas, arum lilies and watsonia; vividly coloured lourie birds dart through the dense forest canopy, while shy duiker and bushbuck hide in the undergrowth below.

The Tsitsikamma Forest

Both options bring you to the turn-off to **Storms River Mouth**, with its forests and unspoilt, rocky shore, its log cabins and suspension bridge. Beautiful **Tsitsikamma National Park** ㉑ lies a little further to the east, stretching for 65 km (40 miles) along the coast. It is home to some especially varied flora and fauna. Inland are wooded ravines, thick with ancient yellowwood trees (some of them up to 50 metres/164 ft high), while the coast is made up of lagoons, dunes, cliffs, beaches and coral reefs. The mouth of the **Storms River** is a good place for swimming and snorkelling.

Experienced hikers are fond of the **Otter Trail** that runs through the park – one the most famous and challenging coastal hikes in South Africa. Allow five days for this 41-km (25-mile) long trek, because there's a lot to do and see – 11 rivers to cross, for example, and sometimes you will need to swim rather than just wade. Overnight accommodation is in hutted camps. Only 12 people are allowed on to the trail on any one day, and you should (indeed must) book up

Map,
pages
180–1

BELOW: "PE", as Port Elizabeth is known, is a popular beach resort.

to 13 months in advance with the National Parks Board in Cape Town (tel: (021) 222810). The waiting list is a lot shorter for the beautiful, 65-km (40-mile) long **Tsitsikamma Trail** (five days, maximum 30 persons per day), which runs along the lower slopes of the Tsitsikamma Mountains, above the Otter Trail (permits available from the Regional Forestry Manager, South African Forestry Company, Private Bag X537, Humansdorp, tel: (0423) 51180). Of course, there are plenty of shorter hikes, too, which don't require permits.

Port Elizabeth began life as a military outpost to guard the first British settlers arriving in 1820. The then Cape governor, Sir Rufane Donkin, named it for his wife.

Port Elizabeth to Grahamstown

The 160-km (100-mile) long trip from Storms River to Port Elizabeth is fairly unremarkable. There is **Jeffrey's Bay** ㉒, of course, legendary among the world's surfing community, but to non-surfers not particularly compelling. The large harbour town of **Port Elizabeth** ㉓, headquarters of the South African motor industry (General Motors, Daimler Benz, BMW and Volkswagen), is where the Garden Route comes to a somewhat disappointing end. Here, a 5-km (3-mile) long **Donkin Heritage Trail** takes you round the town's most important historic buildings, beginning at the Market Place with its imposing **City Hall** (1858). But while the architectural highlights of Port Elizabeth aren't all that exciting, the night-life is quite another story.

You may have failed to spot elephants in Knysna, but the **Addo Elephant National Park** ㉓ (open daily, 7am–7pm; entrance fee; tel: (0426) 400556), 50 km (31 miles) to the northeast on the R335, contains around 200 of them and is a better bet altogether. Elephants used to be plentiful around here, but by 1931, local farmers had hunted them almost to extinction; the last 11 animals, frightened and aggressive, had to be lured to their new habitat with large

BELOW: Addo Elephant Park.

KYNSNA'S ELEPHANTS

Two hundred years ago, great herds of elephants roamed the southern Cape. Today, thanks to ruthless hunting throughout the 18th and 19th centuries, there are only seven left, hidden in the secretive dark-green depths of the forests around Knysna. The persistent hunting has made the tiny herd wary of mankind, with the result that it is extremely difficult to locate. It is known that the herd – the world's most southerly – has managed to adapt to forest conditions; although these beasts belong to the same species as the savannah elephants, their habits and lifestyle are now thought to be more similar to the elephants found in the equatorial forests of Central Africa. The herd's future is by no means assured; three young elephants from the Kruger National Park were introduced in 1994, but one died soon afterwards. Although you have to be very lucky indeed to catch a glimpse of these magnificent animals, the Terblans Nature Walk through the Gouna Forest just north of Knysna is a good bet. Another popular trail is the six-hour Elephant Walk that starts from the Diepwalle Forestry Station, just over a kilometre (half a mile) from the mighty King Edward VII Tree – another giant of the forest; a 46-metre-high (150-ft) yellowwood whose circumference measures a stupendous 9.5 metres (30 ft).

quantities of fruit. Today, over 300 of these marvellous animals can be observed from the park's observation points. Bringing citrus fruits into the reserve is now forbidden, though; the elephants tend to come too close for comfort.

Big-game hunting (with a camera, naturally) can also be done in the private – and pricey – **Shamwari Game Reserve ㉕** (access to overnight guests only; tel: (042) 8511196), 72 km (45 miles) east of Port Elizabeth. Over 26 species of game have been reintroduced here, including elephant, rhino, lion, leopard, buffalo, giraffe and zebra. Don't expect a classic safari amidst thorny bushveld, however: these green hills and valleys with their streams and rivers seem almost too idyllic for a safari park, and the accommodation – especially in the most elegant of the four lodges, an Edwardian manor-house – is actually very reminiscent of England.

The little university town of **Grahamstown ㉖**, located 130 km (80 miles) east of Port Elizabeth, was founded in 1812 by a British soldier, Colonel John Graham. Steeped in British colonial history, whitewashed Georgian and Victorian buildings are in plentiful supply – Merriman House on Market Street, the home of a former bishop of Grahamstown (and where the ill-fated General Gordon of Khartoum spent some nights) is typical. Settlers from many religious denominations built churches here in gratitude for their survival in their new land; a total of close to 40 places of worship give the town one of its nicknames: "City of the Saints". From the 1820 Settlers National Monument on Gunfire Hill, there is a magnificent view down over Grahamstown's flock of steeples. But the town is best known for the arts festival it hosts each year in July, the biggest in South Africa (for more information, tel: (011) 4923010). From Grahamstown, East London is another 200-km (124-mile) drive.

**Map,
pages
180–1**

BELOW: the ostrich farms around Oudtshoorn are a major tourist attraction.

THE GREAT KAROO AND THE WINELANDS

Vast, sunburned plains give way to fertile valleys graced with historic wine farms

Map, pages 180–1

The San called it "Land of the Great Thirst", and it is true that the Great Karoo is dry enough to parch the throat of a desert lizard. For most visitors – and even for South Africans – these wide, dusty plains are a "natural obstacle", something to overcome en route to the lush winelands or frenetic Gauteng. Yet the Karoo's bleakness has a beauty all its own. Dotted with flat-topped *koppies* (hills), it is somehow reminiscent of the South Dakota badlands; a spaghetti western setting enhanced at sunset when the *koppies* – peculiarly light-sensitive – change colour from warm red and ochre to purple and blue. At night the cool, clear air tempts you outside to gaze at the brilliant stars of the southern hemisphere.

The Karoo's origins are still a mystery. It is known that the soft sandstone and shales here were created some 200 million years ago, when vast quantities of mud, clay and sand were first washed into the low-lying, marshy Karoo basin. As the climate gradually warmed, the area was invaded by an ocean, trapping the remains of a temperate forest and creating significant deposits of coal, which are now mined in the northern part of the system. The entire sequence was capped some 130 million years ago by a massive volcanic outpouring of basalt lava. The softer sandstone layers underneath gradually eroded, while the hard volcanic dolerite remained, creating the characteristic flat-topped hills that punctuate the plains.

It is ironic that what was once a gigantic freshwater swamp is today drought-stricken and almost devoid of surface water. Rainfall is quite unpredictable – when it does rain, torrents fall in fierce thunderstorms, often causing destruction and erosion as the water cascades into normally dry water-beds.

Cradock and Graaff-Reinet

In the upper reaches of the Great Fish River lies the town of **Cradock 27**, founded in 1813 as a frontier post to defend the region against Xhosa attacks. Like most other rural towns in South Africa, the stark monumental steeples of the Dutch Reformed church buildings are among its most notable features. Often, these were built as imitations of European churches – in Cradock, the model for the *Moederkerk* was St Martin-in-the-Fields in London's Trafalgar Square.

The little town was first made famous by the writer Olive Schreiner (1855–1920). Her controversial 1883 novel, *The Story of an African Farm*, was a powerful attack on the arrogance and racist attitudes of her fellow whites; later, during the Boer Wars, she was interned for her pains. The house in Cross Street in which she lived between 1867 and 1870 has since been turned into a museum (open Mon–Fri; entrance fee).

LEFT: weirdly-shaped *koppies* dot the Great Karoo. **BELOW:** this arid semi-desert supports a surprising range of wildlife.

The region's main attraction, the **Mountain Zebra National Park** ❷❽ (tel: (0481) 2427), lies 15 km (9 miles) west of the town. The park, which extends over some 6,600 hectares (16,300 acres), was established in 1937 to save the little mountain zebra from extinction. At that time there were only a few of these graceful animals left and it was feared that they may go the way of the related quagga, which became extinct in the 19th century. Through a careful programme of conservation and breeding the park now accommodates about 200 zebras; smaller herds have been transferred to other parks in the province. It is also home to springbok, kudu, lynx and baboon; majestic black eagles can sometimes be seen soaring in the sky above.

With the mountain zebra dismissed by one cabinet minister as just "donkeys in football jerseys", it took a fight by conservationists before they were granted sanctuary in their own park.

The choice of accommodation on offer includes the Victorian **Doornhoek Guest House**, built in 1836 and today a national monument. Roaring fires are an added attraction here – winters in this part of the Karoo are sometimes cold enough for snow to fall. Walkers with three days to spare can follow the 31-km (19-mile) long Mountain Zebra Trail, leading through the Fonteinkloof and Grootkloof gorges and then up Banks Mountain, from where there is a magnificent view of Compass Mountain, the highest peak in the Sneeuberg.

Continue another 120 km (75 miles) east of Cradock, and you'll reach **Graaff-Reinet** ❷❾, "gem of the Karoo", enclosed by a bend in the Sundays River. Founded in 1786, it soon became a hub of political turbulence. In 1795, fed up with colonial rule and inspired by the example of the French Revolution, the inhabitants chased the government representative from town and declared an independent – albeit short-lived – republic.

BELOW: post office, Graaff-Reinet.

Despite all this, Graaff-Reinet looks today like the very model of good order, and differs markedly from the many other provincial towns which clearly grew

up without any overall plan. More than 200 buildings have been declared national monuments, including an entire street – Stretch's Court – now restored to its original 18th-century splendour. The Dutch Reformed Mission Church and the old parsonage – once occupied by one of the country's most noted churchmen, Dr Andrew Murray – have both been converted into museums. In the gardens of the parsonage, now called **Reinet House** (open daily, Sat & Sun am; entrance fee), grows the largest living grapevine in the world. With a girth of 2.4 metres (8 ft) and a height of 1.5 metres (5 ft), it covers an area of 124 sq. metres (1,335 sq. ft) – and still bears fruit. The Drostdy in Church Street, completed in 1806, originally served as the seat of the local magistrate, but at the end of the 19th century it was converted into a hotel. You can no longer spend the night in the Drostdy itself, but you can stay in one of the cottages behind it.

Palaeontologists consider the Karoo basin and its unbroken fossil record one of the world's great natural wonders. An extensive private collection of fossils – some exposed after an entombment of up to 230 million years – can be seen in the **Old Library**, situated on the corner of Church and Somerset Streets (open daily, Sat & Sun am; entrance fee).

Just outside town is a statue of Andries Pretorius, the Voortrekker leader who lived in Graaff-Reinet before joining the Great Trek and leading his people to victory against the Zulus in the Battle of Blood River. About 14 km (9 miles) west of town and definitely worth the detour is the **Valley of Desolation**, part of the **Karoo Nature Reserve** (tel: (0491) 23453) and known for its bizarre rock formations of domes and pinnacles, or dolerites, with heights reaching more than 120 metres (393 ft).

Also worth a visit is the eerie, extraordinary **Owl House** (open Mon–Fri, Sat am; entrance fee) in Nieu-Bethesda. From Graaff-Reinet, take the northbound N9 for Middelburg, then turn off after some 27 km (17 miles) for the village of Nieu-Bethesda. Until a few decades ago, the Owl House in River Street was the private home of a reclusive and enigmatic naive artist, Helen Martins. Working chiefly at night, away from the prying eyes of the neighbours, she covered almost the whole interior of her house – walls, ceilings and some of the furniture – in crushed glass, mixed with cement. Flamboyant murals of suns, moons and stars are emblazoned on the ceilings, while enormous mirrors in all the rooms reflect the glittering whole. Outside, in the vegetable garden, a haphazard jumble of over 300 cement sculptures (camels, peackocks, sun-worshippers and hooded shepherds) turn their faces to the east, while cement guardian owls glare balefully from the garden fence and from perches on the verandah. In 1992, several years after "Miss Martins" committed suicide by drinking caustic soda, the house was turned into a museum.

BELOW: the rare geometric tortoise is only found in the Renosterveld area, southwestern Cape.

Beaufort West and the Central Karoo

Between Graaff-Reinet and Beaufort West, the road stretches for some 210 km (131 miles) on a route whose main virtues are the empty road and wide-open countryside. Keep an eye out for that trademark of the Karoo, its creaking wind-pumps. This ingenious but simple contraption forms the backbone of the region's economy.

Map, pages 180–1

Erected at a borehole and then left to its own devices, the wind-pump continuously churns up water from deep underground to drinking troughs for livestock.

Beaufort West , the "Capital of the Karoo", is a popular winter holiday resort thanks, to its dry climate. It's also the hub of a rich farming district. The area is known for its merino sheep, a breed first brought to the country from Holland in 1789. There are now more than 35 million of the animals; they graze on a diet of shrubs, herbs and succulents, which creates the utterly distinctive taste of Karoo mutton.

In the town itself you can visit three neo-Gothic churches and the **Town Hall** (open daily), built in 1867. A wing of the latter is now a museum, which includes in its exhibits a section dedicated to the town's most famous son, the pioneering heart surgeon Dr Christiaan Barnard.

A cement owl, bright-eyed and inscrutable, guards the entrance to the Owl House in the peaceful village of Nieu-Bethesda.

Most visitors, however, prefer to head for the **Karoo National Park** ⓷, which lies 12 km (8 miles) northwest of Beaufort West. Established in 1979, the park (open daily 5am-10pm; entrance fee; tel: (021) 222810) covers almost 33,000 hectares (81,500 acres). Early hunters and explorers recounted tales of a land where thick swathes of grass stood shoulder-high and where the teeming herds of springbok were so huge that wagons had to be outspanned for two or three days to allow the herd to pass by. But "civilization" brought with it hunters and guns and ploughs and fences and fires. Two animal species – the zebra-like quagga and the bluebok antelope – were shot to extinction, and other herds were decimated and driven into the remotest regions of the arid interior. Today, nature reserves like the Karoo National Park are trying their utmost to preserve some of that fauna and its typical Karoo habitat.

BELOW: you may spot the majestic black eagle in the Karoo National Park.

Visitors are likely to see limited numbers of springbok, gemsbok and hartebeest – reintroduced here by game rangers – as well as smaller predators such as lynx, black-backed jackal and wild cat. A unique feature is the great concentration of tortoises. Both the largest species – the leopard tortoise, weighing in at 45 kg (100 lb), and the smallest, *homophus signatus*, just 100-mm (3-inches) long and weighing 150 grams (5 oz) – can be spotted here.

In spring, the dusty landscape is covered with a colourful carpet of wild flowers. This is a particularly rewarding time to tackle the demanding 27-km (17-mile) **Springbok Hiking Trail**, for which you should allow three days. The route is seldom fully booked, but it is closed between November and February because of the excessive heat. Nights are spent in two simple huts along the route. If you prefer to restrict your walking tour to just a few hours, you can undertake an excursion into prehistory along the **Fossil Trail**, where fossilised remains over 50 million years old can be viewed. The path is also suitable for the blind and for those in wheelchairs.

Continue your journey through the "Land of the Great Thirst" towards **Matjiesfontein ㉜**, some 240 km (150 miles) southwest of Beaufort West. This lovely little Victorian town has been declared a national monument in its entirety. An enterprising Scotsman, Jimmy Logan, was the first to make profitable use of the railway station here, a refilling point for steam locomotives about to embark on the long haul north to Pretoria through the parched Karoo. It wasn't long before he was supplying the trains with water and the passengers with cold drinks and hot lamb chops. Logan's business prospered to such an extent that he was soon able to build the elegant **Lord Milner Hotel**. You can still spend the night here if you wish, and the Karoo lamb still tastes as good as it did in Logan's

Map, pages 180–1

BELOW: the Lord Milner Hotel, Matjiesfontein.

times. During the Boer Wars the little town was a British garrison and the hotel served as a military hospital, with a lookout post in the tower. Today, Matjiesfontein is a popular stopover on the route between Johannesburg and Cape Town; the famous luxury Blue Train also pulls in here.

The Winelands

The route southwest along the N1 from Matjiesfontein leads across the Hex River Mountains, which form a natural barrier between the orchards and vineyards of the Boland – the fertile valleys east of Cape Town – and the sunburned Karoo. The contrast could not be greater. Cupped in the lush valley of the Breede River, **Worcester** ❸ (130 km /81 miles southwest of Matjiesfontein) offers a taste of things to come: elegant Cape Dutch architecture and a beautiful setting at the foot of the Hex River Mountains, highest in the Western Cape, and snow-dusted in winter. On all sides there are vineyards. Worcester lies 100 km (63 miles) northeast of Cape Town and can be reached via the N1, so it is not surprising that the town is overrun by visitors at weekends – as are all the wine-growing towns nearby. It is recommended, therefore, that you make your sightseeing and wine-tasting trips during the week, if possible.

Founded in 1820, Worcester possesses a number of neo-Classical buildings, including the elegant **Drostdy**, probably the finest example of Cape Regency architecture in the country. So-called Worcester gables add an individual architectural accent. Many Cape Dutch gabled houses later acquired Victorian verandahs with wrought-iron railings; the one at No. 132 Church Street, built in 1832, is a fine example. The town's most prominent building is the Dutch Reformed **Moederkerk**, built in 1824 in the neo-Gothic style.

BELOW: life on the road in the Little Karoo.

The Worcester Winelands Association has signposted a wine route for visitors to follow. Here, even the oldest wine producer, **De Wet Wine Cellar** (open Mon–Fri, Sat am; tel: (0231) 92710), situated 8 km (5 miles) north of the town, was not founded until 1946, so although the wines are good, you may find both architecture and landscape more attractive around Stellenbosch or Paarl.

Do not leave Worcester without visiting the lovely **Karoo National Botanical Garden** (behind the golf club north of the town; open daily 8am–5pm). Following rainy spells in spring, the landscape bursts into bloom, sprinkling the gardens with a bright carpet of flowering succulents – but it has plenty of other non-seasonal attractions, too.

Robertson ㉞, which lies 50 km (31 miles) to the southeast, also has a signposted wine route; the local dessert wines and brandies here enjoy a very fine reputation. In the opposite direction, some 35 km (22 miles) northwest of Worcester, lies **Tulbagh ㉟**, a miniature historic gem and small wine centre. Following a series of earthquakes in 1968 that virtually demolished the town, historic Church Street was rebuilt in Cape Dutch style. The restoration work was extremely thorough – perhaps even a little too thorough. Church Street now looks like a huge open-air museum. Nor does the village church serve its original purpose; it has been transformed into the **Oude Kerk Folk Museum** (open daily; entrance fee). On display is a noteworthy collection of Victorian furniture and other household objects.

Elegant **De Oude Drostdy** (open daily, Sun pm; entrance fee), 4 km (3 miles) outside the village, was designed in 1804 by the French architect Louis Michel Thibault. Prisoners once languished in the cellar, which today serves as a storeroom for vintages from the nearby Drostdy vineyards, which you can

Map, pages 180–1

BELOW: a barrier of mountains separates the fertile winelands from the dry Karoo.

taste and buy. Tulbagh, of course, also has its own wine route to offer visitors. The **Theuniskraal** estate (by appointment only; tel: (0236) 300690), to name just one example, produces excellent white wines. It has been in the possession of the Jordaan family since 1927.

Tulbagh once had the quaint name of Tulpiesdorp, *thanks to the profusion of wild Cape tulips that grow in the area.*

From Tulbagh the road passes through the wheat-golden and vine-red "**Land van Waveren**" valley and over the most magnificent of all mountain passes, Bain's Kloof Pass, across the Slanghoek Mountains. Here you will find the wine-growing regions of Wellington and Paarl, both of which have signposted wine routes.

Fifty kilometres (31 miles) south of Tulbagh, **Wellington ㊱** is a small town boasting a Dutch Reformed **Moederkerk** built in 1838 (with an interesting spire added in 1891) and an imposing Town Hall. Particularly recommended amongst the vintners whose properties border the wine route are the **Wellington Wynboerie** (open Mon–Fri, Sat am; tel: (021) 8731163) and the **Onverwacht Wine Estate** (with a Cape Dutch manor-house dating from the 18th century and a restaurant; open Mon–Fri, Sat am; tel: (021) 8643096).

The polished granite domes of Paarl Mountain, rising up behind the town, gave **Paarl ㊲** its name (it is Afrikaans for "Pearl"). On the mountain's southern slope, the slender granite needle of the **Afrikaans Taal** ("Language") **Monument** is clearly visible. It was erected in 1975 to commemorate the centenary of a movement started in Paarl that eventually led to the recognition of Afrikaans as an official language.

BELOW: the Hex River Valley in all its autumn splendour.

Paarl's wine route was established in 1984 and it is particularly popular because it offers not only fine wines, but also a whole series of first-class restaurants. A good place to begin your tasting tour is in the centre of town, at the KWV

A MASTER ENGINEER

Many of the first roads in the Cape were not built, but followed the trails worn into the earth over the centuries by herds of migrating game. Sir Lowry's Pass across the Hottentots-Holland Mountains, for example, was opened in 1830 and for a good deal of its length followed the track used by migrating eland. This meant that right up until the mid-19th century, Cape Town – surrounded as it was by a series of towering mountain ranges – remained virtually sealed off from the rest of the country. Villages which were only 30 km (18 miles) apart, as the crow flies, took over a month to reach over the winding animal trails. In 1848, desperate for access to the interior, the Cape colonial government appointed the Scottish-born Inspector of Roads, Andrew Geddes Bain, to solve the problem. Over the next 45 years, Bain – followed by his son, Thomas – supervised the construction of ten mountain passes into the interior, using only hand-held rock drills, picks, shovels and gunpowder. In terms of scale and logistics, these roads are extraordinary feats of engineering; many (the Swartberg Pass, the Montagu Pass, Bain's Kloof Pass, Prince Alfred's Pass) are still in daily use today. But Bain achieved something else, too; he always insisted on choosing the most beautiful routes. They make very rewarding driving.

Map, pages 180–1

Cellars (open Mon–Fri, Sat am; guided tours Mon–Fri 9am, 11am, 2.15pm and 3.45pm, Sat 10.30am, more frequently in summer; tel: (021) 8073007). Nearby is the estate producing the best-known Cape wines of all, **Nederburg** (open Mon–Fri, Sat am; cellar tours by appointment; tel: (021) 8723605). This huge estate has received countless awards; its wines are to be found on every South African wine list. The Nederburg Auction is held in March or April each year, where the best South African wines are sold to the highest bidder. Also worth a special recommendation are the Merlots and sparkling wines from the **Villiera** cellars (open Mon–Fri, Sat am; cellar tours by appointment; tel: (021) 8822002).

Following the R45 in a southwesterly direction, you'll reach **Franschhoek** ㉞, or "French Corner", a reference to the Huguenots who settled here in the 18th century. The **Huguenot Memorial Museum** (open daily, Sun pm; entrance fee) and the Huguenot Monument, completed in 1943, recall the history of these Protestant refugees, persecuted by Louis XIV because of their religious beliefs.

The wine route leading through the Franschhoek Valley, framed as it is by lofty mountain peaks, is a spectacular one – and not only from a scenic point of view. For one thing, it includes the beautiful 300-year-old **Boschendal** estate (open Mon–Fri, Sat am, Sun am in Dec & Jan; vineyard tours by appointment; tel: (021) 8741031), which makes a Blanc de Noir as spectacular as its setting. It's definitely worth giving in to temptation and sampling the splendid Boschendal Brut too, a champagne in all but name. The estate's restaurant is not at all bad; between November and April you can also indulge in a garden "Pique Nique" before heading off to the cellars.

The Optima Reserve produced by the **L'Ormarins** cellars (open Mon–Fri, Sat am; cellar tours by appointment; tel: (021) 8741026) is a fine blend of

BELOW: gracious Boschendal manor-house, pride of the western Cape.

Map, page 180–1

Cabernet Sauvignon and Merlot with a hint of Cabernet Franc – a full-bodied wine which can profitably be stored for 10 to 15 years. The Cape Dutch-style manor-house on this estate is quite lovely, with the dramatic peaks of the Simonsberg and the Groot Drakenstein rising up in the background. The **La Motte Estate** cellars (open Mon–Fri, Sat am; cellar tours by appointment; tel: (021) 8763119) offers an excellent Shiraz, while the vintners at **Haute Cabriére** (open Mon–Fri, Sat am; tel: (021) 8762630) will ply you with no less than five different sparkling wines.

Heart of the Boland

The final stop and in all probability the highlight of your tour through the winelands is **Stellenbosch ㊴**, 28 km (17 miles) west of Franschhoek via the R45 and the R310. Founded in 1679 by the Dutch Governor, Simon van der Stel, the town lies at the heart of the winelands and is its cultural jewel. It's known for its university, the first Afrikaans-language institution of higher education to have been established in the country, and for having the largest number of Cape Dutch houses of any town in the region. The most harmonious examples are to be found on Dorp Street, Church Street and Drostdy Street.

On and facing Die Braak commonage are the **Rhenisch Church,** the **Kruithuis** or munitions magazine, and the neo-Classical Cape Dutch **Burgerhuis** museum (open Mon–Sat). Heading up Dorp Street, you'll pass the **Stellenryck Wine Museum** (open Mon–Sat, Sun pm), the **Rembrandt van Rijn Art Gallery** (open Mon–Sat, Sun pm), the old Drostdy, Oom Samie se Winkel ("Uncle Samie's Store" – an old-fashioned shop), the Lutheran church, and, finally, the four period houses forming the **Dorp ("Village") Museum** (open Mon–Sat, Sun pm; entrance fee). These are the rather primitive Schreuderhuis cottage (1709), the elegant Cape Dutch Blettermanhuis (1789), Georgian-styled Grosvenor House (1803) and mid-Victorian Murray House (1850).

Stellenbosch's wine route is the oldest in the country. You can sample no fewer than 260 different vintages; making a choice is correspondingly difficult. Should you try the dry Rieslings at **Neethlingshof** (open Mon–Fri, Sat am; cellar tours by appointment; tel: (021) 8838988), or **Kanonkop's** (open Mon–Fri, Sat am; tel: (021) 884 4656) remarkable Pinotage; the outstanding Pinot Noir and Merlot on offer at **Meerlust** (tastings and sales by appointment only; tel: (024) 43587), or perhaps the excellent Cabernet Sauvignon made at **Thelema** (open Mon–Fri, Sat am; tel: (021) 8851924), the latter served complete with a panoramic view of the Groot Drakenstein Mountains?

Simonsig (open Mon–Sat; tel: (021) 8822044) produces 15 sorts of red and white wine, and the **Morgenhof Estate** (open Mon–Sat, Sun Oct–May; cellar tours by appointment; tel: (021) 8895510) has just as large a selection on offer. Most cellars can also provide you with a delicious picnic basket. A good place to finish your oenological orgy is at the **Rust-en-Vrede** ("Peace and Quiet") estate, with a glass of fine Shiraz. What could be nicer before heading back to the highway for the hectic world of Cape Town?

BELOW: traditional staging post, Stellenbosch.

Township life

The street lamps lighting Cape Town's white suburbs at night are still shining when Khayelitsha starts waking up. Cape Town's biggest township is well over an an hour's journey by overloaded minibus taxi from the city centre and industrial areas. The name means "new home" in Xhosa, but for the one million people who live here, it could just as well mean "early start".

As dawn breaks, low mists mask the wood-smoke still rising from last night's cooking fires. The light reveals the extraordinary array of building materials used in Khayelitshan homes, from broken bits of advertising hoarding to garbage bags and flattened tin cans.

Some houses have TV sets resourcefully powered by car batteries; on others, the flimsy roofs are pinned down by rusty upturned wheelbarrows – small protection against the summer southeaster which drives sand into every corner (in winter, by contrast, the roads seldom dry out, and there is mud every-where). "The rich get richer," goes the popular catchphrase, "the poor get Khayelitsha".

Three-quarters of Khayelitsha's residents live in "informal housing", or squatter shacks. After the apartheid legislation which created South Africa's townships was repealed, this was the first community in the Western Cape to be earmarked for upgrading – but while there's now a core of "formal", serviced houses, electricity and running water remain a rare luxury. People wash at communal taps (one per street), and attend the small corru-gated-iron toilets nearby.

Many of Khayelitsha's residents first came to the city because they found it increasingly difficult to survive in the former "homelands", areas ravaged by overcrowding, soil erosion and a grim shortage of opportunity. Their pres-ence here – and it is a similar story in all South Africa's townships – underlines an urgent and ongoing need for more houses, roads, schools, clinics and other services.

Crime statistics – especially for violent crimes such as murder and rape – are fright-eningly high. Yet strangers are greeted warmly, neighbours help each other. At night, the *shebeens* (taverns) are crowded with mer-rymakers; on weekends, the churches resound to gospel choirs. Community halls host jazz concerts, ballroom dancing contests and beauty pageants; dusty streets double up as bumpy soccer pitches.

Unemployment here is about 60 percent, but the sidewalks are crowded with hawkers; a parked minibus acts as a shop, with cab-bages lined up on the roof. Fires line the road-side, roasting "smileys" (half a sheep's head), along with offal and sausages. Thriv-ing *spaza* stores (the name means "hidden" in township slang – a reference to the days when blacks were not permitted to run their own businesses) operate from private homes, selling an amazing range of services from gro-ceries to hairdressing and shoe repairs.

The great majority of South Africans are township-dwellers. They take their feisty, inventive local culture for granted; yet it is a side to the country that few visitors (and indeed, few white South Africans, either) ever explore.

RIGHT: interior, Khayelitsha shack, with walls of soap.

THE WEST COAST

*Dry, bleak and sparsely populated, this coastal strip
is deceptively empty – the region is home to a rich
profusion of flora and fauna*

Map,
page 204

Penguins and lions: you'll get to know both of them along this 2,000–km (1,200-mile) long route through South Africa's vast and desolate western reaches. From a barren but eerily beautiful southern coastal strip – a haven for sea birds – we head north via historic fishing harbours, centre of the crayfish industry. After a diversion inland through fruit groves and forested mountain slopes, the route heads north again through parched Namaqualand, magically transformed each spring into a sea of colour. Thundering waterfalls greet our arrival at the Botswana border, where the journey ends in the wildlife wonderland of the Kalahari.

The first stop along the R27 coastal road is **Bloubergstrand**, 25 km (15 miles) north of Cape Town. Once a small fishing village, it has now been swallowed up by city suburbs. This is where you'll find that classic view of Cape Town with Table Mountain in the background, so beloved of South African postcard manufacturers. Despite the Atlantic's chilly temperatures, the beaches here are very popular with surfers, thanks to the size of the breakers.

Quieter **Melbokstrand**, 11 km (7 miles) further north, also has a fine view of Cape Town; a further 58 km (36 miles) up the coast brings you to the **West Coast National Park ❶** (open daily, 9am–5pm; entrance fee; tel:(02287) 22144) and its lagoon at **Langebaan ❷**. This magnificent wetland is one of the world's most important conservation areas for migrant birds. But most people who visit do so to marvel at another natural phenomenon – the glorious eruption of wild flowers each spring.

The **Postberg** area of Langebaan is a favourite stopover for wild flower enthusiasts – during the spring season, you are permitted to walk across any private land or track here. En route to Postberg, you'll also pass **Church Haven**, a traditional Cape fishing village hugging the salt-marsh shoreline of Langebaan Lagoon. The resort village of Langebaan, on the lagoon's eastern shore, caters for a good range of watersports, including angling, yachting, water-skiing and sail-boarding.

To the north, the lagoon flows into Saldanha Bay, the deepest natural harbour in South Africa. Unsurprisingly, there is a large naval presence at **Saldanha ❸**; it's also a key railway link, where enormous quantities of iron ore are deposited after having been shuttled across the Kalahari from the mines at Sishen. The effect of all the battleship and freighter traffic on the vulnerable ecosystem of the lagoon is worrying enough; unfortunately, plans are now being drawn up for the construction of a steelworks here as well. One wonders whether the mussels that have been farmed in the lagoon since 1984 will taste as delicious once the project goes ahead. The crayfish at **Paternoster ❹**, an unspoilt fishing village located some 30 km (19 miles) further north, can still

LEFT: moonset at sunrise over the Kalahari desert.
BELOW: gameranger, Kalahari Gemsbok Park.

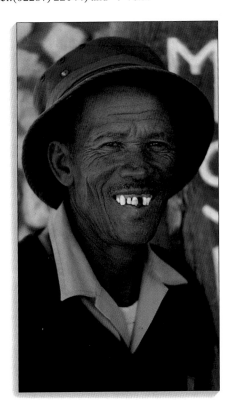

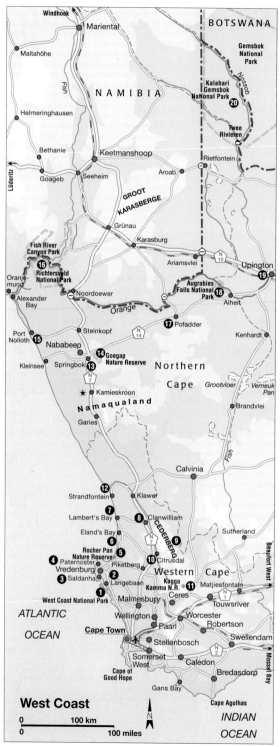

West Coast

0 —————— 100 km

0 —————— 100 miles

ATLANTIC OCEAN

INDIAN OCEAN

be sampled (and are highly recommended) without any problems, nonetheless.

The rocks off Cape Colombine at the southern end of the bay once posed a real threat to sailors; several ships came to grief here before the lighthouse was built. Today, the area around the cape is a nature reserve, a breeding ground for seagulls, cormorants and ibises, amongst others; it's at its most attractive in springtime, when the wild flowers bloom. Also worth a visit is the **Rocher Pan Nature Reserve** ➎ (open daily, 7am–6pm Sep–Apr, 8am–5pm May–Aug; tel: (026) 25727), about 55 km (34 miles) further to the north, which is home to thousands of migrant wading birds. Pink flamingos are the most spectacular.

The birdlife is even more abundant around the picturesque lagoon at **Eland's Bay** ➏. The town itself is not all that interesting, but the beach is excellent, and has become a popular weekend destination for "surfies" from Cape Town.

On the way to the fishing village of **Lambert's Bay** ➐, 16 km further north (Bartolomeo Diaz was the first European to arrive here in 1487), the coast grows increasingly lonely and deserted. If you don't mind the smell and the noise, walk across the stone dam to **Bird Island**, with its nesting colony of around 14,000 Cape gannets. Most of the island is closed to public access, but the observation tower provides a fine view not only of the gannets but also of the jackass penguins who breed here.

The Cederberg

Time to head inland for a change of scene. Sixty-seven kilometres (42 miles) east of Lambert's Bay lies **Clanwilliam** ➑, an orchard town, founded at the beginning of the 18th century and still in possession of some fine historic buildings. One of them, the **Old Jail** (1808), now houses the municipal museum and tourist office (open daily). The famous beverage known as Rooibos or "bush" tea is grown around Clanwilliam, but it's best known as a starting point for excursions into the craggy and wildly romantic **Cederberg Mountains** ➒ – highest of which, the Sneeuberg

(2,000 metres /6,500 ft), does indeed get covered with snow each winter. The mountains are named after a species of cedar indigenous to the area, *Widdringtonia cederbergensis*; sadly, deforestation has now destroyed almost all the trees, and only a few survive up on the more inaccessible slopes. A permit to go hiking and climbing in the **Cederberg Wilderness Area** (home to several leopards), can be obtained from the forest station at Algeria (tel: (022) 9212289), which also has a campsite. To protect the environment, only limited numbers of walkers allowed on each trail at any one time. If you are planning to visit the Cederberg during the busy summer holiday period, you should book hiking permits and accommodation in advance. It's definitely worth the trouble. You'll encounter bizarre sandstone formations, such as the dramatic Wolfsberg Arch, and the weird-looking Malteserkruis; there are fantastic views across stunning scenery; caves decorated with 6,000-year-old San paintings; and crystal-clear rivers to swim in. Once again, the mountains are at their most attractive and colourful during the wild flower season.

Down in the valley you can take a leisurely canoe trip along the Olifant River as far as **Citrusdal ⑩**, the centre of the local citrus fruit industry, which exports thousands of tonnes of fruit each year. The private reserve known as **Kagga Kamma ⑪** (tel: (021) 8638334) can be reached from both Citrusdal and Ceres. As well as such game as kudu and springbok, you can admire some extremely old San rock paintings here. Some distance away from the camp (one lodge, several luxury chalets, superior tents, a restaurant and a swimming pool) lies a reconstructed San village, founded in 1989 with the aim of preserving the traditional lifestyle of this ancient people – or rather, with the aim of showing tourists how they live. Even though the anthropologists who set the village up

Map, page 204

BELOW: flamingo colony, Rocher Pan.

It takes the male crayfish between seven to 10 years to reach a size at which he may legally be caught for human consumption; it takes the female 20 years.

BELOW: a good morning's haul.

have obviously done so with the best of intentions, the whole place still seems very much like an open-air zoo in which the animals are humans.

Namaqualand

The Australians call it the "outback"; the South Africans call it the *sandveld*. Both landscapes have a great deal in common: intense heat, dusty, dry country-side and enormous distances. The *sandveld* region north of the Olifant River, an huge expanse known as **Namaqualand**, is no exception. For most of the year, these stony plains cannot hide the wrinkles and cracks of their age-old skin, or the tattiness of their drab green-grey cover. But, come spring, fields burst forth in colours gay and dazzling. Nature favours these semi-arid scrublands with one youthful cosmetic flush of wild flowers that for a few days in September each year draws people from all over the world. Indeed, the daisies of Namaqualand are one of South Africa's greatest natural attractions.

Coach tours from Cape Town take visitors either on day trips to the edge of the southwestern Cape – the *sandveld* area around Lambert's Bay – or deeper into the heart of Namaqualand to such delightful coastal spots as Tietiesbaai, Hon-deklipbaai, Skulpfonteinput and Kleinsee. As the Namaqualand wild flower extravaganza lasts for only a short time each year and never erupts in the same place all at once, make sure you listen to the weather forecast before you plan your trip (Cape Town flower hotline: (021) 4183705); and bear in mind there are no flowers without rain! Without the reward of the blooms at the end, the long trip along the N7 over the flat, wide plains to Springbok can get very monotonous. Near Klawer comes the last opportunity for many miles to make a detour to the coast at **Strandfontein ⑫**, after which only small corrugated-iron

TAKE ONE CRAYFISH ...

Until the beginning of the 20th century, crayfish were so plentiful in Cape waters that they were viewed with disdain by the upper classes, and used instead as fodder for the inmates of the penal colony on Robben Island. Today, however, crayfish are regarded as a delicacy, commanding top billing and high prices on seafood menus in the most elegant restaurants. Indeed, so valuable has the rock lobster fishing industry become in South Africa that they are often referred to as the "red gold from the sea". The species *Jasus lalandi* is the one most commonly found on the West Coast, and in smaller numbers from Cape Point to East London. To cook crayfish, bring a large saucepan of salted water to the boil. Plunge the live crayfish (one per person) firmly into the saucepan, head end first. This kills them instantly. Cover the pan and boil for about 20 minutes until they turn bright red. Now plunge them into a pan of cold water; when cool, chop off the pincers and split each body lengthways. Remove the small sac at the back of the head (the stomach), the large intestine running from the stomach to the base of the tail, the liver and the lungs on either side of the body. Crayfish are best served as simply as possible. Mayonnaise and brown bread and butter, with lemon quarters, are by far the best accompaniment.

hamlets such as Vanrhynsdorp, Nuwerus, Bitterfontein and Garies add variety to the dusty-brown wilderness.

The next place worth a stop is **Kamieskroon**, boasting not only a petrol station and a shop but also the Kamieskroon Hotel – often booked solid by wild flower enthusiasts right through from July to September. The **Skilpad Wild Flower Reserve** (only open in flower season; entrance fee; tel: (0257) 614), 18 km (11 miles) to the northwest, owned by the South African WWF, gets most of the rain and the flowers here are particularly fine.

Sixty-eight kilometres (42 miles) north of Kamieskroon lies **Springbok ⑬**, the centre of Namaqualand. The town owes its existence to the rich copper reserves in the region, and to something much rarer round here: a spring of fresh water. Some mines are open to the public. The big attraction, however is the **Goegap Nature Reserve ⑭** (open 8am–4pm; entrance fee; tel: (0251) 21880), about 15 km (9 miles) to the east. It is absolutely stunning during flower season, and worth a visit even outside that time of year. In the **Hester Malan Wild Flower Garden**, which forms part of the reserve, you can admire over a hundred species of aloes and succulents, many of which are indigenous to the area. It's a 17-km (10-mile) long round trip if you decide to explore the reserve in your own car, but it's actually more rewarding to book the three-hour guided tour when you arrive; it will take you to more remote and exciting corners. Desert lynx, mountain zebra and springbok are just a few of the animals you may encounter.

There are three hiking paths of around 2–4 hours each through the reserve, designed to show off the best views (in season) across the carpets of flowers. A route for mountain bikes and another for horse-riders have also been set up – though you will, of course, have to supply your own horses and bicycles.

Map, page 204

BELOW: life is hard in the West Coast's fishing villages.

The Diamond Coast

The N7 leads on from Springbok to Steinkopf (52 km/32 miles further north), where you should turn onto the asphalt-surfaced R382 leading over the 950-metre (3,100-ft) high Annienous Pass, down to the coast and **Port Nolloth** ⓕ. The biggest attraction here is the sunsets – utterly magnificent when they aren't obscured by rising sea fog. Port Nolloth used to be a copper port, but today the primary source of income is fishing – and not just for crayfish, either. Diamonds are sucked off the seabed here in large quantities by giant vacuum cleaner-like devices. On its journey past Kimberley, the Orange River gathers up diamond-rich sediments before spewing its precious load up and down the northern Cape coastline, thus creating the world's richest deposits of alluvial diamonds.

The first diamonds were discovered almost by accident in 1926 by an officer in the British-Indian army, Captain Jack Carstens, on an exploratory dig while visiting his parents in Port Nolloth. His discovery proved much richer than anyone could have been imagined. The geologist Hans Merensky subsequently claimed to have found 487 diamonds under one stone alone, and in a single month recovered 2,762 diamonds near Alexander Bay.

As news of the find spread across the world, fortune seekers descended on the area in droves, prompting the government to secure the area and ban private prospecting. The entire coast between Kleinsee and **Oranjemund** is controlled by the De Beers Consolidated Mining Company – founded by Cecil John Rhodes in 1880 – and the public is not allowed off the main road.

The coast is worked by the world's largest armada of earth-moving equipment, constantly pushing the sea back with artificial dunes while the underlying

TIP

Refuse offers from locals who offer to sell you cheap diamonds. Not only are they trading illegally but the stones often turn out to be worthless lead crystal.

BELOW: spring flowers in bloom near Clanwilliam.

Map, page 204

sand is cleared down to the bedrock with shovels and hand-brooms. Every crack and crevice being methodically cleaned out. A vast wealth of diamonds is recovered here each year.

The desert-besieged fishing and diamond towns of the northwest coast are real frontier places, the men as rough as uncut diamonds and as raw as the cheap alcohol they consume in quantity. There are few women, plenty of stray dogs and the only acts considered punishable are illicit diamond dealing, murder and trying to take another man's woman.

The only "resorts" are to be found at Strandfontein near the Olifant River mouth and, at the Port Nolloth extension, McDougall's Bay. These are rudimentary places as resorts go, catering almost exclusively for fishermen and the rough-and-ready local sheep-farming communities. If there is such a place as "the end of the line", then Port Nolloth is surely that place.

From **Alexander Bay**, an unsurfaced and rather bumpy road leads to the **Richtersveld National Park** ⓰ (arrange permits and accommodation in advance; tel: (0256) 8311506). One of the newest national parks in South Africa (it was founded in 1993), Richtersveld is a wild, semi-desert region with virtually no marked routes. Whatever you need here you have to bring yourself and – no less important – take it out with you again when you leave. The park administration rarely lets in more than a few groups at any one time: don't even consider a visit if you have no pre-arranged permit. Winter is the only time it rains here, and in summer the temperature can rise as high as 50°C (122°F) – visits should be avoided during this time as the heat is simply unbearable. It's hard to believe that so much grows in such a harsh environment, but the diversity of succulents here is so rich that botanists are struggling to get them all classified

BELOW: springbok, demonstrating just how it was they got their name.

and described. Some species are known from only one locality or even one specimen, never found again. Others, like the *halfmens* (*Pachypodium namaquanum*) are equally strange; the San people believed they were half-plant and half-human, and anyone who has seen the single, thick tapering stem with its crowning rosette of tightly crinkled leaves will understand why. Also characteristic are the stark tree aloes, or *kokerboom* (quiver trees), whose bark was used by the San to make quivers for their arrows.

The deep pools at the base of the Augrabies Falls are home to shoals of giant barbel – up to two metres long – sightings of which have given rise to rumours of a river monster.

After you've explored the park, there is little choice but to return to Springbok. From here, be prepared for a rather lonely 320-km (200-mile) trip along the N14. **Pofadder** ⓱ is a good place to stop for petrol and a cool beer, but thankfully **Alheit** marks the end of this isolated stretch. Here, the N14 branches off to the left and follows the bank of the Orange River to the **Augrabies Falls National Park** ⓲ (open 6.30am–10pm Apr–Sept, 6am–10pm Oct–Mar; tel: (054) 4510050).

Dominating the entire region is the mighty **Orange River**, making its inexorable way to the Atlantic Ocean like a giant serpent. Carrying almost a quarter of the volume of South Africa's entire river system, the 2,000-km (1,240-mile) long Orange is the life-giving source of the entire region. Its lush, green banks, utilised extensively for the cultivation of cotton, deciduous fruit and grapes, are in stark contrast to the arid surroundings. At Augrabies, the Orange thunders spectacularly over one of the six largest waterfalls of the world.

BELOW: white-water rafting on the Orange River.

In times of drought, the flow is reduced, but every so often flash floods upriver cause the river to burst its banks and the falls become a frightening torrent that gouges out a devastating swathe before it. Then, more than 400 million litres (80 million gallons) of water an hour can gush over the 56-metre

(185-ft) fall into a deep gorge carved out of the granite bedrock. Crashing down a further 35 metres (115 ft) over a series of secondary falls and cataracts, the water sends a vast column of spray into the air, enveloping the area in a heavy mist.

Map, page 204

The true beauty and force of the river and the might of the falls can best be observed from a suspension bridge. Two large pools at the base of the falls are thought to be at least 130 metres (425 ft) deep and contain a great wealth in diamonds carried from the vicinity of Kimberley and washed over the edge – unfortunately, a waterfall is hard to shift.

The park contains a great deal more than just the waterfall. The three-day **Klipspringer Hiking Trail** (40 km/23 miles) here is extremely popular, especially during the local school holidays when it is almost always over-subscribed; during the extreme heat of summer the trail is closed. Three one-hour-long hikes are also available, however, and all you need to bring along is a sturdy pair of shoes. The route from the camp to Arrow Point is particularly recommended; there's a great view from here over two canyons simultaneously. On the Black Rhino Tour organised by the park (maximum seven participants), you can travel by Land Rover and canoe through its less accessible parts. Apart from kudu and springbok, you may also catch a glimpse of a rare black rhino. The park also organises white-water rafting along an 8-km (5-mile) long stretch of river with five sets of rapids.

The route continues now along the banks of the Orange River, to **Kakamas** (8 km/5 miles to the east of Alheit). Artificially-irrigated vineyards and orchards are a feature of the landscape here, as are vast amounts of grapes laid out to dry in the sun. The region is famous for its delicious sultanas, and provides a good deal of

BELOW: the beautiful antelope for which the Kalahari Gemsbok Park is named.

The crescent-shaped pods of the camelthorn tree are a valuable source of food for many species of animal in the Kalahari Gemsbok National Park.

BELOW: you'll spot these magnificent heavily maned lions in the Kalahari Gemsbok Park.

the table grapes exported from South Africa to Europe. The local dessert wines and sherries are also justly celebrated, and can be sampled in the **Oranjerivier Wine Cellars** (tastings by arrangement; tel: (054) 4310830). The town of **Upington ⑲**, which despite its English-sounding name is very Afrikaans indeed, is the largest in the Northern Cape Province and an important tourist centre. Direct flights from Cape Town or Johannesburg shorten the journey here considerably; if you're planning to head off into the Kalahari, this is a good place to rent a four-wheel-drive,or even a mobile home. At the entrance to the Eiland Holiday Resort there's an impressive 1,041-metre (3,415-ft) long avenue of date palms; the trees, numbering more than 200, were planted in 1935.

At the end of a lonely 358-km (222-mile) trip north of Upington, through the most remote area of Northern Cape Province, one of the most fascinating national parks in South Africa is waiting to greet you – the **Kalahari Gemsbok National Park ⑳** (open 6am–7.30pm Jan–Feb, 6.30am–7pm Mar, 6.30am–6.30pm Apr, 7am–6pm May, 7.30am–6pm Jun–Jul, 7am–6.30pm Aug, 6.30am–6.30pm Sept, 6am–7pm Oct, 5.30am–7.30pm Nov–Dec; tel: (012) 3431991). It borders on the considerably larger **Gemsbok National Park** in Botswana, and together they cover an area of some 3.6 million hectares (8.9 million acres).

With its rusty-red sand dunes, the Kalahari is strikingly reminiscent of the Simpson Desert in Australia, but the fauna here is far more varied. **Twee Rivieren** is the only entrance to the park, and it is here at the confluence of the Auob and Nosob rivers that you will see the most animals. The rainwater collects beneath the light sand of the riverbed, which is why the vegetation here

is so lush. It is not unusual to witness a cheetah running down a springbok along the Nossob's dry bed, or a large herd of handsome gemsbok with their rapier horns silhouetted against a sky bruised by thunderclouds. Heavily maned Kalahari lions escape the midday heat beneath thorn bushes, while brilliantly spotted leopards take refuge in the tall camelthorn trees. But it is the park's 200-odd bird species, and most particularly its range of eagles and other raptors, that most impress visitors.

The large camelthorn trees (*Acacia erioloba*) that define the river courses are the life-giving source of the region, providing nests for the sociable weavers and the colony of other birds that cohabit there and offering shade to game and domestic stock. The tree's large crescent-shaped pods also make for nutritious food when they fall. The gum is eaten by animals and used in traditional medicine by local communities. Giraffes can wrap their long, prehensile tongues around the thorn-spiked branches and strip the leaves with seeming immunity to the cruel spines.

The best time of the year to visit is between February and May, just after the small amount of annual rain has fallen. Don't forget to protect yourself against mosquitoes. Bear in mind, too, that at peak time accommodation in the park gets booked up well in advance (booking 13 months in advance is normal). The relatively comfortable main camp is located at Twee Rivieren, but you can also spend the night at Mata Mata Camp (118 km/73 miles to the northwest, after a particularly attractive trip), located not far from the Namibian border which is, however, closed at that point. Camp Nossob, 152 km (94 miles) to the north and on the border with Botswana, is far less attractive. The latter border is marked with boundary stones, but may only be crossed by the animals.

Map, page 204

BELOW: Kalahari salt-pan, with camelthorn tree.

MARVELS OF THE FLORAL KINGDOM

Home to more than 24,000 species – one-tenth of all known flowering plants – South Africa's flora is amongst the richest and most varied in the world

From the weird succulents of the dry Kalahari to the brilliantly coloured blossoms which transform Namaqualand's semi-desert plains in the spring, South Africa is impressively endowed with some spectacular plant life. Most enticing of all for botanists, gardeners and walkers alike is the slender strip of Cape coastline stretching inland in the west as far as Clanwilliam, around the peninsula and then east as far as Port Elizabeth. Dominated by a unique heathland vegetation known as *fynbos* (Afrikaans for "fine bush"), this area enjoys special status as the smallest of the world's six "Floral Kingdoms", and the one with the richest species diversity.

A THREATENED KINGDOM

Characterised by very small or leathery leaves often protected by hairs, the three most common *fynbos* families are Proteaceae (including the national flower, *Protea cynaroides,* or king protea), Ericaceae and the reedy Restionaceae. *Fynbos* grows in some extremely diverse habitats – from arid salt marshes and sand dunes to mountain slopes and crags up in the cloud zone – but the best time to see it is the spring (September and October), when the veld blooms into kaleidoscopic colour. Sadly, as many as 1,326 *fynbos* species are on the endangered list, including the lovely snow protea, which only grows above the snow line in the Cederberg and defies cultivation.

◁ **DELICATE BEAUTY**
The Common Watsonia (*Watsonia densiflora*) is one of the jewels of the *fynbos* region. You can see it in flower in late spring (October–November) throughout the southwestern Cape.

◁ KING OF THE HILLS

Clusters of majestic *Protea cynaroides* growing wild in the world-famous Botanical Garden at Kirstenbosch, Cape Town. In a lovely setting on the eastern slopes of Table Mountain, Kirstenbosch nurtures over 5,600 indigenous plant species. It's one of the best places in the country to see Cape *fynbos* displayed in its dramatic wild mountain habitat.

▽ SOUTHERN SHRUBS

The Cape Floral Kingdom is particularly rich in indigenous heathers – over 600 species, compared to Britain's handful. Characterised by needle-like leaves and pendent, bell-shaped flowers, they make popular garden and pot plants. Look out for this pretty specimen (*Erica versicolor*) on the Robinson Pass, heading over the Outeniqua Mountains from George.

◁ SACRED CYCADS

Sacred to the Rain Queen, ruler of the Lobedu people who live near Duiwelskloof in the Northern Province, the Modjadji cycad (*Encephalar-tos transvenosus*) is a striking feature of the lowveld landscape. These rare plants may reach a height of 13 metres (43 ft), which makes them one of the largest cycad species in the world. Modjadji Nature Reserve has some particularly fine specimens.

◁ FOREST GIANTS

Outeniqua yellowwoods (*Podocarpus falcatus*) are the giants of the Knynsa and Tsitsikamma forests, reaching heights of 60 metres (200 ft). All yellowwood species are now protected by law.

STAR ATTRACTION ▷

Now exported all over the world (it is, for example, Los Angeles' floral emblem), the spectacular Crane Flower (*Strelitzia reginae*) is indigenous to the Eastern Cape and KwaZulu-Natal.

GREAT BOTANICAL GARDENS

Kirstenbosch *(above and left)* is probably South Africa's most famous garden. Equally rewarding, however, are the seven other national botanical gardens ("NBGs"), strategically located in each of the country's major floral zones.

• Founded in 1946, the plantings in Pretoria's sprawling NBG represent every major type of southern African vegetation. The Garden was declared a National Monument in 1979.

• In the Witwatersrand NBG near Roodepoort, a dramatic waterfall provides a backdrop for more than 500 species of highveld aloes, trees and shrubs.

• The Lowveld NBG on the outskirts of Nelspruit has a spectacular series of waterfalls and river gorges, as well as the country's best outdoor collection of indigenous trees, ferns and rare cycads.

• The tranquil Natal NBG in Pietermaritzburg was originally founded in 1872, and features some superb specimens of imported trees.

• The Karoo NBG near Worcester concentrates on plants from the arid semi-desert areas of the country.

• On the outskirts of Bloemfontein, the Free State NBG specialises in frost and drought-hardy plants.

• The beautiful, secluded Harold Porter NBG at Betty's Bay boasts one one of the densest concentrations of *fynbos* in the country.

DURBAN

*East meets West in this cosmopolitan holiday
city, set in sugar country on the edge of a
lush subtropical coast*

Map,
page 218

Durban is South Africa's most popular holiday resort, thanks to a seductive subtropical climate (temperatures reach 32°C, or 90°F, in the summer months), excellent beaches and year-round warm seas. It has more hotels than any other city in the country – unfortunately, many of them the soulless high-rise variety so popular with architects in the 1960s and 1970s. As the "Whites Only" signs have come down from the beaches, its fan-base has started to change: Durban is now a huge favourite with black working-class holiday-makers from as far afield as Gauteng.

This is South Africa's third-largest city, and one of the biggest and busiest ports in Africa, despite never having been afforded so much as the status of provincial capital. First established by the British in 1824 and christened "Port Natal", the name "Durban" was foisted upon it in 1835 in honour of the then Governor of the British Cape Colony, Sir Benjamin D'Urban. Today, it is more commonly known to its Zulu residents as *eThekweni*, or "place of the sea".

All this aside, what really makes Durban distinct from anywhere else in South Africa is its large community of Indian people – around one million strong, of whom 70 percent are Hindus, 20 percent Muslim, and the remainder Christian. Descendants of the indentured labourers who arrived in the 1860s to work in the local sugar cane industry, KwaZulu-Natal's Indians have resisted assimilation into the wider South African society, and enthusiastically maintain their languages, religions, dress codes and even caste system.

The city as playground

The Durban metropolitan area has the highest population density in the country – a fact which becomes apparent during the peak holiday season, when day-trippers from miles around flock to the bathing beaches stretching in a long, blond line north from the harbour entrance. **South Beach** is usually the most densely packed; **North Beach** is somewhat trendier, the surfers' and posers' hangout. On all the beaches, swimming zones are clearly marked; they are also protected by shark nets and patrolled by lifeguards.

For a less crowded experience, head slightly further afield. **Brighton Beach** on the Bluff is good for body surfing; at nearby **Treasure Beach** you can explore an unspoilt stretch of tidal pools, with rare corals and marine life. The Wildlife and Conservation Society conducts tours here for a small fee. Otherwise, head 15 km (10 miles) north of the city to the up-market resort of **Umhlanga Rocks**, which is graced with a long stretch of golden sand.

Heart of the resort area is pedestrianised **Marine Parade** – a brash, busy playground of pools, fountains, amusement arcades and fast food kiosks, flanked by

LEFT: Durban beachfront, the country's holiday playground.
BELOW: winter means summer sunshine here.

luxury high-rise hotels and apartment blocks. Most of the major tourist attractions are found here, clustered along the strip known as the **Golden Mile** Ⓐ, which actually runs for about 6 km (4 miles) along the shore.

Children and adults alike will enjoy **Fitzsimons Snake Park** Ⓑ (open daily; entrance fee) on North Beach, slithering with 80 species of indigenous snake, as well as crocodiles and iguanas. Also very popular, mystifyingly, is **Minitown** (open Tues–Sun; entrance fee), with its miniature replicas of major city landmarks; **Waterworld** (open daily; entrance fee), opposite Country Club Beach, is always packed with thrill-seekers braving the kamikaze water slides and rides. A short walk away at Bay of Plenty beach are the **Amphitheatre Gardens** Ⓒ, a tranquil collection of sunken pools, gardens, lawns and fountains. Nearby, and worth a visit, is the **Sea World** aquarium and dolphinarium Ⓓ (open daily; entrance fee), which has daily dolphin, seal and penguin shows, as well as a comprehensive collection of sharks. The really bold can hire wetsuits and dive in the aquarium.

Around the Point, south of the Golden Mile, **Victoria Embankment** Ⓔ is graced with a number of interesting historical features, including **Da Gama Clock** Ⓕ. It's named for the Portuguese explorer who "discovered" Port Natal for the Europeans on Christmas Day, 1497.

The ornate wrought-iron curlicues of Da Gama Clock, on Victoria Embankment.

Craft markets and malls

The biggest and best of Durban's shopping malls is **The Pavilion**, off the N3 in the district of Westville; most interesting to look at (and easier to get to) is **The Workshop** in downtown Commercial Street – 120 up-market shops in a converted Victorian railway building. Both offer a few good craft shops

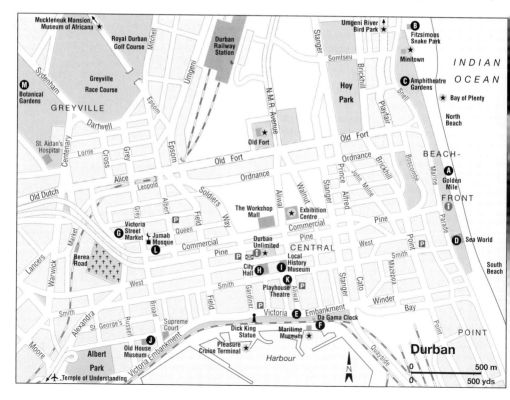

along with standard mall-type fare. By far the most exotic place to shop for curios, however, is **Victoria Street Market** ⓖ, west of the city centre near Warwick Avenue, where both Indian and African craft markets jostle for space alongside fresh produce stalls. Here, you can spend a morning haggling for Zulu assegais and carved masks, Indian silver jewellery and leather-work, or stocking up on spices (try the volcanic "Mother-in-Law" curry powder). If you'd prefer to visit with a guide, numerous companies offers city tours which include this market.

With more than 750 stalls, the **South Plaza Market** (open Sun only) near The Workshop mall in the city centre is one of the largest flea markets in the country; the quality of the jewellery and leather-work, in particular, is generally very good. The **Heritage Market** (open daily), a 20-minute drive from the centre of town in the semi-urban suburb of Hillcrest, sells an eclectic range of crafts mixed in with antiques and tat in a picturesque Victorian-style building.

Mosques and museums

Durban has a surprisingly small number of museums; although each sheds some light on the city's social and natural history, few are exceptional. Make time, nonetheless, for the **Natural Science Museum** (open daily; free), which not only has some interesting wildlife displays (it's especially good on local birds), but is housed in the splendidly neo-baroque **City Hall** ⓗ in downtown Smith Street – it's an almost exact copy of Belfast's City Hall, and worth a visit in its own right. This is also where you'll find the **Durban Art Gallery** (closed Sat; free); a small but handsome collection of local and international pieces.

Map,
page 218

Dick King's epic 10-day ride to Grahamstown in 1842 – to get help for the British garrison besieged by Boers at Durban's Old Fort – is marked by a statue of King on Victoria Embankment.

BELOW: the Durban area is home to the largest Muslim community in the country.

TIP

Take a unusual ride along Marine Parade on one of Durban's famous rickshaws, pulled by a flamboyantly-costumed Zulu driver.

A few minutes' walk away from the City Hall in Aliwal Street is Durban's original Victorian courthouse, now the **Local History Museum** (open daily; free); it tells the story of Port Natal's colonial past.

From here, a short drive west on the Old Fort Road brings you to the district of Berea, set on a ridge; one of its Victorian showpieces is gracious **Muckleneuk Mansion**. It houses some good historical collections, including the **Killie Campbell Africana Library** (open by appointment only), a valuable collection of rare books, maps and manuscripts, as well as the Mashu collection of indigenous Zulu art. Also interesting is the **Old House Museum** (open daily; entrance fee) on St Andrews Street – a detailed replica of a settler home.

The **Playhouse Theatre**, near the City Hall on the corner of Smith and Acutt Streets, is home to the provincial performing arts council, and supports a symphony orchestra as well as ballet, drama and opera companies. The Thursday night philharmonic concerts here are worth attending, but book ahead – they're very popular. Down on Victoria Embankment, a short walk away, the **BAT Centre** arts complex has a fine setting overlooking Durban's small crafts harbour, and an equally good reputation as a supporter of the avant-garde.

Another important element of Durban's cultural make-up – and one of it's best-known landmarks – is the Islamic **Juma Mosque**, on Grey Street, near Victoria Street Market. It's the largest place of worship for Muslims in southern Africa, and famous for its huge golden domes.

Parks and gardens

BELOW: the tropical Mozambique current warms the Indian Ocean off KwaZulu-Natal.

Durban's lush climate supports a healthy number of green spaces and parks. One of the best is the **Umgeni River Bird Park** (open daily; free), on River-

side Road on the north bank of the Umgeni River. It contains a marvellous collection of over 1,000 indigenous and exotic birds, including the rhino hornbill, which sports a foot-long multi-coloured beak.

The futuristic marble **Hare Krishna Temple of Understanding** (open daily; free) just south of the city centre in the suburb of Chatsworth, is the largest of its kind in the southern hemisphere, yet its lush ornamental gardens are a tranquil oasis. It also supports a very good vegetarian restaurant, serving snacks as well as large curries. The **Botanic Gardens** (open daily; free) in Berea may seem a more conventional escape from city heat and dust, but there is a collection of rare cycads and an unusual scent-garden for the blind here, as well as a celebrated orchid hothouse.

"Durbs" after dark

Nightlife in "Durbs", as it's fondly known, traditionally revolves around the hotels, bars, discos and clubs lining the beachfront. Alternatively, a clutch of trendy bars and restaurants have also sprung up in the **Florida Road** area, near Kings Park Stadium, heading inland from Argyle Road.

Seafood lovers in search of local specialities such as crayfish, langoustines and tiger prawns should head for the harbour area. Watch ships sailing by from your table at **The Famous Fish Company** at King's Battery, New Point Waterfront harbour; **Café Fish**, overlooking Durban Yacht Mole off the Esplanade, is another good bet. For a taste of hot and spicy Indian fare, the Ulundi Grill at the five-star **Royal Hotel** in downtown Smith Street has long been regarded as one of the best curry houses in town. **Thirsty's**, back at King's Battery, is rather less pricey, and the perfect place to watch the sun set over Durban Bay.

Map, page 218

TIP

Pleasure cruises around Durban harbour are available from the Gardiner Street Jetty. For details, tel: (031) 3054022.

BELOW: young Zulu maiden in traditional dress, KwaZulu-Natal.

DURBAN TO EAST LONDON

*Sandy shores and lazy lagoons give way to high, green hills
dotted with thatched huts, sweeping down to jagged
cliffs – the traditional land of the Xhosa*

Map, page 224

Johannesburg
SOUTH AFRICA Durban
Cape Town

Sunshine Coast, Hibiscus Coast, Wild Coast – just a few of the lyrical names for the route south of Durban down to **East London**. Some of South Africa's finest beaches stretch out along this shore – yet on the Wild Coast at least, prices are still quite reasonable in comparison with the Garden Route.

The beautiful **Wild Coast** was once part of the "independent" Transkei, created as a Xhosa homeland under apartheid. In the rural areas here, rolling grass hills are dotted with mud-and-grass huts; women walk around with ochre-painted faces, smoking long-stemmed pipes; old men and children urge on teams of oxen to plough the hillside fields.

As you drive through the region, you may spot the occasional teenage boy standing by the roadside dressed in a patterned blanket, his face covered in white clay. According to tribal custom, "a boy is merely a dog" and to attain manhood he must undergo a circumcision and initiation ceremony lasting two to three weeks. Teenage boys are taken to secluded areas where they are tutored by elders and circumcised. The *abakwetha*, as the boys are known, live in spartan conditions in the bush until their wounds have healed. Returning to their villages, they daub their bodies and faces with clay, go naked but for a blanket, and show off their skills in traditional dances. To mark the end of the initiation ceremony, the youths cleanse themselves in a river, and all their old possessions are burned. Finally, they are presented with a new set of clothes, in which they set forth into the world of men.

LEFT: Xhosa matrons enjoy a good smoke.
BELOW: these dramatic rock formations are typical of the Wild Coast.

The Sunshine Coast

From Durban, the well-surfaced N2 leads on for 128 km (80 miles) through a string of popular seaside resorts – Umzumbe, Banana Beach, Sea Park, Umtentweni, Southbroom, Ramsgate and Margate among them – as far as Port Shepstone, where it suddenly veers sharply inland. Here, and along the Eastern Cape border, the coast is made up of a jagged series of steep cliffs and deep bays, most of which can only be reached along tiny unsurfaced footpaths.

Some of the best scuba-diving in South Africa can be had just 22 km (14 miles) south of Durban, at **Amanzimtoti ❶**. Here, regular boats depart for the Aliwal Shoal, a sandbank roughly 5 km (3 miles) from the coast, overgrown with hard and soft coral. At very low tides, passage out to the Shoal may be blocked by a large natural breakwater – but get past that, and you can look forward to exploring natural tunnels, caves and reefs up to 43 metres (140 ft) below the surface. Two wrecks – the *Nebo* and the *Produce* – lie just north of the northernmost tip of the Shoal, known as "the Pinnacles". That part of the seaward side nicknamed "the Outside Edge" is where you'll see ragged-tooth shark,

along with manta rays and moray eels. Only experienced divers should attempt the Shoal's dive sites, however; currents can be very strong. Beginners would do better to dive at nearby **Umkomaas**, a further 19 km (12 miles) down the coast.

The golf course at Umkomaas is just one of many in the region. A game at Selbourne Park course can be great fun, thanks to the water obstacles; the fairways at **Scottburgh ❷** also take some getting used to. For a pleasant day trip from Scottburgh, take the R612 heading inland towards Ixopo through sugar and eucalyptus plantations to reach the **Vernon Crookes Nature Reserve** (open daily; entrance fee; tel: (0323) 42222), which has a good range of scenery from river valleys and coastal forest to swampland. This range of habitats supports plenty of wildlife – over 300 species of bird, including the crowned crane – as well as zebra, blue wildebeest, eland, impala, reedbuck and nyala. If you're visiting in mid-January, there's a good chance of spotting the beautiful snake lily in flower in the reserve's swamp forest.

The wild hibiscus that grows profusely along the roadsides between Hibberdene and Port Edward has given the area its name: Hibiscus Coast.

The Hibiscus Coast

The resorts lying between Hibberdene and Port Edward are hugely popular with South Africans looking for a good-value alternative to the holiday towns of Port Elizabeth, Plettenberg Bay and Knysna down south in the Cape. Accordingly, in December and January, this stretch of coast as far as Port Shepstone gets very crowded indeed. Nonetheless, **Port Shepstone ❸**, the largest town on the Hibiscus Coast, retains a pleasant provincial air. There are several very good (and unbelievably cheap) seafood restaurants here – some specialising in oysters – while the local craft shops are a good bet for high-quality Zulu basketware, handcrafted beadwork and pottery.

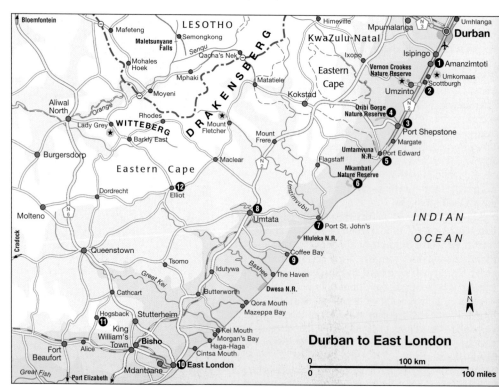

Durban to East London

0   100 km

0   100 miles

Golfers should definitely try out the local course, high above the rocky coast; train fans will enjoy a trip on the **Banana Express**, an old-fashioned narrow-gauge railway that steams its way through banana and sugarcane plantations on a two-hour journey to Izotsha and **Paddock**. Scuba-divers, meanwhile, should head down to the bustling seaside resort of **Shelley Beach**, about 5 km (3 miles) south of Port Shepstone. From here, you can arrange to be taken by launch to some excellent shallow-water reef sites – those at Deep Salmon and Bo Boyi Reefs are particularly recommended. To see the corals and tropical fish at their best, avoid the summer months – visibility tends to be poor after the seasonal rains. If you're a thrill-seeking diver and fancy getting close to hammerhead and Great White sharks, Shelley Beach is also the place to join trips to the deeper waters of Protea Banks, lying 9 km (6 miles) offshore.

The real highlight of any trip to the area, however, is the **Oribi Gorge Nature Reserve** ❹ (open daily; tel: (0397) 91644), 21 km (13 miles) west of Port Shepstone on the N2. Here, numerous hiking routes criss-cross a spectacular canyon. From the vantage point of Overhanging Rock, you can peer gingerly down at the Umzimkulwana River, more than 370 metres (1,200 ft) below.

The Wild Coast

The Wild Coast lies between Port Edward in the north and Morgan's Bay in the south, and its "wildness" is apparent from the moment its deep ravines, steep cliffs and waterfalls come into view. Properly speaking, however, the coast was named after the reefs and rocks some distance offshore, which posed such a danger to shipping in the past. Many of the wrecks submerged around here have still not been thoroughly explored; they issue quite a challenge to divers.

Map, page 224

BELOW: the devil fire fish, an exotic import to South African shores.

The little resort of Coffee Bay received its name when a large cargo of coffee beans was washed up at the mouth of the Nenga River after a shipwreck.

Best-known wreck of all is the *Grosvenor*, a fully laden British treasure ship which came to grief on a stormy night in 1782 off the Pondoland coast. Rumours that the cargo included the glorious Peacock Throne looted from the kings of Persia have sparked off numerous attempts to recover the cargo – all of which have so far come to naught in the restless Wild Coast sea. Ironically, apart from eight cannons salvaged in 1952, the richest haul taken from the ship was its iron ballast, recovered by the ship's blacksmith, who chose to remain on the coast and settle down with two Mpondo wives.

Between May and November, whales with their newborn calves can often be seen offshore, while dolphins are a year-round attraction. This coast also offers some excellent angling opportunities, from fishing the Indian Ocean for enormous reef fish such as musselcracker, to trying your luck in the rivers and lakes, many of which are full of trout.

Unfortunately, in recent years, there have been a number of brutal attacks on tourists along this coast. It's best not to camp on lonely beaches here, and to refrain from travelling at night. Wearing jewellery or carrying a camera slung around your neck should also be avoided. Check with the consulates in Cape Town, Durban or Johannesburg for advice on the security situation.

Port Edward ❺ marks the start of the **Wild Coast Hiking Trail**, one of the most famous trails in South Africa. It takes a full two weeks to hike the 200-km (160-mile) long route as far as Coffee Bay, though the trip can also be split up into shorter sections. The northern part of the trail is rugged and difficult, including such obstacles as steep cliffs, rivers and ravines. The southern section is markedly more easy-going and relaxing; here, you can walk for several days over miles of sandy beach without seeing another human being.

BELOW: the Wild Coast is well named.

Less sporty nature lovers would probably prefer exploring some of the nature reserves scattered along the coast. Largest and finest is the 8,000-hectare (19,750-acre) **Mkambati Nature Reserve** ❻ (open daily; entrance fee; tel: (037) 727 3124), created on the site of an old leper colony about 40 km (25 miles) north of Port St John's. There are two wide estuaries for canoeing; long stretches of deserted, rocky beach; and accommodation in comfortable bungalows between tall shady trees, or in self-catering rondavels right on the seashore. The flora is wonderfully diverse, too, from mangrove swamps to rare species of palm tree growing in a ravine amphitheatre, and numerous species of wild orchid. This is another place where you can walk for days without meeting another soul.

Two of the nicest smaller reserves around here include the **Cwebe Nature Reserve** (tel: (0474) 620247), just south of Coffee Bay, and **Dwesa Nature Reserve** (tel: (0471) 24322), which lies between The Haven and Qora Mouth. Dwesa is a good place to see wildebeest, eland and monkeys; Cwebe provides a habitat for the Cape clawless otter. Plan on being totally self-sufficient if you visit Dwesa, however, as the reserve supplies no provisions of any kind.

After so much rural tranquillity, arriving in **Port St John's** ❼ is like entering a major metropolis. Here, the mighty Mzimvubu – the only navigable river on the Wild Coast – has carved out a most impressive portal for itself as it reaches the sea. The town itself, once a thriving colonial-style outpost, saw an exodus of its white population after Transkei "independence". Today, it survives in somnambulent idleness and indifference. Most of its charm lies in this state of semi-decay, the grand old houses having been abandoned or taken over by new tenants. Not surprisingly, perhaps, it is also home to a flourishing artists' colony.

**Map,
page 224**

BELOW: the area is heaven for hikers.

An abakwetha. *According to Xhosa tribal custom, teenage boys must undergo a circumcision ritual to attain manhood. During this period, the youth's face and body is daubed with clay.*

BELOW: Hole in the Wall, near Coffee Bay.

The R61 now leads back inland for 90 km (56 miles) to **Umtata ❽**, the dusty, unappealing capital of the former Transkei, which today seems to be little more than a large construction site. Still there – but only just, it seems – are a few historic buildings dating from 1879, the year the town was founded, namely the *Bunga* (old Parliament) and the Town Hall.

Between Umtata and East London, several side roads wind their way from the N2 down to the coast. Some of the small resorts they lead to – Cintsa, Cefane and Double Mouth among them – are frequented mainly by local farmers, while Haga-Haga and Morgan's Bay have grown into sizeable resorts with hotels and holiday homes. Their common factors are their small size and situation off the highways. The locals like it this way; it frees some of the pristine lagoons, sun-drenched beaches, and abundant birdlife and fishing resources for their personal enjoyment.

The only surfaced road that branches off this route leads to **Coffee Bay ❾** where another dream beach awaits. An 8-km (5-mile) walk south down the beach brings you to the giant rock formation known as **Hole in the Wall**. In Xhosa, this whaleback island with its huge wave- and river-bored tunnel is known as *esiKhaleni*, or "the place of sound" – for reasons obvious to anyone who stands on the pebbly beach and listens to the booming echo funnelling through the 20-metre (65-ft) hole. But visitors should be forewarned: the rock and the pounding seas that surround it are treacherous and many lives have been lost by the foolhardy.

Well-tended golf courses, hospitable people and some fine 19th-century architecture make **East London ❿** a particularly nice place to visit. Situated on the mouth of Buffalo River, it is the only river port in the country. The two

most popular bathing spots are Orient and Eastern beaches – both suitable for children – while Nahoon Beach is considered an excellent surfing spot. The harbour here has a miniature version of Cape Town's V&A Waterfront – Latimers Landing, complete with shops, restaurants, bars, theatres and even a weekend flea market.

Map, page 224

The whitewashed oriel windows and gables of the imposing City Hall – built in honour of Queen Victoria's diamond jubilee – contrast appealingly with its red-brick walls and bell-tower. Equally attractive, is the Edwardian **Anne Bryant Art Gallery** (open daily except Sun; entrance fee). Formerly a private residence, today it houses a collection of South African art from 1880 to the present.

One of the best natural history collections in South Africa is housed in the **East London Museum** (open daily; entrance fee) on the corner of Union and Lukin Streets. It's strong on the tribal histories of the Xhosa, but the real highlight is a stuffed and mounted specimen of the coelacanth, the world's first. Thought to be extinct for 80 million years, this amazing fish with fins like short, stumpy legs was netted in the nearby Chalumna River in 1938.

Gately House (open daily except Mon; entrance fee), built in 1878 for the mayor of the same name, is an interesting town house museum furnished with Victorian antiques. And down on the Esplanade, you can't avoid the monumental **German Settlers Memorial** – it's quite astonishingly ugly. It's supposed to commemorate the thousands of German-born settlers who settled here in the second half of the 19th century; several of the place names in this area (Hamburg, Potsdam, Berlin) make it clear how strong their influence was in the region.

BELOW: still and secretive mangrove swamps are a Wild Coast feature.

Map, page 224

A good excursion from East London is the six-day, 105-km (65-mile) long **Amatola Hiking Trail**, which begins 75 km (45 miles) north of the city in **Stutterheim** and leads through the wild Amatola Mountains. The Katberg escarpment is the highest point on this range, and in winter its peaks are often capped with snow. But it is **The Hogsback**  that makes the Amatola really memorable. Here, ferns and lichen cling to the trunks of ancient yellowwoods; brambles, wild berries and vines clamber over the forest flora. It was in these woods that the young J.R.R. Tolkien went exploring in his early boyhood. The landscape fired his imagination with the elfin kings, dwarf lords and dragons that were later to populate Middle Earth kingdom in his classic works, *The Hobbit* and *The Lord of the Rings*.

Immediately to the west of The Hogsback (about 25 km, or 15 miles) lies **Alice**, named after the daughter of Queen Victoria. On the outskirts of the town is the **University of Fort Hare**, established in 1916 as the country's first tertiary educational institution for blacks. Among its alumni are some of the country's most influential political and intellectual leaders, including Nelson Mandela. These days, of course, the university is open to all races, and attracts students from all over Africa.

Some 65 km (40 miles) along the R63 to the east of Alice lies **King William's Town** ("King", as it is known to residents). The centre of a thriving agricultural area, the town was founded by the London Missionary Society in 1825 and later became the capital of the colony of British Kaffraria. A stopover should include a visit to the **Kaffrarian Museum** (open daily; closed Sat pm and Sun am). Here, you can view displays devoted to the region's British and German settlers and the culture of the Xhosa and Khoisan people, but the most famous exhibit is undoubtedly Huberta the stuffed hippo. Huberta first captured the country's imagination in 1928, when she took off from Zululand on a 2,000-km (1,200-mile) journey southwards. On her way, she became the most fêted hippo in history, pursued by photographers, journalists and adoring crowds alike. She popped up in cities and towns, wandering through the busy streets of Durban and gatecrashing plush parties. Tragically, three years later, she was shot by hunters while taking a dip in the Keiskamma River, near King William's Town. Her remains were recovered and today take pride of place in the museum.

Back in Stutterheim, take the R61 – which branches off outside the town and leads back onto the N2 – for a rewarding detour into the **Witteberg Mountains**, whose eastern foothills nudge the Lesotho border. This is a popular winter sports region, known rather optimistically as "South Africa's Switzerland". European ski enthusiasts accustomed to long descents will find the South African ones rather shorter.

The range offers all sorts of other attractions, however. Steam train enthusiasts should not miss the ride along 64 km (39 miles) of track between **Barkly East** and **Lady Grey**, where the train ascends an astonishingly steep gradient in just eight loops. Many of the caves up in the mountains here are also bright with San paintings, some of which are thought to be up to 2,000 years old.

BELOW: traditional Xhosa dwellings.

The southern skies

South Africa stretches down from the tropics to about 35° south. Visitors from the northern hemisphere will find all the familiar constellations look upside down here; even the "Man in the Moon" seems to be standing on his head!

The most easily recognised constellation is Crucis, or the Southern Cross. Astronomers have determined that, thousands of years ago, this bright constellation was visible from most of Europe. Today, it is visible from just south of 30° north latitude. On a clear night, it is a simple matter to find south by using the Southern Cross and two stars called the Pointers, which are nearly always visible from anywhere in South Africa – bearing in mind that although the stars change their position during the night, the pattern always remains the same. In your imagination, draw a line in the sky linking the two stars on the main axis of the Cross, and another at right angles to the Pointers. The point where they intersect is directly above due south.

Take care to distinguish the Southern Cross from the "Diamond Cross" and the "False Cross", lying slightly to the northeast.

The Pointers are the two brightest stars in the constellation of the Plough. Alpha Centauri, the brighter of the two, is the fourth brightest star of all, and also – at 4.3 light years – the Sun's closest neighbour. Viewed with a small telescope, it resolves rather startlingly into two separate pinpoints of light; viewed with a larger telescope it reveals a third, fainter, companion.

Conveniently, the five brightest stars of the Southern Cross are arranged clockwise in order of apparent brightness: Alpha, Beta, Gamma, Delta and finally Epsilon.

The Cross is also a convenient reference point for the Milky Way's two satellite galaxies, the Large and Small Magellanic Clouds. Again, extend the long axis of the Cross by about seven times. On either side of this line, you'll see what resembles two small clouds, except that they do not move or change shape. At roughly 200,000 light years away, they are our galaxy's closest neighbours, linked to it not only gravitationally, but via a tenuous "bridge" of hydrogen gas.

The Large Magellanic Cloud (LMC) came into prominence in 1987 as a result of the massive explosion known as Supernova 1987a. A very bright object, known as S Doradus, is prominent in the LMC and is associated with a gaseous nebula known as the Tarantula Nebula, a remnant of a much earlier Supernova event.

Near to the Small Magellanic Cloud, you can spot a hazy white patch with the naked eye. With binoculars it is more prominent; a small telescope resolves it into thousands of stars. This is one of two great globular clusters, consisting of 100,000 stars or more, seen clearly only from the Southern Hemisphere. This one is called 47 Tucanae, and its fellow cluster is Omega Centauri.

The Astronomical Observatory at Sutherland in the Karoo is South Africa's best-known research facility.

RIGHT: to Northern visitors, all the familiar constellations look upside down.

DURBAN TO KIMBERLEY

*A route winding up from the KwaZulu-Natal Midlands
to an eagle's view of the Drakensberg – then down
to the rolling Free State highlands*

Map, pages 234–5

After all the hustle and bustle of Durban, the trip northwest on the N3 is rather a comedown at first – chiefly because it leads through Pinetown, the largest and most depressing slum in the province. In complete contrast is the scenery just beyond the satellite towns of Clermont, Hillcrest and New Germany. Here, a signposted turn-off at Kloof leads to the **Krantzkloof Nature Reserve** (tel: (031) 7643515) and the Inanda Dam. There are some lovely walking trails through this lush forested area, noted for its rare plant species such as cycads. The most spectacular trail brings you to a cliff edge with panoramic views of the Kloof Falls.

Travellers with plenty of time on their hands are advised to follow the old R613 road to Pietermaritzburg. A turn-off at Hillcrest will take you through the romantically named **Valley of a Thousand Hills** ❶, a deeply eroded valley cut through by the Umgeni River cuts on its way to the sea. According to Zulu legend, this was where God grabbed the world and scrunched it up in his hand, on the point of throwing it away. It's easy to believe this story when you look out over the landscape, stretching away towards the horizon like a vast piece of crumpled green velvet. It's known to the Zulus as *emKhabathini*, "the place of the giraffe thorn tree". After a 20-km (12-mile) drive through the valley, a turn-off to the Nagle Dam appears, 4 km (2 miles) before Cato Ridge. This road leads to the foot of KwaZulu-Natal's very own 1000-metre (3200-ft) high **Table Mountain**, standing sentinel at the head of the Valley of a Thousand Hills. It's definitely worth a climb to the summit; the view is quite breathtaking.

The journey picks up pace again as you rejoin the N3, and before long **Pietermaritzburg** ❷ comes into view. Quintessentially English with its white picket fences, precisely-manicured lawns, red-brick paths and trimmed azalea bushes, "Maritzburg" is considered one of the world's best-preserved Victorian cities. Visitors can follow a self-guided trail through the historic heart of the town, starting from the elaborately decorated **City Hall**, the largest all-brick building in the southern hemisphere, which was built in 1893 on the site of the old Voortrekker Parliament. Facing it, on the opposite side of Commercial Street, are two other important buildings: the Legislative Assembly and the old Supreme Court, with its striking portico. The latter now houses the **Tatham Art Gallery** (open Tues–Sun), with paintings by South African and European artists as well as an impressive collection of porcelain, ceramic and glass.

The **Voortrekker Museum** (open Mon–Fri, Sun pm) is situated in the **Church of the Vow**, a small, white-gabled building erected in 1841 to commemorate the Boer's victory over the Zulus at Blood River in 1838.

LEFT: spectacular view, Royal Natal National Park.
BELOW: Zulu *nyanga* (traditional healer).

Giant insects adorn a neo-classical frieze on the façade of Pietermaritzburg's Natal Museum.

It offers some interesting insights into frontier life in the mid-19th century. Next door is the restored home of the Voortrekker hero, Andries Pretorius. Not far away at 237 Loop Street, the **Natal Museum** (open Mon–Sat, Sun pm; entrance fee) has sections devoted to natural history, paleontology and ethnology, along with an excellent reconstruction of a Victorian street.

Another building of note is the Victorian **Railway Station**, which you'll find – unsurprisingly – on Railway Street. This was where the Indian lawyer Mohandas Gandhi (later known as Mahatma, the man who became world-famous for his policy of non-violence) was forcibly thrown off a train in 1893, simply because he had dared to take a seat in a whites-only carriage. The incident sparked Gandhi's desire to fight for human rights which he continued until his death in 1948. A statue to his memory, erected only in 1993, stands opposite the Old Colonial Building.

Boshoff Street leads out of town and across Queen Elizabeth Park, with its magnificent old trees and flowerbeds; it soon arrives at the Green Belt Trails, a network of hiking and horse-riding routes. We are now on the way to **Howick ❸** via the **Midlands Meander**, located between Hilton and **Mooi River ❹**. This is a scenic and very enjoyable driving route dotted with dozens of interesting sites including potteries, art studios, dairies, herb gardens and some of the finest guest-houses in KwaZulu-Natal. Details of all the sites along the route are available from local publicity offices or from the Midlands Meander Association (tel: (0332) 305305).

The **Albert Falls Public Nature Resort** (tel: (03393) 202) lies to the southeast of Howick, 24 km (15 miles) from Pietermaritzburg; its reservoir is very popular with hikers, anglers, yachting and canoeing enthusiasts alike. The

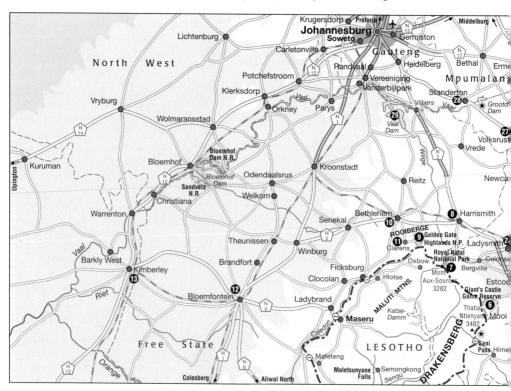

waterfall of the same name is impressive, but upstaged just 20 km (12 miles) away by the **Howick Falls**, which crash 110 metres (360 ft) down a vertical rock face.

Run by the Natal Parks Board, the **Midmar Public Resort and Nature Reserve** (tel: (0332) 302067) is 5 km (3 miles) west of the small town of Howick – which is really only of interest as a starting point for tours into the nearby KwaZulu-Natal Drakensberg. It's definitely worth spending one or two days in the Midmar area, however: there are excellent watersports facilities on the Midmar Dam, while tours can be made through the game reserve, stocked with antelope, rhino and zebra. Another highlight here is the **Midmar Historical Village** (open daily; entrance fee; tel: (0332) 305351) with its Zulu huts and reconstructions of traditional kraal scenes.

The Drakensberg Mountains

The Drakensberg's 1,000-km (620-mile) long mountain ridge – the second-highest in Africa, after the Kilimanjaro Massif in Tanzania – extends from Hoedspruit, west of the Kruger National Park, right down to the kingdom of Lesotho in the south (where it is known as the Malutis), interrupted by just one valley between Harrismith and Barberton. The range separates the coastal plains of KwaZulu-Natal from the highveld of the interior, and nowhere are its jagged cliffs more spectacular than along the border with Lesotho.

The central Drakensberg region can be approached from the N3 near **Estcourt ❺**, and after a 50-km (30-mile) drive you reach the main camp of our first mountain reserve. Originally established to provide sanctuary for the eland – the largest species of antelope – the **Giant's Castle Game Reserve ❻**

Map, pages 234–5

BELOW: rural life, KwaZulu-Natal.

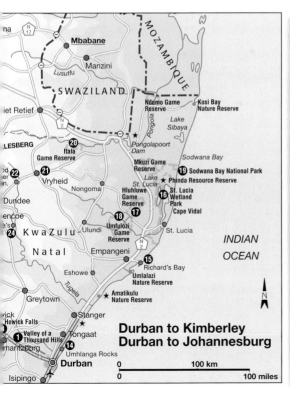

Durban to Kimberley
Durban to Johannesburg

The crested guineafowl is a common sight in the Royal Natal National Park.

(tel: (0331) 471981) is also considered the best place in the country to observe raptors such as the majestic Cape vulture, the lanner falcon, the snake eagle and endangered bearded vulture. Set in high country, dominated by the 3,377-metre (11,076-ft) high Champagne Castle and the Giant's Castle (3,315 metres/ 10,873 ft) mountains, this reserve is ideal for climbers. It also has an extensive network of hiking routes, the most demanding of which is the 40-km (24-mile) trail leading in a series of bends to the very top of Giant's Castle. Hikers may encounter numerous animals, including jackal, lynx and baboon. Keen anglers will already have heard about the enormous rainbow trout in Little Tugela and Bushman's River.

Hundreds of years ago, San communities lived in the basalt caves which pockmark the Drakensberg. More than 5,000 examples of their vivid rock paintings have been recorded; they can be seen at sites such as **Battle Cave** (daily guided tours leave at 9am; entrance fee; tel: (036) 4881050) near Injasuti, an 8-km (5-mile) walk away from the main camp at Giant's Castle Game Reserve.

The climate in the Drakensberg's resorts and hotels is generally mild all year round. However, as you climb, the temperature can drop sharply; visitors should be prepared for unexpected heavy snowfalls during the winter months (May to September). Sudden thunderstorms or blinding mists that rapidly envelop the mountains can also make hiking and climbing expeditions hazardous.

Cathedral Peak and its surrounding nature reserve (tel: (036) 4881880) lies at the centre of a series of free-standing peaks, all of which offer the experienced climber some interesting challenges. Others in the range include the Bell, the Inner and Outer Horn, the Monk's Cowl and the very demanding **Cathkin Peak**.

BELOW: the lush botanical gardens of Pietermaritzburg.

In the southern Drakensberg, the **Sani Pass** (another echo of those diminutive hunter-gatherers, the San) is the only route leading from the east to the independent state of Lesotho. Poor road conditions and treacherous hairpin bends make a four-wheel-drive vehicle essential.

Worth a visit in the northern Drakensberg are the **Royal Natal National Park** ❼ (tel: (0331) 471981) and the adjoining **Rugged Glen Nature Reserve** (tel: (036) 4381051). Situated about 60 km (37 miles) from **Harrismith** ❽ and the N3, this region's dramatic mountain landscape is dominated by the Amphitheatre, a 8-km (5-mile) crescent-shaped stretch of mountain escarpment providing magnificent views. This is where you'll find the country's highest peak, the 3,282-metre (10,760-ft) high **Mont-aux-Sources**. The "Mountain of Beginnings" is so named because five of the country's major river systems – the Orange, the Eland, the Western Khubedu and the Tugela – all have their sources here. A steep two-hour walk, with sturdy chain ladders to ease the ascent, brings you to the summit. For experienced, well-equipped mountaineers there are longer and more challenging routes available.

Within a few kilometres of its source, the Tugela plunges for almost 2 km (1 mile) in a dramatic series of cascades down to the valley floor below. The combined drop of the **Tugela Falls** (850 metres/2,790 ft) makes it the second highest waterfall in the world.

About 25 km (15 miles) to the west of Harrismith, via the N5 and R74, you come to another truly magnificent natural sight – the **Golden Gate Highlands National Park** ❾ (tel: (012) 343 1991). Over the centuries, wind, rain and sunshine have carved the sandstone cliffs here into bizarre formations; these glow golden at dusk, and give the area its unique appeal. Located on the border of the

**Map,
pages
234–5**

BELOW: The Amphitheatre, Royal Natal National Park.

Kimberley's Big Hole, once the world's richest diamond mine.

Free State and Lesotho, the park is named after its "gate" entrance, composed of two massive sections of sandstone. Hikers are in their element here, as are riders: the small Basotho ponies from neighbouring Lesotho have no problems negotiating the terrain.

Heading west from Harrismith on the N5, there are two places worth stopping at en route to Bloemfontein. Pretty **Bethlehem** ⑩, full of distinctive Voortrekker sandstone cottages, was founded in 1864 beside the Jordan River. Today, you'll find restaurants and all the usual tourist amenities here, but they rather jar with the simple architecture. A 30-km (19-mile) diversion south on the R711 brings you to another attractive settlement: **Clarens** ⑪, a village near the western edge of the Golden Gate Highlands National Park, which has become a renowned artists' colony. It's named after the village where Paul Kruger lived after emigrating to Switzerland, and where he died in 1904.

Our route now continues west on the N5 via Senekal and Winburg to **Bloemfontein** ⑫, the capital of the Free State. It dates back to 1840 when a solitary Voortrekker, Johannes Nicolaas Brits, settled in his new *hartbeeshuisie* (a Voortrekker dwelling with thatched roof and dung floor) near a spring surrounded by clover. As others followed his example and the place grew into a settlement, it became known as Bloemfontein, the "spring of flowers".

The town briefly served as capital of the Old Republic of the Free State before it was occupied by the British forces of Lord Roberts during the Anglo-Boer War (1899–1902). The occupation was a mixed blessing. The descendants of the Voortrekkers, who had braved the dangers of the wild unknown to escape the British Empire, had nothing but contempt for the Union Jack hoisted over their town. But British occupancy protected the town from the ravages

of war, ensuring that its architectural heritage remained well preserved – as it is to this day.

A stroll down President Brand Street proves the point; it's widely regarded as one of South Africa's most beautiful streets. Most of Bloemfontein's historic buildings are open to the public. They include the **Old Presidency** (open Tues–Fri, Sat & Sun pm), the **Fourth Raadsaal** (by appointment only; tel: (051) 478898) and the city's oldest building, the **First Raadsaal** (open Mon–Fri, Sat & Sun pm; entrance fee). More contemporary places of interest include the **Sand du Plessis Theatre**, which sparked a major controversy between those locals who favoured modern development and those who argued that its design would detract from the city centre's old-world charm.

The British side of Bloemfontein's character often surprises visitors – this is, after all, the capital of a province widely regarded as an Afrikaner heartland. Yet the city has a substantial English-speaking community, with roots dating back to colonial and earlier times. A number of historical sites – such as Naval Hill and **Queen's Fort** (open Mon–Fri), as well as the Ramblers cricket ground with its clubhouse dating back almost a century – preserve this heritage.

Bloemfontein also holds a very significant place in black South African history. This was the birthplace in 1912 of the South African Native Congress – known as the African National Congress (ANC) since 1923.

Diamond country

About 150 km (90 miles) west of Bloemfontein via the N8 is **Kimberley** ⓭ ("the town that sparkles"), approached along a long, almost dead straight road bordered by vast sunflower fields. It is well past its prime today; when

Map, pages 234–5

BELOW: the former De Beers head-quarters, Kimberley.

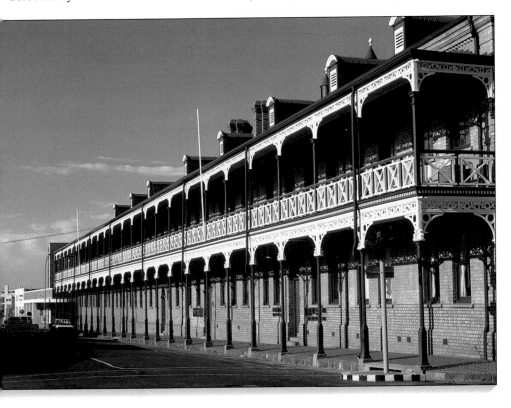

Map,
pages
234–5

you reflect that around 1870 this was a thriving city of bars, bordellos and warehouses inhabited by some 50,000 diamond prospectors, its small-town provincialism is astonishing. Nothing remains of those heady days of diamond mining, as prospecting stopped here as long ago as the 1930s. To get an idea of Kimberley's heyday, visit the excellent open-air **Mine Museum** (open daily, entrance fee), where you can see a collection of 40 original buildings such as Barney Barnato's Boxing Academy, the diggers' tavern, and the custom-built De Beers directors' private railway coach. In De Beers Hall, there is an exquisite collection of uncut diamonds, including the largest in the world (616 carats) and the "Eureka" (discovered in 1866, the first in South Africa).

All the stones in the museum come from the former mine nearby known as **The Big Hole**. Today it's filled with water and the towers are derelict, but between 1871 and 1914, 2,722 kilos (1,237 lbs) of diamonds were excavated from this giant gash in the earth – some 800 metres (2,600 ft) deep and 470 metres (1,500 ft) wide.

On the eastern edge of town is the wealthy suburb of Belgravia, where the diamond barons built their grand houses. Several of these villas are open to the public, furnished just as they were in their heyday. Two of the best examples are **Dunluce** and **Rudd House** (open by arrangement, tel: (0531) 32645).

The **William Humphreys Art Gallery** (open daily, Sun pm) contains one of South Africa's finest collections of 16th- and 17th-century Flemish and Dutch Old Masters. Perhaps the most fascinating record of the city's diamond mining days is in the **Duggan-Cronin Gallery** (open daily, Sun pm). It contains a collection of 8,000 photographs of the mines and the mine labourers, taken between 1919–1939 by Irish mine manager, Alfred Martin Duggan-Cronin.

BELOW: harnessing the wind.

Dorps

The paintbrushes of history have coloured the South African landscape with a rich diversity of villages and hamlets – or "dorps", as the locals call them, from the Afrikaans word for "little town".

Tranquil and traditionally-minded, often poor and distinctly down-at-heel, most dorps are just pinpoints on the map – yet they can be well worth the effort it takes to track them down. There's a timeless quality to these dusty verandahs and sun-baked stone cottages set back in wide main streets, where the rhythms of life are seductively slow and measured. Here, locals greet each other by name; such things as direct telephone-dialling and video shops (to say nothing of racial integration) are but a recent fad, and everything – even the corner café – closes for lunch.

Take the time to delve behind the sleepy façade and you'll find most dorps steeped in romance and folklore, still proudly bearing testament to the colourful cast of characters – outlaws, fortune-seekers, missionaries and pioneers – who helped to shape the country over the last hundred years.

Bathurst in the Eastern Cape has a particularly fine collection of classic old buildings, built by British settlers in the 1820s. Here, the Pig & Whistle – the country's oldest pub – still resounds with bawdy laughter. Lazy creepers climb the walls of the old stone churches which sheltered settler women and children when the town became the focus of a series of bloody frontier wars with the Xhosa.

One of the strangest places anywhere in South Africa is Die Hel ("The Hell"), an isolated hamlet in the remote Karoo valley of Gamkaskloof. First settled by farmers during the Great Trek of 1837, residents contrived to avoid contact with the outside world for more than 50 years. It was only when Boer War guerillas fleeing the British stumbled across the valley that they were discovered – some 20 families, speaking an archaic form of High Dutch, clad in goat skins and only vaguely aware that there was a war on. It took until 1963, 126 years after the settlement was established, for a road connecting the valley to the outside world to be built (until then, all provisions were brought in by pack donkey over a mountain track).

The Northern Province settlement of Nylstroom ("Nile Stream") was named by a break-away sect of Voortrekkers on a mad mission to reach the Holy Land. Having driven their wagons all the way from the Cape, the day came when the doughty trekkers saw up ahead what they thought was a pyramid (actually, a solitary hill) and assumed they were in Egypt – and that the large, flooding river before them was the Nile.

Like so many dorps in the far north of the country, Leydsdorp began life as a mining camp at the turn of the century, part of a colourful "wild west" culture where the local stagecoaches travelling on to Pietersburg were pulled by zebra. Today, in the local cemetery, gravestones bear silent witness to the deadly plague of malaria and blackwater fever which brought the thriving little settlement to its knees in 1924 – and condemned it to the status of a dorp forever.

RIGHT: time moves slowly on these dusty, sun-baked streets.

DURBAN TO JOHANNESBURG

*From St Lucia's lush waterworld to the historic
KwaZulu-Natal battlefields, the road to Gauteng
leads through the heart of Shaka Country*

Like the road south of Durban, the coast to the north of the city is studded with seaside resorts – built, for the most part, on the estuaries of small rivers flowing into the Indian Ocean. Despite their popularity with holidaymakers, it's still possible to find wide, unspoilt beaches here, along with sheltered coves surrounded by tropical palms, bougainvillea and hibiscus. A good way to explore the coastline is to follow R627 northwards from Durban. Alternatively, take the N2 highway and make detours to the various resort towns along the way.

The Dolphin Coast

The 140 km (87 miles) of coast between **Umhlanga Rocks** ⑭ and **Richard's Bay** ⑮ is known as the **Dolphin Coast**: bottle-nosed dolphins are so plentiful that they can usually be spotted from the beaches without much trouble. The **Natal Sharks Board** (phone for demonstration times; entrance fee; tel: (031) 5611001), located on a hill above Umhlanga Rocks, gives fascinating demonstrations on sharks (especially man-eaters such as Great White and tiger sharks) and their importance in the ecological chain, in an effort to remove some of the prejudices felt against these extraordinary creatures. Umhlanga Rocks itself is also worthy of note: an attractive town centre, magnificent beaches and great watersports facilities are all very conducive to a long stay. The Zulu trails running along the coast make for excellent hiking.

More remote sections of coast can easily be reached and explored by car. Plenty of small side-roads branch off the N2, leading to romantic little resorts like Tongaat, Ballito, Salt Rock and Sheffield Beach. The idyll is only briefly interrupted by the industrial town of Stanger, now a sugar cane processing centre but once Shaka's old capital. The **Shaka Monument** on Couper Street commemorates the Zulu king's death – on 22 September 1828, he was murdered here by his half-brothers and arch rivals, Umhlangana and Dingane.

Beyond Stanger the N2 continues to hug the coast, but the picturesque scenery (such as that at Blythdale Beach and Zinkwazi Beach) gradually disappears, apart from **Tugela Mouth** (as the name suggests, a resort on the mouth of the Tugela River) and the **Amatikulu Nature Reserve** (tel: (0331) 946696). The latter, a 2,000-hectare (5,000-acre) area of forested dunes overlooking the sea, contains abundant birdlife as well as giraffe and zebra. If you'd like to explore on foot, the reserve is criss-crossed by a dense network of hiking routes.

North from here the coastal vegetation becomes much more impenetrable. From Gingindlovu the R68 leads off to Vryheid, where the **Battlefield Route**

BELOW: the white rhino – also known as the "square-lipped rhino".

Map,
pages
234–5

begins. We continue along the N2, however, first to Empangeni and then 20 km (12 miles) further to the turn-off for Richard's Bay (pop. 35,000). Lying on the mouth of the Mhlatuze River, this busy port shifts vast quantities of coal, mined in the former gold mines around Witbank and transported here on a seemingly endless series of trains. Away from the grime and grit of heavy industry, nature lovers can explore the **Umlalazi Nature Reserve** (tel: (0353) 401836) which lies about 50 km (31 miles) south of Richard's Bay. It boasts a good selection of walking trails along the banks of a lagoon, across dunes and through a mangrove swamp. It's also possible to explore by canoe. Umlalazi is a breeding ground for several rare species of bird, but be aware of the wild bush-pigs that also live here – they may look sweet but they can get somewhat aggressive.

Parks and game reserves

The route continues via Matubatuba and the R618 to the **Greater St Lucia Wetland Park & Game Reserve ⓰** (tel: (035) 590 1340). This 85-km (52-mile) wide park between the coast and the N2 was founded in 1897, making it one of South Africa's oldest wildlife reserves. Hotels, bungalows and first-class restaurants are all guaranteed to make any stay here a pleasant one.

The heart of the park is extraordinary **Lake St Lucia**, 60 km (37 miles) long, up to 10 km (6 miles) wide and with a maximum depth of just 1.5 metres (5 ft). Fed by the Hluhluwe, Mkuzi and Umfolozi rivers, it lies at the centre of one of the largest and most important wetland areas in Africa. While the lake is home to hippos and crocodiles, the deltas are breeding grounds for rare loggerhead and giant leatherback turtles. An incredible 500 species of bird breed here, too, including pink-backed pelicans, flamingos, spoonbills, fish-eagles and Caspian

Below: hippo in Lake St Lucia.

terns. Comprising more than half the estuarine habitat in South Africa, St Lucia is very important to fish life, and a great variety of freshwater, estuarine and marine species occur here. Anyone taking a boat out on the lake should keep a sharp eye out for hippos; these huge beasts have fixed underwater routes and can become extremely aggressive if their progress is disturbed in any way. One of the best and safest ways to spot hippo is to join a guided tour of the estuary aboard an 80-seater launch.

Hikers have a superb network of routes at their disposal here, right across the park on the promontory between the lake and the Indian Ocean. This forested sand-dune landscape is most impressive (some of the dunes are as much as 150 metres/492 ft high – among the highest in the world). Divers shouldn't miss the coral reefs and the myriads of colourful fish in the **St Lucia Marine Reserve** – a truly unforgettable experience. Away from the reserve, the coast is also very popular with anglers.

The Natal Parks Board operates 10 overnight camps at St Lucia. There are hutted camps at Charter's Creek, Fanies Island, Mapelane and Cape Vidal; three campgrounds at St Lucia Estuary; and campgrounds at Cape Vidal, False Bay, Fanies Island and Mapelane. There is also accommodation in St Lucia's village, which is a base for the St Lucia area.

Just to the north of St Lucia lies another important conservation area – the **Hluhluwe-Umfolozi Game Reserve** (tel: (0331) 471981). Run by the Natal Parks Board, **Hluhluwe ⑰** and **Umfolozi ⑱** were originally separate entities, but they are now administered as one area, joined by a link road (the R618) that passes through the central section of the park and leads northwards as far as Mtubatuba. The animals seem to have become quite accustomed to this

This Nile crocodile is one of an estimated 1,500 which inhabit Lake St Lucia; needless to say, swimming in the lake is forbidden.

BELOW: flamingo, Lake St Lucia.

arrangement, and happily cross the asphalt all the time. Wildlife includes giraffe, warthog, hyena, antelope, zebra, wildebeest, crocodile and hippo, plus 432 species of birds. Hluhluwe is best known for the success it achieved in saving the white (or wide-lipped) rhino from extinction. By the early 1930s, only about 150 white rhinos were left in southern Africa, having been shot almost to extinction. A breeding programme here has succeeded in raising the population to more than 1,000, while a further 3,000 of these magnificent animals have been exported to parks around the world. Today, there is a similar battle taking place to save its cousin, the black rhino – distinguishable only by its narrow upper lip. It took 12 years to erect the 2.8 metre (9-ft) high game-proof fence around the park, a task completed in 1979. It includes old mine cable – the only fencing strong enough to contain rhino.

The Umfolozi Game Reserve Wilderness Trail was established in 1957 (the first of its kind in South Africa) and it is one of the finest ways of exploring the region on foot. Accompanied by experienced rangers who act as guides, the trips can last between three and five days. To minimise the ecological impact of visitors to this unspoilt area, numbers are strictly controlled. Booking ahead is essential, particularly during the busy holiday periods.

Another good place for big-game spotting is the private **Phinda Resource Reserve** (tel: (035) 5620271), owned by the CCA (Conservation Corporation Africa) and supported by a number of wealthy trusts. Small, exclusive and very pricey, you won't find noisy safari vehicles racing around here; there's no mass tourism and no beaten tracks. Nature is still very much intact, and animals have retained their shyness. Lions, cheetah, leopard and elephant abound on the 17,000-hectare (42,000-acre) reserve.

Map, pages 234–5

BELOW: waterbuck, Umfolozi River.

TIP

On the four-day Kosi Bay Hiking Trail, visitors can cross the Sihadla River on a raffia-palm pont and explore palm and swamp forests.

Elephant, rhino and leopard are among the game that can be spotted in the **Mkuzi Game Reserve** (tel: (035) 5730004), which borders the St Lucia Wetland Park to the east. Covering an area of 36,000 hectares (89,000 acres) and run by the Natal Parks Board, this reserve is famed for its aquatic and tropical birdlife: ibises, storks and cormorants are often spotted here, plus rarer species such as Neergard's sunbird and the African broadbill. Because the bush vegetation is so thick, the best place to spot game is from one of the viewing hides dotted across the reserve. These hides overlook watering-holes and are easily accessed by road. A three-night wilderness trail is a good option if you wish to explore on foot. Another of Mkuzi's rare natural attractions is its fig tree forest, which lies beside Nsumo Pan near the eastern edge of the reserve. A 3-km (2-mile) trail leads through the forest, where the trees grow up to 25 metres (82 ft) high.

The route now leads back to the coast and to Lake Sibaya, South Africa's largest freshwater lake at 77 sq. km (30 sq. miles). It's located in the **Sodwana Bay National Park** ⑲ (tel: (035682) 1502), an area of swamp and dense jungle, where the fig and milkwood trees can grow as high as 40 metres (130 ft). While divers head for the stunning coral reefs which lie just off the coast (one of the most renowned dive sites in the country), bird-watchers focus on the lake. Beware of snakes in this park, by the way, and make sure you bring mosquito nets and repellent for the nights. It's extremely important to begin a course of anti-malaria tablets before visiting the area, too.

About 70 km (50 miles) further north, the road brings you to two of the wildest, most remote parks in the region – **Kosi Bay Nature Reserve** and **Ndumu Game Reserve** (tel: (0331) 946696 for both reserves). Bordering on Mozambique in the north and the Indian Ocean in the east, Kosi Bay consists

BELOW: monument to the Battle of Blood River, near Dundee.

of a network of lakes which are home to hippos, crocodiles and an extraordinary variety of aquatic birds, including black egret, fish-eagles, jacanas and the
rare fishing owl. Three thatched lodges house just two, five and six visitors
respectively. While the camp area is accessible to all vehicles, sandy terrain
makes a four-wheel-drive vehicle essential to reach The Mouth, 5 km (3 miles)
from the campsite. A permit is required to explore the reserve on foot or by vehicle, and this can be obtained from the KwaZulu Bureau of Natural Resources.

Ndumu, lying just south of the Mozambique border on the Pongola River
floodplain, was established in 1924 and contains a similar range of wildlife.
Though relatively small, this 10,000-hectare (25,000-acre) reserve is one of the
lushest and most beautiful in the region, and the floodplain offers superb bird-
watching opportunities, especially for large flocks of flamingos and storks. Black
rhino and white rhino are seen, as well as giraffe. The rest camp has seven fully
equipped, three-bedded huts, with a communal ablution block.

The route now leads southwards through the Lebombo Mountains along the
border with Swaziland, following the Pongola River, which feeds a reservoir at
Pongolapoort Dam. From here it is just 50 km (30 miles) to the **Itala Game
Reserve ⓴** (tel: (0338) 65105), perhaps the finest in KwaZulu-Natal. The
scenery in this 30,000-hectare (75,000-acre) reserve is truly breathtaking: dramatic granite cliffs, rolling hills, open savannah, dense forests and romantic
rivers, which all blend together to form a fabulous game-viewing environment.
Before the reserve was established in 1972, the whole area had become seriously overgrazed. Since then, the Natal Parks Board has reintroduced many
indigenous wildlife species, including elephant, white and black rhino, giraffe,
leopard, cheetah and eland. A wide range of accommodation is available, from

**Map,
pages
234–5**

BELOW: the rolling
mountains which
border Swaziland
make splendid
riding country.

luxury lodges and fully equipped self-catering chalets, to simple rondavels and bushcamps. There's also a small campsite located beside the Thalu River.

The battlefields

Vryheid ㉑, 100 km (60 miles) southwest of the Itala Game Reserve, is chiefly remarkable for its tragic history. Set on the Northern Natal Battlefields Route, it lies squarely in the middle of an area where bitter battles were fought first between the British and the Zulus (1879), followed soon afterwards by the Anglo-Boer conflicts of 1880 and 1881. Vryheid was also the capital of the short-lived Boer New Republic (1884–1888), a small piece of land granted to a band of 500 Afrikaner Voortrekkers by the Zulu king, Dinizulu. You can learn more about this period at the old Randsaal, formerly the parliament building, now the **The New Republic Museum** (open Mon–Fri; entrance fee).

The road which leads from Vryheid towards the coal-mining town of Dundee crosses **Blood River** ㉒, and 27 km (16 miles) before actually reaching Dundee a left-hand turn leads 20 km (12 miles) to the **Blood River Monument** (open daily; entrance fee) – a rather crude full-scale replica of 64 Voortrekker wagons made from bronze. It was here that in 1838 a troop of 468 Boers, armed with rifles and cannons, defeated a 10,000-strong Zulu army. The Zulu short spear proved no match for such firepower and more than 3,000 warriors were killed, many of them shot while fleeing across the Ncome River.

The **Talana Museum** (open daily; entrance fee; tel: (0341) 22677), built on the site of the first major battle of the Boer War (20 October 1899) on the northern outskirts of **Dundee** ㉓, has an interesting exhibition charting the various skirmishes that took place around here. The area's industrial heritage

A small memorial on the banks of the Jojosi River marks the spot where Napoleon III's son, the Prince Imperial, died under a hail of Zulu spears in 1879.

BELOW: Inkatha Freedom Party members on the march, KwaZulu-Natal.

THE BATTLE OF RORKE'S DRIFT

When the Centre Column of the British army crossed the Buffalo River into Zululand, troops under Lieutenant John Chard of the Royal Engineers were left to guard the post at Rorke's Drift, a tiny Swedish mission church, storehouse and hospital. On 22 January 1879, news of the disastrous defeat of the 24th Regiment at Isandlwana reached the garrison. Even more alarming was the report that a large Zulu force was approaching at speed. Lieutenant Chard gave orders that Rorke's Drift would stand and defend itself, and arranged for a defensive perimeter of mealie bags, biscuit tins and wagons to be constructed. Only 139 men were stationed there on 23 January (of whom 35 were sick) when, soon after 4pm, a force of some 4,000 Zulu warriors appeared. One furious charge after another was launched, often resulting in hand to hand combat against the barricades, in an attack which continued until dawn. The Zulu forces were supremely confident – yet incredibly, Rorke's Drift proved unassailable, the British defending their position with immense bravery. That terrible late afternoon and night left 17 British dead, while Zulu losses were estimated at a minimum of 500. Eleven Victoria Crosses were awarded to the defenders. Today, a memorial and small museum mark the site.

(mainly coal-mining and glass-making) is also documented. Military history fans can find out more about 50 km (30 miles) further south in the coal-mining town of **Rorke's Drift** ㉔ (*see box, page 248*).

Our route continues on past meadows and fields towards **Ladysmith** ㉕, a pretty place which has preserved many of its 19th-century buildings. Originally established by the Voortrekkers in 1847, Ladysmith soon came under British control. Fifty years later, in October 1899, the British were besieged here by Boer forces. Shelled and starved almost to the brink of defeat, the inhabitants of Ladysmith were finally relieved by a large army of British troops after 118 days. The **Siege Museum** (open Mon–Fri, Sat am; entrance fee) documents life during the Boer War and displays artefacts dating from the siege. Nearby battle sites such as Lombard's Kop, Wagon Hill and Caesar's Camp can all be reached along signposted trails. Ladysmith is also a very good starting point for trips into the Drakensberg.

Eighty kilometres (49 miles) further north on the N11 is **Newcastle** ㉖, a major producer of coal and steel. It was founded in 1864, and its chimneys and smoke are a reminder that Gauteng, the industrial centre of South Africa, is not far away. A welcome scenic diversion lies 16 km (10 miles) to the west of Newcastle on the Mullers Pass road: the **Ncandu River waterfall** is set amidst good hiking territory in a fold of mountains.

Another major battlefield site on our route lies 43 km (27 miles) north of Newcastle on the N11 towards Volksrust. **Majuba** was the site of a humiliating defeat for the British by the Boers in 1881. Two hundred and eighty-five British troops died in the battle, compared to just two Boers. Today, Majuba Hill, the high ground which was of such strategic importance during the fighting, offers superb views over the surrounding countryside.

In **Volksrust** ㉗, a road branches off the N11 and leads through more former battlefields to **Piet Retief**, an unremarkable medium-sized town named after a leader of the Great Trek whom Dingane had murdered. Back on the main route, the industrial town of **Standerton** ㉘ and the adjacent Grootdraai Dam soon come into view. The area around the reservoir has several pleasant hiking possibilities, and is a good place to relax before arriving in Johannesburg via Heidelberg.

Another fine place for outdoor activities – particularly watersports – is the **Vaal Dam** ㉙, along with the banks of the Vaal River between Vereeniging and Vanderbijlpark. The Vaal is the natural border between Free State and Gauteng, and springs from a confluence of small streams and rivulets on the plains of Swaziland. Apart from supplying water to the Witwatersrand, the industrial pulse of South Africa, this vast expanse of water caters to the recreational needs of the millions of people who live and work on the Witwatersrand.

Vanderbijlpark is the main resort area, housing weekend retreats, exclusive yacht clubs and other playgrounds, resorts, campsites, picnic and angling spots. During weekends, yachts, power boats, water-skiiers and sailboards occupy the water, while a riot of colourful bikinis, umbrellas and picnic blankets covers its banks, but the water also draws those seeking tranquil spots far from the madding crowd.

Map, pages 234–5

BELOW: the Vaal Dam is a haven for sailors.

JOHANNESBURG

*This industrial powerhouse contains some of
the country's best museums and galleries –
and a surprising number of parks*

Map,
page 252

E *'Goli*, it is called by the locals – the City of Gold. Johannesburg is the pulsating heart of South Africa's industrial and commercial life, where more than a mile below bustling city traffic, miners dig for the world's most precious metal. At street level, stockbrokers and company directors rub shoulders with street vendors and traditional healers. Ultra-modern corporate towers dwarf noisy pavement stalls. It's the capital of Gauteng province, but many Jo'burgers also see their city as the unofficial capital of South Africa, and fervently defend it as such against the more obvious charms of places like the *visdorpie*, that sleepy fishing-village, Cape Town.

Ever since a fateful day in 1886 when George Harrison, a humble prospector, stumbled upon an outcrop of gold-bearing rock, the region's economy and life have been driven by the pulsating rhythm of the mining industry. The effects are inescapable. Stand on the top floor of the Carlton Centre, the city's highest building, and you see tawny mine-dumps and shaftheadgears dotting the skyline. Walk the streets of downtown Johannesburg, and you find road and building names vividly evoking the gold rush days. Harrison's discovery sparked a gold fever never experienced before or since, anywhere in the world. Prospectors and fortune seekers descended on the area in search of instant wealth. Makeshift shelters and tents mushroomed all over the tranquil veld. A sprawl-

LEFT: *e'Goli*, City of
Gold.
BELOW: Gauteng
street style is the
country's slickest.

ing, rough and raucous shanty town sprang up almost overnight. Within three years, Johannesburg was the largest town in South Africa. A rudimentary stock exchange was established. Men outnumbered women three to one. Hotels and canteens, brothels and music halls were erected throughout the town to satisfy the needs of this boisterous new community.

But it wasn't long before fledgling mining corporations moved in to take control of the industry and swallow up individual claims. "Randlords" like Cecil John Rhodes, Barney Barnato and Alfred Beit quickly accumulated huge fortunes, imposing a semblance of order on the unruly mining town in their wake.

Today, Johannesburg forms the hub of a sprawling metropolis called the Witwatersrand ("Ridge of White Waters"), stretching more than 120 km (75 miles) from Springs in the east to Randfontein in the west, with a rapidly-growing population of almost 5 million. The Witwatersrand is the core of Gauteng, and the place where all the country's major industries are based – making this the undisputed powerhouse of sub-Saharan Africa, if not the entire continent.

City of contrasts

By world standards, Johannesburg is a medium-sized city, but in the African context it is a giant, offering some of the continent's best night-life, hotels and

Johannesburg's famous Market Theatre complex is housed in an old produce market.

shopping opportunities. Yet nowhere are the contrasts that typify the place so forcefully experienced as in the busy downtown area. Just eight blocks west along Commissioner Street from the smart **Carlton Centre Mall** you'll find the traditional charms of **Diagonal Street**. Here, dimly lit "herbalists" such as the **KwaZulu Muti Shop** ❸ sell skins, dried plants and the magic bones thrown by *sangomas* (traditional healers) during divination, alongside tiny stores crammed with household goods and cheap African "art" with a kitsch appeal.

Where the road meets Kort Street lies one of Johannesburg's best-loved Indian restaurants, **Kapitan's Café**. In the early 1960s, this was a favourite haunt of young attorneys Nelson Mandela and Oliver Tambo; it's still serving up some of the finest curries this side of Asia (open lunchtimes only). Just a few blocks further north, on the corner of Pritchard Street – dwarfing the entire street in its shadow – is the ultra-modern, blue-glass **Johannesburg Stock Exchange** ❸ (guided tours Mon, Fri 11am; Tues–Thurs 11am, 2pm; closed pub hols).

Three blocks further west along Jeppe Street you reach one of the city's chief cultural centres, the enormous **Newtown Precinct** ❹. Here, a conglomeration

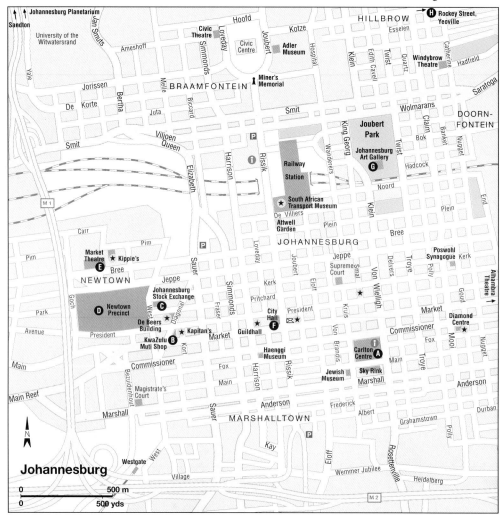

of warehouses stretching across several blocks has been converted into venues for experimental theatre, live music performances, exhibitions and workshop courses for students. It also contains an entire complex of museums.

Map, page 252

Next door to the Precinct is the renowned **Market Theatre** ➒, the home of protest theatre in the 1970s and 1980s and a cornerstone of the intellectual revolution against apartheid. Today, it is an arts complex in its own right, housing art and photographic galleries, a jazz venue and a restaurant.

The **Oriental Plaza** lies a few blocks further west from Newtown Precinct, sandwiched in between Bree Street and Central Avenue. Here, shoppers can bargain for the best prices on everything from silks and spices to herbs and haberdashery, or simply settle down to a leisurely curry. Heading back towards the Carlton Centre, the elegant **City Hall** ➐ on Rissik Street offers a rare glimpse of how this area must once have looked, before the office blocks and concrete flyovers sprang up.

As in any big city, don't carry cameras on your person or wear expensive jewellery; in addition, keep your car doors locked at all times. Regrettably, violent crime is now such a problem in downtown Johannesburg that many local businesses are moving out to the safer northern suburbs of Rosebank and Sandton; it is definitely not advisable to wander about here alone after dark.

Shopping: markets and malls

Johannesburg's flea markets attract a large informal sector of traders from as far afield as Nigeria, Zaire and the Ivory Coast, so pickings are rich as far as tribal crafts are concerned. In the downtown area, **Newtown Africa Market** (open Sat) in Mary Fitzgerald Square, opposite the Market Theatre, is home to

BELOW: commercial heartland.

The mine-dumps, such a common feature of Jo'burg's cityscape, are fast disappearing – they're being reworked to recover the last traces of gold.

the city's original – and most bohemian – "flea". It has around 350 stalls, selling everything from street fashion to arty tat, as well as curios. Producing work on site for some of Johannesburg's most original artisans is the **Mai Mai Market** (open Mon–Fri), popular with migrant workers looking for fancy keepsakes (wooden chests inlaid with illustrated panels; hand-made stools) to take back home after completing their stint on the mines. It's tucked away at the bottom of Anderson Street, and well worth the trouble it takes to find.

A 10-minute drive from the city centre northeast on the airport road brings you to the district of Bruma and **Flea Market World** (daily; small entrance fee), situated on the corner of Ernest Oppenheimer and Marcia Streets, There are more than 600 stalls here and the quality of crafts is generally good, particularly the carved wooden masks and sticks, and the printed fabric. Free entertainment is laid on, too, from buskers to Zulu dancers. On Thursdays and Saturdays, there are activities such as face-painting and bouncy castles for children.

The **Rosebank Mall Rooftop Market** (open Sun and public holidays) lies half-an-hour's drive from the city centre in the smart northern suburb of Rosebank, on the top floor of the mall's parking lot. Bargain hunters will find patience is rewarded here; there are over 500 stalls, including several selling high-quality antique fetishes, spears and carvings. Haggling is expected.

Golden City culture

If you're interested in African art, Johannesburg's commercial galleries are the best in the country. Unfortunately, this doesn't yet hold true for the permanent collections on display at the **Johannesburg Art Gallery ⑥** (open Tues–Sun; free) in downtown Joubert Park. During the apartheid era, the acquisitions

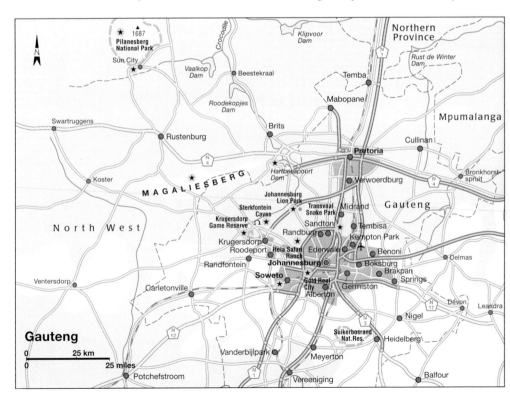

policy virtually ignored black talent. Today, however, all that is changing. Works by South African sculptors add shape and colour to the gallery gardens, while the temporary exhibitions provide a showcase for up-and-coming local artists.

There's an extensive collection of tribal art at the **Gertrude Posel Gallery** (open Mon–Sat by appointment only; closed public holidays; free) in Senate House at the University of the Witwatersrand, a 10-minute drive west of the city centre. Here, you'll see valuable examples of vanishing art forms such as masks, head-dresses, drums and beadwork. The **Everard Read Gallery** (open Mon–Sat; closed public holidays; free) in Rosebank is the best commercial gallery in Johannesburg, covering a variety of work from abstract landscapes to wildlife paintings and tribal art.

The innovative displays at **Museum Africa** (open Tues–Sun; entrance fee; Sun free) in Newtown Precinct depict scenes from Johannesburg's brief but turbulent 100-year history. You may find, for example, a cluster of squatter shacks brought from Alexandra township and painstakingly reconstructed; or displays focusing on the Rivonia Treason Trial, which sentenced Nelson Mandela to life imprisonment on Robben Island; or even a fearsome assortment of home-made weapons confiscated from a miners' hostel.

In the same building are the **Geological Museum**, displaying some of the country's unique mineral wealth; the **Photographic Library and Museum**, and the fascinating **South African Rock Art Museum**, giving an idea of the wide scope of styles and subjects which influenced the San rock artists. Guided tours and lectures are available at all these venues.

Steam train enthusiasts will enjoy the **South African Transport Museum**, on the old concourse of the main railway station in downtown De Villiers Street,

Map, page 252

BELOW: dancers at Bruma Flea Market World.

A contender in one of the weekly "Best-Dressed Man" competitions, a regular feature of township life in Gauteng.

BELOW: model of a police Casspir, relic of the bad old days in Soweto.

which houses the best collection of vintage steam engines in the country, as well as ox wagons and vintage motor cars (open Mon–Fri; 7.30am–3.45pm; free).

Located in the grounds of the **University of the Witwatersrand**, the **Johannesburg Planetarium** is a good place to view the southern skies from a fresh angle. Here, audio-visual shows and multi-media displays take visitors on an astrological journey to distant galaxies (shows Fri, Sat, Sun; entrance fee). At the **South African National Museum of Military History** (open daily; entrance fee) near the zoo in the Herman Eckstein Park in Saxonwold, 12 aircraft and a military submarine vie for your attention with armoured flight vehicles, artillery, small arms and uniforms.

On the wild side

Although nearly all of the city centre is filled with high-rise buildings and space is at a premium, first impressions are deceptive: the city council administers more than 600 parks and open spaces, most of which are dotted around the suburbs.

Visitors can also explore Greater Johannesburg's remaining streams and ridges on a number of self-guided walking trails. Detailed trail brochures, marking sites of historical, archaeological and ecological interest, are available from the Johannesburg Metropolitan Tourism Association. Many city parks are linked by the **Braamfontein Spruit Trail**, which meanders through central Johannesburg, Randburg and Sandton to the Klein Jukskei River – a distance of about 25 km (15 miles) – almost without touching concrete. It can be joined at any point.

The largest park along the trail is the 100-hectare (250-acre) Delta Park, which contains the lovely **Florence Bloom Bird Sanctuary** (open daily; free). Both dams here are rich with birdlife; you can watch from several specially constructed hides.

Other hikes include the Bloubos Trail, the Parktown Urban Walk and the Sandspruit Trail. On the **Randlords Heritage Trail**, you can admire some of the grand homes built for the original Gold Rush pioneers.

The **Melrose Bird Sanctuary** (open daily; free) in the suburb of Melrose includes a dam surrounded by extensive reed beds, providing nests for a large variety of weaver birds. It's part of the James and Ethel Gray Park, a 10-minute drive from the centre of town.

More than 3,000 mammals, birds and reptiles – 30 of them on the endangered list – are housed at the **Johannesburg Zoological Gardens** (open daily; entrance fee) inside the Herman Eckstein Park in Saxonwold. There are enclosures for big cats, elephants, giraffes and large apes, guarded only by moats and free of iron bars. Tours (including night tours) available. Across Jan Smuts Avenue at popular **Zoo Lake**, also in the park, there are rowing boats for hire, a restaurant and children's playgrounds.

For a peaceful stroll away from the noise and dirt of the city, try the **Johannesburg Botanical Garden** (open daily; free) in Thomas Bowler Street, Roosevelt Park Extension, half-an-hour's drive from the city centre on the banks of the Emmarentia Dam. This tranquil spot covers 148 hectares (365 acres), and contains a rose garden, a bonsai garden, pools, fountains and oaks; the dam itself is a pleasant stretch of water, popular with rowers, windsurfers and sailors.

One of the best places to admire Johannesburg's Manhattanesque skyline is **Pioneer Park** (open daily; free), on the banks of Wemmer Pan in Rosettenville. On the northern bank is Santarama Miniland, a contrived but nonetheless very popular miniature city built to a scale of 1:25, depicting all sorts of South African landmarks, including Kimberley's Big Hole.

Nightlife and entertainment

As far as clubs and bars are concerned, Johannesburg's best venues are in and around the trendy suburbs of Melville and Rosebank, and the slightly seedy (but infinitely more exciting) **Rockey Street** in **Yeoville** ⓗ, just east of the city centre. Once one of the hippest districts in the country – where a non-racial culture flourished, long before apartheid collapsed – Rockey Street's now gone somewhat down-market and sports a disreputable, even dangerous, air. However, that, according to *aficionados*, only adds to the appeal.

Thanks to Johannesburg's position at the centre of the South African music industry, most of the country's top bands are based here. At any one time, expect to choose from a rich cross-section of acts, from standard rock, pop and dance music to the snappy sounds of township jive, Afro-jazz and gospel.

Kippies, in the Market Theatre complex in Bree Street, is named for legendary 1950s sax player Kippie Moeketsi, and specialises in township jazz. Rockey Street is a good place to hear music from all over the African continent; it's not unusual to find artists from as far afield as Ghana, the Congo, Zimbabwe and Kenya performing here at assorted venues.

Map, page 252

BELOW: good-humoured banter in a Soweto shebeen.

Local theatre is to a high standard, both in terms of production and theatre facilities. Well-established venues include the Market Theatre and the Newtown Precinct; the cavernous modern **Civic Theatre** in Loveday Street, Braamfontein, stages opera and ballet as well as theatre.

When it comes to eating out, Johannesburg caters to every taste and pocket. Northern suburbs foodies go into raptures over **Linger Longer** in Sandton and **Ile de France** in Bryanston, while at the other end of the scale, the city's large Portugese and Italian communities support a range of unpretentious Mediterranean-style cafés. As for indigenous African cuisine, **Gramadoelas** at the Market Theatre Precinct serves up succulent versions of the rib-sticking Cape Dutch cuisine, including *potjiekos* (stew cooked in a three-legged iron pot) and *melktert*, a creamy custard tart. Hip **Iyavaya** in Yeoville dishes up food and drink from all over Africa – including ostrich steaks and mopani worms – to the heady beat of *zouk* and *kwasa-kwasa*.

One of Gauteng's celebrated "Zola Budd" minibus taxis, which provide transport for the majority of local commuters.

Further afield: the Witwatersrand

It may seem bizarre to treat the townships as a tourist attraction, but to truly appreciate both sides to life in what is still largely a segregated society, they should be visited. One of the few ways to do this safely is on a guided tour. A number of companies run trips to **Soweto** (SOuth WEstern TOwnships), the sprawling city near Johannesburg with close on two million inhabitants; most depart from the Carlton Hotel in the centre of town and include stops at such places as Winnie Mandela's house and a *shebeen* (local tavern).

Wherever you go in downtown Johannesburg, street names reflect the pioneer days – Claim, Prospect, Nugget, Main Reef. A visit to working gold mines

BELOW: Gold Reef City.

outside the city can be arranged through the **Chamber of Mines** – but be warned, it's a sweltering journey 1 km (half a mile) underground, deep into the earth's crust (daily tours; advance booking essential; no-one under 16 years or over 60 years of age admitted; tel: (011) 498 7100).

A less sweaty – but distinctly tamer – way to get to grips with the gold-mining industry is to pay a visit to **Gold Reef City** (open Tues–Sun; entrance fee; tel: (011) 496 1600) at Crown Mines, south of Crown Interchange off the M1 highway, 6 km (4 miles) from the city centre. A lift takes visitors 200 metres (650 ft) down No 14 Shaft – once the richest in the world – as part of a reconstruction of the mining process, from the extraction of the ore to the pouring of the molten gold into ingot moulds. Above ground, an attempt has been made to recreate the rumbustious atmosphere of "gold rush" Johannesburg in the form of a Victorian-style theme park, featuring a funfair and a number of old-style shops and restaurants. Contrived and commercialised it may be, but there are interesting touches, such as the energetic daily demonstrations of *isicathulo* (gumboot dancing) first popularised by migrant workers in the mine hostels.

Nothing beats the experience of visiting a big game park to see lions, elephants, giraffes and antelopes in their natural habitat – but Johannesburg does offer a few scaled-down versions close to the city centre. Up to 60 lions live in an enclosure at the **Johannesburg Lion Park** (open daily; entrance fee per car; tel: (011) 460 1814), about 12 km (7 miles) northwest of Sandton off the Witkoppen Road. You can also see impala, gemsbok, blesbok and ostrich.

The **Transvaal Snake Park** (open daily; entrance fee; tel: (011) 805 3116) on the R101 at Halfway House is home to the world's largest collection of

Map, page 252

King crickets, huge wingless insects more commonly known as "Parktown prawns", are a familiar sight in Jo'burg gardens (and living rooms!). They can grow up to 7.5 cm (3") long.

BELOW: the man-made oasis of Sun City.

SUN CITY

South Africa's answer to Las Vegas lies 90 minutes' drive west of Jo'burg, on the fringes of the Kalahari. This glitzy resort – the most luxurious in southern Africa – contains casinos, cinemas, restaurants, a world-class golf course and numerous hotels. Most over-the-top of all is the Lost City complex, in which a spectacular five-star hotel – a fantasy "African palace" – rises from an imported tropical jungle setting, complete with artificial beach and wave pool. Special effects such as the Bridge of Time – scheduled to shudder and shake every now and again, hypo-allergenic smoke seeping out of its man-made fissures to simulate an earthquake – complete the picture. The brains behind it all? Step forward, Sol Kerzner, the flamboyant boxer-turned-businessman whose hugely successful company, Sun International, operates hotels and gaming resorts around the world. Part of Kerzner's financial genius was in recognising the potential of building resorts in the so-called homelands, which were granted "independence" during the days of apartheid. While South Africa's Calvinist white rulers forbade gambling, you could do pretty much anything in the homelands. Sun City – itself established in the former homeland of Bophutatswana – is complemented by the nearby Pilanesberg National Park.

**Map,
page 252**

Bullfrog Pan in
President Steyn Street,
Benoni, makes an
unusual outing. It's the
second-largest
bullfrog reserve in the
southern hemisphere.
Tel: (011) 8495466.

BELOW: a novel
way to ski: down
a mine-dump.

predominantly African snakes. Here, poisonous vipers are milked daily for
visitors; you can also see crocodiles, alligators and terrapins, all kept in purpose-built pools.

The 1,400-hectare (3,400-acre) **Krugersdorp Game Reserve** (open daily;
entrance fee per car; tel: (011) 9531770) is also worth a visit; less than half-
an-hour's drive from Roodepoort on the R24, about 7 km (4 miles) outside
Krugersdorp, it has white rhino, giraffe, blue wildebeest and several species
of antelope. As well as a guest lodge, there's a camping site and a caravan
park.

About 22 km (14 miles) further west from the reserve off the R563 lie the
Sterkfontein Caves (open Tues–Sun; free; tel: (011) 9566342) – six chambers
with an underground lake said to have special healing powers, first exposed after
lime-quarry blasting towards the end of the 19th century. It was here that anthro-
pologist Dr Robert Broom discovered the fossilized skeleton of the hominid he
nicknamed "Mrs Ples" – short for *Plesianthropus transvaalensis* – in 1936.
There are guided tours every half-hour.

A final point: it's worth bearing in mind that Johannesburg's public transport
system is not very good. There is no underground or light railway network, for
example, and the buses follow limited routes at limited times. Nor is the range
of conventional taxis particularly extensive; nonetheless, enquiries about reputable firms can be made at hotel desks. For the bold, there are also the city's
celebrated "Zola Budds", the minibus taxis favoured by black South Africans.
Unfortunately, while you'll find the atmosphere friendly and the experience
good fun, the driving skills of the operators and the condition of their vehicles
often leave a lot to be desired.

The lure of gold

The gold-mining industry has long been the flywheel of South Africa's economy. Of the 112,000 tons of the metal estimated to have been mined in the world to date, 50,000 tons have come from the African continent, the bulk of it from South Africa. It is the largest producer of gold in the world.

Johannesburg grew from the rough-and-ready diggers' camps that mushroomed here when gold was first discovered in 1886. Today's visitors to Gold Reef City – a popular theme park depicting Johannesburg at the dawn of the 20th century – can take a "cage" some 200 metres (650 ft) underground, to see just how the precious metal is wrested from the rock. But gold has little to do with nostalgia or romance for South Africa's 500,000-odd mine workers.

"The wealth of our gold-mining industry is not so much due to the richness of gold as it is to the poorness of black wages," wrote Alan Paton in the 1960s. Today in the "new" South Africa, despite the minimum wage levels negotiated by the trade unions, the mineworker's life is a tough one.

Most miners begin their day by climbing into the giant metal cages that will take them deep into the belly of the earth for their working shift. Already, South Africa's gold mines probe deeper than their counterparts around the world. In the mid-80s, for example, the Witwatersrand's Western Deep Levels was mining 3,447 metres (2 miles) below the earth's surface – a world record. Working conditions are intensely hot and humid, and despite stringent safety measures, often hazardous. Many of the gold-bearing underground seams are narrow, and the shafts or "stopes" in which the miners work little more than a metre (3 ft) high. Rock temperatures can reach 55°C (131°F), and even though refrigerated air is constantly being pumped through the networks, air temperatures often exceed 32°C (90°F).

Because of the narrowness of the seams, drilling and blasting are usually manual operations. The raw rock is hoisted onto carts which are whisked up to ground level to undergo a series of gold extraction processes – but there is the ever-present danger of rockbursts or earth tremors.

The mining industry has long relied on contract labour as the backbone of its workforce. Johannesburg's bleak hostels and mining compounds were first built to house the thousands of men forced off the land in the early part of this century, who came seeking work in *eGoli* – the city of gold. Mineworkers' traditional songs bear testament to the loneliness and boredom of the mining life, to the harsh, crowded conditions in the single-sex hostels, and to their longings for home life and faraway families.

Inevitably, perhaps, hostels became flashpoints for political violence in the 1980s and 1990s, fuelled by alienation, bitterness and despair. Today, mining companies have been forced to reconsider ways of housing their workers. Behind the glittering images of South Africa's golden treasure, the reality remains: an industry built on back-breaking work and sub-standard conditions.

RIGHT: molten millions.

THE NORTH

*Beyond Pretoria, the highveld rolls on to a
vast escarpment, where wooded cliffs plunge down
to subtropical valleys below*

Map,
page 264

Just a 50-km (31-mile) drive north of Johannesburg, Pretoria's relatively small size disguises its influence as the centre of political decision-making. All state departments and parastatal bodies have their head offices here in South Africa's administrative capital; money may do the talking in the Golden City, but it is in Pretoria where the strings of power are held.

In the past, Pretoria was known as a notoriously dull place, where apartheid's most insular strictures were upheld to the letter and a spirit of killjoy puritanism prevailed. However, all that has altered since the winds of political change swept through South Africa. Now, the city supports a sophisticated international colony of diplomats, politicians and businessmen, and this refreshing exposure to cosmopolitan influences has inspired something of a local cultural renaissance – including the emergence of a thriving gay scene.

It's also known as "Jacaranda City", for reasons that become obvious if you visit in October, when the jacaranda trees' bright mauve blossoms appear. In the city centre alone, 55,000 trees line the streets.

LEFT: the baobab, giant of the African bushveld.
BELOW: detail, Voortrekker Monument.

Historic Pretoria

Many of Pretoria's historic sites commemorate the late 19th-century heyday of Paul Kruger's Zuid-Afrikaansche Republic. In the heart of the city lies **Church Square Ⓐ**, skirted by the Old Raadzaal (seat of the old Republican government); the Palace of Justice and the original South African Reserve Bank. But the chief landmark here is a large, dour statue of Kruger himself, flanked by burgher sentries.

A short walk down Church Street brings you to **Strijdom Square**, dominated by a giant bust of a more recent leader of the Volk, former prime minister, J.G. Strijdom. This time, the surrounding statuary is a group of charging horses, symbolising Afrikaner efforts to establish an apartheid republic.

Kruger House Ⓑ on Church Street West (open daily; entrance fee), the unpretentious home occupied by Kruger and his wife between 1884 and 1901, has now been immaculately restored. Some of the old Calvinist's personal belongings are on display, as well as his private railway carriage and official State coach. Kruger's grave lies nearby at **Heroes' Acre**.

A 15-minute walk to the southwest brings you to gracious **Melrose House Ⓒ** (open Tues–Sun; closed Sun am and public holidays; entrance fee), in Jacob Maré Street opposite **Burgers Park Ⓓ**. Designed and built in 1886, the mansion is one of South Africa's finest surviving examples of Victorian architecture; it is also where the treaty ending the Anglo-Boer War was signed.

Guarding the southern entrance to the city is the **Voortrekker Monument** (open daily; entrance fee), a

The blue crane,
South Africa's
elegant national bird,
can be seen
in Pretoria's
Austin Roberts
Bird Sanctuary.

looming granite structure visible from miles around. Something of a shrine for Afrikaners to this day, it commemorates the Great Trek (1834–1840) that opened up the country's interior for white occupation. Also easily visible from here is the headquarters of the University of South Africa, known among locals as **Unisa**. With more than 105,000 students from across the globe, it is one of the largest correspondence universities in the world.

The government's administrative headquarters are situated in the **Union Buildings E** (tours of the gardens only, by appointment; Mon–Fri; fee charged) on Meintjieskop Ridge, overlooking the city to the east. The image of this stately red sandstone building, designed by Sir Herbert Baker and completed in 1913, adorns souvenir tray cloths, coffee mugs and biscuit tins nationwide. Less prosaically, this was also the setting for Nelson Mandela's historic inauguration on 10 May 1994.

The outdoor life

A short drive north of the city centre brings you to the **National Zoological Gardens F** (open daily; entrance fee) regarded as one of the largest and best of its kind in the world. It's home to about 3,500 southern African and exotic animals; an overhead cableway provides the visitor with a panoramic view of the zoo and the surrounding city. Also outstanding is the **Austin Roberts Bird Sanctuary** (open Sat–Sun and public holidays; free;) in the southeastern district of Muckleneuck, where more than 100 indigenous bird species such as blue cranes, herons, ostriches and waterbirds can be viewed.

Pretoria's magnificent **National Botanical Gardens** (open daily; entrance fee) lie 8 km (5 miles) east of the city centre, containing every major type of

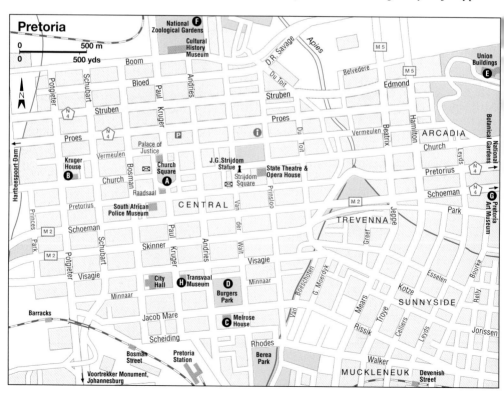

Pretoria

southern African vegetation on display. Conducted tours include a slide show and visit to the nursery. The **Hartebeespoort Dam**, 35 km (22 miles) west of Pretoria, in a beautiful location against the backdrop of the Magaliesberg mountain range, is the setting for numerous small holiday resorts, very popular with Afrikaners from Gauteng and Northern Province.

Map,
page 264

Culture and entertainment

The **Pretoria Art Museum** ❻ (open Tues–Sun; closed Sun am; entrance fee) in the eastern suburb of Arcadia Park houses a good collection of work by (white) South African artists, including such local talent as Frans Oerder, Maggie Laubscher and Walter Battiss. At 218 Vermeulen Street in the city centre you'll find the **Pierneef Museum** (open Mon–Fri; closed public holidays; entrance fee), devoted to the work of another well-known local painter and containing an impressive collection of paintings and graphic art.

The renowned **Transvaal Museum** ❼ (open daily; entrance fee), a 10-minute walk away in Paul Kruger Street, opposite the City Hall, specialises in natural history and houses a famous collection of fossils, as well as one of the country's largest collections of San rock art.

The **State Theatre** on Church Street is the centre of cultural life in Pretoria. A grand total of seven separate auditoriums in the complex provide facilities for opera, drama, ballet and symphony concerts. As far as more informal entertainment is concerned, some of the liveliest nightlife centres around the eastern suburb of Sunnyside. The **Oeverzicht Art Village** in Gerhard Moerdyk Street here houses a lively strip of restaurants, bars and arts-and-crafts shops; in particular, the Provençal cuisine at nearby **La Madelaine** restaurant is much-

BELOW: it's not hard to see why Pretoria is known as the "Jacaranda City".

*Tswaing Crater,
45 km (28 miles)
north of Pretoria, is
one of the best-
preserved meteorite
impact craters in the
world. The water-
filled hole is 1,130
metres (1236 yds)
wide.*

vaunted by the local élite. At **Gerhard Moerdyk**'s in Arcadia, diplomats and politicians wheel and deal over springbok pie and other hearty dishes from a South African menu in an incongruously chintzy setting, complete with crystal chandeliers.

The highveld: eastern grasslands

Leaving **Pretoria ❶** on the N4, the road rolls steadily on through monotonous sun-bleached grasslands. Initially, the journey shows little promise of the hauntingly beautiful eastern escarpment which lies ahead, yet these undulating plains once teemed with herds of wildlife, particularly black wildebeest, zebra and antelope. Today these have been displaced by cattle and sheep farming as well as intensive maize and sunflower monoculture. Occasionally, domesticated blesbok can be seen grazing in game-fenced ranches along the roadside.

The largest coal deposits in the country are found at **Witbank ❷**, providing fuel for nearby power stations. Depressingly, mining here has given rise to growing environmental problems such as air pollution and acid rain.

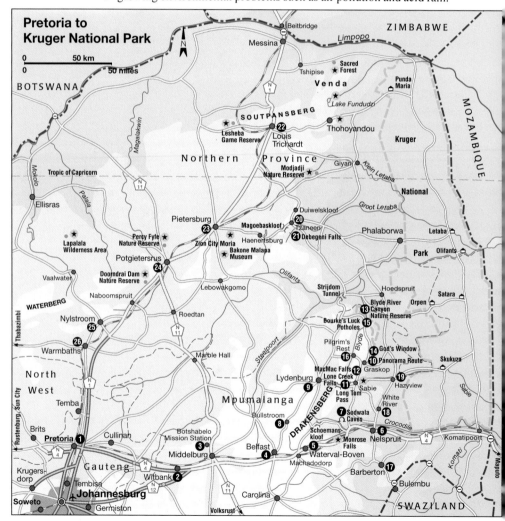

Pretoria to Kruger National Park

This region is the ancestral home of the Southern Ndebele peoples, who are celebrated for their love of colourful and symbolic decoration. Exquisite examples of their geometrically-patterned homes and intricate beadwork on women's costumes can be seen at the restored 19th-century **Botshabelo Mission Station ❸** near Fort Merensky, 13 km (8 miles) north of Middelburg. Guided tours are available from the open-air museum here (open daily; free; tel: (0132) 23897).

Belfast ❹ and **Machadodorp** are two towns that played a pivotal role in the history of the Zuid-Afrikaansche Republic during the Anglo-Boer War. After the evacuation of Pretoria in 1900, the government of President Paul Kruger moved to the railway town of Machadodorp. Later that same year, the last major set-piece battle of the war was fought at **Bergendal**, 8 km (5 miles) outside Belfast. A small memorial marks the battlefield.

On the edge of the escarpment are the two little railway towns of **Waterval-Boven ❺** and **Waterval Onder**, which lie on the rail link between Pretoria and Mozambique. In the mid-1890s, Dutch contractors employed considerable engineering skills in bringing the railway across the escarpment at the point where the Elands River plunges over a spectacular waterfall. The steeply-inclined tunnel and rack-rail can be viewed along the roadside; a further short walk leads to a lovely view of the waterfall.

An alternative route (R539) over the escarpment can be taken just before reaching Waterval-Boven. This follows the course of the Crocodile River for 67 km (42 miles) through the precipitous **Schoemanskloof**. The route meets with the N4 again at the confluence of the Elands and Crocodile rivers, which then tumble down over the beautiful **Montrose Falls**.

Map, page 266

BELOW: scenes from an Ndebele village.

A marker on the Jock of the Bushveld Road, a scenic 12-km (8-mile) route through the Kruger National Park once used by transport riders such as Percy Fitzpatrick and his dog, Jock.

BELOW: recycled beer cans.

The road leads on through lush farmland towards **Nelspruit** ❻, past wayside stalls selling tropical fruits, nuts and curios. Two kilometres (1 mile) beyond the intersection at **Montrose**, a turn-off to the north takes you on a 14-km (9-mile) drive to the **Sudwala Caves** ❼ (open daily; daily tours; entrance fee; tel: (01311) 64152). Nobody knows quite why, but the temperature of the caves stays at a constant 18°C (64°F) throughout the year. Their full depth has not yet been established, but you can explore the enormous chambers with their weird dripstone formations for about 500 metres (1,600 ft) into the mountainside. There is also an exhibition of full-sized model dinosaurs in the caves' gardens.

Pretty **Dullstroom** ❽, 30 km (19 miles) north of Belfast, lies amidst one of the few remaining stretches of pristine natural highveld. Numerous small streams rise in these cool highlands, draining towards the escarpment to the east. All are stocked with trout; fishing is as important in the area as farming. As most of the trout streams are privately owned, seek advice on good fishing spots from the Dullstroom Inn.

Lydenburg ❾ ("Place of Suffering") is a beautiful town that belies the name given to it by survivors of the malaria-stricken settlements in the lowveld. Later, it became the capital of an independent Boer republic; the town's Dutch Reformed church and old school house were built during this period. In the local museum (open daily; Mon–Fri closed 12–2pm; Sat–Sun open 1–4pm; entrance fee), you can see replicas of the "Lydenburg Heads", based on reassembled pottery fragments found in the area dating from AD 500.

From Lydenburg, the road crosses the **Mauchberg** and leads via the **Long Tom Pass** to **Sabie**. Once used by transport drivers, this road's curious name dates from the Anglo-Boer War. During their retreat before the British forces,

the Boers defended the pass with several 150-mm Creusot guns taken from the forts around Pretoria. Nicknamed "Long Tom", these heavy artillery pieces were cumbersome, but effective in slowing the British advance over the mountains.

Map, page 266

The Panorama Route

Throughout the length of KwaZulu-Natal and Mpumalanga Province, the edge of the huge inland plateau of southern Africa swoops abruptly down, providing breathtaking scenic views as well as excellent opportunities for hiking and motoring. The escarpment, or **Drakensberg**, is a spectacular cragged mountain range running south to north for nearly 320 km (200 miles). It is criss-crossed with numerous passes, many pioneered by the transport-riders of the late 19th century, who provided a vital economic link between the land-locked Zuid-Afrikaansche Republic and the Portuguese port of Lourenço Marques (now **Maputo**).

One of these intrepid pioneers was a young man named Percy Fitzpatrick, who, disillusioned with his job in a Cape Town bank, opted for a job carting supplies by ox wagon from Delagoa Bay to the highveld goldfields. Fitzpatrick's closest travelling companion was a cross-breed bull terrier named Jock; the tale he wrote about their adventures, *Jock of the Bushveld* (1907), is now a classic.

The town of **Sabie** lies on the southern reaches of the **Panorama Route ⓾**, 56 km (35 miles) west of Lydenburg. Timber plantations cover the surrounding hillsides; the country's major paper mills are situated here. This is also waterfall country, and numerous short drives lead from the town to picnic and viewing sites such as **Sabie Falls, Horseshoe Falls, Lone Creek Falls ⓫, Bridal Veil Falls** and **MacMac Falls ⓬** (so-called after all the Scots prospectors who camped in the area during the gold rush).

BELOW: the Three Rondavels, Blyde River Canyon.

Visitors interested in taking photographs should bear in mind that almost all of the waterfalls face east and should therefore best be visited before midday.

The 86-km (54-mile) drive northwards from Sabie via **Graskop** to the **Blyde River Canyon** ⓭ should be taken at a leisurely pace: the views are breathtaking. At **Pinnacle Rock, Jock's View** and **God's Window** ⓮, you can stop to look out from dramatically sheer cliff outposts over the expanse of the lowveld. Other sights include the **Lisbon Falls** and the **Berlin Falls** before the road reaches **Bourke's Luck Potholes** ⓯, 66 km (41 miles) from Sabie. Here, paths and footbridges take visitors to viewing sites overlooking an extraordinary example of river erosion.

More is to come. Northwards, the **Blyde River** has carved a magnificent gorge through the mountains. Viewing sites have been created at several points along the canyon, providing superb views of the winding river some 800 metres (2,600 ft) below the summit.

Dominated by three similarly shaped peaks, the **Three Rondavels**, and by **Mariepskop** – one of the highest points in the region – the canyon is a nature reserve (open daily; free) and accessible only on foot. Numerous well-marked trails of varying lengths lead the visitor through tumbling waterfalls and lush, unusual flora, including cycads, giant ferns and rare orchids.

An alternative trip from Sabie is over the **Bonnet Pass** along the R533 for 35 km (22 miles) to **Pilgrim's Rest** ⓰, one of the oldest gold-mining towns in South Africa. Legend ascribes the discovery of gold in this valley (in 1873) to Alec "Wheelbarrow" Patterson, so called because he roamed the hills pushing all his possessions in a wheelbarrow. He stumbled across what was, at the time, the richest deposit of alluvial gold on the subcontinent, and within no time at all a large and motley assortment of fortune seekers had flocked to the area.

Yet within a decade, most of the alluvial deposits had been worked out, and mining operations were taken over by larger companies. In 1883, the independent diggers migrated south to the newly discovered fields at **Barberton** ⓱. Underground mining continued at Pilgrim's Rest until the 1920s, but today the entire town is preserved as a national monument and living museum.

Hiking trails

Perhaps the most rewarding viewing of this picturesque countryside is via the network of hiking trails which traverses the Mpumalanga Province section of escarpment. The **Fanie Botha Trail** was the first National Hiking Way trail to be opened in 1973. It covers almost 80 km (50 miles) of magnificent mountain countryside between the Ceylon Forest near Sabie to God's Window north of Graskop. Short sections of the five-day trail can be taken at a time.

At God's Window, the Fanie Botha trail merges with the 65-km (40-mile) **Blyderivierspoort Hiking Trail**, offering a series of much more leisurely walks along the canyon, ending up at the Three Rondavels.

The region's early mining history can be traced along the **Prospector's Hiking Trail**, which links up with the Fanie Botha Trail at MacMac Falls and leads northwards for 70 km (43 miles) through Pilgrim's Rest and

Anopheles *mosquito, the malaria carrier. Malaria kills more than a million people every year in Africa alone.*

BELOW: Lone Creek Falls.

north to Bourke's Luck Potholes. Pilgrim's Rest is also the starting point for two other routes, the **Morgenzon Trail** and the **Rambler's Trail**, offering a selection of short walks (*see Travel Tips for details*).

The subtropical lowveld

Nelspruit, 355 km (222 miles) from Johannesburg, is the capital of **Mpumalanga** province, the smallest and least-populated in South Africa. This is the base of the escarpment; you'll become aware of the lowveld's heavy, humid air as soon as the lower altitude is reached. Nelspruit's a pretty place, its streets festooned with bougainvillaea and frangipani, but the real showpiece here is the **Lowveld Botanical Garden** (open daily; free; tel: (013) 7525531), set in lovely, lush scenery 3 km (2 miles) outside town along the Crocodile River. It has many rare lowveld plants, including a comprehensive cycad collection.

A 16-km (10-mile) drive north of Nelspruit on the R40 brings you to the attractive little town of **White River** ⓲; **Hazyview** ⓳ is a further 24 km (15 miles) away. The lowveld climate is ideal for the cultivation of exotic subtropical fruit, and you'll notice banana, papaya and mango plantations lining the roadside. Avocados, litchis, citrus and passion fruit are all farmed here, too.

The lowveld was once the site of the major pre-Witwatersrand gold rush. Barberton, 45 km (28 miles) south of Nelspruit, near the Swaziland border, is the product of those wild days of fortunes made and lost overnight. Founded in 1883, it expanded rapidly as rich gold deposits were found in the surrounding hills. Nearby **Sheba Mine** was once the world's richest mine, and a separate town, **Eureka City**, grew up beside it. Eureka is now a ghost town and a half-hour drive from Barberton leads to the ruins past old excavations and mining gear.

**Map,
page 266**

TIP

Find out how to pan for gold on a conducted tour with the Pilgrim's Rest Diggings Museum, just outside town on the Graskop road. Tel: (01315) 81296.

BELOW: the former mining camp of Pilgrim's Rest is now a national monument.

Nelspruit is a mere 105 km (66 miles) west of the Mozambique border and the gateway town of **Komatipoort**, sweltering in the confluent valleys of the Komati and Crocodile rivers. During the 20 years of civil war in Mozambique, Komatipoort lay dormant but for sporadic gunfire. Today, the Nelspruit-Maputo road is being developed with huge amounts of government aid. The intention is to transform the region into a vibrant economic corridor of agriculture, industry and communications, and to restore Komatipoort to its old status as an important gateway to the coast.

Land of the Rain Queen

A 96-km (60-mile) drive from Lydenburg on the R36 brings you to a winding pass, penetrating the steep Drakensberg cliffs through the **Strijdom Tunnel** and dropping down into the hot, baobab-studded flats of **Northern Province**. Soon after the tunnel, the R36 turns off to Tzaneen, 90 km (56 miles) to the west. The main road (now the R527) curves south again to many of the region's private game parks and on to Hazyview, 116 km (73 miles) away.

The great Drakensberg escarpment terminates in the well-wooded slopes around **Tzaneen** ㉑, a prosperous fruit-farming region; tea and timber plantations are also abundant. Showpiece of the area is the spectacularly beautiful **Magoebaskloof**, meandering through indigenous forest up the slopes of the **Wolkberg**. An enchanting 3-km (2-mile) walk through the forests from the main road brings you to **Debengeni Falls** ㉑, which tumble 800 metres (260 ft) into a deep, pot-like natural swimming pool.

A further 20 km (12 miles) north towards **Duiwelskloof** lies the homeland of the Lobedu people, a sub-sect of the Venda, ruled by the mysterious queen,

BELOW: Vernacular creation ...

Modjadji. Since the 16th century, a dynasty of queens has held sway over this region, originally commanding awe and respect even from the warrior tribes among the Zulus and Swazis. In dry seasons she was sent gifts and offerings, together with heartfelt requests to use her secret powers to bring on the much-needed rain. The adventure novelist Rider Haggard based his novel, *She* (1887), on the person of Modjadji. To this day the mystique of the "Rain Queen" remains: the reigning monarch can still only be seen and visited by favoured guests.

Baobab country

The **Soutpansberg** is a relatively small but impressive mountain range just north of the town of **Louis Trichardt** ㉒. A large variety of small antelopes and birds, including raptors, are found on these richly forested slopes. On the northern slopes are rock shelters with vivid wall paintings, indicating that San tribes-people inhabited the area a thousand years ago. One of the most popular ways of exploring these mountains is the five-day **Soutpansberg Hiking Trail**.

Louis Trichardt lies at the foot of the range, 112 km (70 miles) north of Pietersburg. It's named after the intrepid Voortrekker who led the first trek into the interior and on to the Mozambique coastal port of Lourenço Marques (now Maputo). Unfortunately, half of the party – including Trichardt himself – succumbed to the fever.

North of the Soutpansberg, at the top of Northern Province, lies the traditional homeland of the **Venda**. Like the people of Zimbabwe, the Venda were skilled miners, smelters and masons, and the ruins of their intricately patterned stone structures can still be seen here. In earlier centuries, they traded iron, copper and ivory with Arab merchants on the east coast, and historians are only now

Map, page 266

"Duiwelskloof" means "devil's gorge" – a reference to the hazards these muddy slopes posed to transport riders and wagon trains in the rainy season. Thankfully, conditions have now improved.

BELOW: …in a rural community.

beginning to understand the cultural and economic impact of these ancient trade routes on the African hinterland.

In these remote areas, traditional rituals continue to survive; ancestral spirits guard many of the pools and forests in these beautiful mountains. Most important of the holy places is **Lake Fundudzi**. The best way to reach this quiet and beautiful spot is to hike the four-day **Mabuda-Shango Hiking Trail**, which starts from the **Thathe-Vondo Forest Station**, 71 km (44 miles) north of Louis Trichardt. Visitors to these holy forests and lakes should always take care to respect the beliefs of the local people. Swimming and washing in the lakes is forbidden.

From time to time, initiation ceremonies take place in Venda villages, and visitors may, by special arrangement, witness the famous python dance, part of the *domba* or initiation ceremony. Lining up closely behind one another, young girls of the village mime the serpentine movement of a python to the beat of sacred drums. At **Thohoyandou**, fine carvings and other curios can be bought from traders along the roadside.

South Africa's northern border with Zimbabwe is the **Limpopo River**, about 100 km (60 miles) to the north. Copper has been mined in the Limpopo valley since pre-historic times, and the district is rich in archaeological relics.

The bushveld: hot, yellow plains

Heading back southward in the direction of Pretoria, the Great North Road pushes steadily on through a series of hot, yellow plains – this is classic cattle-ranching country. The few towns you pass through here still cling somewhat forlornly to a diehard Voortrekker ethos. About 117 km (73 miles) from plain,

Eugene Marais – celebrated Afrikaner natural scientist, poet and drug addict – farmed in the Waterberg between 1907–1917. His most famous work, The Soul of the Ape, *was based on a study of local wildlife.*

BELOW: rural village, Mpumalanga.

dusty **Pietersburg** ㉓, capital of Northern Province, lies **Potgietersrus** ㉔. Pressing on a further 90 km (56 miles) through sleepy **Naboomspruit** brings you to the agricultural settlement of **Nylstroom** ㉕ *(see "Dorps" feature, page 241).*

Map, page 266

Birdlife around here is among the richest in South Africa, both in numbers and in the variety of species. The little **Nylsvlei Reserve** (open daily; free; tel: (01474) 31074) conserves some of the marshland 16 km (10 miles) north of the town; it attracts more than 400 species of bird and has one of the greatest concentrations of waterfowl in South Africa.

Aeons ago, the Great Rift Valley in East Africa cracked open, pumping masses of molten rock southward and eventually creating the Igneous Bushveld Complex – today regarded as one of the world's richest mineral areas. Traces of these ancient seismic events are still evident around the town of **Warmbaths** ㉖, founded near the largest of several hot mineral springs which erupt from the flat savannah.

Heading south along the N1, it's impossible to ignore the distant mountain massif on the western horizon. This is the **Waterberg** – until recently, a remote retreat seldom visited by tourists. At the privately run **Lapalala Wilderness Reserve**, 130 km (80 miles) from Nylstroom, you can reserve one of the small timber-and-thatch camps spread along the spectacular Palala River gorge and enjoy peace and quiet, hiking, game-viewing, and swimming in the clear river. **Marakele National Park**, 200 km (124 miles) from Gauteng, is home to the world's largest breeding colony of endangered Cape vultures, as well as a rich diversity of plant species including the rare Waterberg cycad. Wildlife includes elephant, and both black and white rhino.

BELOW: heading home from work.

THE BULBOUS BAOBAB

African legend has it that in a light-hearted moment, the gods planted the first baobab upside down. Yet the role of these monster-trees is more important than their weird shape suggests. Their fibrous wood allows them to store huge volumes of water; when chewed by animals, particularly elephants, this can offer critical relief in times of drought. This perpetual supply of water ensures an abundance of leaves every spring, providing both shade and nourishment to animals and insects alike. The soft, well-insulated stems are ideal for hole-nesting birds such as barbets and hornbills. After these have been vacated, the nests are often re-employed as beehives, or retreats for snakes and lizards, so that every baobab is always abuzz with the comings and goings of its many residents. People of the Limpopo River valley attribute fertility properties to the fruits, filled with seeds embedded in a refreshing white "cream-of-tartar" pulp; rock paintings in the region often portray women with baobab fruits instead of breasts. Baobabs can live for 3,000–4,000 years. When they die, the end is swift and dramatic. In a few months, the ancient fibres disintegrate and the tree simply collapses in on itself, disappearing so suddenly that it was once thought that baobabs ignited spontaneously and burned away.

JOURNEYING BY STEAM TRAIN

If travel by steam-hauled train in romantic turn-of-the-century style is the sort of journey that sparks your imagination, South Africa will not disappoint

Electrification of the railways came slowly to South Africa. Because coal was cheap and readily available, the authorities were reluctant to relinquish steam – indeed, by the early 1960s, the South African Railways were still operating a record 2,682 steam trains. The end of main-line steam traction was only officially announced in June 1991.

ALL ABOARD

All this, of course, is very good news for steam train enthusiasts, who can look forward to travelling on a remarkable number of vintage trains which have been preserved as tourist attractions. One of the best-known – and certainly the most opulent – is Rovos Rail's *Pride of Africa*, which plies a route from Cape Town to Pretoria and on to the Victoria Falls and back. These up-market "steam safaris" in immaculately restored 1920s and '30s rolling stock evoke the Edwardian era of luxury rail travel.

A little easier on the pocket are the "Union Limited" steam tours managed by Transnet, South Africa's privatised railway network. Options include a six-day Garden Route trip as well as day excursions from Cape Town. Transnet also manage South Africa's last scheduled mixed steam train service, the *Outeniqua Choo Tjoe*, which works the spectacular lakes and mountains route between George and Knysna (for more details about these and other steam train trips, see *Travel Tips*).

▽ TRAINSPOTTERS' DELIGHT
A brightly polished number-plate from one of the steam locomotives which still regularly ply the Garden Route.

▽ ONE TO PICK
As one of the last countries to operate steam trains commercially, South Africa attracts railway romantics from all over the world. The Eastern Cape's historic 24" gauge *Apple Express* does daily runs from Port Elizabeth to the village of Thornhill, a distance of some 53 km/30 miles. Booking offices can be found in town, at the Greenacres Shopping Centre.

A FINE OLD BOILER ▷
The Greytown Museum's fine collection of railway memorabilia, including this veteran steam engine, reflects the pioneering role played by KwaZulu-Natal in South Africa's railway history.

A ROUTE FROM THE CAPE TO CAIRO

THE RHODES COLOSSUS

It was Cecil Rhodes' most cherished ambition to have a railway line built from Cape Town to Cairo, passing only through British colonies. That way, Britain – rather than her European rivals – would be able to gain possession of Africa's riches. The groundwork for this scheme was laid in 1885, when the first railway trunk routes in South Africa were constructed, linking Cape Town to the Kimberley diamond fields – in which Rhodes' De Beers Consolidated Company just happened to have a very large stake.

Having achieved the wealth that he craved, Rhodes turned his attention to politics, becoming prime Minister of the Cape Colony in 1890. But the discovery of huge deposits of gold on the Witwatersrand – right in the middle of the Boer South African Republic – was to prove something of a stumbling block. A strong SAR, Rhodes reasoned, would constitute a severe threat to British supremacy. The subsequent struggle for control of the gold fields was a long and bloody one, culminating in the Anglo-Boer Wars of 1899–1902. Needless to say, Rhodes' Cape-to-Cairo British line never materialised.

◁ **STAYING ON TRACK**
The railway age first came to South Africa in 1860, when on 26 June, the country's first steam train made its first official journey from Durban to the Point – a distance of some 3 kilometres (2 miles). Today, the railways extend over some 36,000 km (22,000 miles) of largely electrified track, on which nearly 5,000 locomotives are in operation.

△ **SURF AND STEAM**
The most-photographed section of track from South Africa's most famous steam train journey – the *Outeniqua Choo Tjoe*, thundering out onto the long bridge across the mouth of the Kaaiman's River. With daily departures from George, the train arrives in Wilderness after a memorable journey of some two and a half hours, past beaches, lakes and forest.

FULL STEAM AHEAD ▷
Known to steam enthusiasts worldwide, the Garden Route's *Outeniqua Choo Tjoe* gets ready to huff and puff its way out of George station in a blaze of summer sunshine – a sight guaranteed to delight.

THE KRUGER NATIONAL PARK

*Set in classic bushveld wilderness, Africa's
oldest wildlife sanctuary offers a
wealth of natural splendour*

Map,
page 280

I n a roundabout way, it was the mosquito and the tsetse fly which helped safe-guard South Africa's herds of wild game, the highlight of any visit to the country today. Thanks to the malaria and deadly nagana cattle-sickness which these insects spread, hunting parties had to be restricted to the disease-free winter months, while all attempts to settle or civilise the area were doomed.

By the end of the 19th century, however, this was no longer enough to protect the land from farmers with their fences, and "sportsmen" with their guns, who between them took a devastating toll of the area's game. Finally, in 1898, despite considerable opposition from his contemporaries, President Kruger granted the proclamation of the Sabie Game Reserve to conserve the area's dwindling wildlife. This was the core of what later became the much larger Kruger National Park.

In the 1960s and 1970s, a number of drought-stricken farms adjacent to the park were turned into game farms and reserves by their enterprising owners, and so granted a new lease of life. **MalaMala**, **Londolozi** and **Sabi Sabi Game Reserves** are among the the best known of these private reserves, each offering luxurious bush-style accommodation to go with the spectacular game-watching. Many others have subsequently sprang up in their wake; prices are generally high (on a par with five-star-rated hotels) but then so are the standards of service. At night, dinner is set out under the stars in a traditional *boma*, where guests can exchange their experiences of the day around the camp-fire. Night drives are also on the agenda; many reserves will arrange to take visitors to a known lion or leopard kill after dark.

The use of private cars for game viewing is generally discouraged in these reserves, which have their own four-wheel-drive vehicles and experienced game-guides in attendance. Not only does this mean that more game is seen, but much can be learned from the guides, who explain the behaviour of animals, how to track their spoor and how they integrate with the natural environment. The less obvious things in the veld – trees, geology, small animals and birds – are also shown and explained.

In recent years, all of the eastern lowveld game parks (except those that still permit hunting) have removed the fences between themselves and between the Kruger National Park, so that wildlife moves unimpeded across the entire region. **Lekkerlag**, near Timbavati, is one of several game farms offering hunting safaris conducted under the supervision of professional hunters. Licences must be arranged through the Mpumalanga Department of Nature Conservation in Nelspruit.

*Never throw a match
or cigarette butt out
of your car window.
Fire is a constant
hazard in the Park.*

The big game show

The Kruger National Park has an extraordinarily rich and diverse bird and animal life, and this, combined with its tremendous size (it is roughly the size of Israel) is what makes it one of the world's great game reserves. Although it is served by an extensive network of roads and rest camps, this infrastructure barely affects the natural wildness. Regulations governing your activities may seem onerous (there's a strict speed limit of 40 kph, or 25 mph, for example), but they are directed mainly at the well-being of the wildlife.

LEFT: bush-babies
don't sleep at
night.

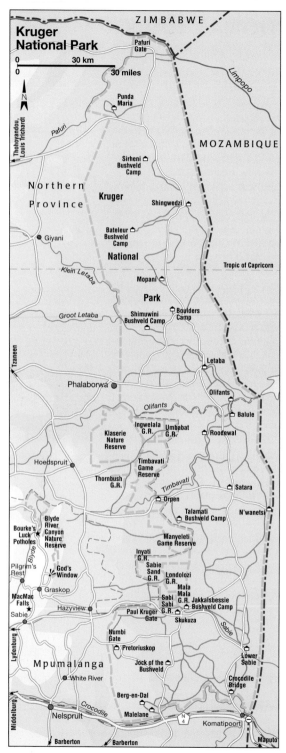

Kruger National Park

Plenty of coach tours of the Kruger National Park are available, but game viewing from a private car is just as enjoyable – and you can go at your own pace.

The best game-viewing is in the morning until about 10am and in the late afternoon. Camps open at dawn (ranging from 4.30am in mid-summer to 6.30am in winter) and it is well worth rising at this hour to get the best sightings. The sweltering midday hours are best spent enjoying a picnic at a water-hole, or in the camps, some of which have swimming pools. Camp gates and park entrance gates close at sunset (6.30pm in summer and 5.30pm in winter) and late-comers are fined.

Frustratingly, this early closing time often means abandoning a game drive just when it holds most promise. However, night drives in special vehicles with knowledgeable driver-guides are on offer in the larger camps.

Camp accommodation

Most people try to visit the park during the winter months – July to August. Temperatures are more moderate then, and the dryness of the veld drives the animals to water-holes, where they can more easily be spotted. Yet the off-peak seasons have much to offer too – not least a reduction in the number of visitors.

In spring and summer the trees and veld flowers are at their best. Birdlife is abundant, thanks to an influx of migratory species, and many of the animals are nursing newborn young.

Most of Kruger's game is spread fairly evenly throughout the park, but the frequency of sightings will obviously be determined by topography and vegetation. Near the southern rivers and watering-holes (Skukuza, Pretoriuskop, Lower Sabie and Crocodile Bridge) hippo, elephant, crocodile, buffalo and small herds of giraffe are often spotted. The central parts (Satara, Olifants, Letaba) are inhabited by large herds of antelope, which in turn attract the larger predators such as lion. In the north (Shingwedzi, Punda Maria) large herds of elephant and buffalo are often spotted, as well as leopard and the elusive nyala.

As well as four small bushveld camps without restaurant or shop facilities (which can provide an exciting experience of self-catered camping in the wild), there are 18 rest camps, varying in size and character. Five of these – **Boulders, Mopani, Jock of the Bushveld, N'wanetsi** and **Roodewaal** – are private and must be taken in their entirety by a single party. They accommodate a maximum of 15 people and are mostly well designed. No catering is provided.

Orpen, **Malelane** and **Crocodile Bridge** are entry-gate camps, used most often as a first base by visitors arriving shortly before the park gates close for the night. **Pretoriuskop**, set in the rolling grasslands of the southwest, is the oldest camp in the park, with a large and welcoming swimming pool. **Skukuza** is the biggest and busiest; a bustling village in its own right. **Lower Sabie** is a beautiful camp located on the banks of a dam on the Sabie River, in the heart of the prime viewing areas of the park. Elephants are numerous in this part and can often be seen from the camp as they visit the Sabie River. The drive along the river towards Skukuza should reward you with sightings of buffalo and bushbuck, as well as lion. Opportunities for bird-watching are also excellent.

The up-market, modern design of **Berg-en-Dal** near the southern border of the park is quite unlike the traditional African rondavels of other camps. Set in a hilly landscape overlooking the Matjulu dam, its extensive, well-fenced grounds are one of the few places where you can walk in the park and enjoy the veld and flora at close quarters. **Satara** is set in the open savannah of the park's central region. **Letaba** and **Olifants** camps are both situated on promontories looking out over a wide river frontage; game-viewing from the comfort of the restaurants and public verandahs here can be simply superb. **Balule** is a small camp about 11 km (7 miles) from Olifants. The north is served by two camps,

Map, see opposite

Because the Kruger Park's population of elephants is culled every year, it has amassed a large ivory stockpile.

BELOW: the Sabie River, lifeblood to big game.

Map,
page 280

Shingwedzi and **Punda Maria**. This part of the park was first proclaimed in the 1920s; Punda Maria in particular has retained plenty of original character.

Although camp restaurants serve meals, guests also have the option of cooking their own on open-air barbecues provided at the accommodation huts. Food and fuel are sold in the larger camps. Crockery and cutlery are not provided.

Kruger by foot

Wilderness hiking trails – where face-to-face encounters with big game are a real possibility – are conducted under the supervision of experienced rangers. Trails operate out of six base camps; they last three nights and two days, starting either on Sunday or Wednesday. The number of hikers on each trail is usually limited to 10, so book well in advance.

Ongoing archaeological research also suggests that Kruger is something of a pre-colonial treasure house. One of the most interesting sites unearthed so far is **Thulamela**, a 16th-century royal village lying close to Pafuri in the park's far north. The Parks Board plans to open Thulamela up to visitors in the near future.

The politics of conservation

In post-apartheid South Africa, people who had been evicted from their homes on racial grounds between 1936 and 1994 are entitled to appeal to a special court for restoration or compensation. A number of such claims have been lodged against the Kruger Park, but only one – that of the Makuleke in the far north – appears to have much substance. In 1969, the Makuleke were evicted from their ancestral grounds between the Levuvhu and Limpopo rivers and resettled on the park's western boundary, so that the fences could be extended as far as the Zimbabwean border. If found to be valid, their claim will probably be settled by means of financial compensation.

BELOW: Kruger, in the Kruger.
RIGHT: *Panthera pardus,* the leopard.

The Makuleke's story reflects something of the extraordinary zeal with which Kruger's administrators carried out their conservation mission during the apartheid era. Indeed, the image most black South Africans had of the park was that it was a kind of armed camp, run by white racists for the pleasure of a privileged elite. Incidents such as that of 1988, when – to cheers from tourists following the scene with field glasses and long lenses – rangers ran to ground a group of guerillas, heading through the bush with a haversack of hand-grenades, only reinforced this view. Because Mozambique was sympathetic to the then-outlawed ANC, the park's sensitive eastern border with that country was patrolled by a quasi-military unit of rangers trained by instructors from the SADF's 111 Battalion.

Even today, a select group of game wardens are still given paramilitary training by former counter-insurgency specialists, to defend themselves against modern-day poachers armed with automatic weapons. In addition, rangers are sometimes called on to act as impromptu border guards, intercepting illegal immigrants from Mozambique who have negotiated a hazardous passage through the bush in order to seek back-door entry into South Africa.

SWAZILAND AND LESOTHO

*These two tiny kingdoms, both enclosed within
South Africa, have a great deal to offer
the adventurous traveller*

Map,
page 290

Listen! The drums, African drums playing out the rhythms of the ancient continent. They tell stories of the people who lived here long, long before the European settlers arrived. Listen to the beat quicken as they tell of Swaziland and Lesotho, for apart from one brief period in Swaziland's history, neither country has ever been ruled by whites.

Lesotho dates back to the time of the first Basotho king, Moshoeshoe. He founded the Basotho nation, uniting a medley of vanquished clans after inter-tribal clashes convulsed much of Southern Africa during the 1820s and 1830s. From his celebrated mountain stronghold, Thaba Bosiu ("Mountain of the Night") he went on to repel countless attacks by Zulu, Boer and British invaders.

Finally, tired of fighting, Moshoeshoe turned to Britain for aid. His kingdom was proclaimed a British protectorate in 1851, and remained so until 1966 when it became an independent democracy with a titular king.

Swaziland's history has much in common with Lesotho's. The Swazi nation started to take shape in the late 1600s under a powerful chief, Dlamini. He forged a nation of Nguni-speaking clans, closely related to the Zulus further south.

The Boers subjugated the Swazis for several decades, but when Britain won the Anglo-Boer War at the turn of this century, it "inherited" Swaziland. Mswati II now rules one of the world's last absolute monarchies – political parties are banned, and ministers are hand-picked by the king.

Highland peaks, wild lowveld

Compared to Lesotho, Swaziland has a good, pre-dictable infrastructure and is a much simpler country to negotiate. It is easy to organise guided tours or car hire for self-drive trips, and it's safe too (in Lesotho, even the weather conspires against you).

The country's attractions divide fairly neatly into two categories: the soft comforts of the Ezulwini Valley, with its smart hotels, restaurants, casinos and craft markets; and then the impressively well-stocked and man-aged game reserves.

Many of the key "sights" are ranged on either side of the capital, **Mbabane ❶**, in the northwest of the country on the South African border. It is not recommended that you stay in Mbabane long – or indeed at all, unless you need to. Although it's a bustling little city, it has more than its fair share of pickpockets and rather less of charm or unique character (although the main market, on **Msunduzu Street**, does offer good craft bar-gains). If you look like a visitor – and most *mlungu* (whites) do – then don't go about alone, especially at night.

Craft-hunters should head for the **Ngwena Glass Factory**, manufacturing decorative and functional

PRECEDING PAGES:
the lion's share;
Swazi mountain
tribeswoman.
LEFT: Swazi
dancers.
BELOW: Mbabane
craft market.

glassware from recycled bottles, and **Phumalanga Tapestries,** where Albert and Marie-Louise Reck weave (and sell) tapestries based on San rock art and bird designs. You'll find both at the border post at **Oshoek ❷**, 23 km (14 miles) northwest of Mbabane.

About 15 km (9 miles) southeast of Mbabane on the MR3, at the end of a tortuous descent down Malagwane Hill, is the lovely **Ezulwini Valley ❸**, the centre of most tourist activity in Swaziland. A sign as you enter proudly declares "*Phuma Lankga Sikose*" ("Long Live the King"), for the 30-km (18-mile) valley ends at **Lobamba ❹**, the Swazi king's Royal Village.

There's a good range of hotel accommodation here, offering just about every holiday activity short of a beach. As well as golf, bowls, tennis, horse riding and a health centre, there's even a glitzy casino.

You'll also find plenty of opportunity to buy Swazi crafts, both at the roadside (bargaining is expected) and in more organised shops. Soapstone sculpture and wood carvings, beadwork and woven articles are the cream of the curios, while the brilliantly coloured "Swazi candles" – shaped like animals – are the pick of the crafts.

Midway along the valley is the **Mlilwane Wildlife Sanctuary ❺**, signposted close to the turning for Mantenga Lodge. Originally used as farmland and for tin-mining, the land has now been regenerated and restocked. You can see white rhino, hippo, giraffe, crocodile, kudu, nyala and eland here, amongst other animals, although the only large predators are leopards, which are rarely spotted. Bird-watching hides have been built overlooking the dams (240 species of bird have been recorded here, including plum-coloured starlings and blue cranes).

BELOW: look out for hippos at the Mlilware Wildlife Sanctuary.

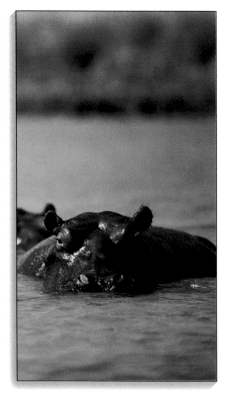

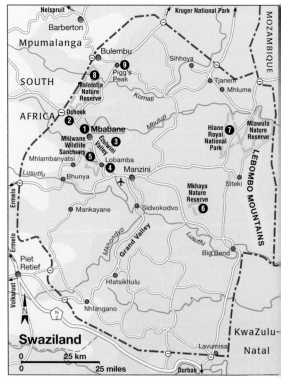

Swaziland

As there are few predators in Mlilwane, you can explore it in your own vehicle, on horse-back, or even by mountain bike, as well as taking game drives or guided walks with park rangers. Mlilwane is an easy day trip from Mbabane; there is also a pleasant rest-camp if you wish to stay longer. Reservations are handled by the tour operator Big Game Parks (*see Travel Tips for contact numbers*).

Map, see opposite

The interior – myriad landscapes

Private and exclusive **Mkhaya Nature Reserve ❻** lies about 90 km (55 miles) southeast of Mbabane, past scenery which changes from the forestry plantations of the highveld and the rolling grasslands around Manzini to dry, flat plains, dotted with thatched huts. Mkhaya itself is set in classic acacia bushveld and offers excellent game viewing, whether you choose guided walks or drives with the rangers. It is one of the best places in southern Africa to see the reticent black rhino.

You'll pass through much the same range of landscapes en route to Swaziland's other chief game reserve, the **Hlane Royal National Park ❼**, about 110 km, or 65 miles, northeast of Mbabane on the MR3. Hlane – pronounced "shlane" – covers 70,000 hectares (173,000 acres) of bushveld, spread among the toes of the Lebombo Mountains. Game includes hippo, elephant, white rhino, giraffe, zebra, impala and – the big news round these parts – lion, successfully reintroduced here for the first time in the country. This is a good place for bird-watching, and for raptor-watching in particular.

The wild north

Spectacular **Malolotja Nature Reserve ❽**, about 35 km (20 miles) north from Mbabane on the road to Pigg's Peak, is Swaziland's northern gem. Wildlife is not

TIP

A good time to visit Swaziland is in January, during the traditional *Incwala* ceremony. The new year is ushered in with much festive singing and dancing.

BELOW: Usutu, the largest man-made forest in the world.

Moshoeshoe asked Queen Victoria to annex Lesotho in 1851 so that his people might be as "the lice in the blanket of the great Queen" – a reference to the all-embracing protection of the British Empire.

BELOW: the Barberton daisy was originally found in the countryside near Barberton, on the Swazi border.

the main attraction here, although game includes blesbok, black wildebeest (gnu), impala and oribi antelope, and a breeding colony of the rare bald ibis near the Malolotja Falls. Instead, this is superb hiking country: from deep, forested ravines and waterfalls to high plateaux, most of which is only accessible on foot (there are 200 km or 120 miles of trails).

The reserve also contains the ancient **Lion Cavern,** believed to the world's oldest mine. Radiocarbon dating techniques have shown that red oxides and haematite were being dug out the earth here as long ago as 41,000 BC. It's situated about 16 km or 11 miles from the park entrance, near the still-active Ngwenya iron ore mine.

Run by the National Trust Commission, accommodation at Malolotja is in in log cabins, adequately equipped with cooking facilities. There is a shop selling basic supplies and a campsite. Further afield, the historic mining village of **Pigg's Peak ❾** (about 24 km or 14 miles further north from the reserve on the MR1) is set amidst green, rolling hills covered in pine and eucalyptus plantations; it makes an interesting half-day excursion.

Lesotho – African Switzerland

This tiny mountain kingdom is an adventurer's dream. Saw-tooth ridges and deep, precipitous valleys glittering with tumbling rivers and falls; mud-and-thatch villages where herders watch over their flocks – it's an African Switzerland, on African time.

The best time to go is between March and April, before it gets too cold to swim, or from October to November, before the summer rains turn the rivers to torrents. These are also good times to see wild flowers – the white and mauve

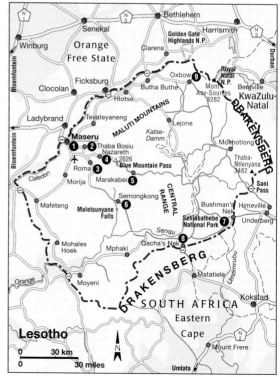

cosmos which creates great bands of colour across the landscape in autumn, and the delicate Afro-alpine species which twinkle on the grassy hills throughout spring and summer.

One of the most popular modes of travel through the rugged interior is by sturdy Basotho pony (but be warned – this does require a certain level of stamina and stoicism). Trekking centres organise tours for riders through breathtakingly beautiful mountain scenery, in accommodation ranging from hotels to village huts. Here, conditions are fairly basic, but perfectly adequate once you get used to no running water, no flush toilets and no electricity. The other way to get round Lesotho is by four-wheel-drive vehicle, either on a self-drive basis or on a guided trip with a tour operator.

The west – mountain cities, painted caves

Most visitors will pass through or be based in **Maseru ❶**, the capital. Just across the border from the South African town of Ladybrand, it may be twice as big as its South African neighbour, but it's also twice as ugly. Nonetheless, the gift and craft shops here serve as a good introduction to the styles of local craftsmanship you'll encounter throughout the country.

Thaba Bosiu ❷, Moshoeshoe's majestic mountain stronghold, lies about 10 km (6 miles) east of Maseru on the B20. You can visit the ruins of the king's residence and his grave after tackling the short, steep climb to the summit. It is compulsory to hire a guide (a small fee is charged) from the Tourist Information Centre at the base of the mountain.

Also worth a visit is the picturesque sandstone town of **Roma ❸**, about 35 km (22 miles) east from Maseru on the A3 route. Home of the National

Map, see opposite

BELOW: Lesotho – African Switzerland.

**Map,
page 292**

*The sturdy Basotho
pony is the product of
careful breeding from
bloodstock
captured by the Sotho
during the Eastern
Cape's Frontier Wars
– over a century ago.*

BELOW: a gathering
of the clans, Thaba
Bosiu.
RIGHT: family outing,
Makhaleng River
Valley.

University of Lesotho, Roma was first established as as a mission centre in 1863. Educational and spiritual matters aside, it is set in a lovely wooded valley, surrounded by mountains that are often snow-capped in winter.

Lesotho's topography consists of a skirt of sandstone, crowned by a massive wedge of volcanic basalt (no point in the country has an altitude less than 1,000 metres, or 3,000 ft). Pocking the soft sandstone are hundreds of caves, once home to those diminutive hunter-gatherers, the San – many are vividly decorated with their paintings.

One of the best-preserved rock art sites is at **Ha Baroana**, about 20 km (12 miles) north of Roma near the mission settlement of **Nazareth ④**. This drive follows a road that winds up from the lowlands into the foothills of the Maluti Mountains, offering dramatic views back over Roma. From Nazareth, it's a 5-km (3-mile) walk from a signposted turn-off to the site. The curator charges a small fee to open the gate.

Peaks and dramatic passes

East from Maseru, a series of magnificent passes soar over the Maluti Mountains, penetrating deep into the heart of Lesotho. The Thaba Tseka road via **Marakabei ⑤** is especially scenic; **Bushman's Pass** (2,268 metres or 7,400 ft) and the dramatic **Blue Mountain Pass** (2,626 metres or 8,600 ft) are just two of the highlights. In between lies Molimo Nthuse Pass, at the top of which is a pony-trekking centre from which ponies may be hired and excursions planned.

South from here lie **Semongkong ⑥** and the **Maletsunyane Falls** – at 192 metres (630 ft), the longest single-drop waterfall in southern Africa. You could fly to Semongkong from Maseru in about an hour, but it takes three days to ride there from the trekking centre at Molimo Nthuse Pass. By four-wheel-drive track from Roma, you could spend anything from a few hours to a few days, depending on the weather. That's Lesotho, and that's why it's such an adventurer's dream.

Isolated, inaccessible and spectacular, **Sehlabathebe National Park ⑦** is the only one in Lesotho. There's very little game there except for the occasional mountain reedbuck, grey rhebuck or oribi, although it's an excellent place to see the rare lammergeyer (bearded vulture) and black eagle.

Situated in the far southeast of the country on the South African border, you can reach the park by four-wheel-drive from **Qacha's Nek ⑧** (about 100 km or 60 miles), or by walking or pony-trekking from the South African border post at **Bushman's Nek**. Either way, there's nothing there but miles of rugged wilderness.

Europeans may find the "ski resort" at **Oxbow ⑨** a bit of a joke, although there's usually a foot or two of snow in mid-winter. Reached via **Butha Buthe**, about 100 km or 60 miles northeast of Maseru on the Sani Pass road, accommodation is rudimentary; nevertheless, young white South Africans love it. Summer visitors can take advantage of the fine trout fishing in the Malibamat'so River here – there's a good site near the Oxbow Lodge, which will advise on permits as well as arrange local guides and treks.

INSIGHT GUIDES

TRAVEL TIPS

Your vacation.

Your vacation after losing your wallet in the ocean.

Lose your cash and it's lost forever. Lose American Express® Travelers Cheques and get them replaced. They can mean the difference between the vacation of your dreams and your worst nightmare. And, they are accepted like cash worldwide. Available at participating banks, credit unions, AAA offices and American Express Travel locations. *Don't take chances. Take American Express Travelers Cheques.*

do more

Travelers
Cheques

CONTENTS

Getting Acquainted

The Place

Situation Lying between the latitudes of 22° and 35° South, South Africa extends from the Limpopo in the north 2,000 km (1,200 miles) to the Cape Peninsula in the southwest and 1,500 km (930 miles) from the semi-desert of Namaqualand in the west to the subtropical east coast of KwaZulu-Natal. To the north, South Africa borders Namibia, Botswana, Zimbabwe; to the northeast, Mozambique. Wholly surrounded by South Africa are the kingdoms of Lesotho and Swaziland, which have never belonged to South Africa – they remained British protectorates until their independence in the mid-1960s.
Area 1.22 million sq. km (471,442 sq. miles) – five times larger than Britain.
Capital Pretoria
Population 38 million, of whom around 76 percent are black, 12.8 percent are white, 2.6

Time Zone

South Africa is two hours ahead of Greenwich Mean Time (GMT), and seven hours ahead of America's Eastern Standard Time. The sun rises in the east, even on the Cape: but it's easy to lose your orientation in the first few days, until you've got used to the sun being in the north. Then, east and west will fall into place for you.
   Attentive visitors will notice

percent are Asian and 8.6 percent are of mixed origin.
Language There are 11 official languages: English, Afrikaans, Zulu, Xhosa, Sotho, Venda, Tswana, Tsonga, Pedi, Shangaan and Ndebele.
Religion 80 percent are Christian, with the rest mostly Muslims, Hindus or Jews.
Currency The currency is the Rand, consisting of 100 cents. In Lesotho, Swaziland, and Botswana, the Rand is generally accepted as payment, in addition to the local currency.
Weights & Measures Metric
Electricity The standard current throughout the country is 220/230 volts. Only sockets with three-pronged plugs are used, so to use European or American applicances you'll have to get an adaptor (which you can find in any electrical appliance shop on the Cape). Some of the larger hotels will loan adaptors to you on request.
Direct Dialling Dial 27 for South Africa, then 21 for Capetown, 31 for Durban, 12 for Pretoria, or 11 for Johannesburg.

Provinces and Regions

The nine provinces are: Northern Cape (capital: Kimberley), Western Cape (capital: Cape Town) and Eastern Cape (capital: Bisho) in the south and west, Free State (capital: Bloemfontein)

that the sun in Durban rises and sets significantly earlier than in Cape Town. The explanation for this is simple: the distance between the two cities is roughly equivalent to that between Birmingham, England and Berlin, Germany. You'll also notice that it gets dark almost immediately – it's pitch-black a mere half-hour after sunset.

in the interior, KwaZulu-Natal (capital: Pietermaritzburg) and Mpumalanga (capital: Nelspruit) in the east, Gauteng (capital: Johannesburg), and the self-explanatory North-West (capital: Mmabatho) and Northern Province (capital: Pietersburg).

THE 21 REGIONS

The Lesotho Highlands, the highest part of southern Africa, straddle the boundary between South Africa and Lesotho and reach an elevation in excess of 3,400 metres (11,000 ft). Much of the area is mountain tundra, receiving regular winter snows.
   The Highveld, a gently undulating, high-lying area of the interior plateau, consists chiefly of grassland and coincides with the largest remaining portion of an ancient plain formed by erosion (the African Surface). It is home to the Witwatersrand urban complex and most of South Africa's gold, coal and maize are produced here.
   Northern Province is of considerable scenic diversity, encompassing the rugged Soutpansberg Mountains and Waterberg Plateau, and the intervening Pietersburg Plain. The Soutpansberg is well-watered and a centre of timber production. Much of the rest is given over to cattle-ranching.
   The Ghaap Plateau, a flat, featureless plain with a semi-arid climate, is devoted almost exclusively to cattle-ranching. A number of powerful springs, such as the Eye of Kuruman, emerge from its dolomite rocks.
   The Bushmanland Plain, the flat, arid expanse of the interior plateau, is sparsely covered by low scrub. Dotted by innumerable seasonal lakes (pans), it is suited to little else but extensive sheep ranching.
   The Bushveld Basin, the world's largest body of basic and ultra-basic rocks, occupies the flat central part of this basin and is a rich treasure-house of

minerals including platinum, chrome, iron and vanadium. Its clayey black turf soils favour the production of cotton, tobacco and other cash crops, while citrus is grown on its margins. The encircling Bankenveld ridges flank the city of Pretoria. The ancient volcanic plug of the Pilanesberg, in the western part of the basin, is the setting for the Sun City resort complex.

The Kalahari Basin, a semi-arid Acacia savannah, this flat sand-covered area was once a sea of desert dunes. The red dune ridges now support a sparse grass/woodland mosaic, which is home to a wide variety of grazing antelopes in the Kalahari Gemsbok National Park.

The Lower Vaal and Orange Valleys are occupied by the major westward-flowing rivers of South Africa. These broad valleys, although semi-arid at best, have attracted a good deal of development. The valley of a major tributary, the Harts River, contains the largest irrigation scheme in the southern hemisphere (the Vaalharts). Kimberley, located between the two valleys, is South Africa's centre of diamond production. Below Upington, the Orange River enters a deep gorge through the imposing Augrabies Falls. Towards the coast, the valley becomes barren and rugged in the extreme.

The Karoo is a vast expanse of semi-arid plains dotted with flat-topped hills *(koppies)*. It is covered by sparse scrub and grass which are well suited to the rearing of sheep.

The northern Drakensberg, part of the Great Escarpment, receives ample rain brought by winds from the Indian Ocean and supports impressive stands of mountainous forest as well as the world's largest plantation of exotic timber in the Sabie area. An early centre of gold production, it boasts spectacular mountain scenery with many resorts and hiking trails.

The southern Drakensberg, along the Great Escarpment, is home to many peaks exceeding 3,000 metres (9,800 ft), making it the premier mountaineering centre of South Africa.

The Cape Fold Mountains, scarcely less spectacular than the KwaZulu-Natal Drakensberg, are home to the unique *fynbos* (macchia) vegetation in the winter rainfall area of the southwestern Cape. Rugged sandstone peaks offer good hiking and rock-climbing, while intervening valleys are the centre of South African wine and fruit production. The scenery of the coastal zone, with its numerous deep bays and sandy beaches backed by majestic mountain chains, is amongst the world's finest.

The Namaqua Highlands consist of arid, rocky mountains and valleys decked by an immense carpet of spring flowers in years of good winter rains. Its remote northern extremity, adjacent to Namibia, is known as the Richtersveld.

The Limpopo Valley and its river form the boundary between South Africa and Zimbabwe. An area of dry savannah woodland, it has numerous game farms and several nature reserves, although large tracts remain devoted to cattle ranching.

The Lowveld, low, undulating plains, separates the foot of the Great Escarpment from the Lebombo Mountains in the eastern parts of Mpumalanga, Swaziland and northern KwaZulu-Natal. With its hot, humid summer climate the Lowveld is a major producer of tropical fruit and sugar. A significant area of natural woodland has, however, been protected in a number of reserves, the largest of which is the Kruger National Park.

The Southeastern Coastal Hinterland, stretching from Swaziland in the north to the Ciskei in the south, is an area of undulating hills crossed by deep river valleys. Ample rainfall produces a run-off which exceeds, in aggregate, that of the Orange River. The warm Mozambique current makes it possible to swim year-round along the KwaZulu-Natal coast.

The Lebombo Mountains mark the eastern border with Mozambique throughout much of their length. Eastward flowing rivers en route to the Indian Ocean traverse it in a series of spectacular gorges.

The Zululand Coastal Plain consists of bush-covered, sandy flats with numerous lakes and estuaries around which several nature reserves have been established. Browsing herbivores dominate the dense woodland, and frequent stretches of water support a diverse population of birds and aquatic creatures.

The Southern Coastal Platform, a raised marine platform stretching from the most southerly tip of the continent to Port Elizabeth, offers picturesque forests and lagoons along the most typical stretch of the Garden Route lying between George and Humansdorp.

The Swartland, a gently rolling plain between the Cape Fold Mountains and the Atlantic coast, has a semi-arid climate and is a major wheat producer.

The Namib, a coastal desert, like the Swartland, is lapped by the Benguela Current whose cold waters support most of South Africa's fishing industry. Barren in the extreme, its sparse scrubland becomes a carpet of flowers after winter rains.

Climate

The Cape Peninsula has a typically Mediterranean climate; the weather in the interior – on the highveld – is moderate. Only the Kruger Park and Northern

Province can really be described as subtropical.

As the seasons are exactly opposite to those in the Northern hemisphere, Christmas comes right in the middle of the hottest season when it is 30°C (86°F) in the shade.

Thanks to the sunshine which graces the Cape's coastal resort areas with 300 more hours of sun each year than the Canary Islands, any time of year is the right time to travel. Particularly ideal are autumn (March–April) and spring (September–October).

Rainfall is an uncertain quantity on the Cape. South Africa is characterised as an arid region (the rate of evaporation is higher than that of precipitation). Two-thirds of the country receives less than 500mm (19 inches) of rainfall a year. In the interior, the precious rain falls mostly in the summer months (October–March), generally in brief but violent showers. The Western Cape receives its precipitation in winter (May–September); along the country's southern coast it could rain at any time of year. The high humidity in KwaZulu-Natal can also make for some truly muggy days.

Snow falls nearly every year in the high mountains, but seldom results in more than a powdery dusting along the ground. The reason for this is lack of humidity rather than the temperature.

Temperatures

The average maximum temperatures for the four major cities are:
Cape Town 80°F/27°C in summer; 69°F/21°C in winter.
Durban 83°F/28°C in summer; 77°F/25°C in winter.
Johannesburg 81°F/27°C in summer; 78°F/26°C in winter.
Pretoria 87°F/31°C; 74°F/23°C in winter.

People

Black South Africans can be divided into nine major peoples, whose cultures, traditions and customs differ significantly. Each group is further divided: the Zulus, for instance, have over 200 different clans or chiefdoms.

Some of the black languages have certain similarities. The largest, the Nguni language family, includes those peoples who moved down the coast from East Africa some 300–400 years ago and ran into the white settlers in the area of Port Elizabeth at the end of the 18th century. The Zulus, Swazis, Xhosa and several smaller groups belong to this linguistic family.

About 8.6 percent of the population are known as coloureds – mixed-race descendants of white settlers and either the Khoikhoi (a cattle herding tribe who farmed the region in ancient times) or the remaining San communities. Descendants of the Malay slaves imported by the Dutch also fall into this category. They live almost exclusively in the west, and speak Afrikaans.

The Indian community first came to work on the sugar cane plantations of KwaZulu-Natal in the second half of the 19th century, and still live for the most part in this region. They still live in accordance with their own traditions, maintaining their music, language and culture. Sixty percent of the Indian community are Hindu and 20 percent are Muslim.

Whites are as mixed a lot as the black population. In the course of the past 350 years, white people have poured into the country from around the world: Dutch and German, British and French, Jews, Portuguese, Greeks, Italians, Poles and others.

Today, Afrikaners – white,

Afrikaans-speaking South Africans – form the majority of the white population (57 percent). These people are descendants of the Dutch, who were the first to arrive on the Cape. English-speaking South Africans comprise some 37 percent of the white population. Of other European nations, Portugal and Germany are the best-represented.

Government

The Constitution, which came into effect on 3 February 1997, is the supreme law of the land. Inter alia, it provides for a Government of National Unity (GNU), three tiers of democratic government (the Executive Authority, the Legislative Authority and the Judicial Authority) and a chapter on fundamental rights.

Parliament consists of a 400-member National Assembly and a National Council of Provinces (NCOP) consisting of 10 representatives for each of the nine provinces. The National Assembly is made up of 200 members from the national representatives list and 200 people from the regional representatives list of the various political parties, elected on the basis of proportional representation.

Ordinary laws are passed by a simple majority in each house and if one house rejects a bill, it must be passed by a majority of the total number of the members of both houses. Finance bills, such as the budget and taxation laws, can be introduced only by the National Assembly. Bills affecting provincial boundaries or the exercise of powers or functions allocated to provincial government must be approved both by the National Assembly and the NCOP.

The head of state is the executive president, Nelson Mandela. The executive deputy

Business Hours

Like so much else in South Africa, regulations governing business hours have loosened up considerably.

Shops are generally open Monday–Friday 9am–5pm, Saturdays 8.30am–1pm. In smaller towns, they are often closed for lunch 1–2pm. Some of the larger shopping malls (with up to 200 shops) don't close until 6pm on Saturday. Supermarkets, too, tend to keep their doors open longer (usually 8am–6pm), and now it has become possible to shop in certain supermarkets and bookstores on Sunday.

Another important element in the Cape, in particular, are the so-called "**cafés**" in every little village. These don't, as you might think, purvey cake and coffee, but rather newspapers, cigarettes, sweets and some groceries;

they are often open 7am–8pm, seven days a week.

Public offices are open Monday–Friday 8am–3.30pm.

Although **banks** don't all observe the same hours of business, they generally only vary by half an hour: Monday–Friday 9am–3.30pm, Saturday 8.30–11am. In the country-side, most banks close for lunch 12.45–2pm.

Opening times for **airport banks** are as follows:

Johannesburg International Airport: open 24 hours.

Cape Town International Airport: open during normal office hours, with the exchange service open two hours before international flights.

Durban International Airport: open regular hours Tuesday, Wednesday, Friday; Saturday 4–6pm; Sunday 9am–1pm and 8.30–10.30pm.

president is Thabo Mbeki. The cabinet is composed of 25 ministerial portfolios.

The priority of the Government of National Unity is the Recon-struction and Development Programme (RDP), which aims not only to build houses, create jobs and feed school children, but also to motivate a demoralised people to rebuild the nation. It involves bringing a sense of purpose to the lives of people who have been marginalised for generations.

The multi-party Government of National Unity will continue to function until 27 April 1999, when the next democratic elections will be held.

Economy

There are few other places in the world where there are such contrasts between rich and poor as in South Africa. On the one hand, the country displays all

the typical third world characteristics of other African countries: explosive population growth (2.3 percent per annum), low productivity, low level of education and training (5 million black youths without any qualification), unemployment, desperate housing shortages, and increasing malnutrition. The other side of South Africa belongs firmly in the first world, with its highly-developed industry, various export technology products and modern telecommunications.

The manufacturing sector breaks down as follows: chemicals, rubber and plastics 22.5 percent; machinery, transport and scientific equipment 21.5 percent; food, beverages and tobacco products 20.6 percent; metal and metal products 14.8 percent; paper products and printing 7.6 percent; textiles, clothing, leather products and footwear

7.2 percent; mineral products 3.3 percent; wood products and furniture 2.5 percent.

The principal crops are maize, wheat, sugar, potatoes, tobacco and fruit (including grapes, which support an expanding wine industry). Of these, sugar, maize and fruit provide substantial export earnings. Wool is South Africa's second biggest agricultural export commodity after maize and its the 10th on the country's list of exports. South Africa is the fourth largest wool producer outside Asia. The country's 27 million sheep include mainly South African Merino for wool and Dorper for mutton. South Africa has approximately 8.4 million head of cattle, consisting of introduced breeds (such as Hereford and Aberdeen Angus) and indigenous breeds (such as Afrikaner). The country's 2 million dairy cows (mainly Friesian) are the base of a progressive dairy industry that produces butter, condensed milk, milk powder and cheese.

For every 1,000 people, there are 144 telephones, 99 passenger vehicles and 44 commercial vehicles.

Planning the Trip

Entry Regulations

Visas and Passports

All visitors need to bring a valid passport, but visitors from the EU, the USA, Canada, Australia, New Zealand, Singapore, Japan, Lichtenstein and Switzerland can travel to South Africa without a visa. However, if any visitors, regardless of passport, travel through Swaziland, a visa is required, which you can get at the border. Visitors from other countries can receive a South African visa free of charge, but must apply at least four weeks before their date of departure. Holidaymakers from countries including Australia, the USA, and Canada (but not the UK, France, Germany or the Netherlands) require a visa for Lesotho.

Transit visas are issued to travellers who plan to go through South Africa to neighbouring countries, whether by air, train or car. Applicants must be able to show a return ticket and a visa for their final destination.

Multiple-entry visas are recommended for all visitors who want a South African visa and also plan to visit Lesotho or Swaziland or other surrounding countries, returning afterwards to South Africa (for their return flight, for example). If you don't decide on such an excursion until you actually get to the Cape, you'll need to apply for a re-entry visa before leaving South Africa. This takes at least a week, and can be obtained from the Department of Home Affairs in Pretoria, tel: (012) 314 8911, or its regional offices in every major city.

A **temporary residence permit** is issued on arrival when you give your reason for, and length of, your stay. If you should want to stay for longer than three months, you'll have to have this permit renewed at the Department of Home Affairs, one of its offices, or a police station; try to do this 10–14 days before the previous permit expires.

Money Matters

Visitors can take 500 Rand each in and out of the country; there's no limit on foreign currencies or travellers' cheques. You can exchange extra Rand into other currencies at the end of your trip, but you have to prove that you brought the money in with you: don't forget to save your exchange receipts.

Travellers' cheques are the safest form of currency. Cheques in German marks and US dollars will yield the highest rate of exchange.

Banks are the best place to exchange cheques or cash; you can take care of this directly at the airport upon arrival. Major hotels also exchange money.

Most hotels, shops, restaurants and travel agencies accept international credit cards: Visa, MasterCard (Eurocard), Diners Club and American Express.

Tax returns You won't have to pay tax if you have your purchases sent directly to your home address. When purchasing diamond jewellery or precious metals from a shop which is a member of the Jewellery Council of South Africa, Johannesburg,

Customs

Items for personal use, such as clothes, jewellery, sports equipment, film, used cameras and video cameras, binoculars, etc. are duty-free. Beyond this, an incoming visitor may bring new or used goods (such as presents) of up to 500 Rand in value into the country, as well as 2 litres of wine, 1 litre of alcohol, 50 ml of perfume, 250 ml of eau de toilette, 400 cigarettes, 50 cigars, or 250 grams of tobacco. Any spirits or tobacco products which exceed these limits are subject to duty, and can't be written off as part of the 500 Rand limit.

A permit is required for **weapons**; this can be obtained from the customs official upon entry, and is valid for 180 days. The visitor must prove that he legally owns the weapon.

For **animals**, you'll need an import permit from the Director of Animal Health in Pretoria, tel: (012) 319 7514. This should be arranged at least two months before your trip. Pets, incidentally, aren't allowed into game reserves.

If you're bringing **cars or motorcycles** into the country, make sure you obtain the necessary documentation from an internationally recognised automobile club.

A special permit is required to bring **plants and animal products** (for example seeds or hunting trophies) into or out of the country. The CITES convention maintains strict control over trade in endangered species of plants and animals.

Generally forbidden: drugs and medication (excepting those prescribed for personal use), and pornography.

tel: (011) 29 6441, the tax is recorded on a separate receipt and credit card slip. When leaving the country, have your departure confirmed at the Jewellery Council counter; the Council will then send a form back to the shop, which will destroy the credit card slip. This practice, however, is only possible with a shop which is a Council member.

What to Bring

As in any warm climate, you'll be most comfortable in light cotton clothing. Most hotels offer a next-day laundry and pressing service, and big cities also have coin-operated laundromats. Holiday centres require only casual dress, although for dinner in a hotel or restaurant one generally dresses more formally.

In winter (June–August), it's generally still comfortably warm in KwaZulu-Natal (Durban). The rest of the country tends to be around 20°C (68°F) in the day's sun; however, at night and in the early morning, it can be cold, even extremely cold. Warm clothing is a "must".

On the Cape and the Highveld (Johannesburg) it can become quite cool, especially in the evenings. Always take a jacket or anorak with you.

When hiking in the game preserves, wear camouflage colours: beige, brown, khaki, or olive green. This isn't only to keep you from being too noticeable to the animals; flies and insects are more attracted to white or colourful clothing. Long-sleeved shirts are also a protection against insect bites.

Rain is termed "lovely weather" in South Africa – an indication that the country's citizens would like to see more of it. When it does rain, however, it pours, and one is quickly soaked through to the skin. It's wise to take a raincoat or umbrella with you.

Topless bathing is taboo on the beaches and at hotel pools; but bikinis are perfectly acceptable.

In addition, don't forget to pack high-factor sun screen and a wide-brimmed sun hat – not only for the beach, but also for hiking, particularly in the interior where the sun can be fierce.

Health

Cholera and smallpox vaccinations are no longer required. Yellow fever inoculations are only necessary for those travelling from an infected yellow fever zone.

Malaria tablets are highly recommended to all visitors to the north of the country, including the Lowveld, Mpumalanga, the Kruger National Park and KwaZulu-Natal. It is essential to consult your doctor about suitable anti-malarial precautions to take before you visit. Typical symptoms are similar to flu, and should show within a week or two. However, the best prophylactic is not to get bitten: that means liberal use of insect repellent and covering with clothing at dawn and evenings, as well as sleeping in mosquito-proof quarters. Use mosquito coils, which you can buy in any supermarket. The critical period is from November to May or June, depending on how late the rains have fallen.

Ticks are found in long grass and can carry tick bite fever (if it should be an infected one that bites you). When walking in long grass it is advisable to wear trousers tucked into boots or long socks.

Snake bites are not very common, because snakes generally try and slither away from "visitors" as fast as they can. Before you take a needle and serum and do yourself any undue damage, you should first look for a doctor or clinic.

Public Holidays 1998

New Year's Day	1 January
Founders' Day	6 April
Good Friday	10 April
Family Day	13 April
Workers' Day	1 May
Ascension Day	21 May
Republic Day	31 May
Kruger Day	10 October
Day of Reconciliation	16 December
Christmas Day	25 December
Day of Goodwill	26 December

Wherever you are in South Africa, medical aid is generally no further than two hours away. The best serum is vigilance: don't sit on any fallen tree or stone without first checking that there are no snakes underneath; walk firmly and look where you're going. If you get bitten then check what kind of snake the culprit was – you can recognise a snake bite by the two adjacent pricks. Don't panic, but calm the patient, lie him down and be reassuring – a snake bite is not necessarily a death sentence!

Put cooking salt and an icepack on scorpion bites to reduce the pain.

Bilharzia is found in virtually every inland body of water in the north, KwaZulu-Natal and Eastern Cape (except in rapidly flowing water or lakes at high altitudes). Don't wade or swim in ponds or brooks. When in doubt, ask about local conditions.

Aids is becoming as major a problem in South Africa as on the rest of the continent; avoid high-risk activities such as unprotected sex.

You don't have to worry about food and beverages – you won't suffer ill-effects from consuming fresh fruit, vegetables, lettuce, fruit juices, ice cream or water from the tap in South Africa.

Getting There

By Air
Most flights to and from Europe are non-stop. It's best, however, to ask when you book – a stop-over can make the flight up to 1.5 hours longer. Johannesburg is southern Africa's transportation hub and it handles the majority of international flights to South Africa. From here, you can fly to Botswana, the Ivory Coast, Kenya, Malawi, Namibia, Zaire, Zambia and Zimbabwe, as well as Mauritius, the Comoro Islands, Madagascar and Réunion. Some international flights also operate directly to Cape Town and Durban.

South African Airways (SAA) fly to South Africa from Amsterdam, Bangkok, Buenos Aires, Dubai, Düsseldorf, Frankfurt, Hong Kong, Miami, Mumbai (Bombay), Munich, New York, London, Paris, Perth, Rio de Janeiro, Sao Paulo, Singapore, Taipei, Tel Aviv, Tokyo and Zurich.

Since the liberalising of air routes in 1992, about 80 other airlines have started competing for the profitable South African international routes. The main operators are Air France, Alitalia, British Airways, Lufthansa, Qantas and Virgin Atlantic.

Your travel agent will be able to provide information about cheaper flights available from charter airlines.

By Sea
The days when you could take one of the weekly mail boats from Cape Town to Southampton, England, for far less than the price of a plane flight are no more. However, there are still a number of shipping companies offering passage to the Cape.

Various cruise liners call at South African ports – detailed information is available from travel agents.

Safmarine, a container ship operator, offers berths for up to 10 fare-paying passengers on its Tilbury (England) to Cape Town, Port Elizabeth or Durban route (via Le Havre or Zeebrugge). The service is available all year, with about two sailings in each direction every month. Book through travel agents or, in the UK, contact: Captain Richard Hellyer, tel: (01703) 334415; fax: (01703) 334416. In South Africa, contact: tel: (021) 408 6911; fax: (021) 408 6370.

RMS St Helena carries up to 128 passengers on its Cardiff (Wales) to Cape Town route, via Tenerife, Ascension Island and St Helena. There are four sailings in each direction every year. UK contact: Curnow Shipping Ltd, The Shipyard, Porthleven, Helston, Cornwall TR13 9JA, UK, tel: (01326) 563434; fax: (01326) 564347. South Africa contact: St Helena Line (PTY) Ltd, 2nd Floor, BP Centre, Thibault Square, Cape Town 8001, tel: (021) 25 1165; fax: (021) 21 7485.

By Rail
It is possible to enter South Africa by train from Namibia, Zimbabwe and Botswana.
• **Namibia**: Windhoek to Johannesburg. Travel time about 45 hours. Departs Wednesday (6.45pm), Saturday (midnight), and Sunday (6.45pm). Change in De Aar to the Trans-Karoo from Cape Town to Johannesburg. The connection is best on the Saturday run. There's only a dining car after De Aar; before that, you can only get snacks.
• **Zimbabwe**: Bulawayo-Johannesburg. Travel time about 24 hours. Departs Thursday mornings.
• **Botswana**: Francistown-Gaberone-Johannesburg. Travel time about 19 hours.

Border Crossings

South Africa: Most crossing points are not open 24 hours a day, so check what time they close before you depart. Information is available from the South African Department of Home Affairs, Private Bag X114, Pretoria 0001, Gauteng, tel: (012) 314 8911; fax: (021) 323 2416.
Namibia: Vioolsdrif (from Cape Town): 24 hours; Ariamsvlei (from Johannesburg): 24 hours; Onseepkans (from the Augrabies Falls): 6am–10pm; Rietfontein (from the Kalahari Chamois Park): 6am–10pm. From Mata-Mata, there's no access to Kalahari-Rietfontein or Twee Rivieren.
Botswana: Ramatlabama (near Mmabatho): 7am–8pm; Skilpadhek (near Lobatse): 7am–5pm; Kopfontein (near Gaberone): 7am–10pm; Stokpoort (from Johannesburg): 8am–4pm; Grobbelersbrug (from Johannesburg): 8am–6pm.
Zimbabwe: Beitbridge: 6am–8pm.
Mozambique: Lebombo (near Komatiepoort): 8am–5pm.
Swaziland: Oshoek (near Mbabane): 7am–10pm; Golela (in the South): 7am–10pm; Mahamba (from Piet Retief): 7am–10pm.
Lesotho: Ficksburg Bridge: Mon–Thur 6am–8pm, Fri–Sun 6am–10pm; Maseru Bridge: 6am–10pm; Van Rooyens Nek (near Wepener): 7am–8pm.
Transkei: Both crossings: 24 hours.
Information about Botswana's Eastern border crossings – controlled by Bophuthatswana – can be obtained from the South African Consulate (Mmabatho), tel: (0140) 32 521.

By Bus

This is faster and cheaper than the train, but you should be ready for lengthy, if comfortable, periods sitting down.

• **Namibia**: The Inter-Cape Mainline goes from Windhoek to Cape Town and Johannesburg. Windhoek–Cape Town Monday and Thursday, 6pm (18 hours); Windhoek–Johannesburg Monday and Thursday, 6pm (21 hours).

• **Zimbabwe**: Translux Harare–Bulawayo–Johannesburg, daily except Thursday and Sunday (21 hours).

By Car

For reasons of insurance and security, you can't go to or from South Africa by way of Zimbabwe and Mozambique in a rented car. In Botswana, you can only drive rented cars on paved roads (with the exception of rented four-wheel drive vehicles). If you want to go to Namibia, Botswana, Lesotho or Swaziland (or are coming from one of these countries), you'll need a written statement from the rental company that you're authorised to take the car over the border.

Automobile Association (AA) services are free to international AA members, on presentation of a valid membership card, and, for a fee, to non-members. The services include car hire (Avis), international motoring advice, route maps, road travel and weather information.

The Automobile Association of South Africa, Dennis Paxton House, Kyalami Grand Prix Circuit, Allandale Road, Kyalami, Midrand 1685, Gauteng, tel: (011) 799 1000; fax: (011) 799 1010.

AA roadside repairs and towing, tel: 0800 010 101 toll-free.

AA Travel Information Centre (Johannesburg), tel: (011) 466 6641.

AA Technical Division: tel: 0800 033 163 toll free.

Practical Tips

Emergencies

During the last few years, there has been an increase in crime in the large cities. Although incidents of violent crime against tourists are rare, sensible precautions should be taken.

Always keep cameras, expensive watches and jewellery concealed when walking about in built-up areas, especially in Johannesburg. If you need to stop to consult a map or guide book, don't draw attention to yourself by looking lost on a street corner – walk into a shop or bank.

As in most countries, walking the streets, particularly alone, at night is not recommended. Car windows should be kept closed and doors locked at all times when driving in Johannesburg. If you are unsure about the safety of visiting a particular area, consult the local tourist information office.

Any loss of valuables should be immediately reported to the police. **The telephone number in all large cities is 10111.**

Disabled

A disabled person with a measure of patience and a sense of humour will enjoy touring South Africa, even though facilities are not always readily available. However, the new South African government is attempting to improve matters and has set up the National Accessibility Scheme. As well as creating a database of accessible amenities and attractions, the scheme promotes awareness of disabled needs throughout the tourism industry. Contact the **South African Tourism Board** (see under Tourist Offices) or one of the following for details:

National Environmental Accessibility Programme
PO Box 1019,
Pine Town 3600,
tel: (031) 701 8264;
fax: (031) 721623.

National Accessibility Scheme
PO Box 3515,
Bloemfontein 9300,
tel: (051) 471362;
fax: (051) 470862.

SA National Council for the Blind
Tel: (012) 346 1190.

Medical Services

The standard of medical aid in South Africa is very high and compares favourably with that of Europe and America. **Doctors** are listed under "Medical" in all telephone directories. One finds all-night **chemists** in all major cities and pharmacies are listed in the Yellow Pages.

Dentists are listed under "D" in all local telephone directories.

There are both private and government **hospitals**. The government hospital telephone numbers are listed under Emergency Services at the front of telephone directories.

There is no National Health Agreement between South Africa and overseas countries, so you will have to pay directly for the service you receive. Travel medical insurance is therefore strongly recommended. Be sure to keep the receipt to submit to your own medical insurance company at home.

Media

Television

South Africa has had television since 1976. Currently, the South African Broadcasting Corporation (SABC) provides three television channels: SABC 1 broadcasts in English; SABC 2 and SABC 3 broadcast in eight African languages and Afrikaans.

The advent of satellite and cable television has increased the choice for viewers who can afford it. M-Net, a private subscription channel accessed with the help of a decoder, broadcasts films, documentaries and most major sports (including rugby, cricket, football and golf). Another subscription service, called Multichoice, offers access to satellite broadcast services. To stay in touch with the competition, SABC is introducing its own six-channel subscription satellite service

Radio

South Africa has radio stations broadcasting in all 11 official languages. As well as SABC's public stations, there are 14 commercial stations and countless community stations.

Print

Newspapers are sold mornings and afternoons on the street corners. European papers and magazines can be found at the booksellers' CNA – at high prices and often several days old.

Postal Services

You can buy stamps at post offices, book shops such as CNA, supermarkets and a host of other outlets. If travelling to rural areas, buy a supply in advance, as post offices can be few and far between.

Post office opening times: Monday–Friday 8.30am–4.30pm, Saturday 8am–midday. Smaller, rural branches close for lunch 1–2pm.

The South African Post Office is not the most reliable postal service in the world. If sending mail other than postcards (especially anything of value), it is probably wiser to use one of the many private postal services available. PostNet is the most widespread of these and details of their nearest bureau can be found in the telephone directory.

Telephones

Using the telephone is fairly cheap. To use public telephone boxes, it's best to purchase a telephone card (available from post offices and supermarkets in R10, R20, R50, R100 and R200 denominations). Local, national and international calls can be made from public telephone boxes.

Hotels generally charge two to three times more than the official rate.

Dialling Codes

International code for South Africa: 27, followed by the area code (without the first zero).

International codes from South Africa: Britain: 09 44; USA: 09 1; Australia: 09 61; New Zealand: 09 64. Directory enquiries in South Africa: 1023 (national); 0903 (international). Free service.

Tourist Information

Most of the larger towns and cities have a **Tourist Information Bureau** which can be identified by a large white "I" on a green background. They provide city maps, information on current events, museums and other points of interest.

In other areas and city centres, the **Publicity Association** fulfils this function, while the **Municipality** provides information in smaller towns. You will find numbers listed in

the telephone directory under Publicity Association or Municipality.

The telephone numbers of some of them are listed below:

Bloemfontein Publicity Association Tel: (051) 405 8490.

CAPTOUR Tel: (021) 418 5202.

Durban Unlimited Tel: (031) 304 4934.

East London Publicity Association Tel: (0431) 26015.

George Publicity Association Tel: (0441) 744000.

Grahamstown Publicity Association Tel: (0461) 23241.

Johannesburg Metropolitan Tourism Association Tel: (011) 337 6650.

Kimberley Information Office Tel: (0531) 27298.

Knysna Publicity Association Tel: (0445) 21610.

Nelspruit Publicity Association Tel: (01311) 55 1988/9.

Northern Province Tourism Association Tel: (0152) 259 2011.

North-West Tourism Council Tel: (0140) 84 3040/6.

Pietermaritzburg Publicity Association Tel: (0331) 45 1348.

Pretoria Information Bureau Tel: (012) 313 7980.

Port Elizabeth Publicity Association Tel: (041) 52 1315.

Western Cape Tourism Board Tel: (021) 418 3705/6.

Tourist Offices

South African Tourism Board (SATOUR).

Head Office: 442 Rigel Avenue South, Erasmusrand 0181, Private Bag X164, Pretoria 0001. Tel: (012) 347 0600; fax: (012) 45 4889.

Australia & New Zealand: Level 6, 285 Clarence Street, Sydney 2000 N.S.W., Australia. Tel: (2) 261 3424; fax: (2) 261 3414.

Canada: Suite 2, 4117 Lawrence Avenue East, Scarborough, Ontario M1E 2S2. Tel: (416) 283 0563; fax: (416) 283 5465.

United Kingdom, Republic of Ireland, Scandinavia: No 5 & 6 Alt Grove, Wimbledon, London SW19 4DZ. Tel: (0181) 944 8080; fax: (0181) 944 6705.

United States (Eastern): 500 Fifth Avenue, 20th Floor, Suite 2040, New York, NY 10110. Tel: (212) 7302929; fax: (212) 764 1980.

United States (Western): Suite 1524, 9841 Airport Boulevard, Los Angeles, CA 90045. Tel: (310) 6418444, (1-800) 7829772; fax: (310) 641 5812.

Zimbabwe: Offices 9 and 10, Mon Repos Building, Newlands Shopping Centre, Harare, PO Box HG 1000, Highlands. Tel: (4) 70 7766/78 6487/8; fax: (4) 78 6489.

Embassies

Australia: Rhodes Place, State Circle, Yarralumla, Canberra ACT, 2600. Tel: (6) 6273 2424; fax: (6) 6273 3543.

Canada: 15 Sussex Drive, Ottawa KIM 1M8. Tel: (613) 744 0330; fax: (613) 741 1639.

United Kingdom: South Africa House, Trafalgar Square, London WC2N 5DP. Tel: (0171) 451 7299; fax: (0171) 451 7280.

United States: 3051 Massachusetts Ave NW, Washington DC 20008. Tel: (202) 232 4400; fax: (202) 265 1607.

Consulates: 333 East 38 St, New York, NY 10016. Tel: (212) 2134880; fax: (212) 2130102. Suite 300, 50 N La Cienega Blvd, Beverly Hills, California, CA 90211. Tel: (310) 6579200; fax: (310) 6573725.

Getting Around

Internal Flights

Increased competition has reduced fares on many of South Africa's domestic routes. Always shop around for the best deals, especially on the busiest routes, such as Johannesburg to Cape Town.

Reduced fares are available for SAA flights. There are midnight flights serving Johannesburg, Cape Town, Durban and Port Elizabeth at a 40 percent reduction on the usual fare. These are very popular, so it is essential to make a booking. Payment is required within 24 hours of booking. These flights operate weekdays.

Confirmation should be obtained regarding weekend flights.

"South African Explorer" is a special package which can be purchased in Europe from SAA or from the national airline of your home country, as well as in South Africa.

Senior Citizens (over 60) receive a 30 percent reduction on airfares.

Family Fares on SAA operate as follows: one Adult (eg father) pays full fare; one Adult (eg mother) pays 60 percent of fare; children 12 and under pay 60 percent of fare; children two and under pay 10 percent of fare.

SAA OFFICES
• **Bloemfontein**, Liberty Life Building, corner of St Andrews and Church Sts. Tel: (051) 408 2922; fax: (051) 408 3331.

• **Cape Town**, International Airport. Tel: (021) 936 2662; fax: (021) 936 2664.

Southern Life Building, corner of Lower Burg St and Thibault Square. Tel: (021) 25 4610.
• **Durban**, Shell House, corner of Smith and Aliwal Sts. Tel: (031) 305 6491; fax: (031) 304 8530.
• **Johannesburg**, Domestic Departures, Terminal 4, International Airport. Tel: (011) 978 3525; fax: (011) 978 4377.
• **Port Elizabeth**, The Bridge, Langenhoven Drive, Greenacres. Tel: (041) 34 4444; fax: (041) 33 7165.
• **Pretoria**, De Bruyn Park Building, corner of Vermeulen and Andries Sts. Tel: (012) 315 2929; fax: (012) 326 8545.

Other domestic carriers operating scheduled services include:
• **Atlantic Air** (for Garden Route), tel: (021) 934 6619; fax: (021) 934 3751.
• **Comair**, tel: (011) 921 0111; fax: (011) 973 3913.
• **Nationwide Air**, Johannesburg International Airport, tel: (011) 390 1660/1/2/3/4; fax: (011) 970 1556. Cape Town International Airport, tel: (021) 936 2050/1/2; fax: (021) 936 2053.
• **SA Airlink**, tel: (011) 394 2430; fax: (011) 394 2649.
• **SA Express Airways**, tel: (011) 978 5569/77; fax: (011) 978 5578.
• **Sun Air**, Johannesburg, tel: (011) 394 7842; fax: (011) 394 9117. Cape Town, tel: (021) 934 0918; fax: (021) 934 9014. Durban, tel: (031) 469 3444; fax: (031) 469 3443.

SPECIALISED CHARTER AIR SERVICES AND SIGHTSEEING FLIGHTS
To visit the more remote spots of South Africa, especially certain games reserves, a light aircraft flight is the best option. There are also many exciting sight-seeing flights on offer, in both light aircraft and helicopter.

Obviously, chartering an aircaft will work out cheaper if you can fill every passenger seat. Here is a small selection of specialised charter operators:
• **African Ramble**, tel: (012) 46 7983; fax: (012) 46 1794.
• **Cape Town Air Operations**, tel: (021) 410 8779. Offer luxurious scenic trips around the Cape Peninsula at sunset in a twin-engined plane.
• **Civair Helicopters**, PO Box 120, Newlands 7725, Cape Town. Tel: (021) 419 5182; fax: (021) 419 5183.
• **Court Helicopters**, PO Box 18115, Rand Airport 1419, Johannesburg. Tel: (011) 827 8907; fax: (011) 824 1660. Cape Town, tel: (021) 25 2966. Court Helicopters operate from Johannesburg and Cape Town. Tours can vary from a lunchtime trip to a two-day tour.
• **Dragonfly Helicopter Adventures**, PO Box 346, White River 1240. Tel: (01311) 5 0565; fax: (01311) 3 2839. "Mountain Magic" is a trip over the highlights of Mpumalanga; "Winged Safari" is a safari at a private game reserve.
• **Executive Aerospace**, tel: (031) 42 6322; fax: (031) 42 7810. First-class charter service for business and leisure.
• **Flamingo Flights**, tel: (021) 790 1010. Trips round the Peninsula, over Robben Island or further afield in a Beaver float-plane.
• **The Flying Company**, PO Box 5231, Cape Town 8000. Tel: (021) 797 3780; fax: (021) 762 2747.
• **Gold Reef City Helicopters**, tel: (011) 4961400. Tours over Johannesburg and Soweto from Gold Reef City.
• **Jetair Charter**, PO Box 259, Lanseria 1748, Gauteng. Tel: (011) 659 1574; fax: (011) 659 2498.
• **Kwena Air**, PO Box 4565, Rivonia 2128, Gauteng. Tel: (011) 803 4921; fax: (011) 803 4566.

• **Rossair**, PO Box 428, Lanseria 1748, Gauteng. Tel: (011) 659 2980; fax: (011) 659 1389.

Trains

Long-distance trains have sleeping berths. The use of the berth is included in the train fare, but a bedding ticket must be purchased. This can be done when making a reservation, or on the train. First Class coupés and compartments carry two and four passengers, while Second Class coupés and compartments carry three and six passengers. Most long distance trains have a dining salon and catering trolleys provide a catering service. It is possible to rent a compartment/coupé at a special price which is about 80 percent of the price of a fully occupied one (some families, for example, do this if they want a compartment to themselves).

Children under seven travel free; children under age 12 pay half price. Senior citizens (over 60) are entitled to a 40 percent discount.

Platform boards can be found on the departure platform on which coach and compartment numbers are listed against the names of the passengers. The

The Blue Train

The distinguished Blue Train is a luxury modern express which transports its passengers in ultimate comfort with excellent service from Pretoria and Johannesburg to Cape Town and back. Accommodation is in compartments for two people, some with their own bathroom. Three meals (included in the price) are served in the dining car and in the lounge car one can enjoy a drink and meet other passengers. Six times a year the train travels from Pretoria to Victoria Falls.

train conductor is also available to assist you.

SPOORNET
State-owned Spoornet operates the long-distance main line routes listed below:
• **The Trans-Oranje (Orange Express)** operates once a week between Cape Town and Durban via Kimberley and Bloemfontein, leaving Cape Town Monday 6.30pm, leaving Durban Thursday 5.30pm, arriving 37 hours later.
• **The Trans-Natal Night Express** operates daily between Durban and Johannesburg, leaving in both directions at 6.30pm and arriving at 8am the next morning.
• **The Trans-Karoo Express** operates daily between Cape Town and Johannesburg. It leaves Johannesburg every day at 12.30pm and Cape Town at 9.20am, arriving 24 hours later.

Other main long-distance express trains are **the Algoa** (Johannesburg to Port Elizabeth), **the Amatola** (Johannesburg to East London), **the Bosvelder** (Johannesburg to Messina), **the Diamond Express** (Pretoria to Bloemfontein), and **the Southern Cross** (Cape Town to Oudtshoorn).

Reservations can be made a year in advance, and it is advisable to book early. The trains leave every Monday, Wednesday and Friday in both directions at 10am (Pretoria) and 10.50am (Cape Town), and arrive 25 hours later.
Blue Train Reservations, PO Box 2671, Joubert Park 2044, Gauteng. Tel: (011) 773 7631; fax: (011) 773 7643.
UK Representative: Leisurail, PO Box 113, Peterborough PE3 8HY, UK. Tel: (01733) 335599; fax: (01733) 505451.

Spoornet will handle all your reservations and enquiries:
• **Johannesburg**, Main Line Passenger Services, PO Box 6135, Johannesburg 2000, tel: (011) 773 8920/774 2082.
• **Cape Town**, tel: (021) 405 3871.
• **Durban**, tel: (031) 361 7621.
• **East London**, tel: (0431) 44 2719.
• **Port Elizabeth**, tel: (041) 507 2400.
• **Pretoria**, tel: (012) 315 2401.

Spoornet's **UK Representative**, Leisurail, issues rail passes for South Africa but not specific point-to-point journeys. Contact: PO Box 113, Peterborough PE3 8HY, tel: (01733) 335599; fax: (01733) 505451.

Buses

Inter-city coach services are offered by **Greyhound Coach Lines**. Contact the Central Reservations Office in Johannesburg, tel: (011) 830 1400; fax: (011) 830 1527. Reservations can also be made through offices in:
• **Cape Town**, tel: (021) 418 4310; fax: (021) 418 4315.
• **Durban**, tel: (031) 309 7830; fax: (031) 309 7746.
• **Port Elizabeth**, tel: (041) 56 4879; fax: (041) 56 4872.
• **Pretoria**, tel: (012) 323 1154; fax: (012) 323 1294.

Translux operates luxury coach services from:
• **Pretoria to Vereeniging, Pietermaritzburg, Durban**; daily, 9 hours.
• **Johannesburg to Umtata, East London, Port Elizabeth**; daily, 13 hours.
• **Johannesburg to Kroonstad, Welkom, Bloemfontein**; 2 times daily, 7 hours.
• **Johannesburg to Cape Town**; Sunday, Monday, Wednesday, Friday, return Sunday, Tuesday, Thursday, Friday, 18 hours.

• **Cape Town (Garden Route) to Port Elizabeth**; daily, 13 hours.
Reservations can be made through: PO Box 1907, Pretoria 0001, **Gauteng**, tel: (012) 315 3492; fax: (012) 315 3572. **Johannesburg**, tel: (011) 774 3333; (011) 774 3871. **Cape Town**, tel: (021) 405 3333.

A good-value, and very alternative, means of getting around South Africa is **Baz Bus**. This is a flexible hop-on, hop-off service that takes in the main tourist areas from Cape Town to Johannesburg. Backpackers are the main customers, especially those wanting to enjoy the Garden Route. Tickets available at youth hostels, or contact Student Travel in Johannesburg, tel: (011) 447 5551; fax: (011) 447 5775.

Other long-distance bus services include:
Intercape, PO Box 618, Belville 7535, Cape Town. Tel: (021) 386 4444. **Springbok Atlas**, PO Box 819, Cape Town 8000. Tel: (021) 448 6545; fax: (021) 47 3835. UK representative: Euro Contacts, Berkshire, UK. Tel: (01628) 773300; fax: (01628) 21033.

Car Rentals

South Africa has a very good network of roads, some 84,000 km (52,000 miles) of tarred roads, and even the untarred roads are usually in good condition. Travelling overland, visitors will enjoy the lack of traffic.
In South Africa, you drive on the left-hand side of the road. Traffic laws are strictly enforced.
When driving through any rural areas be careful of cattle or goats in the road. Rural roads are poorly lit at night; be careful of pedestrians and cyclists.
Speed limits are generally well signposted. The maximum speeds on freeways are: 120

km/h (74 mph); rural roads: 100 km/h (62 mph); in built up areas: 60 km/h (37 mph).
Seat belts must be worn at all times by the driver and passengers.
Car rental firms offer a wide variety of cars from a Volkswagen Golf to an air-conditioned Mercedes 280 SE at three times the rate. Mileage charges are usually extra. Check with the car hire firm for details.
It is often cheaper to arrange your car hire from home. The following companies have offices and representatives in South Africa.
• **Avis Rent-A-Car**, PO Box 221, Isando 1600, Gauteng. Head Office: Johannesburg, tel: (011) 08000 34444 (toll free); fax: (011) 974 2683. Cape Town, tel: (021) 934 0808. Durban, tel: (031) 424 977.
• **Budget Rent-A-Car**, PO Box 1777, Kempton Park 1620, Gauteng. Head Office: Johannesburg, tel: (011) 392 3929; fax: (011) 392 3900. Cape Town, tel: (021) 934 0216. Durban, tel: (031) 423 809.
• **Economy Hire**, PO Box 524, Green Point 8051, Cape Town. Tel: (021) 434 8304/5/6; fax: (021) 434 5560; toll free (SA only): 0800 011257.
• **Europcar**, PO Box 4631, Kempton Park 1620, Gauteng. Tel: (011) 396 1309; fax: (011) 396 1406.
Other vehicles available range from four-wheel-drive jeeps to caravans, campers and campermobiles. For further information, contact: **The SA Vehicle Rental Association** (Johannesburg), PO Box 2940, Randburg 2125, Johannesburg. Tel: (011) 789 2542/3; fax: (011) 789 4525.

Where to Stay

Choosing a Hotel

Visitors to South Africa can expect a wide choice of accommodation: from exclusive five-star hotels to modest city guest houses; efficient motorway motels to tranquil country inns; rustic rondavels (straw-thatched huts) in game reserves to farmhouses offering bed and breakfast. As South Africa is such an outdoor-loving nation, there's an excellent range of camping and caravan sites. For the budget traveller, there are a number of youth hostels, plus **YMCA** and **YWCA** accommodation.

The ultimate in luxury is represented by the **Sun International** hotel and casino group (which includes its flagship, Sun City), and the **Relais et Châteaux** chain with seven upmarket establishments in South Africa.

The **Southern Sun Group** is the largest hotel operator in Africa and you'll find one of its establishments in every large South African city, generally with four or five stars. Bland and rather lacking in character they may be, but you'll find standards of service and customer care consistently high.

Holiday Inns, owned by Southern Sun, is a chain of family-oriented hotels. Apart from the deluxe Holiday Inn Crowne Plaza hotels in the main cities, these hotels can be considered good-value, medium-priced establishments, and not really comparable to their namesakes in Europe and other countries.

Two other dependable medium-priced hotel chains are **Protea Hotels**, with a range of two- to five-star accommodation right across the country, and the smaller group of **Karos Hotels**.

City Lodge Hotels offer no-frills, reasonably-priced accommodation.

Reservations: During the high season (from 1 October to 30 April) accommodation should be reserved well in advance.

HOTEL CHAINS

• **Sun International**: PO Box 784487, Sandton 2146. Tel: (011) 780 7800; fax: (011) 780 7457.
• **Relais Hotels** of the Cape: PO Box 23864, Claremont 7735. Tel: (021) 794 6676; fax: (021) 794 7186.
• **Southern Sun Group** (including **Holiday Inn**): PO Box 782553, Sandton 2146, Gauteng. Tel: (011) 780 0100/0200; fax: (011) 780 0262.
• **Protea Hotels**: PO Box 6482, Roggebaai 8012, Cape Town. Tel: (021) 419 8800; fax: (021) 419 8200.
• **Karos Hotels**: PO Box 87534, Houghton, 2198. Tel: (011) 484 1641; fax: (011) 484 6206.
• **City Lodge**: PO Box 782630, Sandton 2146, Gauteng. Tel: (011) 884 5327; fax: (011) 883 3640.

INFORMATION ON GUEST HOUSES

• **Bed and Breakfast**: PO Box 2739, Clareinch 7740, Cape Town. Tel: (021) 683 3505; fax: (021) 683 5159.
• **Bed 'n' Breakfast**: PO Box 91309, Auckland Park 2006, Johannesburg. Tel: (011) 482 2206; fax: (011) 726 6915.
• **Computicket's Accommodation Bank** Tel: (011) 445 8300. Booking service for hotels, bed and breakfast, self-catering and lodge accommodation.
• **Guest House Association of South Africa (Ghasa)** Tel: (021) 461 0635/(0234)

Hotel Classifications

Hotel classification is based on the South African Tourism Board's National Grading and Classification Scheme, which is listed below:
☆☆☆☆☆ = Outstanding
☆☆☆☆ = Excellent
☆☆☆ = Very good
☆☆ = Good
☆ = Comfortable

42351; fax: (0234) 42418. A non-profit making voluntary association formed by owners of guest houses.
• **Homeshare**: Johannesburg, tel: (011) 907 8206; fax: (011) 907 4031. Durban, tel: (031) 94 1016. A computerised database of over 1000 private homes throughout the country offering bed and breakfast accommodation.
• **South African Farm Holiday Association (Safha)**: PO Box 1140, Oakdale 7534, Western Cape. Tel: (021) 689 8400; fax: (021) 689 1974. Safha (KwaZulu-Natal): PO Box 10592, Scottsville 3209. Tel: (0331) 94 8364; fax: (0331) 94 8368. Farms offering accommodation and hiking trails.

INFORMATION ON CAMPSITES AND MOTORHOME PARKS

• **South African Camping and Caravan Club**, tel: (011) 954 0229.
• **Federation of Caravan and Camping Clubs**, tel: (012) 543 1010.
• Contact the **South African Tourism Board** (see page 306) to obtain a copy of the National Accommodation Guide listing all approved establishments. They will also be able to provide information concerning camping, caravanning and National Park accommodation.

Recommended Hotels

JOHANNESBURG AND SUN CITY

Sadly, street crime has become a serious problem in downtown Johannesburg. Visitors to the city should, therefore, consider booking accommodation in Sandton and the Midrand area (the suburbs lying between Johannesburg and Pretoria).

Chain Hotels

The Balalaika Hotel and Crown Court ✰✰✰✰ Maud St, PO Box 783372, Sandton 2146. Tel: (011) 322 5000; fax: (011) 322 5021. Tranquil setting in the centre of the exclusive suburb of Sandton. Air conditioning, telephone, non-smoking bedrooms, facilities for disabled guests, restaurant. Swimming pool.

City Lodge Johannesburg International Airport ✰✰ Sandvale Rd, Edenvale, PO Box 448, Isando 1600. Tel: (011) 392 1750; fax: (011) 392 2644. Warm and friendly inexpensive hotel close to the airport. Air conditioning, telephone, non-smoking bedrooms available, and facilities for disabled guests. Swimming pool.

City Lodge Randburg ✰✰ Corner of Main Rd & Peter Place, Bryanston West, Sandton, PO Box 423, Cramerview 2060. Tel: (011) 706 7800; fax: (011) 706 7819. Clean and comfortable accommodation conveniently located for the Sandton and Randburg business centres. Air conditioning, telephone, non-smoking bedrooms available, facilities for disabled guests, restaurant. Swimming pool, fitness centre, sauna, squash and tennis courts.

City Lodge Sandton Katherine Street ✰✰✰ Corner of Katherine St & Grayston Drive, PO Box 781643, Sandton 2146. Tel: (011) 444 5300; fax: (011) 444 5315. Value for money hotel in upmarket Sandton. Air conditioning, telephone, non-smoking bedrooms, facilities for disabled guests. Swimming pool.

Holiday Inn Crowne Plaza – Sandton ✰✰✰ Corner of Graystone Drive & Rivonia Road, PO Box 781743, Sandton 2146. Tel: (011) 783 5262; fax: (011) 783 5289; telex: 42 7002. Set in beautiful gardens. Air conditioning, telephone, non-smoking bedrooms available, à la carte restaurant, facilities for the disabled. Swimming pool.

Holiday Inn Crowne Plaza – Sunnyside Park ✰✰✰✰ 2 York Road, PO Box 31256, Braamfontein 2017. Tel: (011) 643 7226; fax: (011) 642 0019. Near the city, but offering the peace and quiet of the country. Air conditioning, telephone, non-smoking bedrooms available. Swimming pool.

Holiday Inn Garden Court Johannesburg Airport ✰✰✰ 6 Hulley Road, Isando, Private Bag 5, Johannesburg International Airport, Kempton Park 1627. Tel: (011) 392 1062; fax: (011) 974 8097; telex: 745 503. Only 1 km from the airport. Air conditioning, telephone, non-smoking bedrooms available, facilities for the disabled. Swimming pool. Pets accommodated.

Holiday Inn Garden Court Sandton ✰✰✰ Corner of Katherine St & Rivonia Road, PO Box 783394, Sandton 2146. Tel: (011) 884 5660; fax: (011) 783 2004; telex: 43 0801. Close to the city. Air conditioning, telephone, non-smoking bedrooms, facilities for the disabled. Swimming pool.

Holiday Inn Johannesburg International Airport ✰✰✰✰ Germiston-Pretoria Highway, Johannesburg International Airport, PO Box 388, Kempton Park 1620. Tel: (011) 975 1121; fax: (011) 975 5846; telex: 74 9534. Convenient for the airport. Air conditioning, telephone, non-smoking bedrooms available, facilities for the disabled. Swimming pool.

Karos Indaba ✰✰✰✰ Hartebeespoort Dam Rd, Witkoppen, Fourways, PO Box 67129, Bryanston 2021. Tel: (011) 465 1400; fax: (011) 705 1709; telex: 43 1161. Large, purpose-built hotel tucked away in one of the leafiest of the city's northern suburbs. Offers some of the best conference facilities in the country, as well as excellent sports facilities. Air conditioning, telephone, non-smoking bedrooms, facilities for disabled guests, restaurant. Swimming pool, fitness centre, sauna, squash and tennis courts.

Karos Johannesburg Hotel ✰✰✰ Corner of Twist & Wolmarans Sts, PO Box 23566, Joubert Park 2044. Tel: (011) 725 3753; fax: (011) 725 6309; telex: 42 2314. Located in the centre of Johannesburg, suitable for businessmen and vacationers. Air conditioning, telephone. Swimming pool.

The Palace The Lost City ✰✰✰✰✰ PO Box 308, Sun City 0316. Tel: (01465) 73000; fax: (01465) 73111. Critics deplore its flamboyant, glitzy presence in one of the poorest regions of the country, but this is nonetheless a top-class hotel in an imported "tropical jungle" setting, complete with artificial beach and wave pool.

Park Hyatt Hotel, PO Box 1536, Saxonwold 2132, Gauteng. Tel: (011) 280 1234; fax: (011) 280 1238. Don't be put off by the prison-like exterior – inside, all is spaciousness, opulence and comfort.

Protea Gardens Hotel ✰✰✰ Corner of Tudhope & 35 O'Reilly Roads, Berea, PO Box 866, Houghton 2041. Tel: (011) 643 6611; fax: (011) 484 2622. Set in lush green gardens. Air conditioning, telephone, non-smoking bedrooms available, restaurant. Swimming pool, fitness centre and sauna.

Sandton Sun Inter-Continental ☆☆☆☆☆ Corner of Alice and 5th Streets, PO Box 784902, Sandton 2146.Tel: (011) 780 5000; fax: (011) 780 5002; telex: 430 338. A luxurious five-star hotel in the heart of Johannesburg's most exclusive business and residential suburb. Air conditioning, telephone, non-smoking bedrooms available, à la carte restaurant, facilities for the disabled, sauna, fitness centre and swimming pool.

Private Hotels
Capri Hotel ☆☆☆ 27 Aintree Ave, Savoy Estates, PO Box 39605, Bramley 2018. Tel: (011) 786 2250/1; fax: (011) 887 2286. Comfortable hotel near the M1 motorway. Air conditioning, telephone, non-smoking bedrooms available, à la carte restaurant.
Carlton Court ☆☆☆☆☆ Main St, PO Box 7709, Johannesburg 2000. Tel: (011) 311 8333; fax: (011) 331 8576; telex: 48 6130. A warm and friendly hotel in the city centre. Air conditioning, telephone, restaurant and non-smoking bedrooms available. No children.
The Devonshire Hotel ☆☆☆ Corner of Jorissen & Melle Sts, PO Box 31197, Braamfontein 2017. Tel: (011) 339 5611; fax: (011) 403 2495. Luxury accommodation close to the business centre and motorways. Air conditioning, telephone, non-smoking bedrooms, restaurant and sauna.
Linfourson Guest House, 58 Curzon Road, PO Box 70318, Bryanston 2021. Tel/fax: (011) 704 2575. This upmarket guest house is outstanding. Five luxurious en suite rooms set in lush gardens, with tennis court, swimming pool and sauna; delightful, friendly service.
Mariston Hotel ☆☆☆ Corner of Claim & Koch Sts, PO Box 23013, Joubert Park 2044. Tel: (011) 725 4130; fax: (011) 725

2921. Aparthotel-style rooms with telephone, restaurant and swimming pool.
Rosebank Hotel ☆☆☆☆ Corner of Tyrwhitt & Sturdee Avenues, PO Box 52025, Saxonwold 2132. Tel: (011) 447 2700; fax: (011) 447 3276; telex: 42 2268. Friendly, prestigious suburban hotel with three restaurants, conference facilities and bar.
Ten Bompas (not yet classified) 10 Bompas Road, Dunkeld West, Johannesburg. Tel: (011) 327 0650. A large

Hotel Classifications

Hotel classification is based on the South African Tourism Board's National Grading and Classification Scheme, which is listed below:
☆☆☆☆☆ = Outstanding
☆☆☆☆ = Excellent
☆☆☆ = Very good
☆☆ = Good
☆ = Comfortable

family home, set in one of the city's oldest suburbs, has been tranformed into a unique boutique hotel. A different designer worked on each of its 10 bedrooms to produce a wonderful mix of neo-African and post-colonial interiors. Natural light and rich ruddy colours dominate. Restaurant.

JOHANNESBURG ENVIRONS
Aloe Ridge Hotel ☆☆☆ Swartkop Muldersdrift, PO Box 3040, Honeydew 2040. Tel/fax: (011) 957 2070. Luxury hotel set in a game reserve with authentic Zulu village, 40 km (25 miles) from Johannesburg. Air conditioning, telephone, restaurant. Fishing, swimming pool, squash and tennis courts.
Heia Safari Ranch ☆☆☆ Swartkop Muldersdrift, PO Box 1387, Honeydew 2040. Tel: (011) 659 0605; fax: (011) 659 0709. Comfortable hotel set in a nature reserve, 40 km (25

miles) from Johannesburg. Telephone, restaurant, fishing, swimming pool, tennis court.

Hostels
Backpackers Ritz, 1a North Road, Dunkeld West, Johannesburg 2196. Tel: (011) 325 7125/327 0229; fax: (011) 327 0233.
Fairview Youth Hostel, 4 College St, Fairview 2094, Gauteng. Tel: (011) 618 2048; fax: (011) 614 2823.
Johannesburg YWCA, 128 De Korte Street, Braamfontein. Tel: (011) 403 3830.
Kew Youth Hostel, 5 Johannesburg Rd, Kew 209, Gauteng. Tel: (011) 887 9072; fax: (011) 643 1412.
Orlando YMCA, PO Box 5, Orlando. Tel/fax: (011) 935 1022.
Rockey Street Backpackers, 34 Regent Street, Yeoville, Johannesburg 2198, Gauteng. Tel: (011) 648 8786; fax: (011) 648 8423.

PRETORIA
Chain Hotels
Holiday Inn Crowne Plaza – Pretoria ☆☆☆☆ Corner of Church & Beatrix Sts, PO Box 40694, Arcadia, Pretoria 0007. Tel: (012) 341 1571; fax: (012) 44 7534; telex: 32 1755. In the centre of Pretoria, good base for businessmen and tourists. Air conditioning, telephone, non-smoking bedrooms available, facilities for disabled guests, restaurant. Swimming pool.
Holiday Inn Garden Court Pretoria ☆☆☆ Corner of Van Der Walt & Minnaar Sts, PO Box 2301, Pretoria 0001. Tel: (012) 322 7500; fax: (012) 322 9429; telex: 32 2525. Located in central Pretoria with comfortable rooms. Air conditioning, telephone, non-smoking bedrooms available, facilities for disabled guests. Swimming pool.
Karos Manhattan Hotel ☆☆☆ 247 Scheiding St, PO Box 26212, Arcadia 0007. Tel: (012)

322 7635; fax: (012) 320 1252. Close to the shopping centre. Air conditioning, telephone, sauna, squash court, swimming pool.

Riviera International Hotel and Country Club ☆☆☆☆
Mario Milani Drive, PO Box 64, Vereeniging 1930. Tel: (016) 22 2861; fax: (016) 21 2908; telex: 74 3217. Exclusive hotel with 18-hole golf course and conference facilities. 45 minutes' drive from Johannesburg. Air conditioning, telephone, facilities for disabled guests, restaurant. Golf course, swimming pool, bowling green, fishing, squash and tennis courts.

PRETORIA, RUSTENBURG AND BOSHOEK

Private Hotels
The Farm Inn ☆☆☆
Lynnwood Road, next to Silverlakes Golf Estate, Pretoria, PO Box 71702, Die Wilgers 0041. Tel: (012) 809 0266; fax: (012) 809 0146. Unusual accommodation in an African stone and thatch palace in a private game sanctuary. Telephone, restaurant. Hiking trails, fishing, horse riding and swimming pool.

La Maison ☆☆☆☆ 235 Hilda St, Hatfield, Pretoria 0083. Tel: (012) 43 4341; fax: (012) 342 1531. This five-bedroomed hotel has an excellent reputation for its cuisine and is just 30 minutes' drive from Johannesburg. Telephone, restaurant and swimming pool.

Marvol House, 358 Aries Street, Waterkloof Ridge, Pretoria. Tel: (012) 346 1774; fax: (012) 346 1776. Small, very comfortable guest house in the white-washed-and-gabled Cape Dutch style. Set on a ridge, with two swimming pools, gym, Jacuzzi and sauna.

Sundown Ranch ☆☆☆
Rustenburg/Boshoek Road, PO Box 139, Boshoek 0301. Tel: (0 142) 73 3121; fax: (0 142) 73 3114. A small country-style hotel with air conditioning,

telephone, restaurant. Horse riding, swimming pool, squash and tennis courts.

Westwinds Country House ☆☆☆ Westwinds Farm Zuurplaat, Rustenburg District, PO Box 56, Kroondal 0350. Tel: (0 142) 75 0560; fax: (0 142) 75 0032. Sometimes called the jewel of the North West. Air conditioning, telephone, restaurant. Hiking trails, horse riding and swimming pool.

Hostels
Kia Ora Embassy Gasthaus, 257 Jacob Mare Street, Pretoria 0001. Tel: (012) 322 4803; fax: (012) 322 4816.

Pretoria Backpackers, 34 Bourke Street, Sunnyside, Pretoria. Tel: (012) 343 9754.

Pretoria YWCA, 557 Vermeulen Street, Pretoria. Tel: (012) 326 2916.

NORTHERN PROVINCE AND MPUMALANGA

Chain Hotels
Hazyview Protea Hotel ☆☆☆
Burgers Hall, PO Box 105, Hazyview 1242, Mpumalanga. Tel: (01 317) 6 7332; fax: (01 317) 6 7335; telex: 33 5737. Luxury hotel 15 km (10 miles) from the Kruger National Park. Air conditioning, telephone, non-smoking rooms available, restaurant. Swimming pool, sauna and tennis court.

Karos Lodge ☆☆☆☆ Sabie River, Kruger Gate, PO Box 54, Skukuza 1350. Tel: (01 311) 6 5671; fax: (01 311) 6 5676. By the Sabie River at the main entrance to Kruger Park. Air conditioning, telephone, non-smoking rooms available, facilities for the disabled, restaurant, hiking trail, tennis court and swimming pool.

Karos Tzaneen Hotel ☆☆☆
1 Danie Joubert St, PO Box 1, Tzaneen 0850, Northern Province. Tel/fax: (0 152) 307 3140. Peaceful hotel set in the Drakensberg foothills. Air conditioning, telephone,

restaurant and swimming pool.

Mabula Game Lodge ☆☆☆
Rooiberg Area, Private Bag X1665, Warmbaths 0480, Northern Province. Tel: (011) 463 4217; fax: (011) 463 4299. Set in 8,000 hectares of private game reserve, two hours north of Johannesburg. Offers game drives, walking trails, horse riding, swimming pool, sauna, fitness centre, tennis and squash courts. Air conditioning, telephone and non-smoking rooms available.

Pine Lake Sun ☆☆☆☆ Main Hazyview Rd, PO Box 94, White River 1240. Tel: (01 311) 3 1186; fax: (01 311) 3 3874; telex: 33 5690. A high-quality resort set in beautiful countryside. Air conditioning, telephone, non-smoking rooms available, restaurant. Fishing, golf course, swimming pool, fishing, hiking trails, horse riding, bowling green, squash and tennis courts.

Protea Park Hotel ☆☆☆
1 Beitel Street, PO Box 1551, Potgietersrus 0600, Northern Province. Tel: (0 154) 3101; fax: (0 154) 6842. Set in peaceful parklands. Air conditioning, telephone, non-smoking rooms available, restaurant and swimming pool.

Sabie River Sun ☆☆☆☆
Main Sabie Rd, PO Box 13, Hazyview 1242. Tel: (01 317) 6 7311; fax: (01 317) 6 7314. Luxury hotel located close to the Kruger National Park. Air conditioning, telephone, non-smoking rooms available, restaurant. Fishing, swimming pool, bowling green, squash and tennis courts.

Private Hotels
Bergwater Hotel ☆☆☆ 5 Rissik Street, PO Box 503, Louis Trichardt 0920. Tel/fax: (015) 516 0262/3. Small, simple with good service. Air conditioning, telephone, non-smoking rooms available, restaurant, facilities for disabled, swimming pool.

Böhm's Zeederberg Country House ☆☆☆ District Hazyview, Box 94, Sabie 1260. Tel: (01317) 6 8101; fax: (01317) 6 8193. Set in the Sabie Valley, near Kruger Park. Air conditioning, telephone, restaurant and swimming pool.

Magoebaskloof Hotel ☆☆☆ Road R71, PO, Magoebaskloof 0731. Tel: (0152 76) 4276; fax: (0152 76) 4280. Small, friendly hotel. Telephone, restaurant, facilities for disabled guests and sports facilities including a swimming pool.

Shangri-La Country Lodge ☆☆☆ Eersbewoond Rd, PO Box 262, Nylstroom 0510. Tel: (01 470) 2381/2071; fax: (01 470) 3188. Small and traditional. Telephone, restaurant, swimming pool.

Hostels

Jock of the Bushveld, Main Road, Sabie 1260. Tel: (013) 42178.

Kruger Park Backpackers, Main Road, Hazyview 1242, PO Box 214. Tel: (0137) 67224.

KWAZULU-NATAL
Hotel Chains

Beverly Hills Sun Inter-Continental Durban ☆☆☆☆☆ 54 Lighthouse Road, PO Box 71, Umhlanga Rocks 4320. Tel: (031) 561 2211; fax: (031) 561 3711; telex: 62 2073. Set right on the coast, just 10 minutes' drive from Durban. Air conditioning, telephone, non-smoking rooms available, restaurant and swimming pool.

Drakensberg Sun ☆☆☆ Cathkin Park, PO Box 335, Winterton 3340. Tel: (036) 468 1000; fax: (036) 468 1224; telex: 64 6106. A spectacular mountain resort in the Cathkin Park area of the Drakensberg Mountains.

Holiday Inn Crowne Plaza – Durban ☆☆☆☆ 63 Snell Parade, PO Box 4094, Durban 4000. Tel: (031) 37 1321; fax: (031) 32 5527; telex: 62 0133.

Located opposite Durban's famous North Beach. Excellent restaurant and luxury hotel facilities.

Holiday Inn Garden Court Durban – Marine Parade ☆☆☆ 167 Marine Parade, PO Box 10809, Marine Parade, Durban 4056. Tel: (031) 37 3341; fax: (031) 32 9885; telex: 62 1448. All sea-facing bedrooms in a hotel just 400 metres from the beach. Also close to the central business district.

Karos Bayshore Inn ☆☆ The Gulley, PO Box 51, Richards Bay 3900. Tel: (0351) 3 1246; fax: (0351) 3 2335; telex: 63 1277. Unfussy hotel set close to the sea. Air conditioning, telephone, restaurant and swimming pool.

Karos Mont-aux-Sources Hotel ☆☆☆ Mont-aux-Sources, Private Bag X1670, Bergville 3353. Tel/fax: (036) 438 6230. Quiet, upmarket hotel with excellent views. Telephone, sports facilities and swimming pool.

Hotel Classifications

Hotel classification is based on the South African Tourism Board's National Grading and Classification Scheme, which is listed below:
☆☆☆☆☆ = Outstanding
☆☆☆☆ = Excellent
☆☆☆ = Very good
☆☆ = Good
☆ = Comfortable

Karos Richards Hotel ☆☆☆ Hibberd Dr, PO Box 242, Meerensee, Richards Bay 3900. Tel: (0351) 3 1301; fax: (0351) 3 2334; telex: 63 1169. Air conditioning, telephone, restaurant and swimming pool.

Karridene Protea Hotel ☆☆☆ Old Main South Coast Rd, PO Box 20, Illovo Beach 4155. Tel: (031) 96 3321; fax: (031) 94 4093. A modern hotel with good sports facilities. Air conditioning, telephone, restaurant, facilities for disabled, swimming pool.

Stilwater Protea Hotel ☆☆☆ Dundee Rd, Private Bag X9332, Vryheid 3100. Tel/fax: (0381) 6181. Good base from which to tour Northern KwaZulu-Natal. Air conditioning, telephone, restaurant and swimming pool.

Private Hotels

Beach Lodge Hotel ☆☆ Marine Dr, PO Box 109 Margate 4275. Tel: (039) 377 5372; fax: (039) 377 1232. Comfortable rooms and restaurant serving traditional German cuisine. Swimming pool. Few minutes' walk to the beach.

Brackenmoor Estate Hotel ☆☆☆ Lot 2013, PO Box 518, St Michael's on Sea, Uvongo 4265. Tel: (03 931) 7 5165; fax: (03 931) 75109. 16-bedroom country hotel with telephone, fitness centre and pool.

Fugitives' Drift Lodge ☆☆☆ PO Rorke's Drift, Rorke's Drift 3016. Tel: (03 425) 843; fax (0 341) 2 3319. Six-bedroom guest house set within a 1,600 hectare (4,000 acre) game reserve, overlooking Isandlwana and Rorke's Drift.

Game Valley Lodge ☆☆☆☆ Ottos Bluff, Pietermaritzburg, PO Box 13010, Cascades 3202. Tel: (033 569) 1787; fax: (033 569) 1795. Luxury game lodge hotel.

Hilton Hotel ☆☆☆ Hilton Road, PO Box 35, Hilton 3245. Tel: (0 331) 3 3311; fax: (0 331) 3 3722. Country-style atmosphere. Restaurant, telephone, non-smoking rooms available and swimming pool.

Oyster Box Hotel ☆☆☆ 2 Lighthouse Road, PO Box 22, Umhlanga Rocks 4320. Tel: (031) 561 2233; fax: (031) 561 4072. Quiet and very comfortable, this is a superb family-run hotel in an upmarket resort. Set right on the beach, it has a good restaurant too, specialising in fresh seafood and enormous steaks. Air conditioning, telephone and swimming pool.

Royal Hotel ✩✩✩✩✩
267 Smith St, Box 1041, Durban
4000. Tel: (031) 304 0331; fax:
(031) 307 6884. Voted the best
city hotel in South Africa for five
consecutive years. Bland
modern exterior, but large,
luxurious and comfortable.
Prides itself on offering the "Last
Outpost of the British Empire"
experience. Seven restaurants,
including the Ulundi which
specialises in fabulous curries.
Air conditioning, telephone,
fitness centre and pool.
**Sani Pass Hotel & Leisure
Resort** ✩✩✩ Sani Pass Road,
PO Box 44, Himeville 4585. Tel:
(033) 702 1320; fax: (033) 702
0220. Set at the foot of the Sani
Pass in 800 hectares (2000
acres) of Southern Drakensberg
countryside. Good for sports
and activity holidays, facilities
include sauna, swimming pool,
golf course, horse riding, tennis
and squash courts.
**Selborne Sun Inter-
continental** ✩✩✩✩✩ PO Box
2, Pennington 4184. Tel: (0323)
9751133; fax: (0323)
9751811. Just 40 minutes'
drive south of Durban, this lovely
country house is decorated with
antiques and fine oil paintings,
set in tropical gardens which are
a bird-spotter's delight. The golf
course is one of the best in the
country.

Hostels
Amazulu Lodge Backpackers,
PO Box 453, Kwanbonambi
3915, KwaZulu-Natal. Tel: (035)
580 1009.
**Backpackers Club
International**, 154 Point Road,
Durban 4001. Tel: (031) 32
0511; fax: (031) 32 0541.
Durban Beach, 19 Smith
Street, Durban 4001. Tel: (031)
32 4945; fax: (031) 32 4551.
Durban YMCA, Anchor House,
82 St Andrew's Street, Durban.
Tel: (031) 305 4496; fax: (031)
305 4499.
Pietermaritzburg YMCA, 1
Durban Road, Pietermaritzburg.

Tel: (0331) 42 8106; fax: (0331)
45 0313.
Summer Place Youth Hostel,
85 Pietermaritz Street,
Pietermaritzburg 3200. Tel:
(0331) 94 5785.
Sunduzi Backpackers, 140
Berg Street, Pietermaritzburg
3200. Tel: (0331) 94 0072.
Wild West Sani Youth Hostel,
PO Box 107, Himeville 4585.
Tel: (033) 702 0340. Set in the
Drakensberg National Park.

<h3 style="text-align:center">EASTERN CAPE</h3>

Chain Hotels
City Lodge Port Elizabeth
✩✩✩ Corner of Beach and
Lodge Rds, Summerstrand, PO
Box 13352, Humewood 6013.
Tel: (041) 56 3322; fax: (041)
56 3374. Value-for-money
accommodation overlooking
Humewood Beach. Air
conditioning, telephone in
rooms, facilities available for
disabled guests, restaurant and
swimming pool.
Country Protea Inn ✩✩✩
Corner of Meintjies and Loop
Sts, PO Box 8, Middelburg, Cape
5900. Tel: (04 924) 2 1126; fax:
(04 924) 2 1681. Country hotel
in the Karoo district. Air
conditioning, telephone in rooms
and restaurant.
Kei Mouth Beach Hotel ✩✩
Beach Road, PO Box 8, Kei
Mouth 5260. Tel/fax: (0 438) 88
0088. Luxury hotel with a
footpath down to the beach.
Good restaurant, watersports,
fishing, trails and golf.
Kennaway Protea Hotel
✩✩✩ Esplanade PO Box 583,
East London 5200. Tel: (0 431)
2 5531; fax: (0 431) 2 1326;
telex: 25 0254. Convenient for
both East London's city centre
and its beaches. Air
conditioning, telephone and non-
smoking rooms available.

Private Hotels
Drostdy Hotel ✩✩✩ 30
Church St, PO Box 400, Graaff-
Reinet 6280. Tel: (0 491) 2
2161; fax: (0 491) 2 4582. An

elegant award-winning hotel built
in the Cape Dutch style. Air
conditioning, telephone in
rooms, restaurant and swimming
pool.
Esplanade Hotel ✩✩
Beachfront, PO Box 18041,
Quigney, East London 5211. Tel;
(0 431) 2 2518; fax: (0 431) 2
3679. Simple yet comfortable
accommodation on the main
beachfront.
Grosvenor Lodge ✩✩✩ 48
Taylor Street, PO Box 61, King
William's Town 5600. Tel: (0
433) 2 1440; fax: (0 433) 2
4772. A homely hotel with air
conditioning, telephone and
restaurant.
Lovemore Retreat, 434
Sardinia Road, Lovemore Park,
Port Elizabeth 6070, PO box
15818, Emerald Hill 6011. Tel:
(041) 36 1708/36 1752; fax:
(041) 36 2304. There's a sad
lack of decent accommodation
here so thank heaven for this
luxurious coastal guest house
on the outskirts of town. Offers
swimming pool, jacuzzi and
steam bath; tranquil beach and
nature walks, too.
New Masonic Hotel ✩✩
Stockenstroom St, PO Box 44,
Cradock 5880. Tel: (0 481)
3115/3159; fax: (0 481) 4402.
Friendly hotel with basic
accommodation.
Tsitsikamma Lodge ✩✩ N2
National Rd, Tsitsikamma, PO
Box 10, Storms River 6308. Tel:
(042) 750 3802; fax: (042) 750
3702. Luxury log cabins in
forest setting. Forest and river
walks. Six special honeymoon
suites with spa baths available.

Hostels
Backpackers Barn, 4 Trollope
Street, Grahamstown 6139.
Tel/fax: (0461) 29720.
East London Backpackers,
128 Moore St, Eastern Beach,
East London 5021. Tel: (0431) 2
3423; fax: (0431) 74 6054.
East London YWCA, 49 St
Georges Road, East London. Tel:
(0431) 29819.

Port Elizabeth Backpackers, 7 Prospect Hill, Port Elizabeth 6001. Tel: (041) 56 0697; fax: (041) 74 6054.

YMCA, 31 Havelock St, Box 12007, Centrahil, Port Elizabeth 6006. Tel: (041) 55 9792; fax: (041) 55 3026.

WESTERN CAPE
Chain Hotels
Far Hills Protea Hotel ☆☆☆ N2 National Road, PO Box 10, George 6530. Tel: (0 441) 71 1295; fax: (0 441) 71 1951. Set in beautiful countryside. Non-smoking rooms available, telephone in rooms, restaurant and swimming pool.

Holiday Inn Garden Court – Wilderness ☆☆☆ N2 National Garden Route Highway, PO Box 26, Wilderness 6460. Tel: (0 441) 877 1104; fax: (0 441) 877 1134; telex: 24 8409. Set overlooking the Indian Ocean and unspoilt beaches. Air conditioning, telephone in rooms, non-smoking rooms available, facilities for disabled guests, restaurant and swimming pool.

Karos Wilderness Hotel ☆☆☆☆ N2 National Rd, PO Box 6, Wilderness 6560. Tel: (0 441) 877 1110; fax: (0 441) 877 0600. Holiday resort-type accommodation with air conditioning, telephone in rooms, restaurant and many sports facilities including a swimming pool.

Knysna Protea Hotel ☆☆☆ 51 Main St, PO Box 33, Knysna 6570. Tel: (0 445) 2 2127; fax: (0 445) 2 3568. Good-quality accommodation on the Garden Route. Air conditioning, telephone in rooms, facilities for disabled guests, swimming pool and restaurant.

Private Hotels
Eight Bells Mountain Inn ☆☆☆ Ruitersbosch District, Robinson Pass, PO Box 436, Mossel Bay 6500. Tel: (0 444) 95 1544/5; fax: (0 444) 95

1548. Family-run country inn set amidst stunning mountain scenery on the Garden Route. Telephone in rooms, restaurant and a wide variety of sports facilities available.

Fairy Knowe Hotel ☆☆ Dumbleton Rd, PO Box 2365, George 6530. Tel: (0 441) 877 1100; fax: (0 441) 877 0364. Basic resort hotel on the banks of the Touws River. Telephone in rooms, bar and restaurant.

Hotel Classifications

Hotel classification is based on the South African Tourism Board's National Grading and Classification Scheme, which is listed below:
☆☆☆☆☆ = Outstanding
☆☆☆☆ = Excellent
☆☆☆ = Very good
☆☆ = Good
☆ = Comfortable

The Plettenberg ☆☆☆☆ 40 Church Street, PO Box 719, Plettenberg Bay 6600. Tel: (04457) 32030; fax: (04 457) 32074. A grand hotel in the English country-house style. Very good food and service, and a relaxing atmosphere. Amazing sea views. Swimming pool.

Riempie Estate Hotel ☆☆☆ Baron Van Reede Street, PO Box 370, Oudtshoorn 6620. Tel: (0443) 22 6161; fax: (0443) 22 6772. Cosy country atmosphere and tranquil setting.

Hostels
Albergo, 8 Church Street, Plettenberg Bay 6600. Tel: (04457) 34434.

George Backpackers, 29 York St, George 6530. Tel: (0441) 74 7807; fax: (0441) 74 6054.

Knysna Backpackers, 42 Queen Street, Knysna 6570. Tel: (0445) 22554.

Mossel Bay Backpackers, 1 Marsh Street, Mossel Bay 6500. Tel/fax: (0444) 91 3182.

CAPE TOWN, THE CAPE PENINSULA AND ENVIRONS
Chain Hotels
Cape Sun Inter-Continental ☆☆☆☆☆ Strand St, PO Box 4532, Cape Town 8000. Tel: (021) 488 5100; fax: (021) 23 8875; telex: 52 2453. Luxury hotel in the centre of Cape Town. Air conditioning, telephone in rooms, non-smoking rooms available, facilities for disabled guests, restaurant, fitness centre and swimming pool.

Capetonian Protea Hotel ☆☆☆☆ Pier Place, Heerengracht, PO Box 6856, Roggebaai, Cape Town 8012. Tel: (021) 21 1150; fax: (021) 25 2215; telex: 52 0000. Friendly hotel on the Waterfront. Air conditioning, telephone in rooms, non-smoking rooms available, and swimming pool.

The Cellars – Hohenort Country House Hotel ☆☆☆☆☆ 15 Hohenort Avenue, PO Box 270, Constantia 7848. Tel: (021) 794 2137/8; fax: (021) 794 2149. Graceful hotel converted from the 17th-century cellars of the former Klaasenbosch wine farm. Set in large landscaped gardens. Noted restaurant and cellar, too. Swimming pool, tennis and walking trails.

Devon Valley Protea Hotel ☆☆☆ Devon Valley Rd, PO Box 68, Stellenbosch 7600. Tel: (021) 882 2012; fax: (021) 882 2610; telex: 52 2558. Set in the heart of the winelands. Air conditioning, telephone in rooms, non-smoking rooms, facilities for disabled guests, restaurant and swimming pool.

Holiday Inn Garden Court – De Waal ☆☆☆ Mill St Gardens, PO Box 2793, Cape Town 8000. Tel: (021) 45 1311; fax: (021) 461 6648; telex: 52 0653 Modern hotel at the foot of Table Mountain. Air conditioning, telephone in rooms, non-smoking rooms available, facilities for disabled guests, restaurant and swimming pool.

Karos Arthur's Seat Hotel

☆☆☆☆ Arthur's Rd, Sea Point, Cape Town 8001. Tel: (021) 434 1187; fax: (021) 434 9768; telex: 52 7310. Mediterranean-style hotel near Table Mountain and Devil's Peak. Air conditioning, telephone in rooms, facilities for disabled guests and swimming pool.

The Lodge Bellville ☆

Corner of Willie van Schoor Ave and Mispel Rd, PO Box 3587, Tygerpark 7536. Tel: (021) 948 7990; fax: (021) 948 8805. Value-for-money accommodation close to the airport. Air conditioning, telephone in rooms, non-smoking rooms, facilities for disabled guests, restaurant and swimming pool.

Marine Protea Hotel ☆☆☆

Voortrekker St, PO Box 249, Lambert's Bay 8130. Tel: (027) 432 1126; fax: (027) 432 1036. Set in a quaint village with reputation for its seafood.

Table Bay ☆☆☆☆☆

Waterfront, PO Box 50369, Waterfront, Cape Town 8002. Tel: (021) 406 5000; fax: (021) 406 5686. Recently opened at a cost of R250 million, this is a spectacular addition to Cape Town's hotels and the first Sun International hotel to open in the city. Handsomely furnished rooms with satellite television and sea or mountain views.

Victoria Junction ☆☆☆☆

Corner of Somerset & Ebenezer Roads, Waterfront, Cape Town 8000. Tel: (021) 418 1234; fax: (021) 418 5678. Boasting a loft-style interior and fitted out to stress the ergonomic aspects of design and decor, this is a bold new addition to the Protea Hotel chain. Witty details include tables that look like surfboards and aerodynamic sofas. The lobby is becoming a must-be-seen social spot for media, film and fashion crews. Just seconds away from the Waterfront precinct.

Private Hotels

The Bay ☆☆☆☆☆ Victoria

Road, PO Box 32021, Camps Bay 8040. Tel: (021) 438 4444; fax: (021) 438 4455. Clean white lines, cool tiled floors, light, bright and airy – this is a refreshingly modern alternative in a town where it's almost obligatory for good hotels to double up as listed monuments. Every room enjoys a spectacular sea or mountain view.

Cedarberg Hotel ☆☆ 67

Voortrekker St, PO Box 37, Citrusdal 7340. Tel: (022) 921 2221; fax: (022) 921 2704. Comfortable accommodation in the Olifants River Valley with air conditioning, telephone in rooms, restaurant and pool.

Grande Roche Hotel

☆☆☆☆☆ Plantasie Street, PO Box 6038, Paarl 7622. Tel: (021) 63 2727; fax: (021) 63 2220. Simply the best hotel in South Africa. A superb setting in a vineyard, sumptuous accommodation, superb service. Bosman's, the hotel restaurant, has classically-trained staff serving haute cuisine and a prize-winning cellar. Swimming pool, tennis and gym.

Le Quartier Francais, 16

Huguenot Road, Franschhoek 7690. Tel: (021) 876 2151; fax: (021) 876 3105. An exceptional country-house guest house just outside Cape Town. It's small and built round a garden court-yard with a pool. Well-placed for tours of the winelands, and the restaurant is highly acclaimed.

Metropole Hotel ☆☆ 38

Long St, PO Box 3086, Cape Town 8000. Tel: (021) 23 6363; fax: (021) 23 6370. City centre hotel in the heart of "antique town" with air conditioning and telephone in rooms.

Mount Nelson Hotel

☆☆☆☆☆ 76 Orange Street, PO Box 2608, Cape Town 8000. Tel: (021) 23 1000; fax: (021) 24 7472; telex: 52 7804. First on anyone's list of Cape hotels, the pale-pink "Nellie" is a grand colonial hotel that has been a favourite of discerning travellers for nearly a century. Even if you don't stay here, taking afternoon tea is a must.

Roggeland Country House

Roggeland Road, Dal Josafat, PO Box 7210, Northern Paarl 7623. Tel: (021) 868 2501; fax: (021) 868 2113. A superb small (eight-bedroom) country-house-style guest house in the winelands. Located an hour from Cape Town, the ambience, the restaurant and the service have placed it firmly in the ranks of the 50 best country-house hotels in the world. The cuisine is South African regional.

Shrimpton Manor Guest

House ☆☆ 19 Alexander Rd, Muizenberg 7945. Tel: (021) 788 1128/9; fax: (021) 788 5225. Excellent cuisine in this manor house, just a few minutes from the sea. Basic rooms and swimming pool.

Victoria & Alfred Hotel

☆☆☆☆ Waterfront, PO Box 50050, Waterfront, Cape Town 8002. Tel: (021) 419 6677; fax: (021) 419 8955. Victorian elegance combined with modern four-star standards. Outstanding restaurant.

Bed & Breakfast

Head South Lodge, Green

Point, Cape Town. Tel: (021) 434 8777. This is a 15-room gem. Chic and retro cool with its Tretchikoff portaits on the walls, rich coloured fabrics and dark wood fixtures, there's a strong whiff of glamorous decadence here. Ironic and fun.

Kirstenberry Lodge, 46

Klaasens Road, Bishopscourt, Cape Town 7700. Tel: (021) 797 1501; fax: (021) 797 2027. An exclusive lodge, sleeping a maximum of 10 guests, overlooking Kirstenbosch Botanical Gardens. Telephones in rooms, swimming pool and walking trails.

Lebensart Guest House and Gallery, 19 Alphen Drive, Constantia, Cape Town 7800. Tel: (021) 794 1013; fax: (021) 794 6641. Charming four-bedroomed guest house offers stylish accommodation surrounded by nature, art and culture. Swimming pool.

Longwood Guest House Corner of Forest Road and Montrose Avenue, 5 Montrose Av, Oranjezicht 8001. Tel: (021) 461 5988; fax: (021) 461 5953. A great example of Sir Herbert Baker design with original teak and yellowwood interior. Magnificent views of mountains, city and bay. Telephones in rooms. Swimming pool.

Hostels

Abe Bailey Youth Hostel, 11 Maynard Road, Muizenberg 7951. Tel/fax: (021) 788 2301.

Ashanti Lodge, 11 Hof Street, Gardens 8001, Cape Town. Tel: (021) 23 8721; fax: (021) 23 8790.

Cloudbreak Travellers Lodge, 219 Buitenkant Street, Cape Town. Tel/fax: (021) 461 6892.

Harbourside Backpacker, 136 Main Road, Kalk Bay 7975. Tel: (021) 788 2943; fax: (021) 788 6452.

The Lion's Den Backpacker's Lodge, 255 Long Street, Cape Town. Tel: (021) 23 9003.

Stan's Halt Youth Hostel, The Glen, Camps Bay 8001. Tel/fax: (021) 438 9037.

YMCA, Burham Drive, Observatory, Cape Town. Tel: (021) 47 6217; fax: (021) 47 6275.

YWCA, 20 Bellevue St, Cape Town. Tel: (021) 23 3711.

FREE STATE AND NORTH-WEST PROVINCE

Chain Hotels

City Lodge Bloemfontein ☆☆ Corner of Voortrekker St & Parfitt Ave, PO Box 3552, Bloemfontein 9300. Tel: (051) 447 9888; fax: (051) 447 5669. Value-for-money accommodation

in landscaped grounds close to city centre. Air conditioning, telephone in rooms, non-smoking rooms available, facilities for disabled guests and swimming pool.

Holiday Inn Garden Court Bloemfontein – Naval Hill ☆☆☆ 1 Union Ave, PO Box 1851, Bloemfontein 9300. Tel: (051) 30 1111; fax: (051) 30 4141; telex: 267 645. City centre hotel with air conditioning, telephone in rooms, non-smoking rooms available, facilities for disabled, restaurant and swimming pool.

Welkom Inn ☆☆☆ Corner of Tempest & Stateway Rds, PO Box 887, Welkom 9460. Tel: (057) 357 3361; fax: (057) 352 1458; telex: 26 3024. Located 5 km from the airport. Air conditioning, telephone in rooms, non-smoking rooms available, facilities for disabled guests, restaurant and swimming pool.

Private Hotels

Indaba Hotel ☆☆ 47 Fichardt St, PO Box 103, Sasolburg 9570. Tel: (016) 76 0600; fax: (016) 76 1938. Central hotel with carvery, bar, function room and swimming pool.

Nebo Holiday Farm ☆☆ Nebo Farm, PO Box 178, Ficksburg 9730. Tel: (05192) 3947/3281; fax: (05192) 286. Two-bedroomed thatched cottage accommodation set in an old English-style rose garden on this large cherry estate. Telephone in rooms, restaurant, sports facilities and swimming pool.

Park Hotel PP, 23 Muller St, PO Box 8, Bethlehem 9700. Tel/fax: (058) 303 5191. Basic hotel with air conditioning, telephone in rooms, non-smoking rooms available, facilities for disabled guests, restaurant and swimming pool.

Hostels

Isibongo Lodge, Olisbiershoek Pass, Harrismith 9880. Tel: (036) 438 6707.

Rustlers Valley Backpackers, Rustlers Valley Farm, Ficksburg 9730. Tel: (05192) 3939/2730; fax: (05192) 3939.

NORTHERN CAPE

Chain Hotels

Diamond Protea Lodge ☆☆ 124 Du Toitspan Rd, PO Box 2068, Kimberley 8300. Tel: (0 531) 81 1281; fax: (0 531) 81 1284. Good standard of accommodation with air conditioning, telephone in rooms, non-smoking rooms available, facilities for disabled guests and bar.

Waterwiel Protea Hotel ☆☆☆ Voortrekker St, PO Box 250, Kakamas 8870. Tel: (054) 431 0838; fax: (054) 431 0836. Small hotel with air conditioning, telephone in rooms and pool.

Private Hotels

Eldorado Motel ☆☆☆ Main St, PO Box 313, Kuruman 8460. Tel/fax: (05 373) 2 2191/2/3. This motel has comfortable rooms with air conditioning, telephone, and a swimming pool.

Kamieskroon Hotel ☆☆ Old National Rd, PO Box 19, Kamieskroon 8241. Tel: (0 257) 614; fax: (0 257) 675. Family-owned hotel in Namaqualand. Specialises in eco-tourism and photographic workshops.

Kokerboom Motel ☆☆ Biesjesfontein, PO Box 340, Springbok 8240. Tel: (0 251) 2 2685; fax: (0 251) 2 2257. Cool, spacious hotel in Namaqualand. Air conditioning and telephone in rooms.

Hostels

Gum Tree Lodge, Bloemfontein Rd, Kimberley 8301. Tel: (0531) 82 8577; fax: (0531) 81 5409.

LESOTHO

Blue Mountain Inn, near Teyateyaneng, PO Box 7, Teyateyaneng, Lesotho. Tel: (00266) 500362.

Hotel Victoria ✰✰✰ PO Box 212, Maseru 100, Lesotho. Tel: (00266) 32 2002/3 or 31 2922.

Lesotho Sun ✰✰✰✰✰ Private Bag A68, Maseru, Lesotho. Tel: (00266) 31 3111.

Malealea Lodge, PO Box 119, Wepener 9944, South Africa. Tel/fax: (051) 47 3200. A self-catering lodge situated in the central Thaba Putsoa range. The staff can organise, or tell you how to organise, just about anything you want to do in Lesotho.

Molimo Mthuse Lodge, contact as for Hotel Victoria above.

SWAZILAND

To book accommodation at Hlane Royal National Park, Milwane Wildlife Sanctuary or Mkhaya Nature Reserve, contact:

Big Game Parks, PO Box 234, Mbabane, Swaziland. Tel: (00268) 61037 or 44541; fax: 40957.

Forester's Arms, PO Box 14, Mhlambanyatsi, Swaziland. Tel: (00268) 74177; fax: (00268) 74051. Not fancy, but full of character. Looks and acts like a faded English country inn.

Highland Inn, Post Office Box, Pigg's Peak, Swaziland. Tel: (00268) 71144. No luxuries to speak of, but cosy, full of country atmosphere and quiet. More character than the nearby casino hotel.

Jabula Inn, PO Box 15, Mbabane, Swaziland. Tel: (00268) 42043 or 42406; fax: (00268) 45855.

Sun International (Royal Swazi Spa, Ezulweni and Lugogo Suns), PO Box 784487, Sandton 2146, Gauteng, South Africa. Tel: (011) 780 7800; fax: (011) 780 7726.

The Tavern, PO Box 25, Mbabane, Swaziland. Tel: (00268) 42361.

Where to Eat

Local Cuisine

Many South African specialties are derived from Malaysian cuisine – a legacy from the 17th century, when Indonesian slaves imported by the Dutch were sometimes used as cooks in white households. In and around Cape Town particularly, mildly spicy Malay dishes have established a firm foothold on the menus of restaurants and hotels.

Bobotie is a sweet-and-spicy dish of ground meat. *Bredie* is traditionally a casserole of mutton and vegetables. *Sosaties* are skewers of mutton or pork with small onions. Chutney is a sweet-and-sour fruit conserve which is served as a condiment with curries. *Koeksusters* are only advised for those with a very sweet tooth:

small cakes fried in fat, then immersed in syrup.

In Durban and the surrounding area, the cuisine has a distinctively Indian flavour. Indentured labourers imported from India to work in the sugar-cane trade in the 1860s brought with them their wonderful curries – spicy casseroles made of vegetables, legumes, lamb, chicken or beef on saffron rice. They're accompanied by such condiments as bananas, tomatoes, chutneys, and particularly grated coconut, which is supposed to take away some of the bite of very hot curries. Catering to timid foreign tastes, curries are also served mild and medium-hot.

Biltong delights the hearts of South Africans living abroad. Resembling dry sticks of wood, these strips of beef are salted, spiced and air-dried. A delicacy is venison biltong: when a game farmer produces his own, this leaves commercially prepared beef biltong in the dust.

Braaivleis (outdoor grilling) is as much a part of the South African way of life as sunshine and rugby. There's hardly a picnic spot, campsite or bungalow in the national parks that hasn't got a barbecue and

Beverages

The local beers are good, with Windhoek, from Namibia, perhaps the best in flavour and purity. Fruit juices and mediocre wine are sold in 3- or 5-litre containers, which have a little tap on the side so that the contents are not exposed to air, and remain fresh. Liquifruit and Monis juices are produced without the addition of sugar.

The flavour of *Rooibos* tea lies somewhere between the better-known herbal teas and black tea. It's made from the fine twigs of the local red bush, and quite refreshing when chilled. You can get it in most

hotels and restaurants, or in any local supermarket.

The local mineral water Skoonspruit (clean spring) is cheaper than the imported product. If there isn't any mineral water, you can always order soda.

If you're fond of liqueurs, make sure you sample Amarula. This mandarin-flavoured liqueur, made from the yellow fruit of the marula tree, is the local equivalent of Cointreau and is extremely sweet. There is also Van der Hum, a golden-coloured mandarin liqueur which is very sweet.

grill. Many hotels also offer *braais* in their gardens on weekends. An important ingredient of *braaivleis* is *boerewors*, a large sausage made of mutton and beef. The best specimens can be purchased at small rural butchers in Free State or Mpumalanga, who make them with the same recipes used by their grandmothers.

Thanks to the country's various climatic and soil conditions, all kinds of fruit are grown in South Africa. On the Cape, there are marvellous grapes, apples and pears; while Mpumalanga and KwaZulu-Natal produce tropical fruits such as paw-paws, avocados, mangos, lichees, pineapples, bananas, and many others. You can get fruit fresh, as juice, or as delicious fruit rolls, fruit pulp dried in thin layers and rolled up – ideal snacks for long car trips.

Restaurant Listings

The restaurants in and around the main cities that are listed below reflect the rich diversity of cuisines available in modern South Africa.

JOHANNESBURG AND PRETORIA
Bodega, Admiral's Court, Tyrwhitt Mall, 31 Tyrwhitt Avenue, Rosebank, Johannesburg. Tel: (011) 447 3210. The best Italian food in Jo'burg. Cool, spacious and airy, with the menu written up on a blackboard. *Moderate*

The Carnivore, Muldersdrift Estate, Muldersdrift. Tel: (011) 957 2099. Vast carvery where the meat is spit-roasted over a huge charcoal fire in the middle of the restaurant. It's wise to starve for a few days before coming here! *Moderate*

Cento, 100 Longeman Drive, Kensington, Johannesburg. Tel: (011) 622 7270. Not only do Al and Val Strick cook Mediterranean food with flair, their cellar

contains the biggest stock of wines in Jo'burg. *Moderate*

Gerard Moerdyk, 752 Park Street, Arcadia, Pretoria. Tel: (012) 344 4856. Old-fashioned, elegant restaurant with flounced silk curtains, antiques and artefacts, heavy tapestries and polished wooden floors. Serves superbly-cooked traditional South African cuisine, such as springbok pie and ostrich. *Expensive*

Gramadoelas at the Market, Market Theatre Precinct, Wolhutter Street, Newtown, Johannesburg. Tel: (011) 838 6960. A magnet for overseas visitors who come for the superb South African cuisine, including such delicacies as crocodile. Beautiful mock-18th century decor. *Moderate*

Ile de France, Cramerview Shopping Centre, 277 Main Road, Bryanston, Johannesburg. Tel: (011) 706 2837. This large, airy space surrounded by windows is a rare oasis for local foodies, who go into raptures over the fine Provençal cooking. *Expensive*

Iyavaya, 42 Hunter Street, Yeoville, Johannesburg. Tel: (011) 648 3500. African cuisine from all over the continent including mopani worms and ostrich. African beers served, too. Great atmosphere and music. *Cheap*

Kapitan's Café, 11a Kort Street, central Johannesburg. Tel: (011) 834 8048. Specialising in delicious curries, this establishment was a favourite haunt of attorneys Nelson Mandela and Oliver Tambo in the 1950s. Open lunchtimes only. *Cheap*

La Madelaine, 258 Esselen St, Sunnyside, Pretoria. Tel: (012) 44 6076. Sensational Provençal food. Simplicity is the watchword of Daniel Leusch's cooking, and it's won him many laurels. *Expensive*

Leipoldt's, 94 Juta St, Braamfontein, Johannesburg.

Tel: (011) 339 2765. Excellent buffet serving traditional South African cuisine, Cape Malay and game dishes. *Moderate*

Linger Longer, 58 Wierda Rd W, Wierda Valley W, Sandton, Johannesburg. Tel: (011) 884 0465. Despite the silly name, a luxuriously appointed restaurant serving really exceptional cuisine. Beautiful presentation, too. *Expensive*

DURBAN AND ENVIRONS
Aangan, 86 Queen Street, Durban. Tel: (031) 307 1366. Delicious authentic South Indian vegetarian dishes. *Cheap*

Billy the BUMS' Bistro and Cocktail Bar, Windermere Road, Durban. Tel: (031) 303 1988. Where the trendy "Basic Urban Socialites" gather. *Moderate*

Café Fish, Durban Yacht Mole, off Victoria Embankment, Durban. Tel: (031) 305 5062. Indoor and outdoor dining at this restaurant on stilts, plus a pub area. *Moderate*

The Colony, First Floor, The Oceanic, Sol Harris Crescent, Durban. Tel: (031) 368 2789. A hot spot for power lunchers, who come for the classic South African cuisine – warthog is a speciality. *Expensive*

The Famous Fish Company, King's Battery, end of Point Road, Point Waterfront, Durban. Tel: (031) 368 1060. Excellent seafood menu. *Cheap*

Joe Kool's, 137 Lower Marine Parade, North Beach, Durban. Tel: (031)32 9697. Popular beachfront bar and restaurant. Where Durban's surfers come when there's no surf. *Cheap*

La Dolce Vita, Durdoc Centre, 460 Smith St, Durban. Tel: (031) 301 8161. Still widely regarded as the best and chicest joint in town after 24 years. Chef/patron Gianni Allegranzi prepares traditional Italian cuisine with elegance and flair. *Expensive*

Le San Geran, 31 Aliwal St, Durban. Tel: (031) 304 7509. Eatery with a lively atmosphere in a lovely pink, listed building. The Mauritian/Creole cooking here is a firm favourite with locals and visitors alike. Outstanding food. *Moderate*

Razzmatazz, Cabana Beach, 10 Lagoon Drive, Umhlanga Rocks. Tel: (031) 561 5847. Wonderful game and seafood dishes, plus daily specials. *Moderate*

Roma Revolving Restaurant, 32nd Floor, John Ross House, Victoria Embankment, Durban. Tel: (031) 37 6707. Enjoy the seafood and pasta menu as you take in panoramic views of the harbour. *Moderate*

Scalini, Marine Sands, 237 Marine Parade, Durban. Tel: (031) 32 2804. Superior Italian cuisine. *Moderate*

Thirsty's, King's Battery, New Point Waterfront harbour, Durban. Tel: (031) 37 9212. Curries and good pub food. Great value and even better views. *Cheap*

Two Moon Junction, 45 Windermere Road, Morningside, Durban. Tel: (031) 303 3078. Buzzing, see-and-be-seen eatery with a picturesque courtyard, serving imaginative contemporary South African cuisine. *Moderate*

The Ulundi Grill, Royal Hotel, 267 Smith St, Durban. Tel: (031) 304 0331. Superb steaks and curries. *Expensive*

CAPE TOWN AND THE CAPE PENINSULA

The Africa Café, 213 Lower Main Road, Observatory, Cape Town. Tel: (021) 47 9553. Authentic African cooking. *Cheap*

Bertie's Big Easy, Bertie's Landing, Victoria & Alfred Waterfront, Cape Town. Tel: (021) 419 2727. Popular for its huge portions of delicious fresh seafood and fine views. Very good value. *Cheap*

Biesmiellah, 2 Upper Wale St, Cape Town. Tel: (021) 230 850. Known for its range of Indian and Cape Malay dishes. The place to come for delicious, hot and spicy food. Muslim-run, so no alcohol on the premises. *Cheap*

Biggsy's Restaurant Carriage and Wine Bar, on the Cape Metro train to Simonstown. Cape Town station, Adderley Street, Cape Town. Tel: (021) 405 3870. Enjoy breakfast or lunch and dine in style as you travel along the stunning False Bay coast. A la carte menu includes seafoods, steaks and curries. Booking essential. *Moderate*

Blues, The Promenade, Victoria Rd, Camps Bay. Tel: (021) 438 2040. Californian-style cuisine in a spacious, airy room overlooking one of the world's most pristinely beautiful beaches. Always packed, so book ahead. *Expensive*

Boschendal Restaurant, Groot Drakenstein. Tel: (021) 874 1252. First-class South African cuisine in elegant surroundings. *Expensive*

Brinjals, 18 Huguenot Road, Franschhoek. Tel: (021) 876 2151. Excellent and very affordable bistro and delicatessen. *Cheap*

Buitenverwachting, Klein Constantia Road, Constantia. Tel: (021) 794 3522. The name means "beyond expectation" and that's a fair description of this wonderful restaurant set on a stunning wine estate. Impressive wine list. Closed Mondays and in August. *Expensive*

Café Paradiso, 110 Kloof St Gardens, Cape Town. Tel: (021) 238 653. Chef Freda van der Merwe dishes up exceptional Mediterranean-style cuisine in this relaxed and friendly café-brasserie, much loved by the local élite. *Moderate*

Col'cacchio, Seeff Building, Foreshore, Cape Town. Tel: (021) 419 4848. Superb pizzas make this a locals' favourite. *Cheap*

Constantia Uitsig, Spaanschemat River Rd, Constantia. Tel: (021) 794 4480. This wine farm restaurant offers fine Provençal cooking where fish and game are specialities. *Expensive*

JB Rivers Café and Cocktail Saloon, Cavendish Square, Cape Town. Tel: (021) 683 0840. New Orleans-style spicy Cajun food plus loads of intriguing cocktails. *Moderate*

Kaapse Tafel, 90 Queen Victoria St (near Museum). Tel: (021) 23 1651. Excellent Cape Malay cuisine served in this small 18th-century town house. *Bobotie* is recommended. *Moderate*

La Petite Ferme, Pass Rd, Franschhoek. Tel: (021) 876 3016. Midday meals and coffee and cakes. *Moderate*

Laborie Restaurant and Wine House, Taillefert St, Paarl. Tel: (021) 807 3095. Gourmet South African cuisine. *Expensive*

Le Quartier Français, 16 Huguenot St, Franschhoek. Tel: (021) 876 2151. Cuisine reflecting influences of the region's original French settler families. *Expensive*

Mama Yama, 15 Shortmarket Street, off St Georges Mall, Cape Town. Tel: (021) 23 0605. Very trendy express sushi bar set in a beautiful art deco building, with a plain and elegant interior. *Moderate*

Mamma Africa Restaurant and Bar, 178 Long Street, Cape Town. Tel: (021) 248 634. Stylishly ethnic. Check out the bar for the biggest reptile in town. *Cheap*

Mano's, 39 Main Road, Green Point, Cape Town. Tel: (021) 434 1090. Hip new restaurant serving some over-the-top cocktails. *Cheap*

Morton's on the Wharf, Victoria & Alfred Waterfront, Cape Town. Tel: (021) 418 3633. One of the best bars and restaurants crowding this thriving – if somewhat touristy – dockside complex. Fine Cajun cooking and a cheery, bustling ambience. *Moderate*

Pavilion Bistro, BMW Pavilion, Granger Bay Blvd, Victoria & Alfred Waterfront, Cape Town. Tel: (021) 418 4210. A waterfront gem, all high-tech steel and chrome. Chef Else van der Nest cooks fabulously imaginative Mediterranean food. *Moderate*

Wangthai, 31 Heerengracht, Foreshore, Cape Town. Tel: (021) 418 1858. Superb Thai cuisine. *Moderate*

Wine Routes

One of the most pleasant ways of exploring the Western Cape is to follow one of the many Wine Routes that have been established in the region. It certainly isn't necessary to be a wine expert to enjoy these routes, as the countryside and architecture one encounters is often every bit as enjoyable as the wine tasting. Routes tend to be clearly sign-posted.

For more information and maps regarding these Wine Routes, contact: **Winelands Tourism Association**, PO Box 19, Somerset West 7129. Tel: (021) 851 1497, or try the AA or Captour.

The Constantia Wine Route is the shortest of the Cape's wine routes, but the nearest one to Cape Town. It includes three estates:

• **Groot Constantia**, Constantia Road, Wynberg. Tel: (021) 794 5067. Open: daily 10am–5pm Feb-Nov; 10am–6pm Dec–Jan. Hourly guided tours of the cellars; Wine Museum; wine tasting. One of the finest examples of Cape Dutch architecture in the country.

• **Klein Constantia**, tel: (021) 794 5188. Open: Mon–Fri 9am–1pm and 2–5pm; Sat 9am–1pm.

• **Buitenverwachting**, tel: (021) 794 5190. Open: Mon–Fri 9am–5pm; Sat 9am–1pm.

Other wine routes include:
Durbanville Wine Route, tel: (021) 96 3453/3020.

Helderberg Wine Route, contact Winelands Tourism Association (see above).

Klein Karoo Wine Route, Klein Karoo Wine Trust, tel: (04439) 6715.

KWV Brandy Cellar, tel: (0231) 20255. The largest in the world, it offers conducted tours.

Olifants River Wine Route, Olifants River Wine Trust, tel: (0271) 33126.

Paarl Wine Route, PO Box 46, Paarl 7622, tel: (021) 872 3605. Has 20 members, most of which arrange cellar tours, wine tastings and sales. Most famous among these is Nederburg, a co-operative producing wines that have taken many international gold medals in the last 20 years.

Robertson Wine Route, The Robertson Wine Trust, tel: (02351) 3167.

Stellenbosch Wine Route, Stellenbosch Tourist Bureau and Wine Route Office, 36 Market Street, Stellenbosch. Tel: (021) 886 4310. A 12-km (7.5-mile), well-marked route around beautiful Stellenbosch brings you to 23 cellars and five wineries, most of which offer guided tours and wine-tastings.

Swartland Wine Route, Allesverloren Estate, tel: (02246) 320.

Tulbagh Wine Route, Tulbagh Wine Association, tel: (0236) 30 0242.

Vignerons de Franschhoek, 66 Huguenot Road, Franschhoek, Western Cape. Tel: (021) 876 3062. A group of 20 vineyards in the Franschhoek area which open for wine tastings and cellar tours.

Wellington Wine Route, tel: (021) 873 4604.

Worcester Wine Route, Worcester Publicity, 75 Church Street, Worcester, Western Cape. Tel: (0231) 71408. The largest wine-making district in South Africa.

Culture

Computicket is an extremely practical and time-saving innovation: a computerised reservation office in every major shopping centre for tickets to major sports events, concerts, plays, opera and the cinema.

In Johannesburg and Pretoria, you can also buy tickets at Computicket for the bus ride to Sun City. **Johannesburg**, tel: (011) 331 9991. **Cape Town**, tel: (021) 21 4715. **Durban**, tel: (031) 304 2753.

Further details can be found in the "Entertainment" listings of the daily papers. *Going Out* is an excellent monthly listings booklet to the Cape region.

Theatre

GAUTENG

Civic Theatre, Loveday Street, Braamfontein. Tel: (011) 403 3408. Contains four stages: the Main Auditorium, the Tesson, the Thabong and the Pieter Roos auditorium.

Johannesburg Market Theatre, The Market Theatre Complex, Bree Street, Newtown, Johannesburg. Tel: (011) 832 1641. Contains three stages: the Main Auditorium, the Barney Simon Theatre and the Laager Theatre. The home of protest theatre in South Africa.

Roodepoort City Theatre, Civic Theatre Complex, Florida Park, Roodepoort. Tel: (011) 674 1356. Venue for drama, ballet and visual arts with an acclaimed resident orchestra, Pro Musica.

State Theatre, Church Street, Pretoria. Tel: (012) 322 1665.

Seven auditoriums with everything from symphony orchestras and opera to contemporary drama.

Victory Theatre, Louis Botha Avenue, Orange Grove. Tel: (011) 483 2793. Alternative theatre.

Windybrow Theatre, Nugget Street, Hillbrow. Tel: (011) 720 7009. Alternative and fringe performances.

CAPE TOWN AND THE CAPE PENINSULA

Baxter Theatre Complex, University of Cape Town, Main Road, Rondebosch. Tel: (021) 685 7880. Contains a theatre, concert hall and Studio Theatre.

Manenberg's Jazz Café, 2nd Floor, Dumbarton House, corner of Adderley and Church Streets, Cape Town. Tel: (021) 23 8304. The place to hear Cape jazz.

Maynardville Open-Air Theatre, corner of Church and Wolfe Streets, Wynberg. Tel: (021) 21 4715. Shakespeare and dance performances under the oak trees in summer.

Nico Malan Theatre Complex, DF Malan Street, Foreshore, Cape Town. Tel: (021) 21 5470. Performing arts centre housing an opera house and several theatres.

Oude Libertas Open-Air Amphitheatre, Stellenbosch. Tel: (021) 808 7474.

Theatre on the Bay, Link Street, Camps Bay. Tel: (021) 438 3301.

DURBAN

Beachhouse, 237 Marine Parade, Durban. Tel: (031) 32 3929. Jazz venue.

Elizabeth Sneddon Theatre, University of Natal, Durban. Tel: (031) 260 3133.

Playhouse Theatre, 231 Smith Street, Durban. Tel: (031) 304 3631. Drama and dance.

Diary of Events

For further information, contact SATOUR (see page 306).

January: Cape Minstrels Carnival, Cape Town.

February: Dias Festival, Mossel Bay, Western Cape.

March: Jeffreys Bay Shell Festival, Eastern Cape.

Harvest Festival of the Sea, Pepper Bay, Saldanha, Western Cape.

March/April: Rand Easter Show (two weeks around Easter), Johannesburg. The largest exposition in South Africa.

April: Mardi Gras Festival, Durban.

Port Elizabeth Splash Festival, Hobie Beach, Port Elizabeth.

Music in the Mountains Festival, Drakensberg Boys School, KwaZulu-Natal.

Game and Wine Festival, Kuruman, Northern Cape.

May: Umtata Cultural Festival, Mditshwa Tsolo District, Umtata, Eastern Cape.

Sabie Forest Fair, Sabie, Mpumalanga.

June: Paternoster Seafood Festival, Paternoster, Western Cape.

Biltong Festival, Showgrounds, Somerset East, Eastern Cape. Country festival.

June/July: National Arts Festival, Grahamstown, Eastern Cape. The largest festival of its kind in Africa – drama, dance, visual arts, music, film, jazz, etc – over two weeks.

July: Knysna Oyster Festival, Western Cape.

Bushveld Festival, Ellisras, Northern Province.

Hibiscus Festival, South Coast, KwaZulu-Natal.

August: Umhlanga (Reed Dance), Badplaas, Mpumalanga.

September: Zululand Show, Eshowe, KwaZulu-Natal.

Whale Festival, Hermanus, Western Cape.

Graaff-Reinet Karoo Festival, Sports Complex, Graaff-Reinet, Eastern Cape.

Groot Marico Arts Festival, Groot Marico, North-West Province.

September/October:

International Eisteddfod of SA, Roodepoort, Gauteng. The largest music/dance festival in the Southern Hemisphere, with participants from all around the world. The event is held every two years.

Magoebaskloof Spring Festival, Magoebaskloof, Northern Province. Celebrations beneath blossoming azaleas and cherry trees.

October: Shembe Blessing Festival, Inyezane Craft Centre & Lodge, Gingindlovu, KwaZulu-Natal. An authentic Zulu song and dance festival near Inanda, originally started by a missionary. Only Zulu dancers can take part; visiting spectators sometimes allowed.

Food and Wine Festival, Stellenbosch, Western Cape. A chance to sample the marvellous wines and culinary specialties of South Africa.

Ostrich Festival, Showgrounds, Oudtshoorn, Western Cape.

Tulbagh Festival, Church Street, Tulbagh, Western Cape.

Jacaranda Festival, Church Square, Pretoria.

November: National Zulu Dance Festival, Wagendrift Dam, Estcourt, KwaZulu-Natal.

Bush Festival, Prieska, Northern Cape. Games and marathon in the bush.

Cherry Festival, Showgrounds, Ficksburg, Free State.

December: Kenton-on-Sea Neptune Festival, Eastern Cape. Knysna Street Carnival, Western Cape.

Xmas Festival, Rustler's Valley, Ficksburg, Free State.

Shopping

Arts & Crafts

With its rich mix of cultures, South Africa has an abundance of artists and craftsmen: painters, graphic artists and sculptors working in wood, bronze and metal; potters who produce work of high artistic quality and craftsmanship; artists who work with leather; jewellery-makers, porcelain-sculptors, glass-blowers, woodworkers and furniture-makers; and weavers and spinners producing hand-knitted garments and individually styled designer clothes.

In the rural areas, traditional crafts abound. The Ndebele paint their houses with certain specific patterns, and produce magnificent beaded jewellery as well as copper and bronze bracelets. The filigree-like chains of Zulu beadwork have an entirely different character. Craft shops also stock grain baskets or sieves woven of grass and reeds, as well as stylised wood carvings of animals.

The Venda produce brightly-coloured clay pots, while the Toriga weave mats from coloured sisal. In Mpumalanga, along the Panorama Route, you can find Leiklip, a soft, shale-like stone with light and dark layers, which is used to make ashtrays and animal carvings.

Arts and Crafts Routes enable the visitor to see the artists and their work in their studios, to meet them over a cup of tea and to experience the environment they live in; perhaps even to buy a piece of art.

Ask the local tourist association for information and maps regarding Arts and Crafts Routes and markets in the area.

EASTERN CAPE

Art by the Sea, Jeffreys Bay. Last Saturday of the month, 10am–5pm.

Bathurst Market, Bathurst. First Saturday of the month, 9am–3pm.

Beacon Bay Arts and Crafts, East London. Every Saturday, 8.30am–12.30pm.

Ikhwesi Lokusa Workshop, Umtata. The Xhosa are famous for the high quality of their handicrafts. Pottery, leather, jewellery and other items are produced here by disabled people.

Izandla Pottery, outskirts of Umtata. The best pottery in the region emanates from this studio where it is also possible to see the potters at work. Next door is Hilmond Weavers, one of the largest hand-weaving shops, producing wall carpets and pillowcases from the pure mohair spun by the pupils of a local school for the blind.

Kei Carpets, Wesley (90 km/56 miles on R72 from Port Alfred). Tel: (0405) 77 1024. Fine hand-knotted carpets. Guided tours can be arranged. Wesley Crafts and Bira Crafts are here too and worth a look.

Lattimer's Landing Flea & Craft Market, East London. Weekends, 10am–4.30pm.

The Provost Craft Market, Grahamstown. Weekdays, 10am–5pm.

FREE STATE

Art Market, Bloemfontein. First Saturday of the month, 8am–1pm.

Cinderella Castle, Clarens. Curio shop in a building made of beer bottles!

Kroon Market, Kroonstad. Last Saturday of the month, 8am–2pm.

Qwa-Hands Centre, outskirts of Phuthaditjhaba. Handicraft centre selling weaving made from mohair and Karakul wool, hand-painted porcelain, bronze work and basketwork.

Westdene Flea Market, Bloemfontein. Every Saturday, 8am–1pm.

GAUTENG

Artists under the Sun, Zoo Lake, off Jan Smuts Avenue, Johannesburg. First Sunday of the month.

Bruma Lake, Bedfordview, Johannesburg. Tue–Fri, 10am–6pm. Bruma Lake is an old mining lake in Kensington, in the east of Johannesburg (not far from East Gate Shopping Centre).

Bryanston Organic Village Market, Culross Road, Bryanston, Johannesburg. A different kind of market with nearly 100 stands selling hand-sewn clothes, jewellery, African batik and pearl creations, minerals and crystals, glass, leather and woodwork, and even organically-grown vegetables. Everything offered here is made of all-natural materials. Thur–Sat, 9am–1pm; Tues nearest the full moon, 6–9pm. For more information, tel: (011) 706 3671.

Crafter's Marketplace, Top Crop Centre, DF Malan Drive, Johannesburg. Daily.

Crocodile River Arts and Crafts Ramble, Johannesburg and Pretoria. Tel: (011) 29 4961. First weekend of every month. The best known of the Arts and Crafts Routes, it meanders along the Crocodile River and includes some of the top artists and craftsmen in South Africa. Studios are open on the first weekend of every month 9am–5pm.

Hatfield Flea Market, Pretoria. Sundays and Bank Holidays, 9.15am–5.30pm.

Jacaranda Route, Pretoria. Tel: (012) 308 7694. Daily, Oct–Nov.

Market Theatre Flea Market, Market Theatre, Johannesburg.

Saturdays, 9am–4pm. The best-known bazaar in Johannesburg, worth a visit for people-watching.

Pretoria Culture Route, Pretoria. Tel: (012) 308 7694. Daily historical tour.

Rooftop Market, Rosebank Mall, Johannesburg. Sundays.

Wag'n Bietjie Route, east of Pretoria in the Bushveld. Tel: (012) 802 0637.

KwaZulu-Natal

Amphimarket, Marine Parade, Durban. Every Sunday, 9am–5pm. The Amphitheatre is transformed into a flea market where you can also watch Zulu dancers. When the old railway station was moved out of the city centre, the locomotive repair shop was left standing; today, it's become a highly original shopping mall, called, symbolically, The Workshop. Dozens of small, intriguing shops make browsing an amusing pastime.

Church Street Market, Church Street, Durban. Daily, 8am–4pm.

Evangelical Lutheran Church Arts and Crafts Centre, Rorke's Drift. Tel: (03425) 627. One of the biggest Zulu art centres in the country, selling hand-woven tapestries, pottery and fabrics.

Illovo River Market, Illovo, Durban. Sundays, 10am–4pm.

German Pioneer Route, tel: (01343) 3456. Paulpietersburg–Piet Retief–Vryheid–Dundee. Daily.

Midlands Meander, tel: (0332) 30 4308. Mooi River to Hilton. Daily, 9am–5pm.

Rogies Park Flea Market, Amanzimtoti. First Sunday of the month, 9am–5pm.

South Plaza Market, corner of Aliwal and Walnut Streets, Durban. Sundays, 9am–5pm.

Traditional Villages

Listed below are a selection of villages where visitors can experience different aspects of authentic South African culture.

Eastern Cape

Kaya Lendaba, Shamwari Game Reserve. Tel: (042) 851 1196. "Place of enlightening talk" – learn about the spiritual significance of sacred places.

Summerhill Pineapple Farm, Port Alfred. Tel: (0464) 25 0833/25 0621. Traditional Xhosa village.

Gauteng

Heia Safari Ranch, Johannesburg. Tel: (011) 659 0605. Traditional Zulu *kraal*; accommodation.

Lesedi Cultural Village, Johannesburg. Tel: (01205) 51394. Different tribes in traditional *kraals*; accommodation.

Loopspruit Ndebele Village, Bronkhorstspruit. Tel: (01212) 20894. Ndebele traditional life and building methods.

KwaZulu-Natal

Dumazulu, Hluhluwe. Tel: (035) 562 0343. Accommodation in huts of different tribes.

Kwabhekithunga, Eshowe. Tel: (0354600) 644. Accommoda-tion in Zulu "beehive" huts.

Midmar Historical Village, Midmar Dam, Howick. Tel: (0332) 30 2067. Display includes traditional Zulu *kraal*.

Ondini Cultural Historical Museum, Ulundi. Tel: (0358) 79 1854. King Cetshwayo's stronghold.

Phezulu Village, Durban. Tel: (031) 777 1208. Living museum illustrating Zulu culture.

Shakaland, Eshowe. Tel: (03546) 912. Accommodation in Zulu huts.

Talana Museum, Dundee. Tel: (0341) 22654. Traditional Zulu village, *muti* (medicinal) garden.

Umgungunhlovu, Eshowe. Tel: (03545) 2254. Reconstructed capital of King Dingane.

Free State

Basotho Cultural Village, Harrismith. Tel: (05861) 31796. Customs, traditions and culture.

Mpumalanga

Botshabelo Historical Village, Middelburg. Tel: (0132) 43 1319. South Ndebele village showing various building stages.

Mpumalanga Cultural Centre – Shabangoland, Hazyview. Tel: Mrs Tinie Snyman (013) 737 8434; (013) 737 7338. Traditional cultural village reflecting Shabango people of Hazyview area.

Northern Cape

Kagga Kamma, Cedarberg. Tel: (02211) 63 8334. Home of remaining South African Bushmen.

Xuu & Khwe Cultural Projects, Kimberley. Tel: (0531) 32680. Visit San communities.

Northern Province

Bakone Malapa, Pietersburg. Tel: (0152) 295 2011. Traditional Northern Sotho *kraal*, customs and skills.

Tsonga Kraal Open-air Museum, Phalaborwa. Tel: (015) 386 8727. Traditional Tsonga lifestyle.

Basadi-Ba-Bapedi, Ga Mphalele. Tel: (015) 619 0030. Rural cultural project manufacturing Pedi traditional goods; music and dancing.

North-West Province

Lotlamoreng Dam Cultural Village, Mafikeng. Tel: (041) 84 3040. Ancient cultural traditions of the tribes including rain ceremonies, story telling and spiritual healing.

Victoria Street Market, Durban. Daily. When Durban's Indian Market moved to its new location between Victoria and Queen Streets (near the mosque), it was renamed the Victoria Street Market. Haggling is expected: you can get discounts of up to 30 percent when buying jewellery, wood-carvings, hand-embroidered clothing or Indian spices. Don't feel guilty: these reductions will have been calculated by the sales-man as part of the sale price.

Wildabout Arts and Crafts Trail, Lower South Coast. Tel: (03931) 22322. Daily, 9am–5pm.

MPUMALANGA

Hall's Gateway Flea Market, Nelspruit. Every Saturday and Sunday, 9am–5pm.

Promenade Centre Flea Market, Nelspruit. Every Saturday, 8am–1pm.

Prorom Square Flea Market, Nelspruit. Fridays, 8am–5pm.

White River, just north of Nelspruit, is home to a number of well-known South African wildlife artists including sculptors, woodcutters, weavers and potters. Ask SATOUR for further information.

NORTHERN CAPE

Art Market, Kimberley. Last Saturday of the month, 8am–1pm.

Kimberley Flea Market, Kimberley, 9am–5pm.

NORTHERN PROVINCE

Ditike Craft Centre, Thohoyandou. Sells clay pots, carvings, basketware and articles woven out of grass or reed of high craftsmanship for which the Vha-Venda are known.

Pietersburg Flea Market, Pietersburg. First and last Saturday of the month, 9am–5pm.

WESTERN CAPE

Contact Captour (page 306) for Arts and Crafts Routes maps.

Akkedis Art Route, near Villiersdorp. Includes 15 artists. Last Sunday of the month.

Constantia Craft Market, Cape Town. Every Saturday and Sunday, 8am–2pm.

Grand Parade Market, Cape Town. Every Wednesday and Saturday.

Greenmarket Square Market, Cape Town. Mon–Sat, 9am–5pm. Cape Town's largest and best-known market offers clothes, jewellery, antiques, leather goods and much more.

Green Point Market, Cape Town. Sundays and Bank Holidays, 9am–5pm.

Hout Bay Craft Market, Hout Bay. Tel: (021) 790 3474. First and last Sunday every month, 9am–5pm.

Noordhoek Art Route, near Hout Bay. First Sunday of the month, 10am–5pm.

Plettenberg Bay Arts and Crafts Route, Plettenberg Bay. 14 shops and galleries.

Three Towns Art Route, Heidelberg, Cape Town. Tel: (021) 851 6166.

Treasure Coast Art Route, Marina da Gama to Seaforth, Cape Peninsula. Includes 21 artists and galleries. First Sunday of the month, 10am–5pm.

Victoria & Alfred Waterfront Arts and Crafts Market, Cape Town. Weekends.

Whale Coast Art Route, Hangklip-Kleinmond-Stanford. Tel: (021) 70 0929.

Whale Routes, False Bay–Hermanus–Ganbaai. Tel: (021) 418 5202.

Antiques

Both Sotheby's and Christie's have branches on the Cape – a clear indication that there's a thriving market for antiques in South Africa.

Most of the real treasures came from Britain by way of the 1820 settlers; also worthy of mention is 17th-century Cape Dutch furniture, usually rustic in style and made of the valuable yellowwood. Cape silver, too, has a good reputation.

Antique and used jewellery can be had for a song in comparison with prices abroad (particularly in the light of favourable exchange rates).

Cape Town and Johannes-burg are best for buying antiques.

In **Cape Town**, browse the shops around Church and Long Streets; the narrow alleys by the Link and Cavendish shopping centres can also be fertile hunting grounds. Ashby's Gallery in Church Street holds auctions every second Thursday.

In **Johannesburg**, Rosebank is the centre of the antiques scene. Flea markets, too, can yield treasures.

In March, Cape Town hosts a major Antique Fair; in October,

there's an Antique and Decora-tor's Fair in Johannesburg.

Visitors should take care to buy expensive items from dealers who are members of the South African Antique Dealers Association (SAADA), a chapter of the international CINOA, which provides a guarantee of the object's authenticity.

Contact: SA Antique Dealers Association, Box 52801, Saxonwold 2132. Johannes-burg, tel: (011) 463 3754; fax: (011) 706 4434. Cape Town, tel: (021) 794 5489. Durban, tel: (031) 368 1414.

Large Parks & Reserves

Practical Points

It is advisable to book accommodation in South Africa's bigger parks well in advance, and to try and avoid the school holidays. Guided trails in the parks must also be booked, as there is often more demand than places. Campers and holiday makers in caravans should book directly with the reserve concerned. Park opening times in all national and provincial parks vary according to the sunrise and sunset.

The speed limits within the parks vary from 25 km/h (15 mph) to 50 km/h (30 mph) and are strictly enforced. Because of stops for photography and the like, you should reckon on an average speed on the asphalt roads of 30–35 km/h (18–21 mph) and 25–30 km/h (15–18 mph) on sand. Maps showing the distances from point to point can be bought at the entrance gates.

Find out beforehand whether the park has restaurant facilities, because many of the smaller ones are only geared to self-caterers. If you're going to be on the road the whole day, it's a good idea to take along your own supply of cold drinks, food, nuts and dried fruit. Note that in the game reserves it is forbidden to get out of the vehicle except in designated areas. Feeding the animals is not only forbidden, but also highly irresponsible.

For more information, contact **National Parks Board**, PO Box 787, Pretoria 0001, Gauteng.

Reservations, tel: (012) 343 1991; fax: (012) 343 0905.
Foreign Desk, tel: (012) 343 2007; fax: (012) 343 2006.
Cape Town Office: PO Box 7400, Roggebaai 8012. Tel: (021) 22 2810; fax: (021) 24 6211.
WWF South Africa, PO Box 456, Stellenbosch 7599, Western Cape.

Guateng

De Wildt Cheetah Research Station, off the R513, near Hartbeespoort Dam. Tel: (012) 504 1921. Until the late 1960s, it was thought that cheetahs did not breed in captivity but at De Wildt this has been proven wrong. Here, researchers discovered that the rare king cheetah (where the spots melt together to form stripes) was not a separate species, but the result of recessive genes in both parents. Wild dog, caracal and brown hyena can also be seen. Advance booking for the two-hour tours is essential.

Suikerbosrand Nature Reserve, Private Bag X 616, Heidelberg 2400. Tel: (0151) 2181. (20 km (12 miles) from Heidelberg on the Nigel/Kliprivier Road, 1 hour from Johannesburg). Open daily: 7am–6pm. Typical Highveld vegetation; numerous birds and various wildlife species live in this reserve. Caravanning and camping; picnic sites; educational centre with film shows; farm-museum with the oldest farm in the region. Trails: 4 km (2.5 miles) self-guided trail; 10 km (6 miles) and 17 km (10 miles) day hike; 6-day, 66-km (41-mile) hike.

Bophuthatswana

Pilansberg Nature Reserve, Box 1201, Mogwase 0302, Bophuthatswana. Tel: (01465) 2 4405. This reserve lies in Bophuthatswana, only 3 hours' drive from Johannesburg on the R565 from Rustenburg. Bounded by volcanic hills, the reserve is home to some 8,000 head of game that roam freely through the 500 sq. km (193 sq. miles). Open daily.

Facilities are:
Kwa Maritane: luxury timeshare and hotel; Tshukudu: luxury chalets; Mankwe: safari tents. Trails of varying duration; tented trail camps. Tel: (014651) 2 1286.

Mpumalanga

BLYDE RIVER CANYON NATURE RESERVE

This reserve lies in the most magnificent scenery, where the Highveld drops approximately 800 metres (2,600 ft) into the Lowveld. The Kadishi Stream here is one of very few active tufa-forming streams in the world. There are two resorts:

Blydepoort Resort, on the R532 from Graskop to Tzaneen, Overvaal Blydepoort, Private Bag X368, Ohrigstadt 1122. Tel: (01323) 769 8005. 75 chalets; caravanning and camping; two restaurants and shop; sport facilities. Trails: short trails and long hikes possible.

Sybrand van Niekerk Resort, on the Lowveld side off the R531 from Acornhoek to Hoedspruit, Box 281, Hoedspruit 1380. Tel: (015795) 5141. Chalets and huts; caravanning and camping; restaurant and shop; sporting facilities. Trails: short trails and long hikes possible.

Loskop Dam Game Reserve, Private Bag X 1525, Middelburg 1050. Tel: (01202) 4184. Fifty-three km (32 miles) north of Middelburg, the reserve supports white rhino, giraffe, zebra, buffalo, kudu and more than 200 bird species and is of particular interest to biologists as it encompasses the transition from Lowveld to Highveld.

Caravanning and camping; fishing; adjoining reserve offers accommodation.

Northern Province

Ben Lavin Nature Reserve, PO Box 782, Louis Trichardt 0920. Tel: (015) 516 4534. Open daily 6am–6pm. At the foot of the Soutpansberg 12 km (7 miles) southeast of Louis Trichardt. Home to rare species such as pangolin, antbear, aardwort, brown hyena, as well as other game. Two hides overlooking waterholes provide fascinating game viewing. Caravan and camping. Trails: Tabajwane trail, circular 8-km (5-mile) route; Fountain trail; circular 4-km (2.5-mile) route.

In the **Tafelkop Nature Reserve**, you will find Emaweni Game Lodge, PO Box 823, Pretoria 0001. Tel: (012) 21 1778 or 325 3601. Some 100 km (60 miles) north of Nylstroom, this lodge is 2 hours' drive from Pretoria. Game-viewing drives are offered to view the wildlife. Luxury chalets; meals available and bar; swimming and fishing.

Hans Merensky Nature Reserve, Private Bag X502, Letsitele 0885. Tel: (015) 3868 632. Seventy kilometres (43 miles) east of Tzaneen, on the southern banks of the Great Letaba River, this reserve of some 52 sq. km (20 sq. miles) has plentiful game, including leopards, hippos, lions and hyenas. Of interest is the Tsonga Kraal Open Air Museum that displays the Tsonga way of life and where craftsmen demonstrate their arts. Facilities at the spa adjacent to the reserve: rondavels, swimming pool and indoor heated spa, tennis and riding. There are bus tours in the reserve and overnight accommodation. Trails: Giraffe trails, circular 35-km (21-mile) route (3 days); Mopanie Interpretative Trail, less than 2 km (1 mile); Letaba Nature Trail, 5 km/3 miles (2 hours); Waterbuck Nature Trails, 15 km/9 miles (4 hours).

Honnet Nature Reserve, 90 km (55 miles) from Louis Trichardt, adjacent to a mineral spa, has large numbers of game roaming between the ancient baobab trees and the bush. There are bus tours and hiking trails, but private cars are not allowed in the reserve. Facilities are at the spa only: hotel; caravan parks; rondavels; shop; sporting amenities. Trails: 10 km (6 miles) Baobab Trail. Reservations: Tshipise Mineral Baths, PO Box 4, Tshipise 0901. Tel: (01553) 9651.

Lesheba Wilderness Area, PO Box 795, Louis Trichardt 0920. Tel: (015) 593 0076. Halfway between Louis Trichardt and Vivo, in an area unique for its high cliffs, deep gorges and curiously weathered rocks, this area has numerous game and a colony of vultures nesting on the cliffs. Two self-catering camps.

Mabula Game Reserve, The Director, Mabula Lodge, Private Bag X 16651, Warmbaths 0480. Tel: (015334) 616/717. Northwest of Warmbaths, one hour from Pretoria, this reserve supports the Big Five, as well as 250 species of birds. Drives in open Land Rovers offer excellent viewing. Hotel and time-share chalets; tennis, swimming and golf; self-guided walks.

MANYELETI GAME RESERVE This 230-sq. km (88-sq. mile) reserve is situated between Timbavati and Sabie Sand on the eastern boundary of the Kruger Park. Khoka Moya Trails operate two camps in the reserve:

Khoka Moya Camp, Safariplan, Box 4245, Randburg 2125. Tel: (011) 886 1810. Twenty km (12 miles) from the Kruger Park (Orpen Gate), this camp offers open-car safari drives by day and night, and hiking trails to view the abundance of game. Four huts; meals available; swimming pool and bar. Trails: hiking trails with armed rangers.

Kruger National Park

There are eight entrances to the park; four (Malelane, Crocodile Bridge, Numbi, Paul Kruger) can be reached from Nelspruit – the latter two via White River. The Orpen and Phalaborwa gates are entrances to the centre of the Park. The northernmost area is accessible via Punda Maria and Pafuri Gates. An airstrip at Skukuza Rest Camp links the park to Johannesburg and Phalaborwa daily.

Accommodation in the park includes self-contained family rondavels, huts with communal washing facilities and a limited number of camps serving group needs. All rest camps offer restaurants, shops, cooking and barbecue facilities.

There are six specific guided Wilderness Trails in the Park: the Wolhuter Trail and the Bushman Trail (between Pretoriuskop and Malelane), the Olifants Trails (in the vicinity of Letaba), the Nyalaland (near Punda Maria), the Metzi Trail (northeast of Skukuza) and the Sweni Trail (east of Satara). Each one includes two days walking in the bush, viewing game, discovering bush-man paintings, bird-watching and three nights in tents. All essential equipment is supplied by the National Parks Board. A maximum of eight people may undertake the trails.

For more information, contact National Parks Board (*see* page 127).

Honeyquide Safari Camp, (reservations as above) 20 km (12 miles) from the Kruger Park (Orpen Gate), is a traditional luxury safari-style tented camp. Hiking trails and night drives are included. Luxury tents; dining room; canvas bar; pool. Trails: hiking trails with armed rangers.

Matumi Game Lodge, PO Box 57, Klaserie 1381. Tel: (015) 793 2452. This beautiful lodge lies 43 km (26 miles) west of the Kruger Park, just off the main road which leads to the Orpen Gate. 16 chalets; meals available.

Percy Fyfe Nature Reserve, Private Bag X2585, Potgietersrus 0660. Tel: (01549) 15678. Lying 26 km (16 miles) northeast of Potgietersrus, this reserve specialises in the breeding of Tsessebe, roan and salbe antelopes. Basic accommodation; no restaurant.

Potgietersrus Nature Reserve and Game Breeding Centre, on the northern outskirts of Potgietersrus, on the road to Pietersburg. This reserve and breeding centre is administered by the National Zoological Gardens of SA. It specialises in rare, endangered African species such as pygmy hippo and scimitar-horned oryx and addax from North Africa, as well as various exotic species from South America and Asia.

<h3 style="text-align:center">SABIE SAND PRIVATE NATURE RESERVE</h3>

This great reservation of 600 sq. km (230 sq. miles) lies south of the Timbavati, bordering on the Kruger Park at the Paul Kruger Gate. The following beautiful game reserves and lodges can be found within this reserve:

Inyati Game Lodge, PO Box 784365, Sandton, 2146. Tel: (013) 735 5381. Set on the Sand River, this lodge offers accommodation for up to 18 guests and dinner is served in "bush bomas", while dancers

accompanied by drums perform traditional ceremonies. Cottages; meals available.

Londolozi Game Reserve, PO Box 1211, Sunning Hill Park 2157. Tel: (011) 803 8421. Situated on the Sand River, this reserve is renowned for its top-of-the-range quality, comfort and service, amid the wild African bush and its unique wildlife. Facilities at Tree Camp (eight guests), Bush Camp (rock cabins, max. eight guests) and Main Camp (en-suite, luxury chalets, max. 24 guests).

The **Sabie Sabie Private Game Lodge**, PO Box 16, Skukuza 1350. Tel: (013) 735 5656, has a reputation for friendly hospitality and high standards. Rich and varied wildlife can be experienced on safari drives, and even near the camp itself. Facilities at Bush Lodge (25 chalets) and River Lodge (20 chalets).

In addition, the **Sabie Sand Private Nature Reserve** encompasses the 300-sq. km (115-sq. miles) Ratray Reserves which are divided into three camps:

Mala Mala, PO Box 2575, Randburg 2125. Tel: (011) 789 2677. This internationally-renowned game lodge, situated 10 km (6 miles) from the Kruger Park (Paul Kruger Gate), offers safari drives to view the Big Five, walks, luxurious camps and a personal guide who looks after the guests' every need including wake-up calls and after-dinner drinks. 26 cottages with 24-hour room service; restaurant and bar; swimming pool and laundry service.

Harry's Camp (reservations as above). Beautiful and unusual, with Ndebele-styled bungalows and an emphasis on outdoor living. A unique bush experience. Three cottages; seven rooms.

Kirkman's Kamp (reservations as above). Perched high above the bushveld, offering a

spectacular view of the river and the surrounding bush and wildlife. Five cottages en-suite; 10 rooms en-suite.

<h3 style="text-align:center">TIMBAVATI PRIVATE NATURE RESERVE</h3>

PO Box 67865, Bryanston 2021. Tel: (011) 463 1990. Situated north of the Sabie Sand resorts and bordering the western boundary of the Kruger Park between Phalaborwa and Orpen Gates, covering 750 sq. km (290 sq. miles) of unspoilt bushveld abounding in wild animals and birds. It is also the birthplace and home of the magnificent white lion. Within the reserve are four lodges offering excellent opportunities for spotting game, be it on drives in open safari cars or on walking trails:

The Motswari Game Lodge, (reservations as above) 97 km (60 miles) from the Kruger Park (Orpen Gate). Offers safari drives by day or by night to view game as small as the chubby antbear and as big as the great African elephant. 18 rondavels and huts; meals included; shop; petrol station; sporting facilities. Trails: guided day hikes.

M'bali Game Lodge, (reservations as above) 9 km (5 miles) from Motswari, M'bali, offers peace and quiet for up to 14 guests in "habitents" situated high above the ground on wooden platforms overlooking a dam on the Sharalumi River. Trails: guided day hikes.

Tanda Tula Game Lodge, PO Hoedspruit 1380. Tel: (015) 793 2435. This lodge lies in the north of the Timbavati Reserve, bordering on the Kruger Park. Tanda Tula (Shangaan for "love of quietness") is home to the Big Five, as well as numerous birds and indigenous vegetation. Visitors enjoy the informality and flexibility of the lodge. 16-bedded game lodge; bar and swimming pool; shop.

Nyala Game Lodge, PO Box 110, Hoedspruit 1380. Tel: reservations as for Tanda Tula Game Lodge. Not far from the other camps in the Timbavati Complex, this lodge offers comfort while you enjoy the wilderness experience. 20 rooms (en suite); "sleep-out" bomas; meals available.

Tshukudu Game Lodge and Nature Reserve, on the R40 between Hoedspruit and Mica. PO Box 289, Hoedspruit 1380. Tel: (015) 793 2476. This family-owned and run establishment accommodates a maximum of eight people and is an excellent getaway spot. Thatched rondavels; tours in open-top Land Rovers.

Wolkberg Wilderness Area, State Forester, Serala State Forest, Private Bag, Haenertsburg 0730. Tel: (015) 276 1303. Accessible along a signposted road off the R71 some 40 km (24 miles) from Pietersburg, this wilderness hiking area covers 170 sq. km (65 sq. miles) of high mountains and deep valleys in the Drakensberg and a section of the Strydpoort Range. Lush forests, great mountain waterfalls and the Mohlapitse River Potholes make this a perfect sanctuary for nature lovers. Camping (permits necessary); no restaurant.

KwaZulu-Natal

KwaZulu-Natal has a subtropical coastline in the east, the majestic Drakensberg in the west and sweeping savannah and rolling hills down the middle. It offers a wide variety of habitats for all kinds of wildlife.

The Natal Parks Board administers 64 game and nature reserves in beautiful spots all over KwaZulu-Natal, but most are concentrated along the north Coast and in the Drakensberg foothills. The Drakensberg has

11 peaks on the KwaZulu-Natal side which top 3,000 metres (10,000 ft), the highest being the 3,409-metre (11,184-ft) high Injasuti, which is in the Giants Castle Game Reserve.

Many of the game reserves offer Wilderness Trails (from a half-day to four days long) under the guidance of armed game-guards. This is an unsurpass-able way of experiencing the bush and its animals. Pony trails are offered on the same basis; in some instances you sleep in caves or under overhangs. The Natal Parks Board offers various types of accommodation from chalets – where everything, from linen to pots and pans and often a cook to prepare your meals, is provided – to rustic huts where you have to bring your own linen and cooking utensils. Food and drinks must be brought along in all parks.

Reservations for all Natal Parks Board reserves and all trails must be done through the Central Reservations Office in Pietermaritzburg: **The Natal Parks Board**, PO Box 662, Pietermaritzburg 3200. Tel: (0331) 47 1981; fax: 47 1980.

Reservations for the caravan and camping sites at the five St Lucia camps is done through **St Lucia Publicity Association**, PO Box 106, St Lucia 3936. Tel: (03592) 225 or 143.

The reserves of Ndumu, Kosi Bay and Baya Camp are administered by the **KwaZulu Department of Natural Resources**, 367 Loop St, Pietermaritzburg, 3201. Tel: (0331) 94 6698; fax: 42 1948.

Albert Falls Public Resort and Nature Reserve, 18 km (11 miles) from Pietermaritzburg, is one of the most beautiful spots in the Natal Midlands. Walks or rides take you around the scenic Albert Falls Dam, across the Umgeni River and to the Gold-Panning Falls, while viewing zebra, impala, blesbok, reedbuck and other small buck.

28 cottages and huts; two camping and caravan sites; swimming; squash, tennis, sailing, riding and canoeing. Trails: several day walks.

Baya Camp, on the shores of Lake Sibaya, accessible via Jozini and Mbazwana. Two hides overlooking dune forests and coastal plains provide excellent bird-watching opportunities. Hut camp; no swimming in the lake due to bilharzia, crocodiles and hippos; fishing (licences obtainable); boat for hire. Trails: guided trails; walking routes. A four-wheel drive vehicle is recommended but not essential.

Bona Manzi Game Park and **Bushlands Game Lodge**, 10 km (6 miles) south of Hluhluwe village, are two private reserves offering accommodation in tree houses and excellent game viewing areas. Facilities are: Bona Manzi: three tree houses, a tree lodge and 10 huts; swimming pool; meals available (unlicensed). Bushlands: eight luxury tree houses; meals provided; swimming pool and bar. Trails: walking trails. Reservations: Bona Manzi, PO Box 48, Hluhluwe 3960, tel: (03562) ask for 3530, or through Bushlands, PO Box 79, Hluhluwe 3960. Tel: (03562) ask for 144.

Chelmsford Public Resort Nature Reserve lies 20 km (12 miles) south of Newcastle, on the Ladysmith road. The resort, dominated by the Leokop Mountain, boasts Egyptian and spur-winged geese, spoonbill, yellow-billed duck, darter and dabchick. The dam attracts game such as rhino and zebra. 12 cottages; camping and caravan sites; fishing and boat trips.

Coleford Nature Reserve is located 22 km (13 miles) south of Underberg, which is one of South Africa's premier trout-fishing areas, and there are excellent trout fishing opportunities in the two rivers that meander through the reserve. There is also some game. 14 cottages; huts; picnic sites; tennis, riding, croquet; trout fishing (permits from camp office). Trails: day walks.

Giant's Castle Game Reserve, 69 km (43 miles) southwest of Estcourt. The 25-km (15-mile) long and 3000-metre (9,840-ft) high wall known as the Giant's Castle is a rugged, but majestic, part of the Drakensberg inhabited by the San until the end of the last century. Close to the main camp is a cave with San paintings; there is also a small museum. Twelve different antelope are found here as well as the very

rare lammergeyer (bearded vulture) which, together with other vultures and birds of prey, can be viewed from a hide.

Facilities at Main Camp (21 cottages/huts), Hillside-Camp (one hut, camping site) and Injasuti Camp (19 huts, camping site); trout fishing. Trails: 50 km (31 miles) of trails; four guided trails; walks and hikes; mountain climbing; 2–3 day guided mountain rides (accommodation in huts and caves).

Harold Johnson Nature Reserve, 24 km (15 miles) north of Stanger. Overlooking the Tugela river mouth and Indian ocean, this reserve has some of KwaZulu-Natal's most beautiful

vegetation. Camping and caravanning. Trails: self-guided trails; educational trails by arrangement. Reservations: PO Box 148, Darnall 4480. Tel: (0324) 6 1574.

Hluhluwe Game Reserve is located about 370 km (230 miles) north of Durban and 17 km (10 miles) west of Hluhluwe village, where you'll also find a hotel, a few shops and a service station. Hluhluwe is quite hilly and, because it lies at the higher altitude of 650 metres (2,130 ft), is cooler in summer than Umfolozi. The diverse vegetation of forest, woodland, savannah and grassland makes the reserve scenically varied; it

Lake St Lucia Complex

On the central Zululand coast, the St Lucia Lake extends for 60 km (37 miles) northwards from St Lucia Estuary which lies 25 km (15 miles) east of Mtuba-tuba. The "lake" is actually an estuary, opening to the sea at the southern end and running parallel to it while separated from it by some of the highest forested dunes in the world – a unique ecological system. In the north, the lake widens considerably and the three interlinked nature reserves encompassing the whole area are an intriguing mosaic of lakes, rivers, pans, swamp forests, open grasslands, dune forests and wide open deserted beaches. The estuary mouth is said to be the only place in the world where you can see sharks, hippos and crocodiles sharing the same habitat.

Though the area is most popular for angling and ski-boat fishing, it has a lot to offer for the nature lover. The trails – from a 3-km (2-mile) self-guided trail to 4-day trails with a guide – have a charm of their own not found in any of the other

reserves. In addition to crocodiles and hippos, the pans are home to reedbuck, bushbuck, the beautiful, elegant nyala and other small game. For bird lovers, it is a paradise: 360 species frequent the lake and its environs. In the northern part of Lake St Lucia, flocks of 20,000 flamingos have been seen and this is also the only breeding colony of pink-backed pelicans in southern Africa. Thousands of fish-hunting birds and other water fowl have found a sanctuary here: the giant goliath heron, saddle-beaked storks, spoonbills, dabchicks (who carry their young on their backs) and scores of others; but the thick bush and reeds are also inhabited by rare birds like the Woodwards batis.

The two trails from False Bay Park are particularly suited for bird watching. The Crocodile Centre of St Lucia has interesting displays and information about the largest of the Earth's reptiles.

Six separate camps are part of the St Lucia Complex: Mapelane, St Lucia Estuary,

Charter's Greek, Fanie's Island, Cape Vidal and False Bay Resort on the northwestern shore of the lake. **Huts and Cottages**: Mapelane (9); St Lucia Village (none in the Park, but plenty of private accommodation and hotels); Charter's Creek (16); Fanie's Island (13); Cape Vidal and Eastern Shores Nature Reserve (23); False Bay Resort (4). **Caravan sites**: Mapelane, St Lucia, Fanie's Island, False Bay.

Camping: in all six resorts, book well in advance for holiday periods through the St Lucia Publicity Association (see previous page). **Restaurants and shops**: only in St Lucia village.

Trails: some are only done April–September as the summer months are extremely hot and humid. Some of the self-guided trails must also be booked in advance. Always be aware of hippos even though they are seldom away from the water during the day. The guided trails start from St Lucia, Cape Vidal, Charters Creek, Fanie's Island and False Bay Park.

contains all the main wildlife species, including black and white rhino, wildebeest, giraffes, buffalo, lions and leopards. Elephants have been re-introduced; bird life is abundant. 25 cottages; huts; Zulu cultural museum; petrol. Trails: self-guided trail and half-day guided walks.

Itala Game Reserve, located in the Pongola Valley, north of Louwsburg, 60 km (37 miles) northeast of Vryheid, is a lovely combination of bushveld, deep valleys, cliff faces, granite outcrops, grassed hilltops and six rivers. It is also home to a large variety of game, plus many birds of prey. 40 chalets/huts; two bush camps; camping; swimming in rock pools; picnic sites. Trails: 3-day Wilderness Trails (March–October); 1-day guided trails.

Kamberg Nature Reserve is 42 km (26 miles) west of Rosetta in the foothills of the Drakensberg. With the Mooi River flowing through it, this peaceful reserve offers excellent trout fishing, interesting trails and wildlife observation. Seven cottages; huts; trout fishing (permit available from office). Trails: Mooi River self-guided trail (4 km/2.5 miles) (designed for visitors in wheelchairs); six other walks and climbs.

Kosi Bay Nature Reserve lies a few miles south of the Mozambique border in the northeastern corner of Zululand. Four crystal-clear lakes are surrounded by the 110 sq. km (42 sq. mile) reserve of mangrove swamps, marshes, swamp forests with umdoni and fig canopy trees and raphia palms. The rare leatherback and loggerhead turtles breed on the stretch of coast south of Kosi Bay and flufftails, palmnut vultures and other interesting birds inhabit this reserve. Four-wheel drive vehicles are essential for sandy roads and river crossings. Swimming in the lakes is not

recommended because of the risk of bilharzia, crocodiles and hippos. Three cottages; camping; fishing and boats for hire. Trails: walks with rangers; overnight trails.

Loteni Nature Reserve, 76 km (47 miles) west of Nottingham Road, is a rugged reserve with a ravine coming down from the 3,300-metre (10,800-ft) high Drakensberg. An abundance of birds and a variety of buck live here. 15 cottages; huts; camping site; trout fishing (permits available from camp office). Trails: Eagle Trail (12-km/7.5-mile trail).

Malachite Camp is a Rattray reserve 8 km (5 miles) southeast of Mkuze village. Named after the malachite kingfisher, this reserve combines outdoor adventure and five-star comfort and lives up to its name, as nearly 400 species of birds have been seen here. There is fishing in the nearby Jozini Dam and game viewing in open Land Rovers. Four thatched double rondavels; meals provided (but unlicensed – so bring your own drinks); fishing (20 minutes away). Trails: walking safaris with ranger. Reservations: Rattray Reserves, PO Box 2575, Randburg 2125. Tel: (011) 789 2677.

Mkuzi Game Reserve, lying some 335 km (208 miles) from Durban on the main North Coast road, has four hides overlooking waterholes and numerous hiking trails through low-lying thornveld, past lakes and fig tree forests. It has an abundance of game, including the elegant and rare leopard, black and white rhino, hippos, crocodiles and, of course, giraffe and antelopes. 21 cottages; huts; camping and caravanning.
Trails: 3-day Wilderness Trail; three-hour walking trails; 3-km (2-miles) Fig Forest Walk and River View Trail.

Midmar Public Resort and Nature Reserve is located 24

km (15 miles) from Pietermaritzburg on the N3. The 28 sq. km (11 sq. mile) reserve surrounds a dam and the resort has a very colonial feel with tea served on the manicured lawns as you watch the yachts on the dam. Wildlife can be viewed by taking a boat ride along the shore line. Adjacent to the resort is the Midmar Historical Village displaying KwaZulu-Natal's pioneering past. 63 cottages/huts; camping and caravan sites; restaurant and bar; swimming (no bilharzia), fishing, sailing, water-skiing, tennis, squash, bowls and riding.

Natal Inland Zulu Bush Safaris, on the R612 between Nongoma and Hlobane, are ideal for bird-watching and game-viewing. Accommodation overlooks the beautiful Msihlengeni waterfall and the river. One lodge (four people); bush camp; swimming pool; self catering. Reservations: SATOUR, tel: (011) 331 5241.

Ndumu Game Reserve, located 470 km (290 miles) from Durban in northern KwaZulu-Natal on the Mozambique border, is a secluded reserve of lush vegetation, fever tree forests, numerous lakes and pans. It is the perfect haven for fish, aquatic birds, colonies of crocodiles and hippos, the robust rhino, the sly striped polecat and many more. Land Rover drives around the pans can be undertaken, as well as guided walks through the reserve which has a very special atmosphere. It is a paradise for bird-lovers, as nearly as many bird species have been recorded here as in the Kruger National Park which is 190 times larger. Open daily 9am–3.30pm. Seven huts. Trails: guided hiking trails.

Oribi Gorge Nature Reserve, located 21 km (13 miles) west of Port Shepston and 128 km (80 miles) south of Durban, includes a 400-metre (1,300-ft) deep spectacular gorge that attracts numerous birds. The gorge is covered in the once widespread indigenous forest, home to leopards, samango monkeys, water monitors and 200 species of birds, including seven eagles. Seven cottages; huts; picnic site; Oribi Gorge Hotel at Fairacres not far away. Trails: 35 km (21 miles) of day walks and trails have been established.

Sodwana Bay National Park, lying some 400 km (248 miles) from Durban and 90 km (55 miles) east of Ubombo, is an angler's paradise (deep sea and shore) as well as the meeting point for divers from all over South Africa. From Cape Vidal (north of St Lucia) to the Mozambique border and three sea miles out to sea, a Marine Reserve has been proclaimed and this, plus the fact that you find the most southern coral reefs here, makes it an ideal area for diving. They even have a resident moraine eel here named Monty, who is so used to divers that he just about shakes hands with them. But the park is also a haven for a great variety of birds that nest in the great fig trees growing in the swampy marshes close to the tidal pools and you can come across a

number of antelope and smaller animals. Facilities: 20 huts; very large camping and caravan site; shop; petrol; deep-sea fishing; diving.

Spioenkop Public Resort and Nature Reserve, 35 km (22 miles) southwest of Ladysmith, is where one of the important battles of the Anglo-Boer War (1900) was fought. Today, the dammed Tugela and the game reserve offer pursuits like horse-riding, yachting, walks and trails in the game reserve and guided tours of the battle fields and a Boer War Museum. 34 cottages/huts; one bush camp; camping and caravan site; pool; boat rides; tennis; riding. Trails: walking trails with game rangers; History Trail (leads to the Spioenkop Battlefield).

Tamboti Bush Camp, 30 km (18 miles) northeast of the village of Hluhluwe, lies in the 40 sq. km (15 sq. miles) of Punata Game Ranch that borders on the Mkuzi Game Reserve and is known for its superb opportunities of viewing game, including rhinos, giraffes and leopards on day and night game drives in open Land Rovers. Four thatched huts; meals provided (but unlicensed); swimming. Trails: walking safaris with

ranger. Reservations: Tamboti Bush Camp, 11 Surrey Lane, Kloof. Tel: (031) 764 0137.

Ubizane Game Ranch, 8 km (5 miles) from Hluhluwe village on Hluhluwe Game Reserve road, is a private ranch overlooking a fever tree forest. Game drives in open four-wheel drives and walking trails allow guests to see white rhinos (bred on the ranch), giraffes and many other animals. Night drives allow for the viewing of nocturnal animals. Three luxury timber bungalows on stilts; meals available (unlicensed, but hotel on same property). Trails: walking trails with ranger. Reservations: PO Box 102, Hluhluwe 3960. Tel: (03562) ask for 3602.

Umfolozi Game Reserve, located 50 km (31 miles) west of Mtubatuba on the R618, 270 km (170 miles) north of Durban, rests between the White and the Black Umfolozi Rivers, and has rugged savannah vegetation. The reserve is famous for its Operation White Rhino in the 1960s, which helped to save the rhinos from extinction by drug-darting and breeding them. All the major animals are found here as well as many lesser known ones, but you are virtually

Royal Natal National Park

The Royal Natal National Park, lying 42 km (26 miles) west of Bergville, looks over the majestic Amphitheatre, one of the most magnificent mountain landscapes in Southern Africa: 8 km (5 miles) wide and cast in one piece of solid rock, it embraces the Tendele Valley below like a Greek amphitheatre. The Tugela is one of five major rivers that have their source on top of the 3285-metre (10,777-ft) high Mont-aux-Sources falls. A series of waterfalls cascade 1,500 metres (4,900 ft) down

the face of the Amphitheatre, one fall being 213 metres (700 ft). The best way to explore this wonderful world is on foot or on horseback on one of the 31 trails, climbs or bridle paths. A 45-km (28-mile) hike leads up to the top of the Sentinel via two chain ladders.

The area also displays a variety of plants: more than a thousand species occur here, and in the adjoining Rugged Glen Nature Reserve you come across yellowwood and Cape chestnuts, ericas and proteas. The rugged cliffs and kloofs are

ideal for all sort of birds of prey and vultures and of course one finds various antelope in the park.

Facilities at the Royal Natal National Park Hotel (just outside the park) and Tendele Hutted Camp (with 16 cottages): lodge; camping at Mahai and Rugged Glen; shop; trout fishing and riding (permits from the camp office); picnic sites.

Trails: 31 walking routes ranging from 3 km (2 miles) to 45 km (28 miles); guided walks.

certain to see white rhino of which there are 900 in the park. Two heated camps; nine cottages; huts; two bush camps, which have to be booked en bloc. Trails: 3-day wilderness trails (April–September); primitive trails (combining Wilderness Trails and backpacking); guided half-day walks.

Umlalazi Nature Reserve is located about 128 km (80 miles) north of Durban, 2 km (1 mile) from Mtunzini. The clear blue waters of the coast can be seen from the quaint log cabins in this lagoon and coastal reserve, which has mangrove swamps and dune forests that attract a wide variety of bird species in addition to bush pig, reedbuck and bushbuck. 13 log cabins; camping site; picnic spots. The Mtunzini Lagoon resort offers water-skiing and boats for hire; shops, petrol.

Trails: two self-guided trails (mangrove and dune forest).

Vergelegen Nature Reserve can be reached from Nottingham Road (all gravel) or on tar via Bulwer and Himeville and then 35 km (21 miles) gravel. To get away from it all, this reserve provides a secluded sanctuary in amongst the deep valleys, pine plantations and green countryside. Two cottages; trout fishing (get permits beforehand). Trails: mapped out day walks.

Vernon Crooke's Nature Reserve is located 15 km (9 miles) west of Scottburgh. Two dams in the reserve attract many birds and game including eland, zebras, blue wildebeest, bushbuck and porcupines. During September/October the reserve is ablaze with wild flowers, almost rivalling Namaqualand.

Zulu Nyala Safaris, off the N2 between Hluhluwe and Mkuze, Zulu Nyala, is the largest privately owned safari ranch in KwaZulu-Natal, encompassing at least five different ecological systems. For bird watchers and photographers, enjoy the sunset river cruises. Three exclusive camps with thatched huts for max. 20 people; meals available (or self catering). Reservations, tel: SATOUR (011) 331 5241.

Eastern Cape

This region of varying beauty – from a weatherbeaten coastline of sandy beaches, silent lagoons and wide river mouths to the lush inland vegetation of enchanting gorges, beautiful mountains, tumbling rivers and dry grassland plains – is still fairly unknown. The area from the mouth of the Kei River to the Umtamvuna River, known as the Wild Coast, is rugged and unspoilt. The 250 km (150 miles) of green thick indigenous forest, hilly grassland and sheer cliffs that fall to the white deserted beaches is one of the most beautiful coasts of the African continent. Hotels are situated in remote villages along the coast.

The Wild Coast Hiking Trails explore this magnificent coast. The route follows the coastline with hiking stopovers in huts along the way. The trail is divided into five sections: Umtamvuna–Msikaba (3 days); Msikaba–Aqate Terrace (7 days); Silaka–Coffee Bay (6 days); Coffee Bay–Mbashe (5 days); Ngabara–Kei River (6 days). The trail is not for the faint-hearted and is a challenge for anyone with a lust for adventure.

Reservations and enquiries for the following reserves (unless otherwise stated): **Transkei Nature Conservation Division**, Department of Agriculture and Forestry, Private Bag X5002, Umtata, Eastern Cape. Tel: (0471) 2 4322 or 24 9309.

For information on parks and trails in the region, contact The National Parks Board or SATOUR.

Bosbokstrand Private Nature Reserve, PO Box 302, Randfontein 1760. Tel: (011) 696 1442. Located 60 km (35 miles) north of East London, the beach has rocky, as well as sandy, stretches and the fishing is regarded as excellent. Clearly marked trails meander through the game area. A-frame chalets; caravan park; shop. Trails: marked walking trails.

Dwesa Nature Reserve lies halfway between Coffee Bay and the Kei River. The fact that it was the Transkei's first nature reserve (1893) says something about the scenic beauty of this part of the coast. The mode of transport in the reserve is by foot and many walks can be undertaken from the camp which only consists of five huts. Fishing is very good, but visitors are not permitted to collect bait. Bungalows. Trails: walks.

L.L. Sebe Game Reserve is situated 20 km (12 miles) from Peddie in the Ciskei and lies between the Fish and Keiskamma Rivers. It offers fresh water angling, game viewing and limited hunting. An enchanting hiking trail meanders along the Great Fish River. Two lodges (one for hikers). Trails: 2-day hike and a few shorter ones.

Malekgonyane Nature Reserve lies in the Drakensberg on the Lesotho border and is beautiful in spring, when the sweeping montainous grassland is covered in fire-lilies, gladioli, red-hot pokers and other wild flowers. There are numerous walks, sparkling streams and waterfalls.

Mkambati Game Reserve, Transkei Department of Finance, Box 574, Kokstad, 4700. Tel: (0372) 3101. Lies halfway between Port Edward and Port St Johns on one of the most beautiful parts of the beautiful Transkei coast; isolated beaches, mysterious forested ravines, swamp forests and awe-inspiring cliffs make this reserve ideal for anyone looking for solitude. A lodge and cottages/rondavels at four different camps; self-catering except for guests of the lodge; shop; ideal for angling; canoes for hire. Trails: short walks to long hikes; guided horse trails.

Mpongo Game Reserve, Officer in Charge, Mpongo Game Reserve, Box 3300, Cambridge. Tel: (04326) 669. Lies 30 km (18 miles) northwest of East London. It has many of the large animals, such as rhinos, giraffes and even lions (in an enclosure), and also has a particularly rich bird life. There are guided trails of 5–20 km (3–12 miles) length and of particular appeal are the night safaris and horseback trails. Caravanning and camping; restaurant and shop; Natural History Museum. Trails: guided trails; night hikes; horse trails.

The Garden Route

Three hundred kilometres (180 miles) of coastline from Riversdale in the west to Storms River in the east, bounded by the Indian Ocean in the south and the Tsitsikamma mountain range in the north, make up the renowned Garden Route. The mountains, the lush indigenous flora, the forests, the many lakes and the meandering rivers make this area a uniquely beautiful haven for all nature lovers.

Addo Elephant National Park lies 7 km (4 miles) north of Port Elizabeth near the Zuurberg Range in the Sundays River Valley. It was established as a refuge for the last 11 remaining coastal elephants – today there are 165 of them. The park, overgrown by a tangle of creepers and small trees, also supports a number of black rhino, buffalo and numerous antelope. Porcupines, antbears and bush pigs are some of the nocturnal animals. No citrus fruits of any kind may be taken into the park (the elephants may become aggressive in order to

Tsitsikamma Coastal National Park

Extending from Plettenberg Bay and the Groot River mouth, near Hurmansdorp, this park is home to the well-known and challenging Otter Trail, which runs through the evergreen forests, the rocky outcrops and the beaches of the Indian Ocean. Small animals and numerous birds accompany the hiker. The park stretches 5 km (3 miles) out to sea and was the first marine national park. The meeting of the warm Agulhas and cold Benguela currents has resulted in an

get at them). Chalets and rondavels; camping and caravanning; restaurant, shop, petrol. Reservations: as above.

Tsitsikamma Forest Park, The Regional Director, Tsitsi-kamma Forest Region, Private Bag X 537, Humansdorp 6300. Tel: (0423) 5 1180. Situated some 100 km (60 miles) east of Knysna, this park with its ancient trees, its lush indigenous forests and gentle streams supports bushbuck, bush pigs, blue duiker and numerous bird species. Caravanning and camping. Trails: trails of varying duration (1 hour–5 days).

Wilderness National Park, National Parks Board. Tel: (021) 343 1991; fax: (021) 343 0905. Stretches along the coast from Wilderness village to the Goukamma Nature Reserve, encompassing several beautiful lakes and *vleis* (wetlands), including the Knysna Lake and the Swartvlei, the largest natural saltwater lake in SA. The rare Cape clawless otter and the exotic Knysna Lourie make the wetlands area their home. This park is an ornithologists' dream, particularly because of the abundance of aquatic birds. Two camps with self-catering chalets and huts; caravanning and camping; launderette and shop;

interesting mingling of tropical and cold water marine life. A snorkelling and a scuba-diving trail have been laid out, the latter only for divers with a valid certificate.

Cottages and holiday apartments; caravanning and camping; shop, restaurant; fishing and diving. Trails of varying duration (1 hour–5 days); underwater trail.

For more information, contact: National Parks Board. Tel: (012) 343 1991; fax: (021) 343 0905.

water-sports, fishing, hiring of canoes. Trails: walking trails.

Zuurberg National Park, information from Port Elizabeth Publicity Association. Tel: (041) 52 1315. This park lies 12 km (7 miles) north of Addo Elephant National Park in the Winterhoek mountains. It shelters some unique plants in its ravines and rolling hills, like the Zuurberg Cycad which is found nowhere else but in this park. It is known for its richness in vegetation and bird life. Accommodation in a nearby hotel. Two short trails.

Cape Town Region

Valleys, coastal plains and rugged mountains characterise the region in which the beautiful city of Cape Town rests. Just north lies Namaqualand, a semi-desert of rocky outcrops, spartan vegetation, space and silence. In spring, the region is transformed into a carpet of brilliant colours when millions of wild flowers open their fragile petals – as if to make up for the drabness of the rest of the year.

Bontebok National Park, National Parks Board, Pretoria (see above) or Regional Office, Cape Town. Tel: (021) 419 5365. Lying 7 km (4 miles) south of Swellendam, this park was established to save the bontebok from extinction. Today, it has some 200 bontebok and other antelope; the park is also renowned for its abundant flora. Late winter and early spring sees the area covered in brilliantly-coloured wildflowers. Four fully equipped caravans for hire; camping; shop. Trails: three short hiking trails.

De Hoop Nature Reserve, Private Bag X16, Bredasdorp 7280. Tel: (02922) 782. Located 60 km (37 miles) east of Bredasdorp, this reserve covers 400 sq. km (154 sq. miles) of very varied habitats. This part of the coast is one of the most important mating and calving areas in the world for the Southern Right Whale, as well as the southern-most vulture breeding area in Africa. Open daily 8am–4.30pm. Two basic chalets; camping. Trails: guided coastal walk (40 km/24 miles); day walks.

Helderberg Nature Reserve, information from the Regional Office of the National Parks Board Cape Town or SATOUR. Tel: (021) 419 5365. The Helderberg mountain stands guard over Somerset West and this small, but picturesque, reserve reaches halfway up its rocky side. Many of the reserve's paths run through mountain-sides of erica and proteas. The best known area is Disa Gorge, where – from January to March – one can see the exquisite "flower-of-the-gods", the red Disa orchid, growing on inaccessible rock faces. A remarkable variety of birds also inhabit this reserve. Open daily 9.30am–6pm. Picnic site; herbarium. Trails: seven trails, 15 minutes–3 hours.

Salmonsdam Nature Reserve, PO Box 5, Stanford 7210. Tel: (0283) 789. Lying 45 km (28 miles) west of Hermanus, this mountainous area, with its deep kloofs, forests and its beautiful waterfall, is coloured by the many species of protea and

erica. Bontebok, klipspringer, other small mammals and numerous birds live here. Open 7am–6pm. Basic hut accommodation; caravanning and camping. Trails: 3 trails (3–5 km/2–3miles).

West Coast National Park Langebaan, information from the Regional Office of National Parks Board or SATOUR or Captour, Cape Town. Tel: (021) 419 5365. Situated about 100 km (60 miles) north of Cape Town, this park encompasses one of the great wetlands of the world, the Langebaan Lagoon. The park is internationally renowned as the world's fourth most important bird sanctuary. This lagoon and the islands in the vicinity are the final destination for up to 55,000 birds after their flight from Greenland and the Arctic regions. There are also large numbers of antelope. In spring, the Postman Nature Reserve (incorporated into the West Coast Park) is ablaze with wild flowers. Langebaan village offers lodge and cottages; caravanning and camping; educational boat trips, canoes for hire, water-sports. Trails: various hiking routes and horseback trails.

North-West & Free State

This area encompasses the highveld of grassy plateaus, largely covered by the farmlands of the Free State, the magnificent Drakensberg mountain range in the east, snow-capped in winter, and the varying habitats along the Orange and Vaal Rivers.

Golden Gate Highlands National Park, National Parks Board. Tel: (012) 343 1991; fax: 343 0905. Situated to the southwest of Harrismith in the foothills of the Maluti mountains near the Lesotho border, this park is known for its strange and fantastic rock formations. In autumn and spring, red hot

pokers, fire lilies and watsonias colour the park magnificently. Although Golden Gate is known for its scenic beauty, birds and game can be seen as well. It is an ideal area for hiking and a number of trails go to particularly beautiful spots. Lodge, chalets, huts; caravanning and camping; restaurant and shop; swimming pool, tennis, golf, bowling. Trails: a 2-day trail and half a dozen short to 1-day trails; horses can be hired.

Rob Ferreira Game Reserve lies on the R29 northeast of Christiana. The Vaal River forms the southern border of the reserve, attracting birds in abundance. The reserve is well stocked with animals, including white rhino and many of the antelopes. Open daily 7am–5pm. Chalets; flats; caravanning and camping; restaurant, supermarket; two swimming pools; mineral bath. Trails: 8-km (5-mile) trail. Reservations: Overvaal Resorts, PO Box 3046, Pretoria 0001. Tel: (012) 346 2288.

Rustenburg Nature Reserve, PO Box 511, Rustenburg 0300. Tel: (0142) 3 1050. Situated 95 km (60 miles) northwest of Johannesburg on the R24, this reserve lies in the beautiful Magaliesberg mountains, taking in part of the plateau on top as well as the northern mountain slopes with their picturesque gorges, waterfalls, sheer cliffs and many an inviting rock pool. The best way of exploring it is on foot, but you can also drive through and – if you're lucky – you'll come across a number of antelope, even sable. Caravanning and camping; visitors' centre. Trails: 3-hour trail and a two-day trail.

Tussen-die-Riviere Game Farm, The Director of Nature Conservation, PO Box 517, Bloemfontein 9300. Tel: (051) 405 5243. 17 km (10 miles) east of Bethulie. This reserve supports more game, including white rhino, than any other reserve in the Free State. During the summer months, the reserve is open to the public (1 November–30 April). From the beginning of May to the end of October, hunters help with the necessary culling. As they receive 20 times as many applications as they need hunters, lots are drawn. Self-catering accommodation. Trails: two nature trails.

Western Transvaal Krugersdorp Game Reserve, The Tourist Officer, Department of Parks, PO Box 94, Krugersdorp 1740. Tel: (011) 660 1076. On the R24, a mere 40 minutes from Johannesburg, this reserve has a great variety of game including giraffes, white rhino, eland, roan, sable, buffalo and many others, as well as a lion camp. Beware of cheeky baboons. Various educational trails (7–10 km/4–6 miles) are conducted by the Wildlife Society. Open daily 8am–5pm. Chalets and huts (bring cooking, caravanning and camping utensils); shop. Trails: guided half-day trails.

Willem Pretorius Game Reserve, PO Box, Ventersburg 9451. Tel: (01734) 4229. Located between Kroonstad and Winburg on the N1, this reserve boasts South Africa's largest herd of wildebeest (some 600) and giraffe; buffalo and white rhino have also been introduced. A large dam is part of the reserve and many of the 200 bird species that have been recorded here are seen in the vicinity. Boat trips are organised and fishing is good. Flats, rondavels, huts; caravanning and camping; restaurant and shop; golf, tennis, bowls.

Namaqualand & Karoo

The Great Karoo, an endless thirsty land with isolated farms, and the Namaqualand of semi-desert vegetation and

springtime floral magnificence, make up this beautiful region.

Akkerendam Nature Reserve, information from The Town Clerk, PO Box 28, Calvinia 8190. Tel: (02772) ask for 11 or 241. This reserve lies less than 2 km (1 mile) from Calvinia, where the flower carpet in spring-time is quite as magnificent as that of Namaqualand. The black springbok and the bat-eared fox are among the mammals found in this beautiful stretch of land, which has three dams. The shorter of its two trails was designed for senior citizens. You need permission to do either of the trails. Trails: two trails (1–2 hours and 6–7 hours).

Hester Malan Nature Reserve, information from Private Bag X1, Springbok 8240. Tel: (0251) 2 1880. In spring, this reserve, which is 16 km (10 miles) southeast of Springbok, is carpeted by colourful wild flowers and is well worth a visit. During the rest of the year, visitors enjoy the beauty of the landscape, a variety of arid region mammals and birds and the collection of Namaqualand succulents. Open daily 8am–4pm. Trails: three short trails.

Kalahari Gemsbok National Park, National Parks Board. Tel: (012) 343 1991; fax: (021) 343 0905. Very different from the coastal and northern reserves, this park of semi-desert lies between the dry river beds of the Nossob and Auob in the northwest corner of South Africa, between Namibia and Botswana. Large herds of wildebeest, springbok and gemsbok move through the sandy and rocky terrain. The Kalahari lions and cheetahs also make this dry area their home. There are three camps at Twee Rivieren, Mata-Mata and Nossob. Huts and chalets (self-catering); caravanning and camping; shop, petrol; restaurant at Twee Rivieren; swimming pool at Twee Rivieren.

Karoo National Park, National Parks Board, Box 787, Pretoria 0001. Tel: (012) 343 1991; fax: (012) 343 0905. Situated just north of Beaufort West on the N1, the Karoo makes an ideal stop-over on the way to Johannesburg. More than 300 sq. km (115 sq. miles) in size, these mountains and the surrounding plains are home to the mountain zebra, caracal and the bat-eared fox. In addition to

Augrabies Falls National Park

Situated 120 km (75 miles) west of Upington on the Orange River, the central feature of this park is the magnificient Augrabies Falls of the Orange River. Although the main falls are 56-metre (183-ft) high, the cataracts before that drop the river another 90 metres (300 ft) and the sheer granite walls of the gorge are up to 250 metres (820 ft) high – an awe-inspiring sight. The area along the Orange, with its kokerbooms (quiver trees), aloes and black basalt rocks, gives the reserve a stark charm all of its own. It can be explored

by car, but you experience this barren, yet beautiful, landscape much more easily by walking. April to October is the most pleasant time (it can get very hot in December and January), but the falls are at their best between November and January. Chalets; caravanning and camping; shop, restaurant, petrol. Trails: Klipspringer Hiking Trail (3 days, April–October) – but you can walk to various view points. For more information, contact: National Parks Board. Tel: (012) 343 1991; fax: (012) 343 0905.

living animals, this park also deals with those that inhabited the area millions of years ago; a fascinating Fossil Walk takes visitors to see half-excavated reptiles which are of particular interest because they were a link between reptiles and mammals. Chalets; restaurant and shop. Trails: Springbok Hiking Trail (3-day, good fitness required).

Karoo Nature Reserve, information from PO Box 349, Graaf-Reinett 6280. Tel: (0491) 2 3453. This must have the most unusual shape of any nature reserve as it encircles the town of Graaf-Reinett. The Vanrhyneveld Pass Dam falls within the reserve and the Valley of Desolation, which is actually more a gorge, is regarded as one of the most beautiful scenic spots in South Africa. No accommodation but facilities in Graaf Reinett. Trails: four trails (2–20 km/1–12 miles).

Mountain Zebra National Park, National Parks Board, Box 787, Pretoria 0001. Tel: (012) 343 1991; fax: (012) 343 0905. Located 27 km (16 miles) west of Cradock in the Eastern Cape, the park is home to a breeding population of black eagles and affords very good game viewing: if you are lucky, even wildcats and Cape foxes. Chalets, old farmhouse; caravanning and camping; restaurant, shop, petrol. Trails: Mountain Zebra Hiking Trail (3 days); short and half-day hikes.

Vaalbos National Park, information is available from SATOUR in Kimberley. Tel: (0531) 3 1434. On the way from Kimberley to Barkley West, this is the youngest of South Africa's National Parks and is still being developed. However, it lies in a very interesting region where Kalahari, Karoo and grassveld mingle. Buffalo and black rhino have already been re-introduced. At present, there is no accommodation.

Flora & Fauna

Parks, Gardens & Zoos

NORTHERN PROVINCE
Johannesburg & Pretoria Aquarium and Reptile Park, corner of Paul Kruger St and Boom St, contains a large assortment of fresh- and salt-water fish, reptiles, and snakes. Open daily 9am–4.30pm.

De Wildt Cheetah Research Centre is located at Silkaatsnek on the R53, some 1.5 hours by car north of Johannesburg. This is a breeding station for cheetahs, wild dogs and hyenas. Guided tours are conducted Saturday 8.30am and 2pm, Sunday 9am and 2pm; advance reservations recommended.

Johannesburg Zoo, Jan Smuts Ave, Parkview, contains more than 3,000 species of mammals, birds and reptiles. Night tours are conducted on Wednesdays and Fridays, 6.30–9.30pm. Tel: (011) 646 2000. Open daily 8.30am–5.30pm.

Pretoria Zoo, Boom Street, is one of the largest zoos in the world, with more than 3,500 species. Visitors can travel via cable car to an observation tower over the cages. A market at the entrance sells arts and crafts. Open daily, 8.30am–5pm.

KWAZULU-NATAL
Aquarium/Dolphinarium, Durban, corner West St and Marine. Parades held daily. In the main tank, fish are fed by a diver twice a day (11am and 3pm); daily tours of the dolphinarium are held at 10am, 11.30am, 2pm, 3pm and 5pm.

The aquarium contains some 1,000 species of fish, including sharks, rays and giant sea turtles.

EASTERN CAPE
East London: the **Aquarium** (feeding times 10.30am and 3pm; shows at 11.30am and 3.30pm) is located on the Esplanade, halfway between Orient and Eastern Beaches. Observe more than 400 kinds of sea creature and fresh-water fish, including intricately-patterned subtropical fish, sea anemones, squid, sharks, sea turtles, penguins and seals.

Queens Park Botanic Garden and Zoo (open daily 9am–5pm) lies on a hill between the city centre and the Buffalo River. In the middle of the beautifully laid-out garden with native plants and trees, the zoo has a special children's section. At 2pm, you can accompany the zoo-keepers on their feeding rounds.

THE GARDEN ROUTE
Port Elizabeth: the main attraction in the **Oceanarium** is the twice-daily dolphin show (11am and 3pm). Seals and penguins are on display as well.

In the **Snake Park**, you can see exotic and native snakes, vipers, crocodiles and other reptiles. Visitors to the **Tropical House** wander through a tropical landscape with waterfalls, rock cliffs and lush vegetation, watching the colourful birds all the while. In the **Night House**, you can observe nocturnal birds and animals by artificial light. Open daily 9am–1pm, demonstrations at 10am, 12.15pm, 2.30pm and 4.15pm.

In **Sea View**, tel: (041) 524138, 15 miles (25 km) west of Port Elizabeth, there's a zoo with lions, leopards and rhinos, plus fishing trips on Saturdays and Sundays. For information about diving excursions, contact the Publicity Association, tel: (041) 521315.

CAPE REGION

Cape Town: South Africa's oldest garden, the **Company's Garden**, at the upper end of Adderly Street, was laid out by Jan van Riebeeck in 1652 to provide passing ships with fresh vegetables. Now, it's a parkland with rose gardens, bird-cages and a sundial dating from 1787. During the legislative period in Cape Town, this is the location of the Parliament and the presidential residence Tuynhuis.

Mariner's Wharf: World of Birds, Valley Rd, Hout Bay, tel: (021) 790 2730, is Africa's largest bird park, containing 3,000 species. Heaven for bird-watchers and photographers. Open daily 9am–6pm.

FREE STATE

Bloemfontein: the **Zoo** contains more different species of ape than any other zoo in South Africa. Most famous, however, is the "Liger" – a cross between a lion and a tiger. Night tours are especially popular. Open daily 8am–5pm.

NAMAQUALAND

Clanwilliam: located 277 km (172 miles) from Cape Town on the N7, this is the centre of a fertile agricultural region which produces fruit, grain, vegetables and Rooibos tea. Tours available, tel. (02682) 64.

At the **Wildflower Garden** in Clanwilliam Damm, you can see the profusion of spring wildflowers from the footpaths. Bidouw Valley, on the way to Wuppertal, is considered a microcosm of Namaqualand because of the variety of its wildflowers.

Birdwatching

Southern Africa is great for bird-lovers: 22 of the 27 living orders are found in this country and some 718 species. One of the reasons for the astounding diversity in bird life is the great variety of vegetation zones.

Below are a list of the major vegetation zones and the nature reserves which are best suited to observing the birds in that particular region.

The Eastern Woodlands (or **Bushveld**) have the richest avifaunas: the Kruger Park and the KwaZulu-Natal Reserves of Ndumu, Mkuze, Hluhluwe and Umfolozi, of which Ndumu is regarded as a bird watchers' paradise. For further information contact: Kruger Park, National Parks Board, tel: (012) 343 1991; and Natal Reserves, National Parks Board, tel: (0331) 47 1981.

Birds of the **Eastern Mistbelt** forests can be seen in Game Valley (Safari World) near Cramond, tel: (03393) 787, and in the Karkloof Nature Reserve, tel: (0331) 47 1981.

Another interesting area is the **Magoebaskloof** between Pietersburg and Tzaneen. For more information, contact the Directorate of Forestry, Northern Province, Private Bag 2413, Louis Trichard 0920. Tel: (01551) 2201.

The birds of the **coastal evergreen forests** of the southern Cape can be seen in the Tsitsikama Forest National Park near Port Elizabeth. More information is available from the National Parks Board, tel: (012) 343 1991.

Birds of the **Highveld** can be seen anywhere along the road, but a stay at Barberspan near Delareyville in North-West Province should be very rewarding; it is the largest waterfowl sanctuary in the region. Information is available from the Barberspan Nature

Identifying Birds

The ornithologist's bible in this part of the world is *Roberts' Birds of Southern Africa*.

Reserve, PO Barberspan 2765. Tel: (0144322) 1202.

The **Willem Pretorius Game Reserve** between Winburg and Kroonstad in the central Free State is also worthwhile for the ornithologist. For more details, contact the Willem Pretorius Game Reserve, Ventersburg 9451. Tel: (01734) 4229.

Mountain birds are most easily accessible in the **Golden Gate Highlands National Park** near Bethlehem, in the eastern Free State – National Parks Board, tel: (012) 343 1991, and the beautiful reserves of the **Natal Drakensberg** – Natal Parks Board, tel: (0331) 47 1981.

The **arid regions** have an extremely rich bird life. The Karoo National Park, near Beaufort West in the Cape, and the Kalahari Gemsbok National Park, in the northern Cape, are among the most convenient reserves to find the birds adapted to these harsh conditions. For more details, contact National Parks Board, tel: (012) 343 1991.

Namaqualand on the Cape West Coast is a bird watcher's, as well as a botanist's, paradise in September when the otherwise arid plains are carpeted with flowers. The Hester Malan Nature Reserve near Springbok is well worth a visit (day-time only).

The Fynbos of the southwestern Cape has several endemic species of birds, which can be seen in the Cape of Good Hope Nature Reserve and the Helderberg Nature Reserve near Somerset West (day visits only).

Tailor-made and group safaris for bird lovers are offered by:

BirdLife South Africa, PO Box 84394, Greenside 2034, Gauteng. Tel: (011) 888 4147; fax: (011) 782 7013.

Lawson's, PO Box 507, Nelspruit 1200, tel: (01311) 4 2257; fax: 2 7482.

Wilderness Safaris, PO Box 651171, Benmore 2010, tel: (011) 884 1458; fax: (011) 883 6255.

Botanical Excursions

Considering its size, South Africa's wealth of flora is remarkable: there are 24,000 flora species, compared with 10,000 in Europe. Keen amateur botanists may be interested to know that The Botanic Institute issues computer printouts which list every species according to family, together with their common names.

The Dendrological Society, one of the largest arboreal organisations in the world, also issues national lists of native (green) and imported (yellow) trees, which you should keep on hand, as all of the number and name-plates in nature preserves and botanic gardens accord with this information. Contact the Dendrological Society of South Africa, PO Box 104, Pretoria 0001. Tel: (012) 57 4009.

Flower Shows

February: Johannesburg (Botanical Gardens): autumn flower show.
April: Durban Exotica, international flower show.
August: Northwestern Cape Namaqualand in bloom.
September: Johannesburg (Botanical Gardens): spring flower show.
Cape Town: wildflower show.
October: Durban: International Orchid Exhibition.
Pretoria: Jacaranda Carnival (with Carnival parade).
November: Johannesburg (Botanical Gardens): Succulent and Cactus Show.

The Botanical Society organises regular excursions for foreign visitors. Contact the Botanical Society of South Africa, Kirstenbosch, Claremont 7735. Tel: (021) 797 2090. Of South Africa's many state and private nature preserves, Richtersveld, south of Namibia, is of interest because it is richer in succulents than any other park in the world and half of the species are endemic, i.e. unique to the area.

South Africa's botanic gardens worth visiting are listed below according to region (those with native plants unique to the area are indicated with an asterisk).

CAPE REGION
Caledon*: Caledon Wildflower Garden; Namaqualand wildflowers.

Cape Town*: Kirstenbosch Botanic Garden, Rhodes Drive, Constantia. Open daily April–August 8am–6pm, September–March 8am–7pm; guided tours Tuesday and Saturday 11am. One of the most important botanic gardens in the world, it is home to most of the 22,000 plant varieties native to South Africa, notably the entire Fynbos family, of which the Protea are members. A bus runs from the city centre three times a day.

Kleinmond*: The Harold Porter National Botanic Garden contains plants of the winter rainfall region.

Stellenbosch: Hortens Botanicus, Neethling St, has a rare collection of local succulents and orchids. Open Monday–Friday 9am–5pm, Saturday 9am–11am.

Swellendam*: Karoo Botanic Garden is located on Roux Road on the N2 motorway, 3 km (2 miles) north of Worcester. In spring, this garden is a veritable sea of flowers.

THE NORTH
Johannesburg: Johannesburg Botanic Garden includes a herb garden. The Wilds, Houghton

Drive, Houghton, is a conservation area devoted to local flora, containing numerous species of wildflower from Namaqualand.

Nelspruit*: Nelspruit Botanic Garden contains African trees. Open in summer Monday–Friday 7.30am–6pm, in winter Monday–Friday 8am–5pm.

Pretoria*: Pretoria National Botanic Garden has various biomes, particularly those of the drier regions of southern Africa (Madagascar, Namibia).

Roodepoort*: National Botanic Garden contains flora of the Highveld (Bankenveld).

Sun City: the Botanic Garden is devoted to "the dramatic and bizarre elements of the plant world".

KWA-ZULU NATAL
Durban: Durban Botanic Gardens, between Syndenham Road and Botanic Gardens Road, Lower Berea, are open daily from 9am. A special feature is the world-famous orchid house, containing 3,000 species from around the world.

Pietermaritzburg: the Natal National Botanic Gardens contain exotic trees and flora of KwaZulu-Natal.

FREE STATE
Bloemfontein: the Botanic Garden is mainly given over to plants native to the Free State, but it's also known for a fossilised tree-trunk said to be at least 150 million years old. The orchid house in Hamilton Park, with its sliding roof and computerised air-conditioning system, is worth a visit. 3,000 orchids are arranged in a fairytale landscape of waterfalls, footbridges and ponds.

Harrismith: Drakensberg Botanic Garden on Platberg presents a cross-section of flora from the Drakensberg Mountains, as well as several lovely walking trails.

Mines & Archaeology

Geological Sites

The classical geological formations of South Africa are of interest to scientists throughout the world. Geological strata (including very old rocks), which in other parts of the world are hidden way down below, are often visible on the surface – creating a sort of hands-on geological history book. The major geological areas are:

Barberton Mountain Land in Mpumalanga – microscopic fossils of the earliest known forms of life found in the chert rocks.

Witwatersrand Basin around Johannesburg – the richest goldfield in the world.

Bushveld Complex north of Pretoria – volcanic layers containing the world's largest reserves of platinum, chrome and iron ore.

Pilanesberg near Sun City – one of the largest extinct volcanoes on earth.

Cape Supergroup in the southern margin – spectacular sandstone mountain ranges including the most famous landmark of all, Table Mountain.

The Karoo stratae, covering nearly half of South Africa, is a massive layered cake of sandstone and rock with a capping of basalt representing the widespread lava flows that accompanied the break-up of Gondwanaland. The picturesque mountain landscapes that characterise the Drakensberg and the Lesotho Highlands are carved wholly within the basalt capping.

Preserved within the sandstones and rocks of the Karoo basin is an unbroken record of vertebrate evolution, from fishes through amphibians and reptiles, including the dinosaurs.

In Mpumalanga, a geological route has been developed which can be hiked by hobby geologists: **the Kaapse Hoop Hiking Trail** in the Barberton/Nelspruit area has boards with geological explanations en route. More of these popular trails are in preparation.

For further information, contact **The Geological Society of South Africa**, PO Box 44283, Linden 2104. Tel: (011) 888 2288; fax: 888 2181. The Society also publishes two journals: *The South African Journal of Geology* and *The Geo-Bulletin Quarterly*.

GEOLOGICAL MUSEUMS

Geological Museum, Johannesburg, tel: (011) 833 5624.

Geological Survey Collection, Transvaal Museum, Pretoria, tel: (012) 322 7632.

Alexander McGregor Memorial Museum, Kimberley, tel: (0531) 32645.

South African Museum, Cape Town, tel: (021) 24 3330.

Mines

Diamonds are, without a doubt, the most exciting precious stones, and the purest, for they're made entirely of carbon. Under enormous pressure, at high temperatures, the stones are formed in the earth's interior over millions of years and forced up towards the surface by volcanic eruptions.

Kimberley, with its Big Hole, is South Africa's most famous diamond mine. Dug in 1871, the world's largest man-made hole is 400 metres (1,300 ft) deep and 500 metres (1,600 ft) in diameter. Up to 30,000 adventurers dig for the shining stones as if possessed. The Kimberley Mine Museum brings pioneer days again to life, as does the small restored city dating from the mine's foundation. The Diamond Museum will make even hardened hearts beat faster. Open daily 8am–6pm (closed on Good Friday and Christmas).Tel: (0531) 3 1557.

The world champion diamond was found in 1905 in the **Premier Mine**, East of Pretoria. The Cullinan weighed 3,106 carats (about 600 grams/1.3 pounds) and was as large as a child's fist. Four of the nine diamonds cut from this stone ornament the British crown jewels, among them the 530-carat Great Star of Africa, the largest-ever cut diamond. Guided tours of the Cullinan Premier Mine are held Monday–Friday at 9am and 10.30am. Pretoria Tourist Information: (012) 313 8259.

The beryl is the most varied precious mineral: its family includes the emerald, the aquamarine, the morganite and the yellow beryl.

Some of the best-known tourmalines are found in Namibia and the northwest Cape. No other precious stone exists in so many colours.

The Rustenburg Platinum Mine, in North-West Province, is the largest in the world. It is possible to visit the mine, but necessary to book in advance. Rustenberg Tourist Information, tel: (0142) 97 3111 ext 3194.

The Blue Mine, to the west of Springbok in Namaqualand, was expanded up until the end of the 19th century. It can be reached on foot.

Phalaborwa, 68 miles (110 km) from Tzaneen on the R71, just outside Kruger Park, is the centre of a rich mining area and an open cast copper mine which can be visited after prior arrangements on Friday afternoons. Phalaborwa Association for Tourism, tel: (01524) 85860. There is also a museum which shows the archaeological, ethnological and mining history of the region.

Archaeology

The Karoo is one of the world's largest fossil graveyards from the age of reptiles and is regarded by scientists as one of the natural wonders of the world.

In the **Karoo National Park** near Beaufort West on the N1 between Cape Town and Bloemfontein, there is a fossil trail which takes the visitor back through 250 million years of geological history. This 440-yard (400-metre) long trail is suitable for wheelchairs and the visually impaired. Information is available from the Park Warden, Karoo National Park, PO Box 316, Beaufort West 6970. Tel: (0201) 5 2828/9.

The Rubidge fossil collection on the farm **Wellwood** in the Graaf Reinet area is, in all probability, the finest private collection in the country.

The **SA Archaeological Society** will assist with information on archaeological sites that can be visited by the public. Visitors are welcome to attend the monthly evening lectures and monthly outings. Further information is available from the South African Archaeological Society, PO Box 15700, Vlaeberg, 8018.

Archaeological Sites

NORTHERN PROVINCE

A park right in the heart of Johannesburg contains the **Melville Koppies**, believed to have been occupied by man 100,000 years ago. An ancient iron-smelting furnace can be seen on top of the hill. Eighty percent of all plant species in the Witwatersrand region can be found in this park, including medicinal and also poisonous varieties.The reserve is open on the fourth Sunday of each month when guided tours are offered. Information and a guidebook are available from the Johannesburg Parks & Recreation Department, PO Box 6428, Johannesburg 2000. Tel: (011) 41 3612.

Suikerboschrand Nature Reserve is close to Heidelberg. There are ruins of stone walled Iron Age villages in the reserve of Sotho/Tswana origin.

The Sterkfontein Caves, not far from Krugersdorp, tel: (011) 956 6342, are limestone caves where archaeological history was made with the discovery of the famous "Mrs Ples" (*Plesianthropus transvaalensis*), the so-called missing link. Guided tours take place every half hour, Tuesday–Sunday 9am–4pm. The caves are closed every year from the second week of January to the first week of February.

The Museum of Man on the turn-off to the Echo Caves in Mpumalanga is an archaeological excavation site with interesting remains reaching back well in excess of 100,000 years. This Iron Age site is situated in the Kruger National Park on the road between Phalaborwa Gate and Letaba Rest Camp. It is well sign-posted and guided tours are available. A kiosk on the site provides information on the site's history and archaeology.

In the **Kruger National Park**, there are many sites with rock paintings in the Stolznek area in the south of the Park.

Ermelo lies 120 km (75 miles) from Waterval Boven, in Mpumalanga, on the R36. There are a number of interesting archaeological sites in the vicinity: e.g. the corbelled stone houses of a tribe that is now extinct; the Goliath Foot Print is a footprint of 1.24 metres (4 ft) and can be seen on a rock in a beautifully wooded area on the farm called Arthur's Seat near Lothair; and on the farm Welgelegen there are many Bushman drawings. Since all these lie on private property permission to view them must be obtained beforehand. For information, tel: (01311) 55 1988.

CAPE REGION

Cape Town: In the lower levels of the Golden Acre shopping complex are the remains of Wagenaar's Dam, built in the 17th century after the Dutch East India Co. established a settlement at the Cape.

Wonderwerk Cave: This important solution cavity is situated on the road between Kuruman and Danielskuil in the Kuruman hills, in the Northwestern Cape. The site is signposted, but the cave itself is protected by a gate and fence.

Buying Rocks

As you'd expect, South Africa has many shops selling minerals and semi-precious stones. The following outlets give you the opportunity to understand the production processes behind your purchases:

Erikson Diamond Centre, 20 Monument Road, Kempton Park, Johannesburg. Tel: (011) 970 1355. Everything you ever wanted to know about diamonds and their production, plus shops selling gems of all shapes and sizes.

Topstones, Dido Valley Road, Simonstown, Cape Town. Tel: (021) 786 2020. One of the largest factories which polish and process semi-precious stones. Shop.

The key can be obtained from the custodian who lives on the farm. The site has been intermittently inhabited for over half a million years and has provided valuable information on Early, Middle and Later Stone Age ways of life.

Postmasburg (Northwestern Cape): Just to the northwest of the town, within its municipal boundaries, lies Blinkklipkop, an ironstone outcrop with an ancient specularite mine. It has been mined for probably a few thousand years by the indigenous people of the area.

Barkley West: Canteen Koppie on the Vaal River, approximately 2 km (1 mile) southeast of the town. This site contains a vast amount of Stone Age implements. It is worth a visit if you are interested in stone implements.

Driekopseiland: This site is in the bed of the Riet River in the northwestern Cape. It consists of large sheets of glacial striated bedrock on which over 3,000 rock engravings are visible.

KWAZULU-NATAL AND DRAKENSBERG AREA

Umgungundlovu (secret plot of the elephant), situated in northern Natal between Melmoth and Babanango, was once the military headquarters of the Zulu king, Dingaan. It was built around 1828 and destroyed by fire in 1838 on the orders of the king. The archaeological excavations have exposed numerous hut floors. Part of the site is being reconstructed.

Ulundi (the high place) is close to and southwest of the modern town Ulundi. This was King Cetshwayo's capital, destroyed by the British army during the Zulu wars of the late 19th century. It has been partially restored and also doubles as a holiday resort where visitors can rent a traditional Zulu hut.

The Drakensberg in KwaZulu-Natal, the Free State and Lesotho have numerous caves and shelters with exquisite rock paintings; sites are often remote and inaccessible and most easily visited by hikers. Directions and permits can be obtained from the officials of these various parks and resorts. Information: Natal Parks Board.

FREE STATE

Willem Prinsloo Game Reserve: This reserve near Winburg contains the ruins of early Tswana Iron Age settlers. Easily accessible, the ruins and are on and next to the road that meanders along the low range of hills on the reserve.

Florisbad: This famous site is situated near Bloemfontein and has a recreation facility. Appointments to visit the archaeological or palaeontological part of the site can be made via the National Museum of Bloemfontein, tel: (051) 47 0609.

BOPHUTHATSWANA

Norlim: The famous limeworks where the Taung skull (*Australopithecus africanus*) was found are situated at this town. The site is open to the public and the position where the skull was found is marked with a little monument.

Caves

You need to obtain a permit to enter a cave on state-owned land. Caves are generally dry, with an average temperature of 16°C (60°F); visitors are advised that histoplasmosis (cave disease) is a danger. It is best to arrange itineraries and access through clubs, which gladly welcome overseas visitors. The following societies will be able to help:

South African Speleological Association, PO Box 6166, Johannesburg 2000.

Cave Research Organisation of South Africa, PO Box 7322, Johannesburg 2000. Tel: (011) 640 4394.

The Cango Caves near Oudtshoorn are the best known South African limestone caves. A small section of the subterranean cave complex is open to the general public on guided tours. The main attractions are the imposing sculptures formed by stalactites and stalagmites. The caves are open December–February and April 8am–5pm, tours every hour; May–November and March 9am–3pm, tours every two hours. There is a museum on site, featuring plants, animals and rock formations from the caves.

The Sudwala Caves in Mpumalanga near Waterval Boven are a network of large interlocking chambers, one of which is used for musical recordings because of the incredible acoustics in the chamber, which measures 67 metres (220 ft) in diameter and 37 metres (120 ft) in height. Within the caves, the temperature remains a constant 17°C all year round. Guided tours take place daily 8.30am–4.30pm. On the first Saturday of each month a six-hour tour is available to the more remote chambers like the fairy-tale Crystal Room.

Outside the caves is a world-famous **Dinosaur Park**. The first of Sudwala's model dinosaurs was commissioned to illustrate the age of the caves (100 million years). Now there are many dinosaurs representing species drawn from around the world; life-size, they inhabit the hillside to the side of the caves and are well worth a visit. The Dinosaur Park is open every day from 8.30am–5pm.

The Echo Caves on the road from Ohrigstad to Tzaneen are the least well known of the limestone caves. The advantage is that fewer people visit them and you may be lucky enough to enjoy this underworld with just your guide. The caves are so-called because the local people used one of the flowstones as a drum to warn of approaching Swazis. As these caves extend for some 40 km (24 miles), the sound travelled for surprisingly long distances and the people could take refuge in the caves. From an archaeological point of view, the caves are fascinating as finds here corroborate the legend that, long ago, strangers in long white robes came to look for gold and to barter with the inhabitants. Some of the finds are exhibited at the Museum of Man on the turn-off from the tar road to the Echo Caves. Both the Echo Caves and the Museum of Man are open daily from 8am–5pm.

Activities

Beach Holidays

South Africa has a coastline some 3,000 km (1,900 miles) long. Along this are beaches of all shapes and characters. In northern KwaZulu-Natal, you will find beautiful and practically deserted beaches stretching for miles; isolated stretches can also be found along the Wild Coast. At the other end of the scale are the main tourist beaches complete with restaurants, entertainment, life-savers – and thousands of sun worshippers during the holiday seasons.

THE KWAZULU-NATAL COAST

From **Kosi Bay (near the Mozambique border) to the Tugela Delta**, there are wonderful beaches. Many, unfortunately, aren't equipped with shark nets and some can only be reached in a four-wheel drive vehicle. Nonetheless, daring swimmers entrust themselves to the calm waters of the Kosi Bay Delta, Sodwana

Bay, Mapelane, St Lucia, Cape Vidal and Richard's Bay. Under no circumstances should you swim in the lakes or lagoons (especially St Lucia Lake), as there's danger from crocodiles and hippos. Campground swimming pools are a safer alternative.

From **Zinkwazi Beach to Transkei**, the larger beaches are effectively protected from sharks. The nets are only lifted during heavy rainfall and during the sardine runs in July.

North of Durban, Umhlanga Rocks, Umhlote Beach and Ballito Bay are the most beautiful stretches of coast. In the holiday season, Durban's beaches are popular resorts, but if you do bathe here, keep an eye on your possessions.

The numerous tidal pools are also very popular: at high tide, the hollows in the rocks fill with water. A favourite is the one at Thompson's Bay (north of Ballito Bay).

On the **South Coast**, in the rock pools along the marvellous beaches, you can find sea urchins, anemones and other sea creatures close at hand. A particularly lovely one is on Treasure Beach.

Dune forests often reach all the way down to the beach in the northern region of the South Coast, providing shady trails for hours of beach walks.

Beach Hazards

Swimmers should beware of the following hazards:
• Backwashes or sidewashes can move you out to sea or along the coast without you noticing it at first.
• A smooth patch amongst an otherwise foaming sea indicates a strong current at that point.
• Never go swimming if you are on your own.
• Sharks are an unlikely, but

not unknown hazard: they do not like murky water, so don't swim near river mouths or after heavy rains. In addition, do not swim at night as that is when sharks feed. Forty-two of the KwaZulu-Natal coast beaches are protected by shark nets.
• Another hazard is blue-bottles: their blue tentacles wrap around your arm or leg and cause an intense burning sensation.

Between **Port Shepstone and Port Edward**, on the border of Transkei, there are 11 large beaches which are protected against sharks.

TRANSKEI, CISKEI AND EASTERN CAPE

The **Transkei and Ciskei** shores are known as the Romantic Coast for a number of reasons: their many bays; inviting, not-too-populous sandy beaches; shallow lagoons; and rivers where you can sail, canoe, or water-ski. However, swim with care in this area: there aren't any shark nets and sharks are particularly fond of river deltas, especially after heavy rainfall, when the water is muddy.

Between **Mzamba and the Umngazi Delta**, there is excellent swimming and the beach near Port St Johns is also very beautiful. East London offers three large beaches and a tidal pool near Fullar's Bay. Between Kidds Beach and the Great Fish River, there are several good places to swim, and Kidds Rock has another pretty tidal pool.

Also between **the deltas of the Boesmans River and the Kariega**, there is over a mile of small beaches of various sizes where you can swim safely and enjoyably. Kenton-on-Sea is one of the loveliest bathing spots in South Africa.

Kei Mouth is at the end of the Kei River, which forms the Transkei border. This broad delta is perfect for swimming and all sorts of water sports; it's also popular with deep-sea and coastal fishermen. The tropical coastal forest is ideal for long walks; those in the mood for adventure can take one of the old ferries over to Kei.

Just south of Kei Mouth, **Morgan's Bay** lies in a particularly impressive stretch of coastal landscape with high cliffs; spray from the breaking waves is thrown up to a height of almost 30 metres (100 ft). The forests and coastal regions are home to a wide variety of birds and, from Haga-Haga, you can embark on interesting coastal walks or an excursion to one of the many tidal pools.

THE GARDEN ROUTE

Kings Beach, Humewood and McArthur Pool are the safest places to swim, overseen by lifeguards.

The stretch of coastline **north of St Francis Bay**, notably Jeffrey's Bay, is especially good for swimming. This is also a popular area for surfing: St Francis Bay is a particular favourite.

Mossel Bay has many sheltered lagoons, such as Hartenbos, Little and Great Brak Rivers, and beaches down to Victoria Bay, with calm waters.

Between Mossel Bay and Plettenberg Bay, **Great Brak River** is a little village on the coast, 20 km (12 miles) east of Mossel Bay, with a lagoon and sandy beach surrounded by wooded hills.

Herold's Bay is located on the N2 National Road, some 25 km (15 miles) southwest of George. A small, sheltered holiday village, it offers a sandy beach and large tidal pools for safe sea bathing.

At **Sedgefield**, on Swartvlei, you can bathe either in sheltered lagoons or on magnificent sand beaches.

Buffels Bay, near Knysna, is known for its picturesque beaches, which extend to Brenton-on-Sea.

The beach at **Noetzie**, east of Knysna, can only be reached on foot or in a four-wheel drive vehicle (the lagoon, too, is safe for swimming).

Oyster Bay is a holiday village with broad sandy beaches, 26 km (16 miles) southwest of Humandorp. In the nature preserve between Oyster Bay and Cape St Francis, you can observe the antics of the sea otters.

St Francis Bay is a magnificent spot on the coast of the Indian Ocean, with broad sandy beaches and excellent facilities for swimming and water sports. The lagoon on the Seekoci and Swart Rivers is known for its extensive bird life, including flamingos and swans by the hundreds. The old, 28-metre (91-ft) tall lighthouse on Seal Point, dating from 1876, is still operational.

Jeffrey's Bay lies a few miles to the north. Its "Super Tube" is on a par with "Bruce" – surf you can rely on the year round. But Jeffrey's Bay is also a paradise for more contemplative souls. Every tide casts a treasure trove of shellfish upon the beautiful beaches; you can even find the chambered Nautilus and Pansies (other shellfish are displayed in the library). Jeffrey's Bay is also known for its variety of arts and crafts.

Kenton-on-Sea is 56 km (35 miles) south of Grahamstown, between the Bushman River and Kariega, which flow into the sea at a distance of over a mile from each other. The coast between these two deltas has sandy beaches, tidal pools and bizarre rock formations. 10 km (6 miles) to the west, near Kwaaihoek, is a replica of the Diaz Cross.

SOUTHWESTERN CAPE

West of **Mossel Bay** are popular beaches near Infanta, Witsand and Stilbaai. There are spectacular walks along the cliffs of Cape Hangklipat Hermanus. June to November, you can spot whales in Walker Bay and other bays in the area.

The western coast near **False Bay** has several lovely beaches, especially south of Simonstown. Sandy Bay is a secret nudist beach (although, officially, nude bathing is not allowed).

On the **Atlantic Coast**, Camps Bay has long, sandy beaches, grassy lawns and a salt-water swimming pool, located at the feet of the Twelve Apostles.

Clifton offers four long, magnificent sandy beaches, separated from each other by huge blocks of granite.

Sea Point is a popular, and thickly-populated, suburb of Cape Town, with a lovely beach promenade almost 3 km (2 miles) long and a large salt-water pool. It's also known for its restaurants.

In the western coastal regions, the beaches of **Strandfontein** (at the level of Vanrhynsdorp) are the most popular among swimmers. The coast before McDougall's Bay, near Port Nolloth, is protected by shallow reefs, and is ideal for swimming.

Spas

NORTHERN PROVINCE

Warmbaths, 100 km (62 miles) from Pretoria on the N1, is a renowned mineral resort with an ultra-modern health complex that includes various pools and hydro-therapy facilities. There is also a nature reserve (with a variety of game) where you can take lovely walks. Accommodation is in chalets, flats, a caravan park and camping site. Contact: Warmbaths Tourist Information, tel: (014) 736 2111.

Boat Trips

Boat trips can be taken from the harbour in **Cape Town** or from **Hout Bay**. Tours include sunset cruises, deep sea fishing and visits to Duiker Island in False Bay, a refuge for seals and birds, including the rare bank cormorant that only inhabits South Africa and Namibian coasts.

Bahari Charters, tel: (021) 689 1504.

Circe Launches, tel: (021) 790 1040.

There are waterfalls of varying height scattered throughout this region: near Sabie is the Bridal Veil falls, plus Horseshoe, Lone Creek and Sabie falls; near Graskop is the Mac falls, plus Lisbon and Berlin falls. All of them are worth a detour.

GARDEN ROUTE

To get to the **Karoo Sulphur Springs**, near Cradock, take the R32 toward Middelburg. There are lovely trails and paths through this area.

CAPE PENINSULA

Montagu Springs have been touted for their curative powers for more than 200 years. These mineral springs are located almost 3 km (2 miles) north of Montagu, in the Cogmans Kloof (Gorge) Nature Preserve. There are many hiking trails in the vicinity. Contact: Montagu Tourist Information Bureau, Bath St, Montagu. Tel: (0234) 42471.

CENTRAL CAPE

Aliwal Spa, on the R30 between Bloemfontein and East London, has mineral springs and thermal baths, plus four open-air and two indoor pools, a bio-kinetic centre and a children's water playground. Bus tours take visitors to see nearby San drawings. For information, tel. (0551) 2951.

Condor Charters, tel: (021) 448 5612.

Drumbeat Charters, tel: (021) 438 9208.

Neptunes, tel: (021) 782 3889.

Sealink Tours, tel: (021) 25 4480.

Teachers Spirit of Adventure, tel: (021) 418 2989.

Waterfront Charters, tel: (021) 25 4292.

Steam Train Journeys

As South Africa is one of the few countries where the steam locomotive is still used, steam enthusiasts come here from all over the world.

The **Transnet Heritage Foundation**, part of the Transnet Museum in Johannesburg, organises a number of steam train safaris each year to different parts of the country to enable visitors to see steam locomotive yards and depots. They last 14 days and the price includes meals and bus tours to places of interest en route. Photo-stops are held at scenic places.

These steam train safaris are run on trains belonging to **Union Limited Steam Safaris**, a company which offers its own programme of steam train journeys. These include day rambles from Cape Town to Franschhoek and Ceres, and a six-day Garden Route tour on the Union Limited Golden Thread. For more information, contact: Union Limited Steam Safaris, PO Box 4325, Cape Town 8000. Tel: (021) 405 4390. Transnet Museum, PO Box 3753, Johannesburg 2000. Tel: (011) 773 9118.

In addition, the Transnet Museum recently took over the **Outeniqua Choo-Tjoe** (Western Cape), which travels between George and Knysna, Monday–Friday, taking 4 hours each way and winding through the most breathtaking mountain scenery. Tickets can be bought at the stations in George and Knysna. For booking and information, tel: (0441) 738288.

The **Magalies Valley Steamer** leaves on the first Sunday of each month from Johannesburg to Hekpoort, more frequently during holidays. Catering car and lounge car; and fires lit for barbeque at Hekpoort; meat and salads for sale. For information, tel: (011) 773 9238.

Hot Air Ballooning

The Magaliesberg valley, northwest of Johannesburg, is ideally suited to ballooning. Flights take place soon after dawn as weather conditions are usually best at this time.

The following companies operate balloon flights:

Bill Harrop's Original Balloon Safaris, Box 67, Randburg 2125, Gauteng. Tel: (011) 705 3201; fax: (011) 705 3203.

Airtrack Adventures, tel: (011) 957 2322. Game viewing over the Crocodile River.

For details of other ballooning companies operating in South Africa, contact: **Aero Club of South Africa**, PO Box 1993, Halfway House 1685, Gauteng. Tel: (011) 805 0366.

Magaliesberg Express, PO Box 3753, Johannesburg 2000. Tel: (011) 888 1154. Departs from Johannesburg Station at 8.45am on Sundays for Magaliesburg (a journey of just under two hours), arriving back in Johannesburg at 5.45pm. There is a lounge car with full bar services and souvenir shop. On arrival, *braai* fires are lit and meat and salads dishes are on sale. Eating utensils and folding chairs must be brought by the passengers.

Since 1906, the narrow-gauge **Apple Express** has been chugging between Port Elizabeth and Thornhill in the fruit-growing area of the Langkloof. It travels this route once or twice a month, and there are also some trips to Loerie and back. For booking and further information, contact: Spoornet Information Centre, The Bridge, Greenacres, Port Elizabeth, tel: (041) 507 2333; or the Port Elizabeth Publicity Association, tel: (041) 521316.

The **Banana Express** (KwaZulu-Natal) travels between Port Shepstone (on the South Coast), historic Paddock and the spectacular Oribi Gorge Nature Reserve. For those seeking a longer steam train journey, there are occasionally rides to Harding too. For information and tickets, contact Hibiscus Coast and Country Publicity, tel: (03931) 22322.

Rovos Rail operates a luxury steam train (the "Pride of Africa"), which is among the most luxurious in the world. There are four main routes: Pretoria to Cape Town (lasting two days, with sightseeing stops at Kimberley and historic Matjiesfontein); Pretoria to Victoria Falls (return trip lasting five days; Cape Town to Knysna (lasting three days, with sightseeing excursion to Oudtshoorn); and Pretoria to Kruger National Park (with additional bus transfers). Rovos Rail also operates an epic 12-day safari from Cape Town to Dar-es-Salaam in Tanzania (via Pretoria, Victoria Falls and Lusaka). None of these trips come cheap, but they certainly represent the highest standards of opulence. For more details, contact: Rovos Rail, PO Box 2837, Pretoria 0001. Tel: (012) 323 6052; fax: (021) 323 0843.

South African National Railway and Steam Museum, Randfontein Estates Gold Mine, near Krugersdorp. Tel: (011) 888 1154/5/6. The museum offers train rides once a month to Magaliesburg.

Eastern Cape Rail Safaris, PO Box 1410, East London 5200. Tel: (0431) 433110. This company offers luxury trips from East London to Aliwal North.

Umgeni Steam Railway Excursions, Tel: (03324) 4110 ext 216. Operated by volunteers at the Natal Railway Museum, Hilton Station, Pietermaritzburg, it organises trips to Howick on the second Sunday of each month, except August and September.

Steam trains are in regular use in the Kimberley region in the Northern Cape. There are departures to De Aar (250 km/155 miles) or to Kraankuil at the halfway point. Contact: Kimberley tourist information, tel: (0531) 27298.

Four-Wheel Drive Rental

Four-wheel drive vehicles are advisable for journeys into Botswana or the more remote beaches of northern KwaZulu-Natal. Rental vehicles are available fully equipped with a long-distance tank, special jack, fridge, 1–2 tents on the roof rack and camping requisites (bedding, cutlery, gas stove and gas lamps). The rental price normally includes insurance and unlimited mileage.

Vehicles are available from:

Campers Corner Rentals, PO Box 48191, Roosevelt PArk 2129, Gauteng. Tel: (011) 787 9105; fax: (011) 787 6900. Cape Town: Tel: (021) 905 1503; fax: (021) 905 4493.

Leisure Mobiles, PO Box 48928, Roosevelt Park 2129, Gauteng. Tel: (011) 477 2374; fax: (011) 477 2321.

If you have your own camping equipment, you can take a Toyota Double Cab with four seats and a cover over the back. Contact: **U-Drive-Rent-a-Car**, Box 23802, Joubert Park 2044. Tel: (011) 331 3735; fax: (011) 331 7116.

As camping equipment is seldom available for rent, tents are best brought from home, although camping and hiking equipment is available for hire in Johannesburg. Contact **Camping for Africa**, PO Box 1938, Randburg 2125. Tel: (011) 787 3498; fax: (011) 787 3524.

Hiking & Camping

Hiking

The best way to discover South Africa's lofty mountains, long, sandy beaches, indigenous rainforests and plantations is on foot. Opportunities range from short rambles suitable for families with young children to week-long expeditions and guided wilderness trails in big game country. A network of self-catering overnight hiking trails traverses the country from the Augrabies Falls National Park in the Northern Cape to the Western Cape mountains and the Soutpansberg in Northern Province. While some trails follow the coastline, others traverse challenging peaks which are often covered in snow during the winter. Some wind through the aromatic *fynbos* vegetation of the Western Cape, others through the grasslands of the Free State. Hiking trails vary in length from two to eight days, although shorter alternatives are usually available on long routes.

Heading the list of South Africa's most popular trails is the **Otter Hiking Trail** along the southern Cape Coast, while the **Blyderivierspoort** and **Fanie Botha** hiking trails in Mpumalanga are other favourites. Of the several wilderness areas available to outdoor enthusiasts seeking solitude and tranquility, those in **the Drakensberg** need little introduction. Although footpaths exist, backpackers are not obliged to stick to a particular route, nor are any facilities provided.

Backpacking requires a degree of experience and self-reliance and, depending on weather conditions, nights are spent either under the stars, in caves or, in many instances, in a small backpacking tent. Other wilderness areas include the Cedarberg, Groot-Winterhoek and Boesmanbos (Western Cape), the Baviaanskloof and Groendal (Eastern Cape), Ntendeka in KwaZulu-Natal and the Wolkberg in the north. For many hikers, however, the ultimate outdoor experience is a guided Wilderness Trail such as those conducted in several game reserves of the Natal Parks Board and the Kruger National Park (information under Large Parks and Reserves).

If you are keen on hiking in South Africa, advance planning is essential since it is almost impossible to get a booking at short notice for popular hiking trails. Contact your nearest South African Tourism Board office for a copy of *Follow the Footprints* which lists trailing opportunities, as well as information regarding duration, capacity, cost, facilities and reservation addresses.

On full payment following a reservation, usually a year in advance, a map is issued which serves as a confirmation of the booking besides giving useful information on climate, geography, flora and fauna of the trails. Keep it safe, as you may need it again.

For more information and bookings, contact:

National Parks Board, Pretoria. Tel: (012) 343 1991; fax: (012) 343 0905.

Natal Parks Board, PO Box 662, Pietermaritzburg 3200. Tel: (0331) 47 1981; fax: 47 1980.

Hiking Federation of South Africa, tel/fax: (011) 886 6524.

National Hiking Way Board, tel: (012) 343 1991.

Drifters offer hiking tours in the spectacular Cedarberg mountains on the Cape West Coast, along the Garden Route and Eastern Cape, the Wild Coast, the Drakensberg, Mpumalanga and the Fish River Canyon in Namibia. The price for 3–8 day hikes includes transport from Johannesburg, a professional guide, accommodation and most meals. For the very detailed brochure and information write to Drifters, PO Box 48434, Roosevelt Park 2129. Tel: (011) 888 1160; fax: (011) 888 1020.

The most useful periodical is the *SA Hiker*, from PO Box 28459, Kensington 2101. Tel: (011) 29 1842; fax: (011) 337 8061.

Mountaineering

South Africa's mountains and marvellous cliff formations are particularly inviting to mountain climbers, whatever the season. Rock-climbers incline towards Northern Province, or the Ceder or du Toits Kloof Mountains in the Cape. Often, the best mountains for climbing are privately owned. Local climbing clubs apply for permits to climb these from the farmers who own them, so it is a good idea to contact these clubs.

The **Magalies Mountains** lie only two hours by car from Johannesburg. On the mountains' north side, the rock faces have been eroded in places into picturesque gorges, lined with clear mountain brooks and giant trees (difficulty rating up to 8b on the French scale). However, **Northern Province** also offers tempting and difficult faces with walls up to 400 metres (1,300 ft) high. For information and an application, contact the **Mountain Club of South Africa**, tel: (011) 786 8367.

KwaZulu-Natal's **Drakensberg Mountains** have a more Alpine character; there are several 3,000-metre (9,800-feet) peaks to scale. The highest mountain in the Drakensberg range is just over the Lesotho border, the 3,482 metre (11,386-ft) Thabana Ntlenyana. Most of the mountains in KwaZulu-Natal which are interesting for climbers lie within nature reserves; before beginning, climbers have to register with the Natal Parks Board.

Montesiel, between Durban and Pietermaritzburg, is held to be the best region in South Africa for hobby climbers. Information: Mountain Club of South Africa, KwaZulu-Natal Section, tel: (031) 72 4074; or Natal Parks Board, tel: (0331) 47 1981; fax: (0331) 47 1980.

Cape Province contains the most popular and best-known mountains for climbers. Leader among these is **Table Mountain**, (1,084 metres/3,556 ft), which boasts more than 500 routes. North of Cape Town, the **Cedar Mountains** enchant visitors with their wonderful rock formations. The **du Toits Kloof Mountains** (Baine's Kloof and Sir Lowry's Pass) are also favourites of climbers.

For further information, contact: the **Mountain Club of South Africa**, 97 Hatfield St, Cape Town, 8001. Tel: (021) 45 3412 (10am–2pm, Friday until 7.30pm).

Sport

For general information on adventure tourism, contact: **The Council of Adventure Travel Associations of Southern Africa**. Tel: (0140) 89 2417; fax: (0140) 2 5775.

Gliding

The north of the country is renowned for its perfect gliding conditions. It offers endless blue skies, stable weather all year round with lots of sunshine and thermals that facilitate very long glides. Gliding tours are offered and clubs may be helpful in organising equipment privately; there are no commercially organised hiring facilities.

Contact the following clubs for more information:

Aero Club of South Africa, tel: (011) 805 0366.

Lifestyle Gliding Adventures, PO Box 67, Randburg 2125, Gauteng. Tel: (011) 705 3201/2; fax: (011) 705 3203. Lifestyle Gliding Adventures take you up on a soaring experience from the Parys airfield. The

rates vary depending on the number of passengers.

Magaliesburg Gliding Club, PO Box 190, Tarlton 1749, Gauteng. Tel: (011) 716 5229.

Witwatersrand Gliding Trust, PO Box 6875, Johannesburg 2000. Tel: (011) 615 2461.

Hang-Gliding

To practise hang-gliding in South Africa, you need to be a member of the South African Aero Club, thereby incurring a liability insurance, but temporary membership is available. Also, check whether your licence system is valid here. The Aero Club will be helpful in that respect. Contact: **The Aero Club of South Africa**, tel: (011) 805 0366.

Equipment may be a problem if you need to hire it. Clubs may be able to help, but there are no regular hiring facilities. For further information, contact the national body, or clubs directly:

South African Hang Gliding & Para-gliding Association, tel/fax: (011) 609 1678.

Hang-gliding is very, very popular in northern areas as a result of good weather all year round.

Cycling

As there are no cycling paths, the sport is more hazardous than in Europe. However, traffic

Parachuting

The superb scenery of KwaZulu-Natal and the Cape region make for fantastic parachuting/skydiving.

The sport involves a very active, social club life. Listed below are some clubs, which offer courses and may also be helpful in other ways.

Aero Club of South Africa, tel: (011) 805 0366.

The Free Fall Factory, PO

Box 87509, Houghton 2041. Tel: (011) 393 1020 (J.H. Visser).

Pietermaritzburg Parachuting Club, PO Box 798, Pietermaritzburg 3200. Tel: (0331) 52 2790 (home Kevin Moore).

Western Province Sport – Parachuting, PO Box 7017, Roggebaai 8012. Tel: (021) 75 6161 (Alan Murray).

on the smaller roads is not heavy. Despite the distances involved, people do cycle from Johannesburg to Cape Town, from Durban to Johannesburg, along the Garden Route and most of all around the Western Cape, which is wonderfully suited for fun cycling as it has magnificent scenery and there is no rain during the summer months (October–April). For organised rides contact:

The South African Cycling Federation, PO Box 271, Table View 7349, Cape Town. Tel: (021) 557 1212.

Mountain Bike Association, tel: (011) 964 2301.

Mountain Bike Information Line, PO Box 1227, Pinetown 3600, KwaZulu-Natal. Tel: (031) 78 4839.

Natal Parks Board, tel: (0331) 47 1981; fax: (0331) 47 1980.

Exploration Society of Southern Africa (ESSA), tel: (011) 614 8883; fax: (011) 482 5050.

Hiring of bikes: **Rent 'n Ride Cycle & Blade Hire**, 1 Park Road, Mouille Point, Cape Town. Tel: (021) 434 1122.

Golf

Golf is very popular in South Africa. A total of 300 registered golf courses are to be found all over the country, offering a wide range of challenges. Many seem to have retained the flavour of South Africa's colonial past, thus membership often requires more than "just" paying subscription fees. Many also incorporate the natural habitat to stunning effect.

From the Milnerton or Mowbray greens, you have a splendid view of Table Mountain, while the Wild Coast Course is laid out with sea water, dunes and plants. The Royal Cape and Royal Johannesburg are graced by beautiful old trees, dating from 1882 and 1890 respect-

Major Golfing Events

• South African Open Championships, January, various venues
• Lexington PGA Tournament, January, Johannesburg
• Sunshine Circuit, January–February, several venues throughout South Africa
• SA Amateur Golf Championships, March, venue not fixed
• Million Dollar Golf Classic, December, Sun City

ively. The Royal George and the Durban Country are said to be the most beautiful golf courses.

It's advisable to call the Club Secretary and ask for a confirmed starting time and dress codes. Jeans are usually unsuitable on the courses. For further information on golf courses that are part of holiday resort accommodation, consult SATOUR's publication on golf and accommodation.

For further information – possibly the planning of a golf safari – contact the **South African Golf Union**, PO Box 1537, Cape Town 8000. Tel: (021) 461 7585.

Horse-Riding

The diversity and spaciousness of the South African landscape, together with the temperate climate, lends itself ideally to horse-riding and horse-riding trails. Horse-riding is within reach of many more people here than it would be in Europe since it is relatively affordable.

Trails are available in various parts of the country, thus offering visitors an experience of this land at a "grass-roots level" – the sensations of what South Africa is about are immediate and alive. Trails in the Drakensberg are organised by the Natal Parks Board and Drifters and take you through scenic grandeur, across natural streams and grassy plains along

the escarpment. The area appears untouched by the 20th century. You may come across rural dwellings or Basothos (people of Lesotho) pursuing the rhythm of their traditional lifestyle. Contact the following for details:

Association for Horse Trails & Safaris in Southern Africa, tel: (011) 788 3923.

Natal Parks Board, PO Box 662, Pietermaritzburg 3200. Tel: (0331) 47 1981.

Drifters, PO Box 484, Roosevelt Park 2129. Tel: (011) 888 1160; fax: (011) 888 1020.

Equus Trails, PO Box 926, White River 1240. Tel: (01311) 51 998; fax: 5 0383. They offer rides through the bushveld in Mpumalanga in the Songimvelo Game Reserve, which lies on the Swaziland border. There are no predators in this game reserve, but there is a wide variety of game and the trail takes you through magnificent mountain scenery (they also offer a Wilderness Trail for hikers).

Glendwoods Magaliesberg Mountain Trail, PO Box 568, Britz 0250. Tel: (01211) 3 1404 (after hours). The Glendwoods Magaliesberg Mountain Trail (only two hours from Johannesburg) is set in one of the oldest mountain ranges in the world. You are likely to see smaller game and the range also has a breeding colony of the endangered Cape Vulture.

Trails in the Cape are scenic, offering a very different landscape that includes lush green surroundings, rolling hills, forests and vineyards.

Equi Trailing, PO Box 1373, Plettenberg Bay 6600. Tel: (04457) 9718 (Mr and Mrs Rowling). This company has organised a trail near Plettenberg Bay in a conservationist paradise.

Sleepy Hollow Horse Riding, tel: (021) 789 2341, gives you the chance to ride in the beautiful surroundings of the

Noordhoek Valley. Join their sunset and champagne rides, moonlight rides with an evening meal, morning rides with a hearty farmhouse breakfast afterwards and lessons. The two-hour beach ride is highly recommended in winter.

Amatola Trails, Hogsback 5721. Tel: (0020) ask for Hogsback 32. Horseback rides through the Eastern Cape.

Marathons

Road running – ranging in distance from 10 to 90 km (6 to 55 miles) – is one of South Africa's most popular sports. Events are held in almost all major towns and cities at weekends.

The highlight of the year is the 90-km (55-mile) **Comrades Marathon** which alternates annually between Durban and Pietermaritzburg on 31 May. The race has an 11 hour time-limit and attracts over 10,000 participants. The runners have to endure a 700-metre (2,300-ft) altitude difference. The 50-km (31-miles) **Two Oceans Marathon** on the Cape Peninsula every Easter Saturday also attracts many runners. Another popular event is the **City to City Marathon** from Johannesburg to Pretoria.

Contact: **Athletics South Africa** (**ASA**), PO Box 15616, Doornfontein 2028, Gauteng. Tel: (011) 402 4973.

Comrades Marathon Association, PO Box 100621, Scottsville 3209, KwaZulu-Natal. Tel: (0331) 94 3510.

Canoeing

South Africans engage with enthusiasm in all forms of canoeing: white water, slalom, sprint and long distance. Olympic canoeists and trainers regard the Highveld as a good training area because of the sunny climate and high altitude

(Johannesburg lies at 1,700m). There are also some very challenging rivers in South Africa. Some clubs hire out equipment. For information, contact:

South African Canoe Federation, PO Box 212005, Oribi 3205, KwaZulu-Natal. Tel: (0331) 94 0509.

South Africa Rivers Association, PO Box 472, Magaliesburg 2805, Gauteng. Tel: (0142) 77 1888.

River Rafting

This is another popular way to enjoy the large African rivers, especially the Orange River. For 4–6 days let this gentle giant

Canoeing Events

Major events are held in Natal in summer and in the Cape in the winter months.
• Umkomaas Canoe Marathon, 3 days, Durban, March
• Orange River Canoe Marathon, 2 days, Hopetown/Cape, April
• Berg River Marathon, 4 days, 300–400 participants, Western Cape, July
• Fish River Marathon (international), 2 days, 400 participants, Craddock, Eastern Cape, October
• Vaal Kayak Marathon, 400 participants, Johannesburg, December
• Duzi Marathon, 2 days, 700–1000 participants, Pietermaritzburg, December/January

take you in rubber rafts or canoes through the most spectacular, unspoilt Richtersveld – cooking on open fires and sleeping under the African desert sky – a unique way of letting go of the stresses of civilisation. The wonderful thing is that no canoeing experience is required and even children can

take part (especially in the rubber raft trips). The following organisations offer rafting and canoeing trips:

South African River Rafters Association, Cape Town, tel: (021) 762 2350; Durban, tel: (031) 47 2015.

South Africa Rivers Association, PO Box 472, Magaliesburg 2805, Gauteng. Tel: (0142) 77 1888.

Felix Unite (Tugela, Orange, and Breede Rivers – canoes), PO Box 1524, Sandton 2146. Tel: (011) 463 3167/8; fax: 706 1614.

Orange River Adventures (Indian Mohawk canoes), c/o 5 Matapan Road, Rondebosch 7700. Tel: (021) 685 4475.

River Rafters (Orange River – rubber rafts), PO Box 1157, Kelvin 2054. Tel: (011) 82 5407.

River Runners (rafts, canoes, kayaks), PO Box 583, Constantia 7848. Tel: (021) 705 6229.

Sunwa Ventures (Tugela River and Vaal Dam), PO Box 41952, Craighall 2024. Tel: (011) 788 5120.

Diving

Diving in the waters around South Africa is a great way to explore the rich marine life (2,000 species) from the icy waters of the west coast (the Benguela current of the Atlantic) to the subtropical east coast (the Agulhas current of the Indian Ocean).

On the Atlantic coast, divers can harvest rock lobster (crayfish), perlemoen, black mussels and others. As the warm Agulhas current can be felt further up the Eastern Cape coast, the marine life changes: flame coral, starfish, feather stars and other exotic and colourful sea creatures abound. People without diving experience might consider making use of diving courses offered here to

acquire diving qualifications. For further information contact:
South African Underwater Union, PO Box 557, Parow 7500. Tel: (021) 930 6549; fax: (021) 930 6541.
Sea Fisheries Research Institute, tel: (021) 439 6160.
National Monuments Council, Tel: (021) 462 1502; fax: (021) 462 4509. (For information on wreck-diving.)

From **Cape Vidal** (on the level of St Lucia Lake) to the Mozambique border, an aquatic reserve stretches for 5 km (3 miles) out into the sea. Divers are drawn by the world's southernmost coral reefs and the colourful marine life. At Sodwana Bay are the **Sodwana Dive Retreat** and **Sodwana Lodge Charters**. These diving resorts offer training, sale and hire of equipment, speciality diving (such as night dives) and accommodation. The area has a beautiful sandy beach with a dune forest. The bay is sheltered by a ridge jutting seaward from the dune headland. Contact **Sodwana Dive Retreat**, tel: (031) 86 6266 (ask for Don Rennie); fax: 305 7430, or **Sodwana Lodge Charters for Diving**, tel: (031) 29 0972; fax: (031) 29 4805.

The region between **Umhlanga Rocks** and **Salt Rock**, with its shallower reefs close to the coast, lends itself especially to spear fishing. Vetch's pier is more for beginners.

The Durban Underwater Club, tel: (031) 32 5850, offers excursions from Umkomaas and Rocky Bay. **Trident Diving School** in Durban, tel: (031) 305 3081, organises dives to the Aliwal Shoal 4 km (2 miles) off the coast of Umkomaas just south of Durban. **Underwater World** in Scottburgh, tel: (031) 32 5820; fax: (031) 37 5587, offers diving excursions.

The diving businesses in **East London** are good places to organise diving trips. Countless

Spear-Fishing

Much the same can be said about spear-fishing as about diving: the best marine fauna are found in the area where the warm Agulhas current meets the cold Benguela current off the south coast. The best month overall for diving in South Africa is March.

However, there are regulations that need to be observed such as the closed seasons on particular species, protected areas, size and number restrictions on the fish caught and also permit requirements. For such information, contact the **SA Underwater Union**.

reefs between the Great Fish River and Kidd's Beach provide excellent diving. Diving is popular around East London as so many vessels have foundered along this stretch of coast. For information, tel: (0431) 2 6015.

The area around **Port Alfred** is only suitable for experienced divers. Information can be obtained from the **Kowie Underwater Club** in Port Alfred. Less experienced divers can brave the deep around Algoa Bay. **The Dolphin Underwater Club** in Humewood offers courses.

At the **Tsitsikamma National Park**, east of Plettenberg Bay, a snorkelling trail and a scuba diving trail have been established which explore this silent world. It is like diving in a gigantic aquarium. For information on the Tsitsikamma diving trails contact the **National Parks Board**. Tel: (021) 22 2810.

The numerous rugged stretches of coast in the south-western Cape make diving a fascinating proposition almost everywhere. You may well discover old wrecks between **Danger Point** and **Waenhuiskrans**. Further information can be obtained from the **Bredasdorp**

Publicity Association, tel: (02841) 4 2584. Cape Hangklip near Cape Town is another popular diving area.

Fishing

Trout fishing is pursued by many South Africans all over the country. You need a licence, which is not transferable from province to province. The licence is issued by a magistrate's court or sometimes by the office of the nature reserve where the stream is located. You also require the prescribed trout tackle. The season is all year round, peaking in autumn and spring. In the north, the favourite areas are **Dullstroom, Pilgrim's Rest, Graskop, Sabie** and **Lydenberg**, all in Mpumalanga.

The KwaZulu-Natal trout areas are all along the **Drakensberg Escarpment** and rivers in the **Umgeni** and **Himeville** districts. In the Cape popular trout fishing areas are around **Stellenbosch, La Motte, Bain's Kloof** and **Maden Dam** near King Williams Town.

South African Freshwater Angling Association, PO Box 377, Welkom 9460, Free State. Tel: (0171) 352 2755.

Federation of South African Fly Fishermen, PO Box 2142, Pietermaritzburg 3200, KwaZulu-Natal. Tel: (0331) 45 3700.

ROCK AND SURF ANGLING

This is a favourite pastime all along South Africa's interesting coastline with its varied conditions concerning water temperatures, winds and currents, all of which affect the type of marine life. Fishing permits are required for particular areas such as **Table Bay** (obtainable from harbour authorities). No licences are required to fish off the **Natal** coast or in estuaries. Taking rock life such as crayfish does require a licence. For further information contact: **South**

African Federation of Sea Angling and South African Federation of Deep Sea Angling, PO Box 35936, Menlo Park, Pretoria 0001, Gauteng. Tel: (012) 46 1912.

Popular coastal strips include **Durban Harbour, North and South Pier, St Lucia, Mapelane, Cape Vidal, Mission Rocks, Umfolozi** and **Sodwana Bay**. The best season here is June–November.

The **Garden Route coastline**, the **Peninsula coastline** and **False Bay** up to Milnerton (north of Cape Town) and from **Gordon's Bay** around Cape Hangklip are popular areas. The season is all year round.

GAME AND DEEP SEA FISHING

This has a special thrill for many anglers. June marks the famous **Sardine Run** which is accompanied by hundreds of game fish, while in the Cape the two main runs are the tunny run in October and the runs of snoek in autumn and winter. For further information contact:

South African Marlin and Tuna Club, Jubilee Square, Simon's Town 7975, Western Cape. Tel: (021) 786 2762.

Ski Boat Light Tackle Game and Fishing Association, PO Box 4191, Cape Town 8000. Tel: (021) 21 3611 (ask for Mr Steyn).

The best areas of the **KwaZulu-Natal coast** include the south coast, off Durban harbour and the north coast at Sodwana, Richards Bay and St Lucia (season December–June).

Major Fishing Events

• Master Angling Tournament, mid-March, Cape Town
• Cape Boat and Ski Boat International Tournament, October, Cape
• Mpumalanga Billfish Tournament, November, Sodwana Bay

Cape areas include **Hout Bay, Simonstown** and **Hermanus**, while the season stretches mid-October–November and March–mid-May. In KwaZulu-Natal the best season for marlin and sail fish is November–April, while in the Cape the long fin and yellow fin tunny are in season September–April.

Sailing

With a 3,000-km (1,860-mile) coastline of sandy beaches, bays, lagoons, cliffs and rock shorelines, the South African seas offer the sailing enthusiast the full spectrum of challenges in conditions from the Cape of Storms to calm seas bathed in sunshine. On average the winds are in the 15–25 knots range.

Yacht club facilities are excellent, from clubs with 50 to those with 3,000 members. Most yachts in South Africa belong to the cruising category in the 10–15 metres (50–80 ft) range, of which the majority are built locally to stringent standards. Offshore sailing requires that you belong to a recognised yacht club and that you comply with harbour regulations (licence, permits, registration, etc.). The national body to which you can turn for information is situated in Cape Town:

The Cruising Association of South Africa, PO Box 5036, Cape Town 8000. Tel: (021) 439 1147; fax: 434 0203.

Royal Cape Yacht Club, PO Box 772, Cape Town 8000. Tel: (021) 21 1354/5.

Point Yacht Club, 3 Maritime Place, Durban 4000, KwaZulu-Natal. Tel: (031) 301 4787.

The organisations listed below offer courses in sailing, as well as chartered tours that are scenic and offer activities such as fishing:

Table Bay Sailing Academy, PO Box 32296, Camps Bay 8040. Tel: (021) 438 8242.

Lifestyle Travel Luxury Yachting Adventures, PO Box 67, Randburg 2125. Tel: (011) 705 3201; fax: 705 3203. They offer everything from lunch and sunset charters to 5-day cruises in 13-metre (45-ft) and 16-metre (53-ft) sailing boats off the Cape coast and in the best wetland and wildlife sanctuaries.

DINGHY SAILING

Dinghy sailing (that is, sailing in a boat under 6 metres (20 ft) with raisable centreboard) is popular mainly on the inland dams. Clubs welcome visitors and may be helpful in getting you a sail. The **Vaal Dam** is the largest venue (420 km/260 miles), with 700 km (430 miles) of shoreline, and the season is year round. The major event is the Lion Week Vaal Dam, October. Contact the **South African Yachting Association**, Private Bag 0004, Germiston South 1411. Tel: (011) 827 3508; fax: (011) 827 0538.

Surfing

South Africa has beautiful sandy beaches and great surf. **Durban**, South Africa's surfing centre, hosts most of the surfing competitions since weather and water are warm all year round. Further south lies **Jeffrey's Bay**, well known for its dangerous but exhilarating waves. Even more challenging are the **St Francis Bay** waves known as "Bruce's". However, they are not as consistent as the waves at Jeffrey's Bay; many only work on a few winter days a year. West of **Port Elizabeth**, the long breakers abound right down to **Cape Town**'s big solid waves. While the landscape is spectacular, the waters are freezing. Major events are the National Amateur Championships (July, venue changes) and the Gunston 500 (July, Durban).

Equipment and information on local conditions is available from surf shops in urban centres. For information contact: **United Surfing Council**, PO Box 799, East London 5200, Eastern Cape. Tel: (0431) 35 3069.

Windsurfing

South Africa's sunny weather all year round, together with the many beautiful sandy beaches and the huge expanses of water of the inland dams, offer many opportunities for the windsurfing enthusiast. Not only are temperatures ideal, wind conditions, too, facilitate the sport. Access to the water is very good and South Africa's rescue operations are very well organised. All you need worry about is whether you can handle the strength of the wind. Some areas require permits for offshore windsurfing. Below are some of the popular areas in Mpumalanga, KwaZulu-Natal and the Cape.

The North: Bona Manzi Dam (near Bronkhorstspruit), Vaal Dam, Ebernezer Dam (near Tzaneen).

KwaZulu-Natal: Midmar Dam; Suitable coastal areas are few: Warner Beach (Scottburgh), Amanzimtoti (for experienced windsurfers), lagoon at Zinkwazi, northern Richards Bay, lagoon at Mtunzini.

Cape: Plettenberg Bay, Struisbaai, Swartvlei (inland near George), and many more.

For further information, contact **South African Windsurfing Class Association**, Private Bag X16, Auckland Park 2006. Tel: (011) 726 7076.

Inland Watersports

Sailing, windsurfing, speed-boating and water-skiing can be enjoyed at the **Midmardamm** lake, northwest of Pietermaritzburg on the N3, and at the **Hartebeesport Dammk**, north of Johannesburg on the R511.

Spectator Sports

CRICKET

This is one of the major team sports in South Africa. The standard is very high, and the game is strongly promoted. Cricket has led the way towards integrated sport in South Africa by hosting Rebel Tours, while at the same time trying to break the international sanctions which were imposed on all sport before apartheid began to be dismantled. Now sport is theoretically open to all South Africans.

The game was introduced to the continent by the British colonials. The fact that since 1858 the Queen's Birthday has been officially celebrated by a cricket match testifies to its long popularity amongst the English community.

Major events are the **Castle Cup Cricket Final** in February (venue changes) and the **Benson & Hedges Cricket Final** in March (venue changes).

For more information, contact: **United Cricket Board**, PO Box 55009, Northlands 2116, Gauteng. Tel: (011) 880 2810.

FOOTBALL

This sport is hugely popular amongst all South Africans. At club level, football is well organised. There are many clubs and all are a part of the league structure. The clubs represent all sections of the population from varsity students to manual workers from townships. Soweto boasts a few large football stadiums and several professional clubs.

For information, contact: **The South African Football Association**. Tel: (011) 494 3522.

HORSE-RACING

Competitive horse-riding is a popular spectator sport. Some of the major horse racing events attract large, glamorous crowds, most famously the Rothmans July Handicap.

RUGBY

Despite the years of sanctions against South African sport, rugby remained strong and competitive at the provincial level and has now made a strong international comeback. This is partially thanks to the high standing that rugby has at the school level; schools channel players into club rugby which then feeds them into provincial rugby.

Major Rugby Events

• Currie Cup (senior provincial teams), league ends in an October final
• Lion Cup, senior provincial knock-out, July
• Sanlam Bank Trophy (also called Piennaar Competition) played by provincial teams not in the Currie Cup, October
• Gold Cup sub unions, ends in final, month not fixed

For more information, contact: **South African Rugby Football Union**, PO Box 99, Newlands 7725, Cape Town. Tel: (021) 685 3038.

ART & PHOTO CREDITS

INSIGHT GUIDE
South africa

Editorial Director **Brian Bell**
Maps **Polyglott Kartographie**
Cartographic Editor **Zoë Goodwin**
Production **Mohammed Dar**
Design Consultants
Klaus Geisler, Graham Mitchener
Picture Research **Hilary Genin**

Index

Note: page numbers in italics refer to illustrations

The Insight Approach

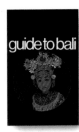

The book you are holding is part of the world's largest range of guidebooks. Its purpose is to help you have the most valuable travel experience possible, and we try to achieve this by providing not only information about countries, regions and cities but also genuine insight into their history, culture, institutions and people.

Since the first Insight Guide – to Bali – was published in 1970, the series has been dedicated to the proposition that, with insight into a country's people and culture, visitors can both enhance their own experience and be accepted more easily by their hosts. Now, in a world where ethnic hostilities and nationalist conflicts are all too common, such attempts to increase understanding between peoples are more important than ever.

Insight Guides:
Essentials for understanding

Because a nation's past holds the key to its present, each Insight Guide kicks off with lively history chapters. These are followed by magazine-style essays on culture and daily life. This essential background information gives readers the necessary context for using the main Places section, with its comprehensive run-down on things worth seeing and doing.

Finally, a listings section contains all the information you'll need on travel, hotels, restaurants and opening times.

As far as possible, we rely on local writers and specialists to ensure that information is authoritative. The pictures, for which Insight Guides have become so celebrated, are just as important. Our photojournalistic approach aims not only to illustrate a destination but also to communicate visually and directly to readers life as it is lived by the locals. The series has grown to almost 200 titles.

Compact Guides:
The "great little guides"

As invaluable as such background information is, it isn't always fun to carry an Insight Guide through a crowded souk or up a church tower. Could we, readers asked, distil the key reference material into a slim volume for on-the-spot use?

Our response was to design Compact Guides as an entirely new series, with original text carefully cross-referenced to detailed maps and more than 200 photographs. In essence, they're miniature encyclopedias, concise and comprehensive, displaying reliable and up-to-date information in an accessible way. There are almost 100 titles.

Pocket Guides:
A local host in book form

However wide-ranging the information in a book, human beings still value the personal touch. Our editors are often asked the same questions. Where do *you* go to eat? What do *you* think is the best beach? What would *you* recommend if I have only three days? We invited our local correspondents to act as "substitute hosts" by revealing their preferred walks and trips, listing the restaurants they go to and structuring a visit into a series of timed itineraries.

The result: our Pocket Guides, complete with full-size fold-out maps. These 100-plus titles help readers plan a trip precisely, particularly if their time is short.

Exploring with Insight:
A valuable travel experience

In conjunction with co-publishers all over the world, we print in up to 10 languages, from German to Chinese, from Danish to Russian. But our aim remains simple: to enhance your travel experience by combining our expertise in guidebook publishing with the on-the-spot knowledge of our correspondents.

"I was first drawn to the Insight Guides by the excellent "Nepal" volume. I can think of no book which so effectively captures the essence of a country. Out of these pages leaped the Nepal I know – the captivating charm of a people and their culture. I've since discovered and enjoyed the entire Insight Guide series. Each volume deals with a country in the same sensitive depth, which is nowhere more evident than in the superb photography."

Sir Edmund Hillary

The World of Insight Guides

400 books in three complementary series cover every major destination in every continent.

Insight Guides

Alaska
Alsace
Amazon Wildlife
American Southwest
Amsterdam
Argentina
Atlanta
Athens
Australia
Austria
Bahamas
Bali
Baltic States
Bangkok
Barbados
Barcelona
Bay of Naples
Beijing
Belgium
Belize
Berlin
Bermuda
Boston
Brazil
Brittany
Brussels
Budapest
Buenos Aires
Burgundy
Burma (Myanmar)
Cairo
Calcutta
California
Canada
Caribbean
Catalonia
Channel Islands
Chicago
Chile
China
Cologne
Continental Europe
Corsica
Costa Rica
Crete
Crossing America
Cuba
Cyprus
Czech & Slovak Republics
Delhi, Jaipur, Agra
Denmark
Dresden
Dublin
Düsseldorf
East African Wildlife
East Asia
Eastern Europe
Ecuador
Edinburgh
Egypt
Finland
Florence
Florida
France
Frankfurt
French Riviera
Gambia & Senegal
Germany
Glasgow

Gran Canaria
Great Barrier Reef
Great Britain
Greece
Greek Islands
Hamburg
Hawaii
Hong Kong
Hungary
Iceland
India
India's Western Himalaya
Indian Wildlife
Indonesia
Ireland
Israel
Istanbul
Italy
Jamaica
Japan
Java
Jerusalem
Jordan
Kathmandu
Kenya
Korea
Lisbon
Loire Valley
London
Los Angeles
Madeira
Madrid
Malaysia
Mallorca & Ibiza
Malta
Marine Life in the South China Sea
Melbourne
Mexico
Mexico City
Miami
Montreal
Morocco
Moscow
Munich
Namibia
Native America
Nepal
Netherlands
New England
New Orleans
New York City
New York State
New Zealand
Nile
Normandy
Northern California
Northern Spain
Norway
Oman & the UAE
Oxford
Old South
Pacific Northwest
Pakistan
Paris
Peru
Philadelphia
Philippines
Poland
Portugal
Prague

Provence
Puerto Rico
Rajasthan
Rhine
Rio de Janeiro
Rockies
Rome
Russia
St Petersburg
San Francisco
Sardinia
Scotland
Seattle
Sicily
Singapore
South Africa
South America
South Asia
South India
South Tyrol
Southeast Asia
Southeast Asia Wildlife
Southern California
Southern Spain
Spain
Sri Lanka
Sweden
Switzerland
Sydney
Taiwan
Tenerife
Texas
Thailand
Tokyo
Trinidad & Tobago
Tunisia
Turkey
Turkish Coast
Tuscany
Umbria
US National Parks East
US National Parks West
Vancouver
Venezuela
Venice
Vienna
Vietnam
Wales
Washington DC
Waterways of Europe
Wild West
Yemen

Insight Pocket Guides

Aegean Islands★
Algarve★
Alsace
Amsterdam★
Athens★
Atlanta★
Bahamas★
Baja Peninsula★
Bali★
Bali *Bird Walks*
Bangkok★
Barbados★
Barcelona★
Bavaria★
Beijing★
Berlin★

Bermuda★
Bhutan★
Boston★
British Columbia★
Brittany★
Brussels★
Budapest & Surroundings★
Canton★
Chiang Mai★
Chicago★
Corsica★
Costa Blanca★
Costa Brava★
Costa del Sol/Marbella★
Costa Rica★
Côte d'Azur★
Crete★
Denmark
Fiji★
Florence★
Florida★
Florida Keys★
Gran Canaria★
Hawaii★
Hong Kong★
Hungary
Ibiza★
Ireland★
Ireland's Southwest★
Israel★
Istanbul★
Jakarta★
Jamaica★
Kathmandu *Bikes & Hikes*★
Kenya
Kuala Lumpur★
Lisbon★
Loire Valley★
London★
Macau
Madrid★
Malacca
Maldives
Mallorca★
Malta★
Mexico City★
Miami★
Milan★
Montreal★
Morocco★
Moscow
Munich★
Nepal★
New Delhi
New Orleans★
New York City★
New Zealand★
Northern California★
Oslo/Bergen★
Paris★
Penang★
Phuket★
Prague★
Provence★
Puerto Rico★
Quebec★
Rhodes★
Rome★
Sabah★

St Petersburg★
San Francisco★
Sardinia
Scotland★
Seville★
Seychelles★
Sicily★
Sikkim
Singapore★
Southeast England
Southern California★
Southern Spain★
Sri Lanka★
Sydney★
Tenerife★
Thailand★
Tibet★
Toronto★
Tunisia★
Turkish Coast★
Tuscany★
Venice★
Vienna★
Vietnam★
Yogyakarta
Yucatan Peninsula★

★ = *Insight Pocket Guides*
with Pull out Maps

Insight Compact Guides

Algarve
Amsterdam
Bahamas
Bali
Bangkok
Barbados
Barcelona
Beijing
Belgium
Berlin
Brittany
Brussels
Budapest
Burgundy
Copenhagen
Costa Brava
Costa Rica
Crete
Cyprus
Czech Republic
Denmark
Dominican Republic
Dublin
Egypt
Finland
Florence
Gran Canaria
Greece
Holland
Hong Kong
Ireland
Israel
Italian Lakes
Italian Riviera
Jamaica
Jerusalem
Lisbon
Madeira
Mallorca
Malta

Milan
Moscow
Munich
Normandy
Norway
Paris
Poland
Portugal
Prague
Provence
Rhodes
Rome
Salzburg
St Petersburg
Singapore
Switzerland
Sydney
Tenerife
Thailand
Turkey
Turkish Coast
Tuscany
UK regional titles:
Bath & Surroundings
Cambridge & East Anglia
Cornwall
Cotswolds
Devon & Exmoor
Edinburgh
Lake District
London
New Forest
North York Moors
Northumbria
Oxford
Peak District
Scotland
Scottish Highlands
Shakespeare Country
Snowdonia
South Downs
York
Yorkshire Dales
USA regional titles:
Boston
Cape Cod
Chicago
Florida
Florida Keys
Hawaii: Maui
Hawaii: Oahu
Las Vegas
Los Angeles
Martha's Vineyard & Nantucket
New York
San Francisco
Washington D.C.
Venice
Vienna
West of Ireland